GEORGE II

ANDREW C. THOMPSON is fellow and director of studies in history, Queens' College, Cambridge. He is the author of *Britain, Hanover and the Protestant Interest* (2006) and a number of articles on eighteenth-century politics and diplomacy.

Also in the Yale English Monarchs Series

*Available in the U.S. from University of California Press

GEORGE II

KING AND ELECTOR

Andrew C. Thompson

YALE UNIVERSITY PRESS
NEW HAVEN AND LONDON

For Victoria

First published in paperback in 2012

For information about this and other Yale University Press publications, please contact:
U.S. Office: sales.press@yale.edu   www.yalebooks.com
Europe Office: sales @yaleup.co.uk   www.yalebooks.co.uk

Set in Baskerville by IDSUK (DataConnection) Ltd
Printed and bound by CPI Group (UK) Ltd, Croydon, CR0 4YY

Library of Congress Cataloging-in-Publication Data

Thompson, Andrew C.
  George II: king and elector/Andrew C. Thompson.
    p. cm.
  Includes bibliographical references and index.
  ISBN 978–0–300–11892–6 (cl:alk. paper)
  1. George II, King of Great Britain, 1683–1760. 2. Kings and rulers—Biography.
3. Great Britain—History—George II, 1727–1760. I. Title.
  DA501.A3T46 2011
  941.07'2092—dc22
  [B]

                                                                    2011006394

A catalogue record for this book is available from the British Library.

ISBN 978–0–300–18777–9 (pbk)

10 9 8 7 6 5 4 3 2 1

CONTENTS

CONTENTS

ILLUSTRATIONS

PREFACE AND ACKNOWLEDGEMENTS

This book could not have been completed without the help and advice of a number of people. Material from the Royal Archives is cited by the permission of Her Majesty Queen Elizabeth II and I am also grateful for the help that I received from Pamela Clark and the staff of the Royal Archives. Much of the German material used in this study comes from the personal archives of the princes of Hanover, held in the State Archive in Hanover itself. I acknowledge the access granted by His Royal Highness Prince Ernst August and the support of Kirsten Hoffmann and her colleagues at the State Archive. Closer to home, Adrian Wilkinson facilitated access to the Berkeley diaries in the Lincolnshire Archives. I would also like to thank Nigel Aston for drawing this new source material to my attention and for discussion of it. I continue to benefit from the time I spent at the Lewis Walpole Library in Farmington, Connecticut, not least from their wonderful collection of images.

Institutionally, I have been fortunate to be based at Queens' College, Cambridge for a number of years. Two terms of sabbatical at a crucial stage enabled me to get much of the writing of the book done and relief from my administrative, as well as my teaching, responsibilities was incredibly helpful. Within Queens', I have benefited from discussions in the Combination Room with a number of individuals but Richard Rex, Craig Muldrew, James Campbell, Andrew Zurcher, Martin Crowley, Ian Patterson and Jonathan Spence have been especially helpful. One term of my sabbatical was funded by an early career fellowship from the Centre for Research in the Arts, Social Sciences and Humanities (CRASSH) within Cambridge and Mary Jacobus and my fellow fellows made that a conducive atmosphere in which to present some of my initial findings. Simon Werrett proved particularly helpful in discussions about fireworks.

More generally I have had useful conversations and exchanges over various aspects of early Hanoverian history with Nigel Aston, Jeremy Black, Elaine Chalus, Robin Eagles, Holger Hoock, Clyve Jones, Matthew Kilburn, Larry Klein, James Lees, Matthew Neal, Torsten Riotte, Michael Schaich, Hannah Smith, Grant Tapsell, David Vickers and Lucy Worsley. I have been particularly helped by John Andrews in relation to all matters Handelian. Rosamond McKitterick invited me to contribute a session on the 'Hanoverian court' to her part I course on 'Royal and Princely courts' and I have valued the opportunity to try out some of the ideas that found their way into the finished book on her and several cohorts of students who undertook that course. The students' comments and questions were, as always, invaluable. Clarissa Campbell Orr has been an indefatigable supporter and provider of dynastic references. Tim Blanning remains a source of advice and inspiration. Brendan Simms and Hamish Scott have been encouragers, as well as readers and critics. Stephen Taylor first suggested that I undertake this project and has helped at various stages along the way, including commenting on it in draft. Needless to say, any remaining errors are my own.

Robert Baldock and his staff at Yale, particularly Beth Humphries and Tami Halliday, have been unfailingly helpful and efficient and I am grateful that I was given the opportunity to undertake this project in the first place.

The arrival of Elizabeth and Charlotte at the point at which I was supposed to be bringing the project to completion brought both challenges and rewards. While I would not necessarily recommend combining first- (and second-)time fatherhood and writing, it did lead to a certain focusing of the mind. George II commented in his later years that he had not perhaps paid as much attention as he should have done to his children when they were young – I hope that I have not made the same mistake. That I was even able to contemplate undertaking both tasks at the same time is due in no small part to the love, patience and support of Elizabeth and Charlotte's mother so this book is for Victoria.

Cambridge
August 2010

ABBREVIATIONS

Add. MSS	Additional Manuscripts
BL	British Library, London
CHW	Charles Hanbury Williams papers, Lewis Walpole Library
EHR	*English Historical Review*
Hervey, *Memoirs*	John, Lord Hervey, *Some materials towards memoirs of the reign of King George II*, ed. Romney Sedgwick (3 vols, London, 1931)
HJ	*Historical Journal*
HMC	Historical Manuscripts Commission
LC	Lord Chamberlain's department, National Archives
LS	Lord Steward's department, National Archives
LWL	Lewis Walpole Library, Farmington, Connecticut
NA	National Archives, Kew
NHStA	Niedersächsisches Hauptsstadtsarchiv, Hanover
Cobbett, *Parliamentary History*	*Parliamentary history of England,* ed. William Cobbett (36 vols, London, 1806–20)
RA	Royal Archives, Windsor
SP	State Papers, National Archives

Genealogical table of the early Hanoverians

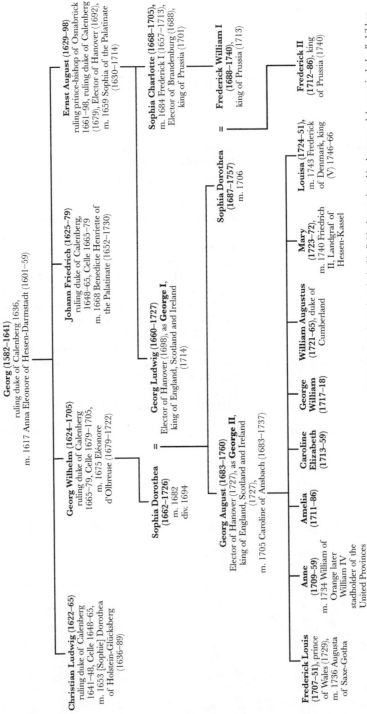

Georg (1582–1641)
ruling duke of Calenberg 1636,
m. 1617 Anna Eleonore of Hessen-Darmstadt (1601–59)

Christian Ludwig (1622–65)
ruling duke of Calenberg
1641–48, Celle 1648–65,
m. 1653 [Sophie] Dorothea
of Holstein-Glücksberg
(1636–89)

Georg Wilhelm (1624–1705)
ruling duke of Calenberg
1665–79, Celle 1679–1705,
m. 1675 Eléonore
d'Olbreuse (1679–1722)

Johann Friedrich (1625–79)
ruling duke of Calenberg
1648–65, Celle 1665–79
m. 1668 Benedicte Henriette of
the Palatinate (1652–1730)

Ernst August (1629–98)
ruling prince-bishop of Osnabrück
1661–98, ruling duke of Calenberg
(1679), Elector of Hanover (1692),
m. 1659 Sophia of the Palatinate
(1630–1714)

Sophia Dorothea (1662–1726)
m. 1682
div. 1694

=

Georg Ludwig (1660–1727)
Elector of Hanover (1698), as **George I**,
king of England, Scotland and Ireland
(1714)

Sophia Charlotte (1668–1705),
m. 1684 Frederick I (1657–1713),
Elector of Brandenburg (1688),
king of Prussia (1701)

Georg August (1683–1760)
Elector of Hanover (1727), as **George II**,
king of England, Scotland and Ireland
(1727),
m. 1705 Caroline of Ansbach (1683–1737)

**Sophia Dorothea
(1687–1757)**
m. 1706

=

**Frederick William I
(1688–1740)**,
king of Prussia (1713)

**Frederick Louis
(1707–51)**, prince
of Wales (1729),
m. 1736 Augusta
of Saxe-Gotha

**Anne
(1709–59)**
m. 1734 William of
Orange later
William IV
stadtholder of the
United Provinces

**Amelia
(1711–86)**

**Caroline
Elizabeth
(1713–59)**

**George
William
(1717–18)**

**William Augustus
(1721–65)**, duke of
Cumberland

**Mary
(1723–72)**,
m. 1740 Friedrich
II, Landgraf of
Hessen-Kassel

Louisa (1724–51),
m. 1743 Frederick
of Denmark, king
(V) 1746–66

**Frederick II
(1712–86)**, king
of Prussia (1740)

This table only shows the principal individuals mentioned in the text and does not include all children.

INTRODUCTION

Any biographer has to worry about the merits of the subject. Is there enough intrinsic interest to justify a study devoted to a particular individual, especially in an age where historians have tended to prefer general, synoptic studies to the narrow concentration on a single life? These fears are partly allayed when the subject is a monarch. The history of an eighteenth-century king was almost inevitably the history of his kingdom as well. Yet for George II some of the doubts remain.

George II can rightly be described as a forgotten king. He figures not at all in Sellars and Yeatman's immortal guide to British history, *1066 and All That*. He has also not been well served by previous generations of biographers, although his fortunes seem to have undergone a mini-revival in recent years.[1] Understanding the reasons for this relative neglect, unusual for a British monarch in any age, shed interesting light on why a new study is necessary now.

There are two main difficulties that George II's prospective biographer faces: one archival and the other historiographical. The raw material that George left behind is relatively scarce. There is nothing approaching the collection of letters of his grandson, George III, which forms a substantial, multi-volume work in its printed incarnation. Indeed, the irony is that George III's purchase of the Stuart Papers means that, for the early eighteenth century, there is more material in the royal archives covering the Jacobite claimants than the Hanoverian monarchs. That which is preserved at Windsor, particularly the financial records, is extremely useful for understanding George's life but it is insufficient by itself.

George's own attitude towards letters and papers is unhelpful in several respects. When he came to the throne in 1727 it is widely thought that he filleted his father's private papers, stored in his bureau in the royal closet. Something similar may have happened to his own papers – it was not uncommon for letters to be returned to the family of a deceased person on their death by the recipient so that they could be disposed of appropriately. George also had a tendency towards economy in relation to correspondence as he did in so many other aspects of his life. He would

---

[1] Book-length studies of George are very thin on the ground. The twentieth century produced a couple – J.D. Griffith Davies, *A king in toils* (London, 1938) and Charles Chenevix Trench, *George II* (London, 1973) – and the twenty-first has already yielded two more: Mijndert Bertram, *Georg II.* (Göttingen, 2003) and Jeremy Black, *George II* (Exeter, 2007).

note a reply on the original letter and then return it to the sender. This can be seen in several cases where the notes survive in the papers of his leading ministers, such as the duke of Newcastle. More crucially, though, George's standard mode of operation militated against the easy recovery of his thoughts.

George was a king who still took an active role in governing. Ministers would see him individually in his closet and receive his instructions and discuss with him the correspondence he had received. This was an intensely oral style of governing so the king's thoughts tend to be preserved at second hand – in the letters that ministers wrote to each other. Therefore, reconstructing the king's views involves the careful analysis of the surviving papers of a number of key individuals, like Newcastle, his political confidant, Philip Yorke, the first earl of Hardwicke, and other leading ministers. It is sometime easier to work out what was going on when the king was absent from London, on one of his visits to Hanover, because the physical separation of ministers forced them to communicate by letter, rather than in person.

The other major archival difficulty reflects the dual nature of the king's role. George became king of England, Scotland and Ireland in 1727 but he had only come to Britain in 1714. He had been born in the north-west German duchy of Calenberg which, by the time of his journey across the North Sea, had become, through some territorial consolidation, the Electorate of Hanover. While his family's connection to Britain began with the Protestant succession, he was a member of one of the most ancient of European ruling dynasties, the Guelphs. Like his father before him and his grandson and great-grandsons after him, George was to be both king and elector – a monarch and a sovereign prince of the Holy Roman Empire. The 'personal union' of Britain and Hanover was to continue until 1837 when the differing succession laws in the component territories left the British thrones to Victoria and the Hanoverian crown, as it had become in 1815, to her uncle Ernst August. One of the effects of the dissolution of the personal union was that the records of the *Deutsche Kanzlei* (German chancery) in London were sent back to Hanover. The *Deutsche Kanzlei* was the link between the absentee ruler and his ministers back in Hanover. When the records were returned to Hanover, about half of them were destroyed, thus making the historian's task more difficult.[2]

Two further factors add even more layers of complexity. The first is the difficult history of the familial records of the Guelph dynasty when it returned to Hanover.[3] Hanover fell victim to Prussian advances in 1866 and the exiled George V became embroiled in a protracted argument with

[2] For the early history of the 'Deutsche Kanzlei', see Rudolf Grieser, 'Die Deutsche Kanzlei in London, ihre Entstehung und Anfänge', *Blätter für deutsche Landesgeschichte*, 89 (1952), pp. 153–68. On the history of its records, see *Übersicht über die Bestände des Niedersächsischen Staatsarchivs in Hannover* (4 vols, Göttingen, 1965–92), ii, pp. 171–2.

[3] For a discussion of the Guelph archives, see Torsten Riotte, 'The kingdom of Hanover and the Marienburg sale', *Court Historian*, 12 (2007), pp. 49–61. The destruction of material in Hanover is discussed in *Übersicht*, i, p. 7.

the Prussian authorities about his assets and title. Some of the family's archives were eventually transferred to the state archives in Hanover where they are now catalogued under two separate deposits. The family retained other records and some of these have recently been sold. The Hanoverian state archives suffered considerable damage from Allied bombing during the Second World War and were subsequently the victim of a serious flood in 1946. Consequently, much material relating to history of the eighteenth-century Electorate has been destroyed, although imaginative use of the surviving material means that the situation is not as bleak as it might appear at first glance. In short, the reconstruction of George's life and times requires careful consideration of a diverse and dispersed set of sources in several languages. So far, so typical for many biographical subjects, but difficult primary material only provides part of the explanation as to why George's life has not attracted the attention that it deserves.

George II needs to be rescued from the enormous condescension of Whig historiographical posterity. This may appear to be a surprising claim, given that George's contemporary supporters were more often drawn from among the Whigs than their Tory opponents. Yet as the grand narrative of Whig history developed in the years after George's reign, the king was increasingly marginalized. In its crudest form, the Whig story was one of the progress and triumph of representative institutions. Its telos was often seen as the forms of representative government with an increased franchise that emerged in Britain during the nineteenth century. Within this narrative, 1688 marked a major turning point. After the Glorious Revolution, the importance of the monarchy declined. Britain became a constitutional monarchy and parliament rose to a sovereign position rapidly. Much emphasis was placed on the importance of Sir Robert Walpole – the first British prime minister – and his 'reign' from 1721 to 1742 in establishing the future course of political developments. In this story it was vital for the king to play a subordinate role: how could George III be portrayed as a tyrant in the 1760s if he was simply following established constitutional practice? In short, for the Whigs, to play up the importance of Sir Robert Walpole, it was necessary to play down the role of George in politics.

George's allotted part within this scheme required him to become a mere cipher, dominated by those around them. This subordination could be to the powerful Whig aristocrats, who viewed themselves, unfairly, as superior to the arriviste Guelphs. It could also be to the various women in his life – wife and mistresses – with the implication that the king had somehow been emasculated. All in all, and George's occasional outbursts added to the impression,[4] there seemed reason to believe that George really was a 'king in toils'.

While influential, this view does not tell the whole story. There have always been dissenters. John Owen's work on the construction of a stable

[4] See below, p. 144.

administration in the aftermath of Walpole's resignation made him
very aware of the importance of George as a political player and this
was reflected in an important subsequent essay.[5] An early essay by
Jeremy Black showed the significance of George as an active participant
in foreign policy in the 1730s, and Aubrey Newman's inaugural lecture
at the University of Leicester shed intriguing light on what a proper
study of the king might look like.[6] It is in the light of this work that the
present study will rehabilitate the king and counter the overwhelming
tendency identified by German, as well as British, historians to view the
Hanoverian dynasty in negative terms.[7]

    This revision of George's role will take place on a number of levels.
Central to the claim is the discussion of foreign policy. The supposed preference of the king for his German territories over his British kingdoms has
clouded previous work on the subject. Put simply, the accusation was that
George was prepared to sacrifice British interests to Hanoverian ones. The
extension of this argument was that it was unwise for Britain to be
involved so heavily in continental politics and that it should instead
concentrate on imperial expansion. With the benefit of hindsight, nineteenth-century historians, such as Sir John Seeley, claimed that history had
proved George's critics right and George wrong because Britain had
become an imperial power with little interest in the continent.

    By contrast, it will be argued here, in line with other recent work on the
subject,[8] that British interests were not necessarily contradictory to those
of Hanover. Rather the two could be married, even if the relationship
went through its ups and downs. Moreover, a significant number of British
ministers was prepared to toe the king's line when it came to foreign policy,

---

[5] J.B. Owen, *The rise of the Pelhams* (London, 1957) and 'George II reconsidered', in
A. Whiteman, J.S. Bromley and P.G.M. Dickson, eds, *Statesmen, scholars and merchants*
(Oxford, 1973), pp. 113–34.

[6] Jeremy Black, 'George II reconsidered. A consideration of George's influence on the
control of foreign policy, in the first years of his reign', *Mitteilungen des österreichischen
Staatsarchivs*, 35 (1982), pp. 35–56 and Aubrey Newman, *The world turned inside out: new views
on George II* (Leicester, 1987).

[7] For German surveys of British attitudes to their German kings, see Edgar Kalthoff, 'Die
englischen Könige des Hauses Hannover im Urteil der britischen Geschichtsschreibung',
Niedersächsisches Jahrbuch für Landesgeschichte, 30 (1958), pp. 54–197, Angelika Müller, 'Das Bild
der Hannover-Könige des 18. Jahrhunderts in der neueren und neuesten englischsprachigen
Geschichtsschreibung', in Heide N. Rohloff, ed., *Grossbritannien und Hannover: die Zeit der
Personalunion, 1714–1837* (Frankfurt/Main, 1989), pp. 194–226 and Torsten Riotte, 'Das Haus
Hannover in der angelsächsischen Forschung', *Niedersächsisches Jahrbuch für Landesgeschichte*, 79
(2007), pp. 325–34.

[8] See, in particular, Brendan Simms, *Three victories and a defeat* (London, 2007). Jeremy
Black has suggested that this trend 'has the makings (for good and ill) of a new orthodoxy'
(Black, 'Debating Britain and Europe, 1688–1815', *British Scholar*, 1 (2008), p. 39). For
my own modest contribution to the recent revival of interest in the European aspects
of eighteenth-century British politics, see Andrew C. Thompson, *Britain, Hanover and the
Protestant interest* (Woodbridge, 2006).

either because of intellectual agreement or because of the pragmatic realization that to do otherwise was foolhardy. George, therefore, enjoyed
considerable freedom of manoeuvre when it came to directing foreign
policy. His early career and encyclopaedic knowledge of genealogy and
military matters gave him a head start, as did his penchant for hard work.
He was more confident and expert in this area than many, if not most, of
his ministers. Additionally, his trips to Hanover gave him the opportunity
to conduct his diplomacy in person by consultation with his own and
visiting diplomats. British ministers found it much more difficult to interfere with George's plans beyond British shores.

A good deal of attention is devoted in this work to George as a creator
and director of foreign policy. This approach has a number of consequences. It leads to a rebalancing of interest in both people and period.
Foreign policy was never a particularly strong suit for Robert Walpole and
much of the most interesting and divisive foreign policy decisions were
taken after his resignation in 1742. His importance for George's reign is
therefore de-emphasized but not, of course, ignored. Instead the succession of ministers who held the office of secretary of state receive relatively
more attention, as do the years after 1742. Throughout the sometimes
tortuous ministerial crises of the 1740s and 1750s the king's desire to make
sure that his foreign political aims were met remained prominent. The
origins of domestic political crisis often lay in foreign political action.

Restoring George to his position at the centre of foreign policy also
serves as a reminder of the similarity between his position and that of a
number of his contemporary European monarchs. The parallels between
George and other European rulers do not stop there. The revival of interest
in court studies in recent years has led to renewed attention being paid to
the people and structures immediately around the monarch and the ways
in which these could be used to project royal power. It has become common
to see the history of the British courts in the eighteenth century as being at
variance with that of most of their continental counterparts. In their
different ways both John Brewer and Hannah Smith have argued that as a
cultural and political institution the court was becoming less important in
the eighteenth century.[9] The corollary of arguments that see the court as
less influential has tended to be that the monarchy was also losing its trac-
tion as the ultimate cultural and political arbiter. While accepting that
monarch and courtiers might no longer have enjoyed the monopoly of
cultural power that they once had, it is necessary to remember, as Clarissa
Campbell Orr has recently pointed out, that ministers and courtiers were
often the same people wearing different hats. So, to understand politics in

---

[9] John Brewer, *The pleasures of the imagination* (London, 1997) and Hannah Smith, 'The
court in England, 1714–1760: a declining political institution?', *History*, 90 (2005), pp.
23–41. Smith sees the court retaining its function as a venue for politics, even if its institu-
tional importance had declined.

the period properly, it is necessary to look at a triangular set of relationships between the monarch, his courtiers and parliament.[10]

Moreover, thinking about George at the apex of a court necessitates discussing not just how he coped with the increasingly commercialized world of cultural London but also how he spent his time when in Hanover. The argument made in what follows is that George was particularly adept at adapting to circumstances. While in London, he could take advantage of the blossoming of consumer society to associate the monarchy with cultural activity without having to foot the entire bill – as a patron of the Royal Academy of Music and a regular attendee at the Theatre Royal or the new Royal Opera House in Covent Garden. This was an arrangement that suited both sides. George had a strong sense of economy in all aspects of his life. Theatrical proprietors, on the other hand, were aware of the economic value of the royal moniker. Royal attendance was a good way to advertise performances and usually guaranteed a large audience. The king's various dealings with Handel, whose works accompanied most important dynastic occasions during the reign, also illustrate the value of the royal connection to both patron and client. Unfortunately, there is no evidence to support the story often associated with George that he began the tradition of standing for the Hallelujah Chorus during performances of the Messiah.[11]

George's life as a monarch was not defined simply by his time in London. He spent significant amounts of time in Hanover – about one summer in three over the course of his reign. A proper understanding of his courtly and political activities needs to pay attention to these visits. Although some work has been published on the visits in the first half of his reign,[12] the later period is largely uncharted territory. George's active interest in the management of his court in Hanover, even when he was not there, and the rich and varied cultural life he experienced during his visits provide an important contrast to his behaviour in London. George had an acute awareness of the differing expectations in his two territories – living with the consequences of the Protestant succession in one and continuing to be an active *Landesvater* in the other – and acted accordingly.

In one respect, George was a little different from some of his continental counterparts. He displayed relatively little interest in portraiture and his image. He was painted in Hanover, prior to 1714, and he sat for Kneller

---

[10] Clarissa Campbell Orr, 'New perspectives of Hanoverian Britain', *HJ*, 52 (2009), pp. 516–17.

[11] Donald Burrows, *Handel* (Oxford, 1994), p. 300. There is no evidence that George ever attended a performance and, for the reasons outlined above, it is extremely unlikely that royal attendance would have gone unadvertised in advance or unremarked subsequently.

[12] See, in particular, Uta Richter-Uhlig, *Hof und Politik unter den Bedingungen der Personalunion zwischen Hannover und England* (Hanover, 1992) and, more generally, Hans Patze, 'Zwischen London und Hannover. Bemerkungen zum Hofleben in Hannover während des 18. Jahrhunderts', in Peter Berglar, ed., *Staat und Gesellschaft im Zeitalter Goethes* (Cologne and Vienna, 1977), pp. 95–129.

once he became prince of Wales. After Kneller's death, the job of principal painter was taken over by Charles Jervas so it was he who produced the coronation portraits of George and Caroline in 1727. Subsequent official portraits were painted by Enoch Seeman and John Shackleton but George only retained copies of Seeman's work. Shackleton's more elaborate image was distributed widely in the 1750s (a version was presented to the Foundling Hospital, for example). The portrait generally held to be the best likeness, by Robert Edge Pine, was not completed until after the king's death.[13] Yet, if the king did not often commission his own image, others were prepared to do so. The Lord Chief Justice commissioned a portrait for the Court of Common Pleas in 1744. The artist was Thomas Hudson. George's military exploits in the 1740s were commemorated visually. He liked martial images, particularly equestrian ones. The university of Cambridge commissioned a statue of the king, in Roman garb, which now stands in the entrance hall to the university library.

Biographers are probably more likely to develop an empathy for their subjects than other writers are. In George's case this is especially important as his character has attracted significant criticism. It is worth assessing how appropriate the traditional picture is. The king's detractors have accused him of being stubborn, petulant, routine-orientated, mean, quick to anger and slow to praise, boorish, weak and indecisive. One recent historian has gone so far as to suggest that he displayed behaviour indicative of his being a sufferer from Asperger's syndrome. Others have commented on his penchant for big wigs and shoes, implying that he was over-compensating for his slight stature.[14] Victorian commentators tended to decry the absence of interest in the arts displayed by William III, George and his father, perhaps because they had become used to the connoisseurship of Georges III and IV.[15]

It would be foolish to deny that, on occasion, George showed a number of these characteristics. However, there are several points that can be made in his defence. The first is that they tell some, but not all, of the story. Accusations of parsimony need to be balanced by the king's unostentatious use of his own funds in support of worthy causes. When his wife died in 1737, George continued to pay all the pensions that she had granted and retained all her servants.[16] He gave £2,000 to the Foundling Hospital in 1749, prompted probably by the connection with Handel.[17] More

[13] Oliver Millar, *The Tudor, Stuart and early Georgian pictures in the collection of Her Majesty the Queen* (2 vols, London, 1963), i, p. 26.

[14] Hervey, *Memoirs*, i, pp. 250–5, 261, 276–8; ii, pp. 484–94; iii, pp. 750–2, 769–72, Horace Walpole, *Memoirs of King George II*, ed. John Brooke, (3 vols, New Haven, 1985), i, pp. 116–20, Tracy Borman, *Henrietta Howard* (London, 2007), p. 35 (Asperger's reference), Bertram, *Georg II*, p. 38.

[15] See the editorial comment in Robert Phillimore, ed., *Memoirs and correspondence of George, Lord Lyttelton* (2 vols, London, 1845), i, p. 278 to this effect.

[16] W.H. Wilkins, *Caroline the illustrious* (2 vols, London, 1901), ii, p. 365.

[17] Burrows, *Handel*, p. 300.

generally, he displayed a willingness to live within his means that had much in common with George III but differed dramatically from other eighteenth-century princes of Wales like his own son Frederick and the future George IV. Perhaps this should be seen as another example of the differences and consequent conflict between the Guelph generations.

More importantly, though, the issue of character raises questions about whether the king's alleged failings impeded his ability to do his job: effective leaders are not necessarily nice people. In this respect, accusations of indecision are probably the most damaging and there are examples of George taking a while to determine what course of action to take. It should also be said, though, that while George may have displayed his irritation at small matters, he had the ability to remain calm in a crisis, such as during the 1745 Jacobite invasion.

Criticisms of George need to be noted, but the following account seeks to rebalance the existing historiographical picture by offering a more thorough account of the king's role in government and a more positive assessment of his merits. To do this, it considers a broader range of sources than any previous account of the king's life. It takes advantage of the publication and discovery of several new accounts of George's court in the 1750s to counter the impression created by the more hostile pictures of the king that can be found in the pages of the memoirs of John, Lord Hervey and Horace Walpole.[18] Both Hervey and Walpole were closely connected to Robert Walpole – Hervey a friend and Horace a son. In their different ways, both can be seen as representative of the Whig historiographical tradition from which George needs to be rescued. By contrast, the memoirs of James, second Earl Waldegrave and the diary of John, fifth Baron Berkeley of Stratton, which has only recently become available to researchers, provide a rather more nuanced picture of what George was like.[19]

The approach adopted in the ensuing narrative is unashamedly chronological. Each chapter seeks to tell the king's story but also includes broader perspectives on issues like the shape of court life in Britain and Hanover or how government was developing in the period. It seeks to place George in his own time, rather than seeing him either as a brake on what was to develop subsequently or as a relic of a bygone age.

George, as many of those around him were never tired of pointing out, retained considerable affection for the lands of his birth. This affection manifested itself on several levels, from a preference for hunting wild boar over deer, through a liking for Hanoverian game on his table, to an

[18] For details, see note 14, above.
[19] Waldegrave's memoirs first became easily available in J.C.D. Clark, ed., *The memoirs and speeches of James, 2nd Earl Waldegrave, 1742–1763* (Cambridge, 1988). On Berkeley of Stratton's diary, see Nigel Aston, 'The court of George II: Lord Berkeley of Stratton's perspective', *Court Historian*, 13 (2008), pp. 171–93. This material forms an integral component of my account in chs 8–9.

impatience for parliamentary business to be dispatched as quickly as possible to allow him to depart for his 'country seat' at Herrenhausen.[20] Yet for all his bluntness and desire to play the German soldier-prince, George showed himself able to assimilate himself into a new political culture after 1714. Although mocked for his foibles, he displayed a remarkable dexterity in realizing what the constitutional limits of his new role were. Long-lasting changes in the way that Britain was governed occurred during his reign, although, as the account of the development of the cabinet offered in Chapter 7 shows, these might be seen as unintended and surprising. Thinking about the king's 'German' as opposed to his 'British' interests is unhelpful. As a member of an ancient ruling house, George's perspective and outlook were European and he thought in terms of his domains and territories, rather than about national boundaries. This is the primary lens through which his life should be viewed.

---

[20] For the penchant for Hanoverian game and the pressure this put on his huntsmen, see Patze, 'Zwischen London und Hannover', p. 114.

Chapter 1

INHERITANCE AND EXPECTATION

George of Braunschweig Lüneburg was born on 10 November 1683 NS. He was the eldest son of Georg Ludwig, prince of Calenberg and his wife, Sophia Dorothea of Celle and took his names from his father and paternal grandfather. Like all elite marriages in late seventeenth-century Germany, his parents' union had been contracted to achieve dynastic and political aims, rather than for more humdrum, romantic reasons. There was little expectation that the boy born in the Leine palace in Hanover would one day inherit the thrones of England, Scotland and Ireland yet it was already clear that George's familial prospects were on the up.[1] His parents' union, solemnized in 1682, was a further development in a complex process that George's grandfather, Ernst August, hoped would significantly enhance the power and prestige of his own branch of the Braunschweig Lüneburg family.

ERNST AUGUST AND THE RISE OF HANOVER

Nestled in the north-west of the Holy Roman Empire, the territories of Braunschweig Lüneburg represented the remainder of the lands that Henry the Lion, the great Guelph leader, was able to retain after he was deposed by Frederick Barbarossa as duke of Saxony in 1180. The Holy Roman Empire covered an area larger than that of modern Germany, stretching into Bohemia and Moravia as well as Burgundy at its height, and was a hotchpotch of political entities with the emperor as the ultimate feudal overlord. The emperor, who since the middle of the fifteenth century had been a member of the Habsburg family, enjoyed more control and influence in some parts of the empire than in others. The various princes, dukes, counts, landgraves and margraves who ruled over the 300-odd units[2] that made up the empire were keen to preserve their status and

---

[1] The *Oxford Dictionary of National Biography*, repeating the claim in the original dictionary, lists George's place of birth as the Herrenhausen palace, just outside the town of Hanover. I have been unable to find a German source to confirm this. Indeed, Wilhelm Havemann, *Geschichte der Lande Braunschweig und Lüneburg* (3 vols, Göttingen, 1853–7), iii, p. 516 places George's birth in Hanover itself and this is supported by Georg Schnath's observation that the Hanoverian court tended to spend May to late autumn in Herrenhausen before returning to the Leine palace in the town itself for the winter (Georg Schnath with contributions from Rudolf Hillebrecht and Helmut Plath, *Das Leineschloss: Kloster, Fürstensitz, Landtagsgebäude* (Hanover, 1962), p. 82).

[2] This number excludes the imperial knights and their territories in the south-west of the empire.

rights. At the imperial diet or parliament in Regensburg (the Reichstag) there were three separate assemblies, representing the imperial Electors, the princes and the imperial free cities respectively.

Two distinct territorial divisions emerged when Henry the Lion's diminished inheritance was split in 1267. In many ways, the history of the territories over the next few centuries is indicative of how fragmented central Europe could become and how the empire had developed in the way that it did. The senior branch of the family ruled as dukes of Braunschweig Wolfenbüttel and had been resident in Wolfenbüttel itself since the middle of the fifteenth century. By the seventeenth century the cadet branch of the family controlled the duchies of Celle and Calenberg, which included Göttingen, but again, it was different branches of the family that ruled in each duchy. Ernst August's prospects for self-advancement seemed limited. Born in 1629, he was the youngest of four brothers. His father, Duke George, had moved his residence to Hanover and begun the construction of the Leine palace in 1636 but he had died in 1641, leaving the Calenberg territories to his eldest son, Christian Ludwig. In 1648, Ernst August and Christian Ludwig's uncle Frederick died without sons so the Celle portion of the territories was left to Christian Ludwig. He decided that Celle was preferable to his existing territories so vacated Calenberg, leaving it to his younger brother Georg Wilhelm. Bringing the territories of Celle and Calenberg back within the same family was one reason why 1648 was ultimately to prove so fruitful for Ernst August and his offspring. Another was the small gains that Braunschweig Lüneburg made in the treaties of Westphalia which brought the Thirty Years War to an end. Unlike some of its neighbours, such as Brandenburg, the Guelphs' territorial acquisitions were modest in 1648. They simply gained the right to appoint alternate bishops of Osnabrück.

The idea of a Protestant prince ruling as a bishop in an ecclesiastical territory might appear a little odd. Yet it was in many ways symptomatic of the Westphalian treaties, which sought to bring the religious conflict that had torn central Europe apart over the previous three decades within a mutually acceptable legal framework for Protestants and Catholics. Ernst August was to become the first post-Westphalian Protestant bishop of Osnabrück in 1661, succeeding a Bavarian Wittelsbach – the Wittelsbachs had virtually cornered the market in Rhine bishoprics by the seventeenth-century. By the time that Ernst August had become a ruling prince in his own right he had also acquired another crucial prop for successful state-building, a fertile spouse.

The circumstances of Ernst August's marriage were unusual, even by seventeenth-century standards.[3] He and his elder brother, Georg Wilhelm, took considerable (sybaritic) pleasure in travelling to Venice at carnival

---

[3] What follows draws on Ragnhild Hatton, *George I: elector and king* (London, 1978), ch. 1, Karin Feuerstein-Praßer, *Sophie von Hannover* (Regensburg, 2004), pp. 61–80 and Maria Kroll, *Sophie: electress of Hanover* (London, 1973), pp. 52–79.

time. This was not uncommon for men of their wealth and social status. En route to one such visit in 1656 the two brothers had stopped at the Electoral court in Heidelberg. There they had met Sophia, granddaughter of James I and VI and one of the many children of Frederick V and Elizabeth Stuart, the Winter King and Queen. Sophia, who had been born in 1630 after her parents' exile in The Hague, was living at her brother's court, following his restoration in 1648. She was relatively old for an unmarried princess but her lowly position in the family (last daughter and twelfth of thirteen children) combined with the impoverished state of her family after the deprivations of the Thirty Years War probably accounted for her single status. Nevertheless, Georg Wilhelm took a shine to the sharp Palatine princess to the extent that he indicated his willingness to marry her. He was under a certain amount of domestic pressure to marry as his estates were not happy that his elder brother had converted to Catholicism and so wanted some guarantees that a Protestant line might be preserved.

The two brothers continued their journey to enjoy the pleasures of the south. Perhaps it was the return to Venice that made Georg Wilhelm realize that he was not quite ready to give up the bachelor lifestyle to which he had become accustomed. Whatever the reason, it left Georg Wilhelm's family in a bind. To break marriage contracts without good cause was both legally difficult and reputationally problematic. In an attempt to salvage familial honour, Ernst August agreed to fulfil his elder brother's commitment and marry Sophia. Ernst August's co-operation came at a price, though. Aware that none of his three elder brothers had produced offspring yet, Ernst August sensed that there was a chance to advance his branch of the family if he could guarantee that his elder siblings remained childless. One means to do this was to extract the promise from Georg Wilhelm that he would remain unmarried and thus increase the likelihood that some of the familial territories might devolve to Ernst August or his children. This was, however, only a first step. It would still be necessary for either Christian Ludwig or Johann Friedrich to lack male heirs for Ernst August to become the ruler of one of the Brunswick duchies. Unencumbered by any particular desire to settle down, Georg Wilhelm agreed to his side of the bargain and Ernst August and Sophia were married in the autumn of 1658. Their union was rapidly blessed with children. George's father, Georg Ludwig, was born in May 1660 and six further children survived into adulthood, including a number of males, capable of inheriting territory and continuing the line themselves.

Ernst August was able to advance his hopes a little further during the course of the 1660s. In 1665 his eldest brother, Christian Ludwig, died childless. Georg Wilhelm promptly decided that he wished, as his brother had in 1648 and as was provided for in his father's will, to exercise his right to choose between the two duchies and rule in Celle instead of Calenberg. Johann Friedrich, the next brother, initially resisted this, asserting his own rights to inherit Celle directly but eventually an agreement was reached and Georg Wilhelm moved his court to its new home. This was not before Ernst August had sided with Georg Wilhelm and put a regiment of Osnabrück troops at his brother's disposal, in case the fraternal dispute escalated. Ernst August was rewarded with control of Diepholz by Georg Wilhelm, thus giving him for the first time some territory that he could pass on to his heirs. Georg Wilhelm and Ernst August remained on reasonable terms. Unlike their brother, who had converted to Catholicism in 1651, they were suspicious of the rising power of Louis XIV. Whereas French influence was growing at Johann Friedrich's court in Hanover, his brothers looked elsewhere for allies. Georg Wilhelm, in particular, was a strong supporter of William of Orange during the 1670s.

Yet for all the progress that Ernst August thought he was making, there was a small cloud upon the horizon. Much of his hopes for familial advancement relied upon Georg Wilhelm keeping his side of the 1658 bargain and remaining unmarried. Georg Wilhelm had, however, met someone who had taken his fancy. Visiting the court at Kassel, he had encountered Eléonore Desmier d'Olbreuse, a French Huguenot of noble extraction, who was in the entourage of the princess of Tarente. Georg Wilhelm was so taken with her that he persuaded Ernst August to invite Eléonore and her companion Mademoiselle de la Motte to join Sophia's suite for their journey to Italy in the winter of 1664–5. Mademoiselle de la Motte agreed but Eléonore preferred to follow her mistress to The Hague. Georg Wilhelm was besotted enough to abandon his Italian excursion and travel to the United Provinces instead. He then persuaded Ernst August to ask his wife to invite Eléonore to Osnabrück as a lady-in-waiting, which she did. Eléonore accompanied Ernst August and Sophia to Celle where she entered into a morganatic marriage with Georg Wilhelm. Ernst August had reassured himself before agreeing to this course of action that the 1658 agreement would remain in place. Such reassurance proved to be not only necessary but perhaps also inadequate. Eléonore gave birth to a daughter, Sophia Dorothea, in September 1666. Although Eléonore's subsequent pregnancies miscarried, Georg Wilhelm now had an heir, albeit a female and illegitimate one. Ernst August and Sophia began to worry that plans for familial advancement might yet be curtailed by older relatives.

From the dynastic perspective, Georg Wilhelm's infatuation with Eléonore was problematic. The duke of Celle was able to use his good standing with the Holy Roman Emperor, following his support for anti-French elements in the empire, to have his morganatic bride raised to the status of imperial countess in 1671. In April 1675 Georg Wilhelm went a step further. He married Eléonore and ensured that Sophia Dorothea was retrospectively legitimized. Despite Georg Wilhelm's further promise that the agreement of 1658 still stood, Ernst August and Sophia began to fear that things were not working out as they had planned. When it emerged that Sophia Dorothea had been betrothed to August Friedrich, the son of Anton Ulrich of Wolfenbüttel, later in 1675 the apprehension of the bishop of Osnabrück and his wife reached new heights. Sophia Dorothea was a mere nine years old at this point. An expansion of Georg Wilhelm's family was therefore not imminent in that generation but the newly legitimized Eléonore was hardly past her child-bearing years. Sophia Dorothea's potential spouse was killed at the siege of Philippsburg in 1676 but the line of potential suitors was hardly diminished. Georg Wilhelm's wealth and the size of his army made a coupling attractive for a number of German princely families.

Ernst August's own fortunes were boosted somewhat in 1679 when Johann Friedrich died, leaving only daughters. Ernst August inherited his brother's territories and quickly moved from Osnabrück to take up residence in Hanover. Slowly it was becoming clear to Ernst August and Sophia that the only way to guarantee that they could provide significant territory for their offspring was for their oldest son to marry his first cousin. This would ensure both that Celle and Calenberg would be brought together under one ruler and that a broader ambition might be contemplated as well. For Ernst August was not content simply to establish himself as a territorial ruler in the north-west corner of the empire. He wanted his family to join the empire's elite tier and gain Electoral status.

Imperial Electors, as the name suggests, were those princes who had the right to elect the emperor. Traditionally, there had been seven – the archbishops of Mainz, Trier and Cologne and the secular rulers of Saxony, Brandenburg, Bohemia and the Palatinate. Yet the earlier history of the seventeenth century had made clear that this number was not fixed. Bavaria had been raised to Electoral status by the Habsburgs following the staunch support that the Wittelsbachs had provided for the Catholic cause during the trials and tribulations of the Thirty Years War. Electors were second only to the emperor in the hierarchy of the empire and they came immediately after monarchs in the pecking order of European rulers. Beyond status, the imperial offices they held were lucrative.

It was to membership of this club that Ernst August now aspired. The union of Celle and Calenberg would provide a territorial unit large enough to have Electoral pretensions. In the interim, the military support that the combined forces of Osnabrück, Celle and Calenberg could provide for the emperor in the ongoing conflicts with the Ottomans and the French was a useful reminder to the emperor of how valuable friendship with Ernst August was. Ernst August's conduct was typical of any politician or statesman operating within a patron/client-based society. He was perfectly happy to do what he could to help out his patron, the emperor, but there was an expectation that such aid would not go unnoticed and that the reciprocity on which such interactions were based meant that Ernst August would gain something for himself as well.

For Ernst August, the dynamic dynast, therefore, significant hopes were invested in his eldest son, Georg Ludwig. Georg Ludwig had begun his military training in the campaigns of the 1670s and had become quite an accomplished soldier. On his father's accession to the dukedom of Calenberg, it was clear that Georg Ludwig now needed to be trained properly as a ruler. Georg Ludwig had travelled around Europe, including a trip to London in 1680 where some had thought that he was seeking the hand of Princess Anne. However, Ernst August's immediate ambitions were more local, so negotiations were begun with Georg Wilhelm in Celle and agreement was eventually reached in September 1682 on the terms of the union between their two eldest offspring. Ernst August agreed to accept a dowry of 100,000 taler, with Sophia Dorothea being paid a yearly allowance of 4,000 taler (to be put at her husband's disposal) by her father.[4] The marriage was celebrated in November 1682 and their firstborn arrived a year later.

GEORGE'S BIRTH AND UPBRINGING

George's father had been away on campaign for much of 1682 but he had returned in time for his son's birth. George's grandfather was pleased with his gender: a male heir provided some sort of guarantee of territorial succession into the second generation and strengthened the Calenberg claim of credibility in relation to potential Electoral status. Before pursuing the campaign for the Electoral cap further, Ernst August thought that it was important to decrease the likelihood of a further splintering of the territories he had worked so hard to bring back together. He decided that the best way to achieve this was to introduce the principle of primogeniture: all his lands should be passed to a single, male heir. For the tiny George, the eldest son of an eldest son, such a move by his grandfather would be beneficial to his own future prospects. George's uncles were less impressed, feeling, not entirely unjustifiably, that their father was cheating them out of their rightful inheritance. Ernst August persisted with the scheme and was slowly able to persuade most of his other sons to agree to it. For the disaffected, the imperial army or rival courts, such as Wolfenbüttel, offered alternative career paths or opportunities to cause further embarrassment for their father. Sophia was disappointed at the tensions within her family but understood the dynastic imperatives that had brought them about. George's parents meanwhile produced another child – a daughter, Sophia Dorothea, in March 1687.

Information on George's early years is scarce. His father remained an active solider for much of the 1680s and 1690s. How involved his mother was in his upbringing is unknown. Surviving accounts suggest that George was particularly close to his grandparents, especially Sophia and Georg Wilhelm.[5] George's early education was placed in the hands of a series of preceptors and tutors. His grandfather, Ernst August, was probably influential in determining who these people were and what they taught. Initially, George was under the care of his grandmother's *Oberhofmeisterin*,

---

[4] Hatton, *George I*, pp. 40–1.

[5] George told Hervey about his closeness to Georg Wilhelm in the aftermath of his wife's death in 1737. See Hervey, *Memoirs*, iii, p. 917.

Frau von Harling, who had also looked after his father. Sophia was left to keep a grandmotherly eye on him when his mother travelled to Italy to see his father, who was taking a break from campaigning in 1685. Johann Hilmar Holsten acted as George's tutor after the boy's fourth birthday, teaching him, among other things, German because he had previously only spoken French.[6] Holsten reported that George had a good memory but was a somewhat impatient pupil and that he had to make special efforts to interest him in German. The young prince was also instructed in genealogy and heraldry and spent his mealtimes listening to improving fables and proverbs from biblical and classical sources.[7]

In a set of instructions for George's tutor, Phillip Adam von Eltz, in June 1692, Ernst August emphasized the critical importance of a thorough grounding in the Christian religion. The court preacher was to ensure that the young prince attended divine service not just on Sundays but during the week as well. George should be kept away from gambling and should instead spend his time in conversation with honourable and appropriate persons.[8] A later set of instructions from 1696 stated that Georg Michael Bacmeister, the new under-governor, needed to live close to George (the room next to his was specified) to ensure that he could keep him away from dangerous influences and instil in him respect for his father and grandfather.[9] Interestingly, an almost identical set of instructions was adopted by Georg Ludwig when he came to stipulate how George's oldest son was to be educated.[10]

How successful this educational process was is an open question. Certainly, there were some who felt that it could have been stricter. Writing to her aunt, Sophia, in 1706 Liselotte of the Palatinate, the wife of Louis XIV's younger brother, Philip, duc d'Orléans, noted that she felt that George's current fits of temper were a product of not having been disciplined more severely as a boy.[11] There is little doubt that George was possessed of both a sharp tongue and a strong temper – observations of this sort are a consistent feature of accounts of his character throughout his life. Whether it was a lack of discipline that lay at the root of these traits is debatable. Moreover, he could also be charming, as William III noted when he met George for the first time in 1698. William was also

---

[6] Mijndert Bertram, *Georg II* (Göttingen, 2003), p. 25.

[7] Georg Schnath, *Geschichte Hannovers im Zeitalter der neunten Kur und der englischen Sukzession, 1674–1714* (4 vols, Hildesheim, 1938–82), ii, pp. 498–9.

[8] Havemann, *Geschichte der Lande Braunschweig*, iii, p. 516.

[9] Schnath, *Geschichte Hannovers*, ii, p. 499.

[10] Ibid., iii, p. 781. These instructions for Frederick were published in C.E. von Malortie, *Beiträge zur Geschichte des Braunschweig-Lüneburgischen Hauses und Hofes* (6 vols, Hanover, 1860–72), v, pp. 27–38.

[11] Elisabeth Charlotte to Sophia, Marly, 1/7/1706 (Letter 608) in Eduard Bodemann, ed., *Aus den Briefen der Herzogin Elisabeth Charlotte von Orléans an die Kurfürstin Sophie von Hannover* (2 vols, Hanover, 1891), ii, p. 138.

impressed by George's knowledge of Christianity so perhaps his tutors had been partially successful.[12]

Previous biographers have tended to blame George's upbringing, in a rather loose sense, for his reactions in later life. One line of argument is that his mother was disengaged from rearing her son so in some deep psychological sense he lacked love and affection.[13] The problem with such assertions is twofold. The evidence simply does not survive to permit an accurate diagnosis of how involved (or not) Sophia Dorothea was with George. Moreover, it is easy to overlook the fact that patterns of child-rearing were very different in princely families in the early modern period than they are today. Contacts between George and his mother was limited.[14] If it is difficult to blame the general circumstances of George's early years for his later attitudes, there is little doubt that a specific incident must have had a considerable impact on him, although again it is hard to speculate on what precisely that impact was.

THE KÖNIGSMARCK AFFAIR AND ITS AFTERMATH

George's parents had not been brought together by mutual affection but by the exigencies of practical politics. In such circumstances anything more than plain toleration of the other partner was considered a bonus. For princely males, having produced an heir, there was no necessity or indeed expectation that they would remain monogamous; Georg Ludwig was no exception in this regard.[15] The sexual double standard, rooted in the fear that an heir might not really be entitled to his father's property, meant that such freedom was not extended to women. Sophia Dorothea, however, decided that if her husband could take a mistress then there was nothing to stop her from taking her own lover. Count Philipp Christoph von Königsmarck was a Swedish noble in Hanoverian service when he first met Sophia Dorothea.[16] The couple began an exchange of letters and

---

[12] Schnath, *Geschichte Hannovers*, iii, p. 779.

[13] Charles Chenevix Trench, *George II* (London, 1973), p. 5.

[14] Schnath, *Geschichte Hannovers*, ii, pp. 496–7. There is only one mention of her children in Sophia Dorothea's surviving correspondence with her lover, Count Königsmarck, and that is to her daughter rather than her son, although references to other members of the family are frequent.

[15] Hatton, *George I*, pp. 49–51 discusses the most important of Georg Ludwig's mistresses, Ehrengard Melusine von der Schulenburg.

[16] The tale of the affair has intrigued numerous authors. Accounts include A.F.H. Schaumann, *Sophie Dorothea, Prinzessin von Ahlden und Kurfürstin von Hannover* (Hanover, 1879), W.H. Wilkins, *The love of an uncrowned queen* (London, 1900) and most recently Eleanor Herman, *Sex with the queen* (London, 2006) – although Sophia Dorothea's actions ensured that any chance of her becoming a queen disappeared. The definitive account of the affair remains that of Georg Schnath whose knowledge of the surviving evidence was unsurpassed – see Schnath, *Der Königsmarck-Briefwechsel* (Hildesheim, 1952) which combines commentary with a critical edition of the surviving letters and his three essays, grouped together as the 'Sophie-Dorotheen-Trilogie' in idem, *Ausgewählte Beiträge zur Landesgeschichte Niedersachsens* (Hildesheim, 1968), pp. 52–257.

it was perhaps this that gave the game away. However the news leaked out, various members of the court became aware that something was going on. Both were warned that the relationship must stop. Whether it was her husband or her father-in-law who determined that something should be done to curtail this liaison is not known. What is apparent is that on a hot July night in 1694 when the court was back in Hanover for Sunday service, and thus staying at the Leine palace rather than Herrenhausen, Königsmarck was intercepted on his way to Sophia Dorothea's apartment and was never seen again. A group of four Hanoverian courtiers, including George's erstwhile tutor von Eltz, found themselves rewarded for their part in the events of that evening.[17]

Georg Ludwig himself was conveniently (and probably intentionally) absent from Hanover. It is almost certain that Königsmarck's body was disposed of in the neighbouring Leine river, although Horace Walpole claimed in his *Reminiscences* that the body had been buried within the palace. Walpole said that he had heard this story from George's wife, with the additional piquant detail that the body had actually been unearthed during construction work in the palace after Georg Ludwig's death.[18] This anecdote is typical of Walpole's style – gossipy and very rarely favourable to either George or his father. While it is not entirely implausible, Walpole had to admit that when he mentioned this story to George's long-term mistress, Henrietta Howard, she disavowed all knowledge of it. Caroline herself never returned to Hanover after 1714 so could not have witnessed the grisly discovery with her own eyes.[19] However, the primary point is that Königsmarck's disappearance was the trigger for decisive action to be taken against Sophia Dorothea. In the face of incontrovertible evidence of her infidelity, divorce proceedings were quickly set in motion. Ernst August agreed with his brother that Sophia Dorothea should be confined to a castle in Ahlden. All contact with her children was to cease and traces of her presence were systematically removed from the Hanoverian court. Sophia Dorothea's father agreed to support her, while her dowry was to be retained by Ernst August and used for George and his sister.

George was in his eleventh year on the last occasion that he saw his mother. Perhaps unsurprisingly a number of stories were later to circulate implying that he had felt the loss profoundly. Walpole, for example, noted that when his father died in 1727, portraits of his mother that George had kept hidden appeared for the first time.[20] Henrietta Howard claimed to Walpole that George would have either freed his mother from Ahlden and brought her over to Britain or left her in charge of Hanover, had she

---

[17] Georg Schnath, 'Der Fall Königsmarck', in idem, *Ausgewählte Beiträge*, pp. 68–89.

[18] Horace Walpole, *Reminiscences written by Mr Horace Walpole in 1788 for the amusement of Miss Mary and Miss Agnes Berry* (Oxford, 1924), p. 22.

[19] Schnath ('Der Fall Königsmarck', pp. 88–9) is equally dismissive of Walpole's claims, adding the practical consideration that it would have been very difficult to disguise the presence of a decomposing body for that long.

[20] Walpole, *Reminiscences*, p. 23.

outlived his father.[21] There is no evidence for the rumour that George made an abortive attempt to visit his mother while out on a hunting expedition, leaving his companions, only to be pulled back before he reached Ahlden. The Hanoverian authorities kept copious records on all visitors to Sophia Dorothea and, given the tense nature of George's later relationship with his father, it is highly unlikely that such an attempt would have left no official trace.[22]

ELECTORAL STATUS AND ITS IMPLICATIONS

His mother's departure left something of a gap in the young George's life. Yet, other than the messy collapse of Georg Ludwig's marriage, the fortunes of Ernst August's clan seemed to be on the up in the 1690s. With the help of not a little pressure and plenty of cash, Ernst August had finally persuaded the emperor to grant Hanover Electoral status in 1692. All that remained now was to convince the other Electors that they should agree to Hanover's elevation. As part of Ernst August's push for increased status other aspects of life in Hanover were being improved.

To be taken seriously as a prince in the empire, or in Europe more generally, in the late seventeenth century, there were various strategies that a contender could adopt. One was to increase the size of one's military power, which in effect meant having a large army. Armies cost money so there were implications for how the state was organized to extract revenue most effectively from the population at large. A number of German princes operated a system of putting their regiments out to tender to the highest bidder. The key purchasers of German regiments in this period were the French Bourbons and Austrian Habsburgs who had invariably found themselves on opposite sides in all major international conflicts of the previous two centuries. One of the reasons that Ernst August's brothers had been keen to ditch the duchy of Calenberg for Celle at the first opportunity was that Celle was perceived to be wealthier and, therefore, potentially the more important military power. Georg Wilhelm had done much to enhance Celle's military reputation through his friendship and alliances with William of Orange.[23]

Military power was not the only form of power, however. Or rather, it was possible to signal military strength through means other than simply the number of men that could be put into the field in any given campaign. Conspicuous display and consumption were other ways for a prince to make an impression on the European scene. The audience for such display was twofold. On the one hand, it served to remind subjects, both high and

---

[21] Ibid., p. 22.

[22] Schnath, 'Die Prinzessin in Ahlden', in idem, *Ausgewählte Beiträge*, pp. 197–8.

[23] For the importance of soldiers and the efforts that rulers went to in order to obtain them, see Peter H. Wilson, *German armies* (London, 1998), Schnath, *Geschichte Hannovers*, ii, pp. 226–8.

low, of the power and importance of the prince and, as practised by Louis XIV at Versailles, showed the social distance between the monarch and even the highest-born of his subjects. On the other hand, the large palace, the lavish decorations, the expensive cultural entertainments all helped to persuade visiting diplomats that the court to which they had been sent was a wealthy one (and consequently also a militarily powerful one).

This system of display has been termed 'representational culture'.[24] The name relates to the notion that the power of the prince is displayed to the people and they are expected to be passive recipients of culture, rather than to engage actively in discussions of the relative merits of different ideas. Much of the work on the spread of representational culture has focused on the extent to which Louis XIV's court provided a model for all other aspirant representational rulers in Europe.[25] Signs of a court trying to ape Versailles might be the construction of a new palace, such as Schönbrunn in Vienna or Charlottenburg in Berlin where the architectural influence of Versailles is clear. A greater degree of ritual and ceremony might also be introduced, as might attention to the arts as means of promoting princely power.

For Ernst August, there were several ways in which he could harness the power of representational culture in a more general attempt to increase the status of his family and territories. Building was one. The Leine palace in Hanover was altered to create a space large enough for court festivities.[26] More importantly, a new opera house was constructed in 1688–9 within the palace. The finished product could seat 1,300 spectators and was generally acknowledged to be one of the finest in Europe. It had been built so quickly partly as a response to the news that the court at Wolfenbüttel was also constructing an opera house. It was critical that the one in Hanover should be bigger and better than that of the neighbouring territory to reinforce the signal that power had slipped away from the senior to the junior branch of the Guelphs.

The first production in 1689 was *Enrico Leone* by the court's Kapellmeister, Agostino Steffani, a Catholic cleric, composer and diplomat. The choice of subject indicates why opera was so important for representational culture. Through the plot of the opera, about the grandaddy of the Guelph dynasty, Henry the Lion, the power and prestige of the Guelphs, in both history and contemporary politics, could be projected to the audience. It was partly a means of massaging the ego of Ernst August who was, of course, present for the first performance, but it was also a way of reminding

---

[24] For an excellent summary of the ideas of 'representational culture' see T.C.W. Blanning, *The culture of power and the power of culture* (Oxford, 2002), pp. 1–25. Jürgen Habermas, *The structural transformation of the public sphere* (Cambridge, 1989) and Norbert Elias, *The court society* (Oxford, 1983) have exercised an important influence on studies of this topic.

[25] On Versailles, see Peter Burke, *The fabrication of Louis XIV* (New Haven, 1992).

[26] Schnath, *Leineschloss*, p. 67.

the wider audience that Ernst August's ego ought to be massaged and his power acknowledged. Opera, with its classical and historical plots easily amenable to allegorical interpretation, was an ideal medium in this regard.[27] Subsequent historians of the Hanoverian court have tended to see Ernst August's reign as the apotheosis of this type of baroque power.[28] It is true that Georg Ludwig was less keen on the flamboyant display of representational culture than his father. After 1714 both Georg Ludwig and George were to become occasional visitors to, rather than permanently resident in, Hanover and therefore a certain diminution in courtly activity occurred. Nevertheless, George, as subsequent chapters will make clear, was perfectly prepared to make use of the full gamut of cultural festivities to emphasize his own Electoral and regal power.

The new-found brilliance of the court in Hanover was partly a reflection of the force of Ernst August's personality and ambition but it was also the result of the cultural and intellectual prowess of his consort, Sophia. Sophia has been portrayed as a smart and canny woman by her biographers.[29] Her association with Leibniz, who had been appointed to a post by Johann Friedrich in 1676 but remained in Hanover after Ernst August's accession, has reinforced the notion of her intellectual interests. Sophia's other major achievement was the construction of the baroque gardens at Herrenhausen, where she enjoyed spending considerable time walking and wandering. Sophia was a dominant personality in the Hanoverian courtly world and the young George probably came under her influence.[30]

Sophia's impact, or otherwise, on George's nurture is important because of her attitude to George's mother. The pop psychological view has been that Sophia never quite got over the fact that Georg Wilhelm rejected her in the 1650s. Consequently she felt an antipathy towards both Eléonore and Sophia Dorothea as the child of that union.[31] Even without jealousy, there were reasons why Sophia might have been wary of her son's wife. Like her husband, Sophia had had to struggle to obtain recognition. None of the advantages associated with being a first-born had been hers. Therefore, anything or anybody that might endanger the plans that she and Ernst August had put together for advancing their branch of the family was deeply suspect. Sophia Dorothea's earlier projected marriages fell into precisely that category.

---

[27] For the history of the opera house in Hanover, see ibid., pp. 69–75 and Rosenmarie Elisabeth Wallbrecht, *Das Theater des Barockzeitalters an den welfischen Höfen Hannover und Celle* (Hildesheim, 1974), pp. 45–54. For the importance of opera to representational culture, see T.C.W. Blanning, *The triumph of music* (London, 2008), pp. 73–81.

[28] Heide Barmeyer, 'Hof und Hofgesellschaft in Hannover im 18. und 19. Jahrhundert', in Karl Möckl, ed., *Hof und Hofgesellschaft in den deutschen Staaten im 19. und beginnenden 20. Jahrhundert* (Boppard am Rhein, 1990), p. 241.

[29] Feuerstein-Praßer, *Sophie*, pp. 7–9 is typical.

[30] Havemann, *Geschichte der Lande Braunschweig*, iii, p. 516 goes as far as to attribute the pattern of George's upbringing largely to Sophia's influence.

[31] Schaumann, *Sophie Dorothea*, p. 22.

Beyond fear and jealousy, there was also a large dose of snobbery. Eléonore came from a noble family but she was hardly of equal social status to Sophia, whose parents and grandparents were monarchs. One story aptly illustrates Sophia's acute concern with status, as well as indicating the importance of etiquette and marks of recognition within this world. The type of chair in which one was permitted to sit was one way in which social distinction was articulated. In the presence of monarchs, all but the most important would have to stand anyway. Those who were allowed to sit could be offered three sorts of chair, which signified ascending degrees of social importance: a stool, a backed chair and an armchair. Sophia is alleged to have refused the offer of a stool when visiting Louis XIV because she had already been offered a backed chair when visiting the empress.[32] Given that within the pecking order of European royalty, the Holy Roman Emperor (and Empress) were generally agreed to rank above the kings and queens of France, it would have been insulting to accept a lesser mark of status from a lesser ruler, having already been given a higher honour by the empress. Just as Sophia was not prepared to be snubbed by Louis XIV, she was equally concerned to ensure that Eléonore knew her place. She claimed that Eléonore never sat in an armchair in her presence, overt recognition of Eléonore's social inferiority.[33] In the correspondence between Sophia and her niece Liselotte, snide remarks about Eléonore's background and malign influence were frequent. In March 1698, Liselotte commented that George's temper must have been inherited from his mother, because his paternal relatives were all so well mannered.[34] When Sophia reported that George had been spending a considerable amount of time with his new wife and shutting himself away from court society, Liselotte tartly responded that this was yet another example of George's failure to understand the necessary 'grandeur' with which he, as an Electoral prince, had to act. The source of this failure was genetic – he had too much of his grandmother Eléonore's 'noble' (as opposed to royal) blood.[35] The final example of Liselotte's emphasis on nurture being unable to overcome nature can be found in a letter of 1710. Liselotte was comparing the characters of George and his cousin (and future brother-in-law) the crown prince of Prussia. While the crown prince came from a pure bloodline, with George the 'mouse droppings had been mixed into the pepper' so although seemingly the same, it was little wonder that they behaved so differently.[36]

[32] Britta Hegeler, 'Sophia von Hannover – ein Fürstinnenleben im Barock', *Niedersächsisches Jahrbuch für Landesgeschichte*, 74 (2002), p. 185. The incident is described in Sophia's memoirs, printed as Adolf Köcher, ed., *Memoiren der Herzogin Sophie nachmals Kurfürstin von Hannover* (Leipzig, 1879).

[33] Schaumann, *Sophie Dorothea*, p. 21.

[34] Elisabeth Charlotte to Sophia, Versailles, 9/3/1698 (Letter 334), in Bodemann, ed., *Briefen der Herzogin Elisabeth Charlotte*, i, p. 325.

[35] Idem to idem, Versailles, 10/2/1707 (Letter 628), ibid., ii, p. 154.

[36] Idem to idem, Versailles, 27/10/1710 (Letter 740), ibid., p. 258.

It is difficult to be sure how much Sophia's apparent dislike of her daughter-in-law might have coloured George's childhood. Ragnhild Hatton maintained that much of the stress on the antipathy between the two Sophias had been overdone, at least at the time of the marriage itself.[37] In the post-divorce bout of recriminations, it seems unlikely that George was not made painfully aware of his mother's failings. She was, after all, the obvious scapegoat. Whether George's perceived misdemeanours could actually be attributed to his mother's less than elevated status is hardly the point. What such comments reflected was the complicated familial situation that the young prince found himself in following his parents' split. Liselotte's final dramatic denunciation of George's genes was prompted by a report from Sophia that George had left the dinner table to spend some time with Eléonore.[38] More generally, efforts were made to minimize the amount of unsupervised time that George spent with his maternal grandmother because of fears of what she might say or do.[39] Sophia probably had felt snubbed on this particular occasion but equally George may also have felt that he could not completely forget the other half of his family simply because his mother was now *persona non grata* with his father and grandparents.

Indeed, there is some evidence that Georg Wilhelm was rather fond of his grandson. George was a guest at his grandfather's court in October 1698 when William III came to visit his friend and ally the 'good old duke' of Celle.[40] Ernst August had died in January 1698, making Georg Ludwig the duke of Calenberg and Elector of Hanover and George now rejoiced in the title of Electoral prince. Regular conferences took place between officials of the two courts to ensure that the Braunschweig-Lüneburg duchies could present a united front to the world. It had been decided that George should spend some time at either Georg Wilhelm's hunting lodge at Göhrde or in Celle itself during William's visit. The initial suggestion had been that George should visit Göhrde to be introduced. George's father and his officials were keen not to do much more because they were anxious not to be dragged into making commitments about the future of the Spanish succession at a time when William was negotiating the first partition treaty. They wanted to win William's support for their own concerns, specifically the enforcement of the primogeniture clauses of Ernst August's will which would ensure that his inheritance would remain undivided and for wider recognition of Hanover's Electoral status. Their efforts were hampered by the fact that Georg Ludwig was refusing to dine with William, his claims for an armchair in the king's presence having been met with a stout refusal.

[37] Hatton, *George I*, pp. 40–1.
[38] Elisabeth Charlotte to Sophia, Versailles, 27/10/1710 (Letter 740), in Bodemann, ed., *Briefen der Herzogin Elisabeth Charlotte*, ii, p. 259.
[39] Schnath, 'Die Prinzessin in Ahlden', pp. 198–9.
[40] The best account of this visit is Schnath, *Geschichte Hannovers*, iv, pp. 9–15.

THE PROTESTANT SUCCESSION

Whether George joined in the hunting trip is uncertain. He was present in Celle where William arrived on 17 October. George had been invited, along with his sister and grandmother Sophia, and William III was very taken with both the Electoral prince and his sister. Leibniz was later to claim, in a letter to George's wife, that he had always intended that the question of what would happen to the succession in Britain should be raised during William's visit. There is little suggestion in the surviving evidence that this view was held more widely and it seems unlikely that Georg Ludwig or Georg Wilhelm had conceived of such an ulterior motive in arranging the visit. Nevertheless, Eléonore, prompted by Leibniz, raised the prospect of George's sister as a possible spouse for the duke of Gloucester (the son of William's heir) his sister-in-law, Anne. William did not seem averse to the idea and Leibniz was not reprimanded for taking such a bold step without his master's specific approval.

Throughout George's childhood his family had been trying to establish its position in north-west Germany. His early manhood was to be dominated by Hanover emerging on to the broader European stage. The death of the duke of Gloucester in August 1700 meant that William and Anne would have to think very carefully about the fate of the British thrones, given that by this stage it was highly unlikely that Anne would have any more children. Although not a particularly close blood relation of William and Anne, Sophia was a Stuart, and a Protestant one at that. In London, thoughts began slowly to turn towards her as a possible successor. One of the more obnoxious elements of James II's rule had been his Catholicism. The Bill of Rights (1689) had dwelt on James's perceived crimes and established the principle that Catholics should be excluded from the line of succession. Confession was, therefore, important when it came to determining how best to deal with William and Anne's childlessness. At first Sophia was a little reluctant to contemplate acceding to the British thrones. She had been upset by the mid-century upheavals in Britain which had led to the execution of one of her relatives and the exile of his family. As an exile herself, Sophia was keen that regal rights should not be altered by popular clamour. There is also some evidence to suggest that she thought that a restoration of the (Catholic) Stuarts was the right thing to do and she would not have wanted to be regarded as a usurper.[41] It was clear, though, that acquiring the British thrones would result in an even greater enhancement of the prestige of the Guelphs than even Ernst August could have envisaged.

---

[41] Ibid., pp. 17–19 for a careful discussion of Sophia's reaction to the news of the death of the duke of Gloucester and the ensuing semi-official approach to her which raised the possibility of her succeeding. Schnath is sceptical that Sophia was particularly worried about trespassing on her Stuart cousins' rights, arguing instead that the thrust of her response was noncommittal and cautious.

Georg Wilhelm and Sophia seem to have realized the potential advantages for the Guelphs much earlier than Georg Ludwig. Sophia travelled to the United Provinces in autumn 1700, accompanying her daughter Sophia Charlotte of Prussia and the Prussian crown prince, Frederick William. William seemed to admire greatly the Prussian crown prince. Georg Wilhelm was anxious that George might also have the chance to meet William again, pressing Georg Ludwig, to allow George to make the journey to the Netherlands with him. Georg Ludwig, when asked again, said that he did not want George to get any ideas about an English succession so felt that the trip was a bad idea.[42] The Elector proved immovable and the trip was abandoned. Georg Ludwig's relations with his mother were not improved by the fact that a letter in which she suggested that he was reluctant to contemplate a move across the Channel became public.[43]

George was becoming increasingly entwined with the succession question almost regardless of what he wanted for himself. In December 1700 reports reached Hanover that there were rumours circulating that the English nation was wary of giving the throne to a queen, and so there was talk of naming George directly as Anne's successor. Despite their recent disagreements over tactics, Georg Ludwig instructed his representative in London to make clear that such a move could only take place following a formal renunciation by his mother of her rights to the throne. Moreover, Georg Ludwig wanted to assert his own rights over those of his son. William responded that he could see that Sophia's advanced age might prove something of a barrier to her succeeding in her own right. However, he wanted a positive declaration from Georg Ludwig of his own willingness to accept the throne and a promise that George would be sent to Britain to acquaint himself with English practices and customs. The Elector was reluctant to agree to this, although he could see that there would be advantages to George acquiring the language. He did not want his son to reside permanently in Britain, and reminded William of the number of occasions on which he had travelled back to the United Provinces himself. Should George marry and produce male heirs, Schütz, the Hanoverian representative, could hint that Georg Ludwig might reconsider the residence question but, in the interim, his absence from Hanover could only be temporary.[44] This exchange was abruptly halted in February 1701 when Georg Ludwig stated that he was not willing to speculate on an uncertain future. Regardless of the Elector's wishes, a contemporary report from the imperial envoy, Wratislaw, also alluded to the desire to see the succession passed directly to George, although this must be conditional on him giving up his Hanoverian rights.[45]

[42] Ibid., pp. 19–20.
[43] Hatton, *George I*, p. 73.
[44] Schnath, *Geschichte Hannovers*, iv, pp. 23–4.
[45] Ibid., p. 25.

While William's notions of George spending a large amount of time in England were considered impractical and undesirable by both Georg Ludwig and Georg Wilhelm, the process of passing a measure to regulate the succession proceeded when the parliamentary session opened in February 1701. Georg Ludwig's Hanoverian ministers were quick to grasp that the prospect of the British thrones might be a useful incentive when it came to trying to marry George off. It was just one of the additional advantages that might be derived from the succession.[46]

The Act of Settlement was given the royal assent in June 1701. Its provisions named Sophia and 'the heirs of her body being Protestants' as successors to William and Anne. Catholics and those married to Catholics were excluded, thus removing the claims of some fifty closer blood relations to the throne. The Act also enshrined the principles that the monarch must be a member of the Church of England, that he (or she) could not leave Britain without parliamentary permission and that titles could not be granted to those who were not British subjects. Several of these provisions reflected unhappiness with the way in which William III had behaved, with his frequent absences from Britain, either on campaign or visiting the United Provinces. Yet they had also been included with an eye to the future in the hope that the Guelphs would not (or would not be able to) behave in a similar fashion.

The immediate impact of the Act of Settlement on George's life was quite small. He was present for the official presentation of the Act to his grandmother by the earl of Macclesfield on 15 August 1701 in the Leine palace. Naturally, such an occasion was celebrated with a banquet and a ball.[47] His maternal grandfather renewed pressure on his father to allow George to accompany Georg Wilhelm to Het Loo to hunt and to meet William III again. Georg Wilhelm also suggested that his grandson might accompany him on a visit to Britain early in the next year. Georg Ludwig conceded that the trip to the United Provinces might be appropriate on this occasion but remained adamant that George could not travel to Britain until he had produced male heirs.[48] George is said to have made quite an impression on those of William III's English courtiers who were present at Het Loo in the autumn of 1701. It was also at about this time that he began, at his grandmother's behest, to learn English properly. By March 1702, Sophia was reporting that he had made rapid progress.[49] Sophia was now being presented with a number of works designed both to improve her knowledge of the customs and constitution of Great Britain and to alert her to the patronage claims of the respective authors. Some of these were probably passed on to her grandson as well. Sophia's own knowledge of English was rusty but she was able to recall it quickly.

[46] Ibid., p. 37.
[47] Ibid., p. 42.
[48] Ibid., pp. 45–6.
[49] Ibid., p. 61.

The path from the Act of Settlement to the eventual fulfilment of its provisions in August 1714 was to be a bumpy one for nearly all those involved. William's death in 1702 brought the issue into sharp relief. Talk of George being sent to Britain temporarily diminished, not least because Anne, unlike her brother-in-law, was strongly opposed to the idea. The succession question was to remain a cause of dispute within British domestic politics, both between Whigs and Tories at Westminster and as one of the causes of dispute between England and Scotland that was only partially resolved by the union of 1707. In Hanover how best to pursue and protect the Guelph claim was to cause tensions between Sophia and her son and George would find himself used as a pawn in these arguments.

MARRIAGE PLANS

Before tracing further the highs and lows of George's relations with his future kingdoms in the first two decades of the eighteenth century, it is necessary to explain George's domestic situation. As much of the preceding discussion has emphasized, being a prince brought with it a number of serious responsibilities, chief amongst them being the necessity of producing an heir to ensure that the family firm would continue to flourish into the next generation. Selection of an appropriate partner was therefore a crucial part of the political calculation of both rulers and their ministers. Georg Ludwig was of course determined that George should not be allowed to reside for long outside Hanover before an heir was born. George was now of an age when the question of an appropriate match was high on his father's agenda.

Georg Ludwig had strong ideas about his son's future wife when he succeeded his own father in 1698.[50] The marriage was a matter of hope and concern. Hanover's increased status, which the granting of the Electoral cap entailed, had made George more of a catch on the international marriage market. However, the enforcement of the primogeniture clause meant that the perpetuation of the dynasty was now entirely reliant on George, assuming that Georg Ludwig himself did not remarry and have more sons. Georg Ludwig's choice of partner for his son had fallen upon Ulrike Eleonore, the younger sister of Charles XII of Sweden. Born in 1688, she was just ten when Georg Ludwig first thought of her as a match for his fifteen-year-old son.

Ties to the Swedish royal family were important for strategic reasons. Sweden was still a major power in the Baltic and north Germany. Moreover, a Swedish alliance would provide a useful counterweight to Danish power. Hanoverian relations with Denmark, its near neighbour, were usually antagonistic. In December 1698 Georg Ludwig instructed his representatives in Sweden to discover whether Ulrike Eleonore had a 'healthy complexion' and whether the prospects of her producing heirs

[50] Ibid., iii, pp. 230–47.

were good.[51] There was, however, competition for Ulrike's hand –
Frederick III of Brandenburg hoped to marry the Prussian crown prince
to Ulrike and one of his daughters to Charles XII. Hanoverian efforts to
complete the Swedish match intensified, even when negotiations with
Charles XII became difficult following the outbreak of the Great
Northern War in 1700. Georg Ludwig dispatched Colonel Balthasar von
Klinckowström to join Charles XII's army in July 1701 and von
Klinckowström remained with the Swedish king until March 1702. The
marriage negotiations were not the only reason for Klinckowström's
mission – Georg Ludwig was anxious to secure Swedish support for a
projected strike by Hanover and Celle against Wolfenbüttel – but he
pursued them vigorously.

Something of the strength of Georg Ludwig's desire to secure the
Swedish match can be seen in the change of tactics that took place in
the summer of 1702. In July 1702 Duke Frederick IV of Holstein-Gottorp,
the husband of Charles XII's elder sister Hedwig Sophie, was killed in
battle. Hanoverian attention immediately switched to her as a potential
wife for George. Two years older than the Electoral prince, she could
marry immediately. Moreover, she had already given birth to a son so the
prospects of securing the dynasty looked sound.[52] Although Swedish diplomats suggested that Hedwig did not find George objectionable, she was
unwilling to enter into a rapid second marriage because of her concerns
about her son's claims to the Swedish throne and her own position as
regent, given her brother's continued absence on campaign. Hanoverian
officials also sought to reassure their Swedish counterparts that the Act of
Settlement's requirements for an English monarch to be Anglican should
not be seen as a barrier to a match with George because there was virtually no difference between Anglicanism and Lutheranism (the crown prince
of Prussia's Calvinist faith was, however, highlighted as a good argument
against that particular option!). Hanoverian officials even suggested that
Hedwig Sophie's son's claim to the Swedish throne might be enhanced,
rather than diminished, if his stepfather were to become king of England.
The negotiations dragged on, not helped by Charles XII's own refusal to
marry or think about providing his own successor. By February 1705 Georg
Ludwig's patience had been exhausted and he made clear that he would
look elsewhere for a bride for his son.

MARRIAGE ACHIEVED

The woman who was to become George's bride did not come from
nearly so illustrious a background as the Swedish royal family. Born in
March 1683, Wilhelmine Caroline of Ansbach-Bayreuth was the daughter
of Margrave Johann Frederick of Ansbach and his wife, Eleonore of

---

[51] Ibid., p. 234.
[52] Ibid., p. 241.

Saxony-Eisenach. Her father died in 1686 and her mother then entered into an unhappy second marriage with Elector Johann Georg IV of Saxony. Caroline, as she was invariably known, lost her stepfather in 1694 and her mother two years later. She then moved to Berlin, to the court of her guardian, Elector Frederick III of Brandenburg, who later became Frederick I of Prussia.

As an orphan, Caroline's only hope of advancement seemed to be through a good marriage. Her blond hair and blue eyes worked to her advantage in this respect and she attracted the interest of the imperial court in Vienna. The future emperor, the Archduke Charles, visited her en route to Spain to assert his right to the Spanish crown in October 1703 and considered her to be a worthy bride. The only sticking point was Caroline's Protestantism. Ferdinand Orban, the Jesuit confessor of the Elector Palatine, was dispatched to persuade Caroline of the errors of her Lutheran faith and the wisdom of conversion to the mother church. But, as John Gay was later to put it, 'she scorned an Empire for religion's sake' and refused to be persuaded by Father Orban's casuistry.[53]

Caroline's decision would later prove to be to her long-term advantage, not least by endearing her to the vehemently anti-Catholic British. Yet, given her background and lack of opportunities, it must have seemed foolhardy in the extreme even to her close relations that she should forgo the chance to become queen of Spain simply for the sake of the Protestant faith. Princely conversion to achieve secular advantage was a relatively common practice within the empire in this period. Augustus of Saxony had converted to Catholicism in order to be elected king of Poland and Elisabeth of Wolfenbüttel also converted, albeit somewhat reluctantly, to become Charles VI's wife. Interestingly, one of the few people to praise Caroline for her principles was Georg Ludwig in a letter to his mother in November 1704.[54]

By this point, Georg Ludwig must have been thinking that his Swedish plans might not be brought to fruition and an alternative arrangement might have to be made. Although Sophia was later to protest, perhaps a little too much, that she had never given serious thought to Caroline as a bride for George, she would have had the perfect opportunity to observe her during her own regular visits to Berlin to see her daughter.

These circumstances need to be remembered when assessing the traditional accounts that place much of the initiative for finding his future bride squarely on the shoulders of George himself. He left Hanover in June 1705, accompanied by his former tutor Philipp Adam von Eltz. Although his destination was unknown, the English envoy Sir Edmund Poley suspected that it might be Cassel, Zeitz or Ansbach.[55] Using the pseudonym of von dem Bussche, George met Caroline in Ansbach and convinced himself that

[53] John Gay, 'Epistle I – to a lady, occasioned by the arrival of her Royal Highness', line 134 in *The poetical works of John Gay* (3 vols, London, 1797), ii, p. 9.
[54] Schnath, *Geschichte Hannovers*, iii, p. 249.
[55] Poley to Stepney, Hanover, 14/6/1705, BL, Add. MSS 7072.

she was the only one for him. He hurried back to Hanover, eager to ask his father if negotiations for her hand might be opened. The speed with which Georg Ludwig agreed to his son's request suggests that it was not entirely unexpected. He promptly ordered von Eltz to return to Ansbach to make discreet enquiries about Caroline's availability and willingness to enter into a match with his son. Caroline was able to offer the necessary reassurances that the projected match with the Archduke Charles was definitely off and the marriage contract was signed by the end of July 1705. The contract stipulated a dowry of 20,000 Frankish guilders. George agreed to provide Caroline with a sum of 6,000 talers (or 300 talers a year for life). Fourteen thousand talers would be provided for Caroline in the event of George's demise and this sum was to be transferred to the Herzberg region where the castle of the same name could also serve as a dower house. The treaty even went so far as to provide accounts for Herzberg to show that it would indeed yield the sums intended.[56]

The speed and secrecy with which the negotiations had been conducted meant that Caroline's guardian, Frederick I of Prussia, was presented, to his irritation, with a *fait accompli* when news of the match was publicly announced. The marriage itself was concluded quickly. It took place on 2 September 1705 in Hanover. Court mourning for the death of Georg Wilhelm on 28 August 1705 was suspended for two days to allow the marriage to be celebrated properly. Pleased as he undoubtedly was on his wedding day, George still managed to sleep through some of the sermon, allowing the ever acid-tongued Liselotte to remark that at least it meant he would be well rested before the exertions to follow.[57]

George's marriage was to be a long and, by contemporary princely standards, successful one. Caroline proved to be a great support and her presence did much to establish the dynasty in Britain after 1714. Yet there seem to have been some rocky moments at the start of the relationship. Liselotte had told her aunt a story about the archbishop of Paris's vineyard shortly after the wedding.[58] The story went that the archbishop was willing to give his vineyard to any married couple who could complete the first year of their union without ceasing to love each other or regretting their decision. Liselotte noted that the archbishop was still in possession of his vines and, a few months later, opined (presumably on the basis of Sophia's reports of George's behaviour) that she was sure George would not be claiming the property from the French cleric.[59] Liselotte's view in this, and

[56] For the treaty itself, NHStA, Dep. 84 A, 42. There is another copy in NHStA, Dep. 84 B, 365, fos 9–18. See also the discussion in Schnath, *Geschichte Hannovers*, iii, p. 251.
[57] Kroll, *Sophie*, p. 216.
[58] Elisabeth Charlotte to Sophia, Versailles, 29/10/1705 (Letter 588), in Bodemann, ed., *Briefen der Herzogin Elisabeth Charlotte*, ii, p. 118. For an English version of the same letter, see Elborg Forster, trans. and ed., *A woman's life in the court of the Sun King: letters of Liselotte von der Pfalz, 1652–1722* (Baltimore and London, 1984), p. 160.
[59] Elisabeth Charlotte to Sophia, Versailles, 21/2/1706 (Letter 595), in Bodemann, ed., *Briefen der Herzogin Elisabeth Charlotte*, ii, p. 128.

a subsequent letter, was that Georg Ludwig should be told about George's failings. What good was it if he knew all about the Greeks and Romans and yet could not behave like a prince?[60] She did admit, though, that she thought that George and Caroline would start to get on better soon and her observation that Sophia seemed to have been less irritated by George before his marriage suggests that perhaps his grandmother was finding the change of status difficult as well.

The Electoral prince's affection for his new wife was readily apparent, though. When Caroline contracted smallpox and pneumonia in 1707, George nursed her through the illness, remaining at her bedside and endangering his own health. Liselotte's complaints about George locking himself away from the court with his wife appeared in a letter of February 1707.[61] This was shortly after Caroline had given birth to their eldest son, Frederick Ludwig. Frederick's safe arrival was a release to George in several ways. The pressure on him to ensure the survival of the dynasty was reduced and the chances of his being able to fulfil his frustrated military ambitions were increased.

SOLDIER AT LAST

George deeply resented his father's refusal to allow him to go off and fight before his dynastic duty had been completed. Georg Ludwig had gained extensive military experience at a similar stage of his career, although the fact that he had younger brothers probably meant that Ernst August felt that allowing him to do so was less of a risk than it was for George, an only son. The opportunities for young princes to test their leadership capabilities through military command were as ample in the early eighteenth century as they had been in the late seventeenth. Despite the best efforts of William III and Louis XIV to anticipate a solution to the childless state of Charles II of Spain, conflict had erupted on his death in November 1700. Louis XIV wanted to further the claims of his grandson, while Emperor Leopold I pushed those of his second son, the Archduke Charles. Fighting had, therefore, been going on for some time when Georg Ludwig consented to George's participation in it.

The instructions that Georg Ludwig drew up prior to George's departure in May 1708 noted that his main aim should be to acquire a solid knowledge of the art of war through conversation with experienced generals and officers; he added that, while true bravery was praiseworthy in those of high social status, it was unbecoming to be unnecessarily daring.[62] George was sent off to the headquarters of the duke of Marlborough, accompanied by von Eltz, Colonel Oeynhausen and two gentlemen-in-waiting; they arrived on 22 June

[60] Idem to idem, Versailles, 25/3/1706 (Letter 597), ibid., p. 130.
[61] Idem to idem, Versailles, 10/2/1707 (Letter 628), ibid., ii, p. 154.
[62] For a copy of the instructions (19/5/1708), see L. von Sichart, *Geschichte der königlich-hannoverschen Armee* (5 vols, Hanover, 1866–98), ii, pp. 297–8.

1708.[63] The French had pushed into Flanders and Marlborough was engaged in a series of manoeuvres to head off further French advances, following the fall of Ghent and Brugge. The Electoral prince had been attached to the Hanoverian regiment of von Bülow that formed part of a contingent commanded by the British soldier and diplomat Colonel William Cadogan, who had been a close confidant of Marlborough throughout both the Nine Years War and the War of the Spanish Succession. Cadogan had been placed in command of the advance guard by Marlborough. George accompanied Cadogan in a series of marches until eventually Cadogan led his troops across the Scheldt on 11 July at Eename near Oudenarde. This bold move had taken the French by surprise but they still heavily outnumbered Cadogan's forces. However, with skilful deployment of his troops, Cadogan secured the bridge-head, enabling Marlborough to bring the main allied army across. George was involved in the early stages of battle. He led the life squadron of von Bülow's dragoons as the allied attempt to cross the river was countered by the French cavalry. In the ensuing melee, George's horse was shot from under him. Seeing the danger that the Electoral prince was in, Colonel Johann Albrecht von Lösecke leapt from his own horse and, in the effort of helping George on to his, received a fatal wound. When it was suggested to George by von Bülow that the danger was so great that he should withdraw, George responded that he had promised his uncle (probably Ernst August, Georg Ludwig's youngest brother who had made a name for himself as a soldier) that he would uphold the family's honour so he immediately returned to the fray. Lösecke's family would subsequently receive a pension from George so he undoubtedly felt a debt of gratitude for Lösecke's bravery. Yet George's own courage was commended and commented upon. Marlborough wrote to Georg Ludwig, commanding allied forces on the Rhine, that George had shown exceptional bravery in charging at the head of Georg Ludwig's troops.[64] George remained with Marlborough's forces for the rest of the campaigning season, taking part in the siege of Lille. But he was not to see action on the scale of Oudenarde again. His request to rejoin allied forces in 1709 was firmly refused by his father.[65]

The impact of the battle on George is interesting for several reasons. One is that it prompted the prince to write to Caroline to reassure her of his survival in one of the few of their letters to be preserved.[66] On 12 July, George informed his wife of the allied success of the previous day. He described his own contribution to the battle and the loss of Lösecke, at his side. Unfortunately, his baggage had not yet caught up with him so he was

[63] Alexander Schwencke, *Geschichte der Hannoverschen Truppen im Spanischen Erbfolgekriege, 1701–1714* (Hanover, 1862), p. 139.

[64] Ibid., p. 143. There are some letters between Marlborough and George in BL, Add. MSS 61234 but these are mainly taken up with Marlborough keeping George informed of the progress of his campaigns between 1708 and 1710 and contain no further reports of George's action at Oudenarde.

[65] Schnath, *Geschichte Hannovers*, iii, p. 783.

[66] George to Caroline, Oudenarde, 12/7/1708, NHStA, Dep. 84 B, 365.

having to use Marlborough's quarters to write to her. He asked Caroline's pardon for failing to provide more details of the battle but he hoped she would understand that he had not slept in twenty-four hours and so felt unable to talk much about it.

GEORGE AND THE PROTESTANT SUCCESSION IN BRITISH POLITICS

Outside the circle of his family, George's conduct in the field was a useful addition to the armoury of those trying to defend the Protestant succession in Britain. He had become the focus for efforts, particularly by the Whigs, to ensure that enough was being done within Britain to safeguard the succession. A brief detour into British partisan politics is necessary to understand the significance of this. The names of Whig and Tory to describe the major political groupings within the House of Commons date from the reign of Charles II.[67] Although often referred to as parties, neither grouping was much like a modern political party. Family ties, patronage and association were just as important as an ideological platform in holding the groups together. Nevertheless, there were some key principles that served to unite them. The nomenclature reflected two sides of the political fears of the Restoration political nation. A Tory had originally been an Irish brigand. When applied to politics, the word was designed to suggest that emphasis on the hereditary rights of monarchs, the doctrine of non-resistance and a strong defence of the Church of England as the only Protestant church might have dangerously 'popish' tendencies and suggest a lack of limit to the exercise of power that was seen as one of the major reasons why it had been necessary to break with the Church of Rome at the Reformation. A Whig, on the other hand, was a Scottish Covenanter who opposed the engagement with Charles I in December 1647. The word was used to conjure up the image of a group similar in intent to those who had executed a monarch in the 1640s, who espoused dangerously republican principles and who were willing to admit that the Church of England might not have a monopoly on religious truth. The two groups had arisen in the course of the struggle during the later years of Charles II's reign about who should succeed him. Whigs had been determined to exclude Charles's Catholic brother, James, duke of York, arguing that a Catholic monarch would destroy English liberties in church and state. This quest had ultimately been unsuccessful, although it could be argued that the Whigs had had the wry last laugh when James's policies after 1685 seemed to show that their fears had been entirely justified. The Glorious Revolution, or last successful invasion of Britain as it might also be called, was, among other things, a brief moment of unity between Whigs and Tories in agreement that the threat to the English

---

[67] Tim Harris, *Politics under the later Stuarts* (London, 1993), chs 3–4 provides a succinct introduction to the origins of party.

political nation from Catholic rule was greater than the dangers posed by allowing varieties of Protestant faith. All rulers in this period tended to associate religious toleration with political unrest, partly because they saw their own rule as divinely sanctioned. If the religious underpinnings of society could be questioned, then it was possible to attack the form of secular government as well.

In the aftermath of 1688 the vast majority of Whigs and Tories had agreed that monarchs should henceforth be Protestant and this principle had been established in the Bill of Rights in 1689. The Act of Settlement had reaffirmed this view. Thus, although later generations of (mainly Whig) historians were to see the events of 1688 as vital in showing the centrality of parliament, in general, and the House of Commons, in particular, as the keystones of English constitutional arrangements, for contemporaries it was at least as important that the principle of Protestant monarchy had been firmly established. After the passing of the Act of Settlement the Whigs had been the most vociferous advocates of the Hanoverian solution to the British monarchical problem. This reflected their own origins in the Restoration period and their continuing suspicions that the Tories, for all their advocacy of the rights of the Church of England, were little more than closet supporters of the exiled Stuarts. Regardless of whether the charge was true or not, in the public mind there was an indelible association between a return of the Stuarts and the introduction of 'popery and arbitrary government'. While some hoped that the Stuarts might renounce their Catholicism in order to recapture the British thrones, both politics (particularly bankrolling by Catholic monarchs and later the papacy) and personal piety meant that neither James II nor his heirs thought that London was worth more than a mass.[68]

Debate within British politics in the first decade of the eighteenth century centred on a number of interrelated areas, all of which were amenable to both Whig and Tory interpretations. There were fears that the Church of England was coming under attack from the growth of Protestant dissent. Tories tried to pass legislation to ensure that the loopholes that Dissenters were exploiting to hold public office were closed. Whigs argued that Catholics continued to pose a greater threat to domestic security and that political energies were better spent on the struggle against Louis XIV's France. For Whigs, the War of the Spanish Succession represented the continuation of the struggle instituted by William III to ensure that Europe did not fall entirely under the shadow of a Catholic monarch. Tories, on the other hand, thought that the war was both expensive and had gone on too long. It was impoverishing the landowners of the Tory squirearchy who were facing increased land tax

---

[68] For an excellent discussion of Jacobite policy, see Edward Gregg, 'France, Rome and the exiled Stuarts, 1689–1713', in Edward Corp (with contributions from Edward Gregg, Howard Erskine-Hill and Geoffrey Scott), *A court in exile* (Cambridge, 2004), pp. 11–75.

bills to pay for the conflict. Moreover, the war was enriching a new class of financiers, most of them of a Whiggish inclination, who had arisen in the aftermath of 1688 when such changes as the foundation of the Bank of England in 1694 vastly increased the ability of the state to borrow and, by extension, to wage war. All of these issues could be used to fan the flames of political argument but the issue of the succession in many ways brought them into sharp relief. The Guelphs were foreign princes and therefore likely to favour continued active involvement in war on the European continent. They were Lutherans, rather than Anglicans, so it was possible to stoke up fears about dangers to the Church of England that they might pose.

Whig supporters of the Guelphs, therefore, wanted to do all that they could to portray Sophia and her family in the best light possible. Having George brought across to England to learn about the lands he might one day inherit was a perennial pet project of some of the most activist Whigs. Whigs feared that some Tories thought that the Act of Settlement could be reversed. Partisan controversy about the succession led to two further pieces of legislation in the session of 1705–6 designed to increase the likelihood of a smooth transition to Guelph rule. A Regency Act, listing a named group of individuals who would ensure the safe transition from Anne to Sophia and her heirs, was passed eventually, as was a Naturalization Act that made Sophia and her family, provided that they were Protestant, British.[69] Anne herself tried to steer a middle course between competing Whig and Tory claims, although her instincts were probably more Tory. She had a mixed ministry for much of the first decade of the eighteenth century. She was not keen, however, to have George in Britain. Nevertheless, Anne was prepared to show some further marks of favour to one of her presumptive heirs. Now that he had been naturalized, it was thought appropriate to grant George some English honours.

In June 1706, during Lord Halifax's mission to Hanover, George was invested as a knight of the Garter by Sir John Vanbrugh as Clarenceux King of Arms. Halifax was appointed as George's proxy for the official installation in St George's Chapel, although this was not to take place until 1710.[70] George had written a formal Latin note to Anne in 1706 to thank her for the award – he had been able to take up the place left vacant by the death of his grandfather, Georg Wilhelm, the year before.[71] In addition to the Garter, George, as a naturalized British subject, was also granted a title, or rather titles. He was created Baron Tewkesbury, earl of Milford Haven, Viscount Northallerton and duke and marquess of

---

[69] Geoffrey Holmes, *British politics in the age of Anne* (revised edn, London, 1987), pp. 83–4, Schnath, *Geschichte Hannovers*, iv, p. 143.

[70] The programme for the installation, dated 22/12/1710, including a plan of the stalls is in NHStA, Dep. 84 B, 365.

[71] The letter, without date or place, can be found ibid.

Cambridge in December 1706. Both George and his father were some-what reluctant to accept these honours formally, suspecting that they were a mere sop to avoid doing anything practical about securing the succession, although Howe, the English envoy, was eventually granted an audience to make the necessary presentations.[72]

In this context of heated debate about the succession, George's achieve-ments on the battlefield at Oudenarde could be used to good effect. George's exploits were commemorated in verse:

> Not did so behave
> Young Hanover brave
> In the bloody field, I assure ye:
> When his war-horse was shot,
> He valued it not
> But fought it on foot like a fury.[73]

Indeed, this impression of the heroic young soldier was to be one of the most persistent features in accounts of George's character and exploits. Georg Schnath, the foremost historian of Hanover in this period, suggested that George's popularity in the aftermath of Oudenarde led some Whigs to think again about inviting him to come to London but, once more, Anne's reaction was such that nothing came of the plans.[74] Halifax had used accounts of George's bravery as an excuse for writing a congratulatory note to Sophia in which he drew a sharp distinction between the behaviour of George at Oudenarde and that of James Edward, the Stuart claimant or Old Pretender, who had witnessed the battle from the sidelines.[75]

While George was becoming better known to his future subjects, rela-tions closer to home were more problematic. Conflict between Guelph fathers and sons was almost a fixed point in the eighteenth century (except with George III, whose father died young, so he argued with his grandfa-ther, George, instead). Many explanations have been offered for this conflict, some specific and some general. In the case of the relationship between George and Georg Ludwig, the impact of divorce has frequently been invoked. There are, however, some more structural reasons which need to be remembered. First, the relationship between a ruler and his heir was always likely to be a tense one. For the ruler, the desire to preserve the heir and continue the line could easily lead to over-protection (this can be

---

[72] Schnath, *Geschichte Hannovers*, iii, p. 781.

[73] The ballad in question, entitled 'Jack Frenchman's Defeat', is sometimes attributed to Jonathan Swift. However, Countess Cowper attributes the ballad to William Congreve and reported that George wanted to thank Congreve, having been told of his authorship after his arrival in Britain. See Spencer Cowper, ed., *Diary of Mary Countess Cowper, lady of the bedchamber to the Princess of Wales, 1714–1720* (London, 1865), p. 24.

[74] Schnath, *Geschichte Hannovers*, iv, p. 207.

[75] Ibid., p. 206.

seen clearly in Georg Ludwig's reluctance to allow his son to earn his spurs). From the perspective of the heir, once adulthood has been achieved, life could quickly become little more than waiting for one's father to die. Finding a role, in other words, was exceptionally difficult. Such tensions were easily exacerbated when close physical proximity led to a sense of being stifled. The Leine palace was not especially large by contemporary European standards and it contained all the administration of the Electorate, as well as apartments for Sophia, Georg Ludwig, George and Caroline. George and Caroline's family continued to grow, putting even more pressure on space. Anne was born in 1709, Amelia in 1711 and Caroline in 1713. Anne's birth prompted George to write a particularly affectionate letter to his wife. He was only a little angry that the birth had caused her pain because she should know that 'everything that concerns you is infinitely precious to me'. Having passed on the greetings of various family members, George concluded, 'Adieu, my dearest heart, for God's sake take care of yourself, and of the young family . . . the peace of my life depends on knowing you in good health, and upon the conviction of your continued affection for me. I shall endeavour to attract it by all imaginable passion and love, and I shall never omit any way of showing you that no one could be more wholly yours.'[76]

The vexed question of the Protestant succession rumbled on. Changes in British domestic politics, as well as the conduct of the War of the Spanish Succession, were beginning to make both leading Whigs and the Hanoverians themselves a little nervous. The general election of 1710 had brought a considerable number of Tories into the House of Commons. Although the size of the electorate in the early eighteenth century means that the result cannot be taken as a measure of popular feeling in any but the vaguest sense, it was indicative of a change in mood in the political nation. Concerns about the continuation of the war coupled with disquiet at the campaign that the Whigs were pursuing against the leading High Churchman, Henry Sacheverell, seemed to favour the Tories, with their staunch support for the Church of England and desire to bring the war to a conclusion. The new ministry of Robert Harley and Henry St John was much more Tory in complexion than its predecessor. Georg Ludwig was concerned when it became clear that the new ministry intended to pursue separate peace negotiations with the French, potentially leaving other members of the Grand Alliance, the coalition of princes and states that had sought to limit Louis XIV's power since the 1690s, high and dry. Many of these fears were justified when the treaty of Utrecht was finally signed in 1713: several of the issues that Georg Ludwig and the emperor had hoped the peace would resolve were left open and they had to struggle

---

[76] R.L. Arkell, *Caroline of Ansbach* (London, 1939), p. 46. The translation is Arkell's own. The German source was destroyed during the Second World War so the translation cannot be checked.

to conclude a further treaty with the French at Rastatt in 1714 which finally brought hostilities to an end.

Georg Ludwig regarded the treaty of Utrecht as a betrayal and it did little to calm suspicions in Hanover and among the Whigs that the Tories might be thinking about Stuart, rather than Hanoverian, options. How far either Anne or the Tories or Louis XIV were actively pursuing a policy of support for the Stuarts is uncertain. The climate of suspicion was such that fears were magnified out of all proportion. The problem was becoming more significant because Anne's health was clearly in decline. She had been very ill in the winter of 1713–14, which led both supporters and opponents of the Protestant succession to become more active. The issue of whether the Protestant succession in the house of Hanover was safe was debated in the House of Lords in April 1714. Given the furore, the succession's supporters reverted to type and argued that now would be a good time for a member of the Guelph dynasty to travel to Britain. The call for George to come to Britain was, therefore, renewed. The means by which this was to be achieved was the demand that a writ of summons be issued for the new duke of Cambridge to take up his seat in the House of Lords.

Schütz, the Hanoverian envoy, was instructed to pursue the matter but received short shrift from Anne. Schütz was forced to leave London and a very blunt letter was sent to Sophia stating that none of her family would be welcome in London while Anne lived. The letter was received by Sophia on 5 June. Three days later, as she was walking in the gardens of Herrenhausen accompanied by Caroline and Johanna Sophie, countess of Schaumburg-Lippe, Sophia was taken ill and died. Anne survived Sophia by a mere six weeks. Her death in August 1714 was to lead to significant changes for George and his family.

Chapter 2

KING-IN-WAITING

Anne's death brought enormous upheaval for George and his family. News of his father's changed status reached Hanover quickly. Georg Ludwig was not in any hurry to make the journey to his new lands. As was traditional, heralds had proclaimed him king on the day of Anne's death. The list of regents that had been left in London for the occasion had been opened and the regency council it created had begun to act.

Before departing for London, it was necessary to put in place arrangements to ensure the smooth government of the Electorate in the absence of its Elector. Georg Ludwig drew up a detailed set of instructions for what his Hanoverian officials could and could not deal with by themselves.[1] George and his family would accompany Georg Ludwig to London. However, Georg Ludwig decided that his German subjects could not be left completely bereft and decided that Frederick, second in line to the throne after George, should stay in Hanover as the family's representative. Georg Ludwig's youngest brother (and the only one with whom he was still on good terms, following the recriminations from the primogeniture dispute), Ernst August, was also to remain in Hanover. Perhaps it was envisaged that Ernst August would act as the senior member of the family, educating Frederick in the arts of government. Unfortunately, the death of Charles Joseph of Lorraine, Elector of Trier and bishop of Osnabrück, in December 1715 meant that the bishopric of Osnabrück again needed to be filled by a Guelph and Ernst August seemed to be the obvious choice. Consequently he spent less time in Hanover after his installation in Osnabrück.

THE NEW KINGDOMS: LEARNING THE ROPES

George and his father travelled to London via the United Provinces, where Georg Ludwig was able to talk to members of the Dutch elite, traditional allies of both Hanover and Britain. Crossing the Channel on a yacht provided by the Royal Navy, the royal party landed at Greenwich on the evening of 28 September 1714 NS. Having knighted Captain Sanderson, who had commanded the ship on their crossing from Holland, both Georg

---

[1] For the text of the *Reglement* see Richard Drögereit, ed., *Quellen zur Geschichte Kurhannovers im Zeitalter der Personalunion mit England 1714–1803* (Hildesheim, 1949), pp. 5–15.

Ludwig and George received various dignitaries at Greenwich the next morning, before proceeding in a festal procession to London. Cannons sounded at the Tower of London to mark their entry and contemporary reports noted the size of the crowds that came out to welcome the new monarch and his son.[2] George dined in public on several occasions during his first few days in London. Caroline and his daughters were initially left in Hanover but they had travelled to London in time for Georg Ludwig's coronation in October 1714.[3] Both George and Caroline participated in the coronation ceremonies. George was the first prince of Wales to be present at a coronation for a significant length of time. Caroline's presence was even more of a novelty – there had not been a princess of Wales since Catherine of Aragon's short marriage to Henry VIII's elder brother, Arthur. In the rush to organize the coronation, compromises had to be made so George had to make do with the crown used by Mary, William III's wife, at her earlier coronation.[4] The new prince of Wales and his spouse were quickly established in a set of apartments at St James's Palace on the side of Paradise Court opposite to those occupied by Georg Ludwig.[5]

The country in which the prince and princess now found themselves was not altogether alien to them. Both had achieved a reasonable grasp of English before their arrival in London. In addition, a growing number of Britons had journeyed to Hanover in the years prior to 1714 in an effort to find grace and favour with the future royal family through the acquisition of place in their respective households. Royal households, and the court more generally, were significant employers. For those of noble birth, the quest for preferment made attendance at court a virtual necessity. There were opportunities for those further down the social scale too. The Irish writer and philosopher John Toland, who travelled to Hanover as secretary to the earl of Macclesfield on his mission to present the Act of Settlement to Sophia, published an account of his experiences at the courts of Hanover and Berlin which included characters of Georg Ludwig, Sophia, George and, for the edition published in 1714, of Caroline as well.[6] No doubt Toland hoped that by bringing news of both Hanover and its rulers to a wider British audience, the subjects of his work would look more kindly on one of their potential subjects.

---

[2] For an account of George's entry with his father in 1714 see Hannah Smith, *Georgian monarchy* (Cambridge, 2006), pp. 98–9. There is an excellent German account in NHStA, Hann. 91, v. Hattorf, 54, fos 22–7. Johann Philipp von Hattorf, whose diary covers the royal entry, was a Hanoverian official who became chief Hanoverian minister in London in 1728.

[3] Details of arrangements for their journey can be found in NHStA, Dep. 103, XXIV, 2643.

[4] Ragnhild Hatton, *George I* (London, 1978), p. 129.

[5] H.M. Colvin, J. Mordaunt Crook, Kerry Downes and John Newman, *The history of the king's works: volume V, 1660–1782* (London, 1976), pp. 239–40.

[6] John Toland, *An account of the courts of Prussia and Hannover* (London, 1714). The work had originally appeared in 1705. For Toland's attitudes towards Hanover, see Nick Harding, *Hanover and the British empire, 1700–1837* (Woodbridge, 2007), pp. 17–21.

Another couple who made the journey to Hanover in search of fame and fortune were Charles and Henrietta Howard. Henrietta came from a Norfolk gentry family, the Hobarts, and she had married Charles Howard, youngest son of the fifth earl of Suffolk in 1706, who had like many younger sons of the nobility embarked on a military career. Charles Howard sold his commission soon after the marriage but was irritated to discover that much of his new wife's inheritance had (wisely as it turned out) been placed in trust to protect her from unsuitable husbands. The couple's impoverished state eventually led them to travel to Hanover in the hope of securing patronage. In this Henrietta had some success: it seemed likely that she would become a bedchamber woman to either Sophia or Caroline when the Protestant succession took place.[7] Henrietta's expectations were fulfilled – she travelled back to London in Caroline's entourage in October 1714 and was appointed a woman of the bedchamber soon afterwards. Her husband, meanwhile, gained a place as a gentleman of the bedchamber to the new king. Henrietta's relationship with both George and Caroline was to be long-lived.

Those who did not travel to Hanover might stake their claims for recognition in other ways. Edmund Gibson, an Anglican cleric who had already received some recognition as chaplain to Archbishop Tenison, wrote to Caroline in March 1714 enclosing a copy of his *Codex juris ecclesiastici Anglicani* on the government and discipline of the Church of England. The work showed, Gibson noted, how the Protestant succession had been vested in Caroline's family and detailed the laws against popery. Gibson, who was widely perceived as a prominent Low Churchman and partisan Whig, hoped that Caroline would believe that 'noe Subject of Great Britain does more cordially wish the honour and enlargement of your Illustrious House' than himself.[8]

Nevertheless, even allowing for their linguistic aptitudes, there was much that was alien to George and Caroline in their new home. For one thing, the system of government was a little different. Although the accusations made by opponents of the Protestant succession that the Guelphs were used to ruling in an absolutist fashion and so would introduce nasty absolutist ways into Britain turned out to be unfounded, it was the case that the estates of Georg Ludwig's Electoral territories had much less say in government than parliament had within Britain. For a venerable tradition of Whig historians, the accession of the Guelphs was further evidence that the power of the monarchy within Britain was in terminal decline, the initial blow having been dealt when the convention chose to offer the throne to William III in 1689. In such accounts political power was conceived as a zero-sum game so any increase in parliamentary power and authority must have been accompanied by a decline in more traditional

---

[7] Tracy Borman, *Henrietta Howard* (London, 2007), p. 42. Borman's work is the most recent biography of Henrietta Howard.
[8] Gibson to Caroline, London, 25/3/1714, NHStA, Dep. 84 A, 365.

sources of authority, such as the monarchy and the Church of England. There undoubtedly was a sense among many of the great aristocratic families that they were more ancient and, therefore, superior to the new royal family and that they had a right to be consulted on all the important decisions affecting the nation. Yet this is a long way from a view of Britain inevitably marching towards greater political participation and the more populist politics of the nineteenth century that traditional Whig accounts suggest. The reigns of the first two Georges were to lead to a growth in the power of the executive, as distinct from the monarch, but not for the reasons that many have suggested.

To unpack this claim, it is necessary to say a little about parliament in the early eighteenth century and the position it enjoyed within the British constitution. Mention of parliament now is likely to lead to images of dispatch boxes and party leaders facing off against each other during set-piece debates. It is often taken to be shorthand for the House of Commons but in the eighteenth century the House of Lords remained at least as important as the Commons, if not more so. MPs with pretensions to national importance hoped that a seat in the Commons would not be the pinnacle of their achievements. Elevation to the peerage was the reward for the most able but for many direct royal favour was unnecessary: as sons of the nobility they could hone their political skills in the Commons before taking up their fathers' seats in the Lords when the title passed to them.

The chief power that the Commons did enjoy was that of control of the purse-strings. This power had, in many ways, increased in the aftermath of 1688. Faced with a new land and new set of customs, William III had to work quickly within existing arrangements to gain finance for his wars against Louis XIV. The Stuarts had tried very hard to survive for long periods without calling parliaments to grant direct taxation, relying instead on traditional monarchical revenues, such as customs, foreign subsidies and what they could get away with. As an incomer, William III did not enjoy the luxury of having taxes granted for life. He also faced huge bills for a foreign policy of European engagement. Regular parliaments were the price that he had to pay for grant of supply. Parliament had, therefore, begun to change from an event – as it had been prior to 1688, when summoned simply at the will of a monarch and often when all other options had been exhausted – into an institution. This transition was reinforced by the other financial changes that were introduced to help fund William's wars.[9]

Encapsulated in the phrase 'financial revolution', the foundation of the Bank of England and the switch to a situation in which government debt was institutionalized had a transformative effect on many aspects of British

---

[9] For useful short introductions to the political and financial history of Williamite England, see Julian Hoppit, *A land of liberty? England, 1689–1727* (Oxford, 2000), ch. 2 and Craig Rose, *England in the 1690s* (Oxford, 1999), ch. 4.

society in the 1690s.[10] The shift towards a system of government finance based on permanent borrowing vastly increased the state's ability to wage war. The consequences for political debate were important as well: could the new financial instruments be trusted and what would the rise of wealth based on bits of paper do to those whose wealth was based in more tangible property like land? From the point of view of the House of Commons, the ability to approve taxation was crucial to the smooth functioning of the new system. Those who were lending to the government wanted to know that there were funds available, via the tax system, to pay the interest on their loans. Moreover, they were concerned that the ministry had a plan for how the debt would eventually be repaid so the role of the Commons in scrutinizing government expenditure was to become increasingly important as well. Those who were investing in government debt were very often those with political power. Therefore, in many ways, MPs were behaving in a self-interested manner in ensuring that the system worked because they might not only have to pay the taxes that they were passing but could also take advantage of the financial opportunities offered by the credit economy themselves.

From the point of view of the ministry, parliament was there primarily to ensure the smooth running of the financial system on which the functioning of the state relied.[11] There was some space to debate issues, particularly those related to foreign policy because MPs thought, not unreasonably, that if the vast bulk of government expenditure was devoted to foreign policy then they ought to have a say in its direction. The formulation of foreign policy was, however, still considered a matter for the royal prerogative and George and his father were able to develop strategies to ensure that what they regarded, with absolute constitutional propriety, as their foreign political business was not overly interfered with or influenced by the mewings of MPs in the Commons. For MPs themselves, the Commons was an arena in which legislation on areas of more local or regional concern might be passed but the initiative for this would come from an individual or group of individuals, rather than a party platform or central government.

Beyond the legislature, the executive contained a number of levels. Much of the machinery and personnel of government were directed towards either the efficient extraction and collection of taxation or the management of the army and the navy. Places on the various commissions, boards and committees that ran these enterprises were sometimes open to talents but were often awarded as sinecures for those deemed worthy of patronage. At the top of the executive were the ministers themselves, many of whom held titles reflecting their traditional roles. Financial

[10] The classic study of these changes is P.G.M. Dickson, *The financial revolution in England* (London, 1967). For more recent discussions, see Henry Roseveare, *The financial revolution, 1660–1760* (London, 1991) and John Brewer, *The sinews of power* (London, 1989).

[11] See also, Jeremy Black, *Parliament and foreign policy in the eighteenth century* (Cambridge, 2004), pp. 1–12.

management was entrusted to the commissioners of the treasury, led by the first lord of the treasury. Yet, arguably, the most important of these ministers were the two secretaries of state. Entrusted with the conduct of diplomacy, their remit was split geographically with a department devoted to the north and one to the south. The northern department dealt with the Scandinavian courts, Russia and the empire, and the southern with France, and the Iberian and Italian peninsulas.

Ministers met in council to discuss policy and to offer advice to the monarch. Ragnhild Hatton has shown that Georg Ludwig continued to preside at this cabinet council himself, as well as seeing his ministers in private, or the closet, as contemporary parlance put it. At first George was present at these councils and so would have got to know both how the system worked and the personalities involved. However, continuing the practice that he had grown used to in Hanover, George was not present when his father saw his ministers in private.[12] The monarch, therefore, was still a key player in early eighteenth-century government. He was at the centre of decisions about foreign policy which was the primary focus of governmental activity. Georg Ludwig, in some ways, enhanced, rather than diminished, this trend. Like William III, Georg Ludwig was an experienced soldier-ruler who was used to meeting the great and the good of Europe and had an extensive network of contacts in addition to the resources provided by Hanover's own diplomatic machinery. Consequently, he had an ability to conduct diplomacy himself that Anne had lacked.

PRINCE OF WALES: SEARCHING FOR A ROLE

Even though the monarch might still have been a key player in politics, George was to discover that there was little more in the way of a defined role for the prince of Wales than there had been for the Electoral prince of Hanover. He was still, to a large extent, living in his father's shadow. Events early in his father's reign were to reinforce this point. The Jacobite uprising of 1715 was important in a number of respects.[13] A rising by some of the Scottish clans under the earl of Mar was put down by John Campbell, second duke of Argyll. The Old Pretender arrived in Scotland too late to have any real influence on the conduct of the campaign. From the point of view of domestic politics, the uprising presented a golden opportunity to the Whigs. Georg Ludwig's initial instincts had been to adopt Anne's tactic and construct a mixed ministry with a combination of Whigs and those Tories, like Nottingham, who had supported the Hanoverian succession. The Whigs used the uprising as an opportunity to persuade Georg Ludwig that the Tories were not to be trusted, arguing that under every Tory bed lurked a Jacobite, and that therefore the king

[12] Hatton, *George I*, pp. 129–30.
[13] For a comprehensive history of the uprising, see Daniel Szechi, *1715: the great Jacobite rebellion* (New Haven and London, 2006).

needed to entrust his government to their sole care. Tories were removed from their positions at court, in the ministry and in local government and replaced by ardent Whigs. With a few execeptions, the Whigs were to enjoy a monopoly of patronage and place for the next half-century.

From George's point of view, the uprising was a bitter reminder of how little he could do. He was unable to take command of his father's troops – the argument about the danger to the heir was probably invoked – so he had to twiddle his thumbs at St James's. Conditions in the palace were cramped although George and Caroline did have their apartments redecorated and enlarged.[14] Relations between George and his father remained strained. George was, however, developing his social profile. Unlike his father, he seemed comfortable with some of the social responsibilities of the monarchical role. He was happy to dine in public, to attend the theatre and to participate in the drawing rooms and balls that were the fixed points of court life.[15] Having a wife at his side and young children around him helped as well. The very domesticity of the new prince and princess of Wales mitigated the sense of strangeness that a new dynasty brought with it.[16] The couple were shouldering the task of establishing the public profile of the Hanoverian monarchy practically by themselves. Georg Ludwig, continuing the pattern that had developed when he became Elector, was much less interested in court ceremonial and tended to shy away from formal occasions and appearances when at all possible.

Social popularity was hardly a substitute for political power, though. Relations between the king and his heir worsened in 1716. Conflict manifested itself in several ways, but its roots lay in Georg Ludwig's desire to return to Hanover for the summer. The British ministers were less than keen on the idea, arguing that his departure would be unwise, given how recently the rebellion in Scotland had finished. Unfortunately, the provisions of the Act of Settlement that had required parliamentary permission for monarchical absence from the realm had been repealed in 1716 as unbecoming to the royal prerogative. There was little that ministers could do, other than complain. However, they still wanted to prevent any unnecessary political intrigue during the king's absence. Military matters were something that both Georg Ludwig and George had a strong interest in, and control over military patronage was jealously guarded by both. Marlborough, the hero of the War of the Spanish Succession and builder of Blenheim, was still commander-in-chief but he suffered two strokes in 1716, and thoughts therefore turned to his successor. The choice lay between William Cadogan, George's commander at Oudenarde, and the

[14] Colvin et al., *King's works*, p. 240.

[15] Dudley Ryder, *The diary of Dudley Ryder, 1715–1716*, ed. William Matthews (London, 1939), pp. 76–7 [15/8/1715].

[16] Christine Gerrard, 'Queens-in-waiting: Caroline of Anspach and Augusta of Saxe-Gotha as princesses of Wales', in Clarissa Campbell Orr, ed., *Queenship in Britain, 1660–1837* (Manchester, 2002), pp. 146–7.

duke of Argyll. Cadogan had replaced Argyll at the end of the campaign against the Scottish rebels in 1715, after claiming to Marlborough that Argyll had showed excessive leniency towards them. The ministers were inclined to favour Cadogan but feared what Argyll's reaction might be (Argyll was a sharp negotiator – he had managed to get himself promoted to the rank of general at the age of just twenty-five in 1705 as a condition for his help in ensuring the smooth running of the Scottish parliament in the difficult years prior to the Union of 1707). Moreover, Argyll held the position of groom of the stole in George's household and it was feared that he could use his closeness to George to foment trouble in the king's absence. Georg Ludwig forced George to dismiss Argyll before his departure.[17]

George was unhappy at the interference in the management of his household. He was, however, left with little choice in the matter. Georg Ludwig made clear that unless George accepted the decision, Ernst August would be brought across to act as guardian of the realm in the king's absence in Hanover. It was probably this that was the cause of George's anger in 1716, rather than the absence of the title of 'regent' that some accounts have claimed lay at the root of the resentment between father and son. As Ragnhild Hatton and Graham Gibbs have shown, the formulation 'guardian of the realm' was an appropriate one and should not be seen as a deliberate snub by the king against his son.[18] Georg Ludwig envisaged an arrangement akin to those he had put in place for the government of Hanover after 1714: during his absence from London minor matters could be settled by George but important decisions and appointments had to be referred to the king. George could preside at cabinet meetings but he could not create peers. He could confirm army appointments and grant pardons but only to a certain point: treason cases and high-ranking commissions were reserved for the king. These arrangements probably seemed sensible to Georg Ludwig – they provided George with an opportunity but allowed him little scope to make large mistakes – and reflected the ways in which he had been introduced to the government of Hanover by his own father. Yet for a frustrated prince, looking for a role, they must have seemed yet another example of the shackles his father was placing upon him.

Despite the constraints on his governmental powers, George made use of his father's absence to score a number of public relations points.

---

[17] Patricia Dickson, *Red John of the battles* (London, 1973), pp. 195–200. For contemporary confirmation of ministerial worries about the influence of Argyll over George, see Spencer Cowper, ed., *Diary of Mary Countess Cowper, lady of the bedchamber to the Princess of Wales, 1714–1720* (London, 1865), p. 58. For evidence of George's close friendship with Argyll, see Ryder's report of their discussions at the theatre in March 1716, *Ryder Diary*, p. 195.

[18] Hatton, *George I*, p. 197 and G. C. Gibbs, 'George I (1660–1727)', *Oxford Dictionary of National Biography*, Oxford University Press, Sept 2004; online edn, May 2009 [http://www.oxforddnb.com/view/article/10538, accessed 14 July 2009].

He spent the summer at Hampton Court, where he dined in public frequently.[19] Together with Caroline, he appeared at a series of celebrations which combined the regal with solid English rusticity. There were rural sports and reports of the royal couple discoursing easily with the locals. George and Caroline's participation in English country dances was also noted.[20] George's public activity was not confined to Hampton Court. He travelled in the south-east during September 1716, visiting Kent, Sussex, Hampshire and Surrey. George first visited the earl of Dorset's seat at Knowle before proceeding to Tunbridge Wells, where he took the waters and 'took a turn in the walks'. He stayed with the duke of Newcastle then moved on to Lewes. Having visited the earl of Scarbrough's estate at Stansted Park, George travelled to Portsmouth, where he inspected several regiments and boarded some of the ships in the dockyard. Both his arrival and his departure were marked by salutes from the guns of the fort and ships in the harbour. On his way back to Hampton Court, he stopped in Guildford where the houses were illuminated, the streets strewn with flowers and the populace most welcoming. The official report of the four-day tour noted that those who had met him had been pleased by the prince's 'gracious and affable manner' and the poorer sort were grateful for his 'bounty and charity, which was very liberally bestowed among them'.[21]

The impression gained by many was that he was trying to create an identity and a following separate from that of his father. Countess Cowper reported, admittedly at second hand, some of the comments that George had been making about his new home and its inhabitants in March 1716. Mrs Clayton, one of Caroline's ladies of the bedchamber, had been entertaining the assembled company with George's thoughts on the English, whom he had described as 'the best, the hansomest, the best shaped, the best natured, and lovingest People in the World, and that if Anybody would make their Court to him, it must be by telling him he was like an Englishman'. The reaction of the foreigners at the table had been a strong one, with Schütz, the keeper of the prince's privy purse, retorting that he believed there was not 'one handsome woman in England'.[22] Whether Whigs like Robert Walpole and Viscount Townshend wanted to portray his actions as such or whether it was the result of a definite plan on George's part, the impression was that George was trying to represent

---

[19] *Cowper Diary*, p. 125, *Ryder Diary*, pp. 298–9, John M. Beattie, *The English court in the reign of George I* (Cambridge, 1967), p. 229.

[20] Gerrard, 'Queens-in-waiting', p. 148.

[21] *London Gazette*, 5472, 25–29/9/1716.

[22] *Cowper Diary*, p. 99. Such disputes between German and English courtiers were not unusual: a few pages later Cowper reports an exchange between the countess of Schaumburg-Lippe and the Countess Deloraine in which the former contended that English women did not hold themselves properly and the latter retorted that because English women had birth on their side, they did not need to stick their breasts out (ibid., p. 102).

himself as distinctively British in this period. Some, such as Christine
Gerrard,[23] have argued that the responsibility for pushing a sense of
British identity should be attributed primarily to Caroline. The precise
origins of the strategy, if it can be called such, are obscure. George's motivation for pursuing it are also unclear. Perhaps it was a bid for popularity
on the prince's part or perhaps it was simply to irritate his father.

Two events in December 1716 helped to increase the prince's popularity even further. While he was attending the theatre at Drury Lane, a
Mr Freeman attempted to enter George's box and when he was stopped
from doing so, discharged a shot which went over the prince's shoulder.
Freeman was apprehended and discovered to be carrying several loaded
pistols about his person. Described by contemporary newspaper reports as
mad, Freeman may not have been a particularly serious potential assassin
but George's coolness in the face of danger enhanced his reputation.[24] In
addition to personal courage, George also opened his wallet to help those
in need. Following a serious fire in Limehouse, he provided £1,000 for the
victims.[25]

POLITICAL TENSIONS

George's new-found popular touch may have been one reason for a
further round of disputes with his father but a broader political crisis had
an impact as well. The early years of Georg Ludwig's reign had been
marked by a series of dramatic foreign political moves.[26] Together Georg
Ludwig and his secretary of state, James Stanhope, had engaged in negotiations which had secured an alliance with France and they entertained
grand plans to bring peace to both the north and south of Europe. Few
would dispute the benefits of peace. More controversial was the sense that,
amidst all these negotiations, Georg Ludwig was pursuing a particular
foreign political course for Hanoverian, rather than British, ends. These
worries were acute in relation to Georg Ludwig's policy on the Baltic. The
Great Northern War had been going on since 1700 and involved Russia,
Denmark and Saxony-Poland in an attempt to undermine Swedish dominance in that part of Europe. Georg Ludwig, wearing his Electoral cap,
had long extended a greedy eye towards some of Sweden's possessions
within the empire, namely the duchies of Bremen and Verden. Following
his accession to the British thrones, the king hoped that the resources of
the Royal Navy might be used to further this aim. The method proposed
was to send a squadron to the Baltic to protect the forces attacking the
Swedes and ease their supply routes. While there were undoubtedly
benefits that might accrue to Hanover from Sweden's demise, there were

[23] Gerrard, 'Queens-in-waiting', p. 147.
[24] *Weekly Journal or British Gazetteer*, 8/12/1716.
[25] *London Gazette*, 5498, 25–29/12/1716.
[26] For the background, see Hatton, *George I*, pp. 180–92.

good strategic reasons for British involvement, not least the protection of British shipping.[27]

Not all Georg Ludwig's ministers were convinced by these arguments. Walpole and Townshend had expressed their disquiet at the direction of Georg Ludwig's policy and this led to Townshend's dismissal as secretary of state for the north in December 1716. Anxious not to splinter his ministry entirely, Georg Ludwig offered Townshend the post of lord lieutenant of Ireland – a post with insufficient power to be really important but prestigious enough for a politician who needed to be moved sideways, rather than completely excluded. The king had been persuaded to do this by Stanhope although Charles Spencer, third earl of Sunderland had wanted even firmer action. Sunderland had a long career in Whig politics behind him and felt that he had not received the recognition he deserved in 1714. He had been particularly offended that Townshend had been appointed secretary of state when he had only been offered the lord lieutenancy of Ireland. Protesting ill health, Sunderland had never quite got round to travelling to Dublin and had been appointed lord privy seal in 1715. During the summer of 1716 he had travelled to the continent, ostensibly to take the waters at Aachen, but had continued to Hanover. Sunderland was able to persuade Georg Ludwig and Stanhope both that Townshend was opposed to the direction of their negotiations and that he was conspiring with George who, it was claimed, was deliberately courting popularity while Georg Ludwig was away.

George was now embroiled in a split between two different factions of Whigs, both determined to maintain their hold on power. The struggle was played out in the early months of 1717. Georg Ludwig had promised on his accession that he would try to remove some of the disabilities that Protestant Dissenters laboured under as a result of legislation passed during Anne's last Tory administration. The laws in question were the Occasional Conformity Act of 1711 which prevented Dissenters from taking communion in the Church of England once a year and thereby gaining the necessary qualifications to hold civil office, and the Schism Act of 1714 which restricted Dissenters' ability to run educational establishments. The Dissenters had been staunch supporters of the Hanoverian succession and so some concessions in relation to their legal position were seen, not least by them, as just recompense for their efforts. George, however, let it be known that he supported the efforts of some of the bishops to block the repeal of the legislation.[28] His sympathy for the

---

[27] This point is made persuasively and at greater length in Brendan Simms, *Three victories and a defeat* (London, 2007), chs 4–5.

[28] For the background, see Norman Sykes, *William Wake* (2 vols, Cambridge, 1957), ii, pp. 114–16 and Andrew Starkie, *The Church of England and the Bangorian controversy, 1716–1721* (Woodbridge, 2007), ch. 2. Archbishop Wake was anxious to preserve his status as Caroline's spiritual adviser.

Church of England may have been yet another attempt to reinforce an identification with his new home.

In early April 1717 the ministry asked parliament for a large vote of funds to support Georg Ludwig's anti-Swedish strategy. The ministry hoped that the revelation of the Gyllenborg plot, which had been uncovered in January 1717, would help to ensure that the funds were forthcoming. Gyllenborg, the Swedish envoy, was arrested and his papers seized on suspicion that he, and Swedish diplomatic colleagues in other European capitals, had been engaged in Jacobite plotting. The aim was to commit Charles XII to active military support of the Jacobite cause, in exchange for Jacobite funds. Charles's interest in the Jacobites was more related to finding means to nullify Georg Ludwig's intervention in the Baltic than to solid ideological commitment. At the same time, Georg Ludwig probably hoped that funds for his anti-Swedish designs might increase the chances of Hanover acquiring Bremen and Verden. The prince of Wales made it clear that he did not care about Bremen and Verden.[29] The ministry's majority dropped dramatically when the vote on funds was taken. Most of the prince's household abstained and many of the parliamentary supporters of Walpole and Townshend voted against. It was alleged that Spencer Compton, the Speaker and a close ally of George, had done much to ensure the narrowness of the vote.[30] Questioned by his father's Hanoverian minister, Bernstorff, about his behaviour, George claimed not to be acting against the king, but the behaviour of his followers in the Commons suggests otherwise.[31] Furthermore, the fact that the prince had stopped attending meetings of the cabinet council by this point suggested that relations were far from harmonious.

An open break between the prince of Wales and his father did not happen quite yet but Townshend's behaviour could not go unpunished. He was dismissed and Walpole promptly resigned as well. The next few years were to be difficult ones for the Stanhope–Sunderland ministry.[32] They faced opposition in the Commons from the Walpole–Townshend grouping which occasionally allied with Tories but was more dangerous when it was working with the prince of Wales. This period is usually described as 'the Whig split'. It was also the first example of what was to become a common eighteenth-century political phenomenon – the reversionary interest. For politicians who had fallen out of favour with the

---

[29] Hatton, *George I*, p. 199.

[30] Jeremy Black, 'Parliament and the political and diplomatic crisis of 1717–18', *Parliamentary History*, 3 (1984), pp. 79–80.

[31] Hatton, *George I*, p. 201.

[32] Clyve Jones has cogently argued that the usual description of the ministry should be reversed to reflect the greater experience and seniority of Sunderland ('The "reforming" Sunderland/Stanhope ministry and the opening of the 1718–19 session of parliament in the House of Lords', *Historical Research*, 78 (2005), p. 60) but I persist in the traditional designation because of my emphasis on the primacy of foreign relations in the first half of the eighteenth century.

monarch, one way to ensure that they might regain some of their lost power and influence was to side with the next likely incumbent, regardless of partisan affiliation. Hence the court of the prince of Wales, in times of acute political division, was often the breeding ground for opposition for those dissatisfied with the existing regime. The first three Hanoverian monarchs were all relatively long-lived so being prince of Wales could be both boring and frustrating.

FAMILY SPLITS AND RIVAL COURTS

Throughout the summer of 1717, efforts were made to reconcile the king and his son. Georg Ludwig's Hanoverian ministers, Bernstorff and Bothmer, acted as go-betweens, sometimes talking to Caroline and some-times to George directly. Much of George's animus seems to have been directed against Sunderland, whom he thought had been needlessly offensive to him. The king, on the other hand, was unwilling to force Sunderland into making an apology. In an effort to shore up his own popularity, Georg Ludwig decided to postpone his intended visit to Hanover in 1717, much to the relief of his British ministers. Instead, it was decided that he would spend the summer at Hampton Court and use the opportunity to show that he, too, could live lavishly and support a brilliant court. During his three-month stay, Georg Ludwig dined in public on Thursdays and Sundays and was much more willing to engage in court life than he had been previously.[33]

The prince and princess of Wales also spent the summer at Hampton Court, although the prince's new allies, the Walpolean Whigs, were notable by their absence. Caroline was in reasonably frequent attendance on her father-in-law but observers noted that relations between the prince and his father still seemed strained. George went hunting by himself and it was suspected that his supporters were encouraging him to remain independent of his father, perhaps in the hope that he might be able to summon the parliamentary strength to force out Stanhope and Sunderland when parlia-ment reconvened in November.[34]

Conflict was, therefore, very much in the air when Caroline's preg-nancy was brought to a seemingly successful conclusion with the birth of a son in October 1717. Sons were, of course, more important than daugh-ters from the dynastic perspective and a second son for the prince and princess added to the sense of security about the long-term future of the Hanoverian dynasty. Nevertheless, the new prince rapidly became a source of contention. First, there was the issue of his name. Caroline wanted to call the child William. Georg Ludwig, as one of the godfathers, was initially happy with this choice but the British ministers contended

[33] Beattie, *English court*, pp. 264–7, Smith, *Georgian monarchy*, pp. 199–200.
[34] Hatton, *George I*, p. 205.

that the new prince should be named after his grandfather (and father) instead. George William was suggested as a compromise and the duke of Newcastle, the lord chamberlain, was dispatched to tell the prince and princess the news. The question of who the boy's other godparents should be was the next cause of disagreement. George and Caroline were keen to ask George's uncle, Ernst August, the bishop of Osnabrück, to take on the role. Ernst August had no heirs of his own, being unmarried and he was unlikely to have any. He seemed, therefore, to be a good choice: providing for younger sons (and daughters) was always a matter of concern within royal families. The British ministers, however, insisted that the lord chamberlain had traditionally been nominated as one of the godfathers of royal princes and that the king should insist on preserving precedent. The prince and princess tried to defer the baptism in an effort to find some way of avoiding this, after their suggestion that Newcastle could stand proxy for Ernst August at the christening was refused. Concerns, kept secret from British ministers, about Georg Ludwig's health meant that his Hanoverian advisers were also anxious to get the matter resolved quickly because they hoped the parliamentary session could be kept short to enable the king to depart for the continent as soon as possible to take the cure at his favourite spa.[35]

The previous history of tension and conflict needs to be borne in mind when assessing the impact of events at the christening itself which were the ostensible cause of the break between father and son. The christening took place on the evening of 28 November. On its conclusion, George accompanied his father out of the room before returning to the assembled company. He proceeded to take Newcastle aside and accused him of acting dishonourably in the affair. Most accounts claim that in his anger towards the duke, George said that he would 'find him' but his thick German accent meant that the timorous Newcastle interpreted this as 'fight him' and thought the prince had challenged him to a duel. The frightened duke informed the king and ministers of the alleged challenge, which led to a deputation being sent by the king to his son the next day to ascertain what had happened. The dukes of Roxburghe, Kent and Kingston were charged with discovering whether it was true that the prince was proposing to engage the king's chamberlain in a duel. The prince pointed out that this was not so but he reiterated his anger that he had not been able to choose the godfather for his own son. His anger at the duke was related to the slight that he felt Newcastle had made against him. As a mere subject, Newcastle should have politely declined to do something that he knew was against the prince's wishes. The prince claimed, however, that he still had the utmost respect for his father.[36]

---

[35] Ibid., p. 207.

[36] George's letters to his father were printed, and the copies preserved in the Vienna archives were reproduced in Wolfgang Michael, *England under George I* trans. Annemarie and George MacGregor (2 vols, London, 1936–9), ii, pp. 309–10.

Georg Ludwig and his ministers were not, or refused to be, satisfied with this. George was told to leave St James's, although he did so only when he received a note to this effect in the king's own hand.[37] Perhaps naïvely, the king had assumed that Caroline would remain at St James's. She chose instead to follow her husband. Theirs was a solid political and emotional partnership. The pair found refuge down the road from the palace in a rented house in Albemarle Street. When this turned out to be too small, they bought Leicester House, which stood on the north side of what is now Leicester Square. The fate of George and Caroline's children in all this was fraught. The king had made clear when he gave George his marching orders that the children were to remain at court, under the care of the countess of Schaumburg-Lippe. George tried to visit them without telling the king that he was doing so, which caused the king to ban any visits without prior notice. George's attempts at law to get his children back failed: the judgment was that royal grandchildren were the property of the crown so the king was entirely within his rights to determine how they should be educated.

The king indicated that anybody who attended his son and daughter-in-law at what was to become, in effect, a rival court would not be welcomed by him, thus creating difficulties for those who had allegiances to (or indeed places with) both. This was a particular problem for some of Caroline's women of the bedchamber whose husbands held posts in the royal household and were therefore faced with a stark choice about whose side they were going to take. Countess Cowper, for example, had to decide whether to prioritize her husband's career and chances of preferment or her own friendship with the princess. Her husband, Lord Cowper, was to resign as lord chancellor in 1718, having failed to effect a reconciliation between the king and his son, although as Hatton argues, his discontent with the religious policies of Stanhope and Sunderland was more important than concern about the fate of the royal grandchildren in his decision.[38]

Two other women of the bedchamber facing difficult choices were Mrs Clayton, whose husband was an MP and close associate of Marlborough (and therefore inclined to side with Sunderland and Stanhope in the disputes between the Whigs) and Henrietta Howard. Henrietta's husband, Charles, was a groom of the bedchamber to the king. Henrietta was happy to stay with the princess. Part of the reason for that was probably her growing intimacy with George, who had been a frequent guest at supper parties held in Henrietta's apartment at Hampton Court during his sojourn there in the summer of 1716. Her choice to stay with Caroline angered Henrietta's husband and he demanded that their son remain with him.[39]

[37] For contemporary newsletter accounts detailing the dispute see HMC, *Report on the manuscripts of his grace the duke of Portland* (10 vols, London, 1891–1931), v, pp. 541–50.
[38] Hatton, *George I*, p. 208.
[39] Borman, *Henrietta Howard*, ch. 6.

Despite the public break with his father, George was not to take full advantage of his new freedom by launching an all-out assault on the ministry in parliament. If anything, members of Georg Ludwig's court suspected that bringing the disputes into the open had weakened the prince's position. Suspicions that the prince might create difficulties in the parliamentary debate on the Mutiny Bill (a classic occasion for causing trouble because the necessity of passing an annual bill of this sort went to the heart of the issue about whether the king was entitled to maintain a standing army) were ill founded as George left the Lords before the vote was taken.[40]

The split between father and son nevertheless remained and, despite the efforts of Lord Chancellor Cowper and others, it was not to be healed quickly. Those, such as Friedrich Ernst von Fabrice, who had known George for a long time, found it difficult to resist visiting him, even when on a diplomatic mission to his father's court and when it had been made clear by the king's German ministers that such a visit would be inappropriate.[41] Means were found, however, to ease the pain of separation from George and Caroline's children a little. The countess of Schaumburg-Lippe was permitted to go daily to Leicester House to give news of how the children fared and, when little George William became ill, he was taken to Kensington so his parents could visit him there. He did not survive – a post-mortem revealed a polyp on his heart.[42] The countess of Schaumburg-Lippe's letters suggest that Caroline was able to visit the children discreetly well before the split was brought officially to an end.[43] Instructions issued by the king to Jane, dowager countess of Portland, who was the governess to Anne, Amelia and Caroline, before his departure for Hanover in 1719 confirm that this was the case. George and Caroline were to be permitted to visit the children as often as they wished, provided that all visits took place in the children's apartment and the prince was only accompanied by his immediate bedchamber servants. Should any of the children become ill, it was important that their parents were kept informed of their state of health.[44]

Some semblance of a parliamentary opposition to the ministry centred round the prince was to continue. It found most obvious expression in opposition to various aspects of the Stanhope–Sunderland ministry's plans

[40] Hatton, *George I*, p. 209.

[41] See Fabrice's account of his mission to London on behalf of Charles XII of Sweden in Rudolf Grieser, ed., *Die Memoiren des Kammerherrn Friedrich Ernst von Fabrice (1683–1750)* (Hildesheim, 1956), pp. 120–1.

[42] BL, Stowe 231, fo. 53.

[43] See countess of Schaumburg-Lippe to Sophie Catharina von Münchhausen, Kew Green, 27/5.7/6/1718 and idem to idem, St James's, 13.24/1/1719, Friedrich-Wilhelm Schaer, ed., *Briefe der Gräfin Johanna Sophie zu Schaumburg-Lippe an die Familie von Münchhausen zu Remeringhausen, 1699–1734* (Rinteln, 1968), pp. 52–3, 57–9.

[44] Instructions for the countess of Portland, St James's, 4/5/1719, BL, Add. MSS 61492, fo. 226.

during the 1718–19 parliamentary session. Sunderland had been working on the bishops' bench and hoped that he might now be able to get both the Schism and Occasional Conformity Acts repealed. In addition, there was some prospect that the Dissenters might be able to gain further relief through the repeal of the Test Act which would have removed the need for civil office holders to be communicant members of the Church of England. Given his earlier opposition to repeal even of the Schism Act, it is unsurprising that the prince opposed repeal of both the Occasional Conformity and Schism Acts, now arguing, as he told Lord Perceval, that it would lead to 'disobliging, as he believed, nine parts of the nation to gratify the tenth'.[45] The prince was present in the Lords when the Repeal Bill was introduced and voted against it when it was moved that the Bill should be committed. Subsequently, the prince was present in the gallery when the Bill was debated in the Commons.[46] The Bill was eventually passed, although ultimately no attempt was made to repeal the Test Act as Sunderland thought it impractical.

The new year brought another piece of legislation in which the prince had a particular interest. An attempt was made to pass a Peerage Bill which would in effect, have, fixed the number of peers in perpetuity: it allowed for the sixteen elected Scottish peers to be replaced by twenty-five hereditary peers, envisaged six further English creations but then limited new creations to the extinction of existing titles. MPs were less than happy at the prospect of further social advancement being closed off to them. The prince was irritated as well. Such a measure would limit the royal prerogative and his future ability to reward his friends once he became king. It was widely said that Sunderland was behind the measure and it was yet another affront to the prince. George, however, found his interests aligned on this occasion with a sufficiently large group to ensure that the measure did not pass, although the Lords were perfectly happy to restrict future membership of their elite club. It was withdrawn in April 1719 and a second attempt to introduce it in the 1719–20 session failed as well.[47]

Sunderland was clearly not a fan of the prince of Wales. His efforts to contain the heir seem to have gone beyond simple legislative means. Papers from this period, preserved for some reason by Georg Ludwig, and found later by George and Caroline, indicate that Sunderland and

[45] Quoted in G.M. Townend, 'Religious radicalism and conservatism in the Whig party under George I: the repeal of the Occasional Conformity and Schism Acts', *Parliamentary History*, 7 (1988), p. 36.

[46] Ibid., pp. 37–8.

[47] For the background to the Peerage Bill, see Clyve Jones, ' "Venice preserv'd; or a plot discovered": the political and social context of the Peerage Bill of 1719', in Clyve Jones, ed., *A pillar of the constitution* (London, 1989), pp. 79–112. The strength of George's personal parliamentary following, based around his household, as opposed to the larger group of opposition Whigs, was relatively small. Sedgwick (*The House of Commons, 1715–1754* (2 vols, London, 1970), i, p. 85) lists ten MPs who were attached directly to George in 1717 and voted consistently against the ministry.

his secretary, Charles Stanhope, a protégé and relation of Sunderland's ministerial partner, had suggested that desperate measures were talked about, even if there was little likelihood that they would ever have been acted upon. Stanhope is alleged to have drawn a comparison between George and Christ, arguing that even God had been willing to sacrifice his own son for the good of humanity. Another item hinted that the prince could be taken on board a boat and transported to wherever the king thought fit.[48]

Although the prince was able to maintain something of a following after his split with the court, the lure of patronage remained strong. Argyll deserted George in early 1719 and was rewarded with the lord stewardship of the household and an English title by the king. Walpole and Townshend were sharp observers of the political situation. The first opportunity to return to power, once their rivals had been routed, would be seized with alacrity. Some Tories also had hopes that the prince might advance their cause but they needed incentives to keep them loyal. Some of the prince's servants were won away from him by offers of advancement from the other side. One such was James Craggs, who had been the prince's cofferer prior to the split but was enticed over by the offer first of the secretaryship at war in 1717 and then the post of secretary of state when Stanhope and Sunderland rearranged the ministry in 1718. Craggs junior was to mastermind the passage of the legislation through the Commons that converted government debt into South Sea stock.

The attempt by the South Sea Company to break the Bank of England's monopoly on the issuance and financing of government debt was to give rise to one of the most dramatic speculative bubbles of early capitalism. The company had been established in 1711 as a means to fund £9 million of government debt accrued during the War of the Spanish Succession by exchanging debt for shares in a company granted the sole rights to trade with South America. The government granted an annuity to the company, meaning that the holders of shares had some guarantee of a return on their money. George had become governor of the company in 1715, replacing the disgraced Harley, who had fallen from favour after the Hanoverian succession because of his support for the treaty of Utrecht. The prince had entertained hopes at that point that he might be able to improve his independence by increasing his income. However, following the Whig split, the company moved rapidly to distance themselves from somebody now regarded as a political liability. George was replaced as governor by his father. The bubble resulted from the attempts in 1719–20 to convert even more of the national debt into South Sea stock.

[48] Sedgwick, *Commons*, i, pp. 31–2. The animus between George and Sunderland features prominently in Arthur Onslow's account of the politics of the period. See HMC, *Fourteenth report, Appendix, part IX. The manuscripts of the earl of Buckinghamshire, the earl of Lindsey, the earl of Onslow, Lord Emly, Theodore J. Hare esq., and James Round, esq.* (London, 1895), pp. 506–10. Onslow entered the Commons in 1720 and was Speaker from 1728 to 1761.

The problem was that there was little or no underlying trade with South America to keep the company afloat. Whilst the government could benefit from a reduced interest rate, the company needed to raise further share capital to keep itself afloat. This was done by a clever marketing campaign and by allowing various elite shareholders to buy stock without actually having to part with the cash for it and then sell it on when the price rose. This fuelled an unsustainable demand for stock and by September 1720, prices were tumbling.

Both the king and the prince had been induced to take a certain amount of South Sea stock. One reason for George's willingness to do this may have been that the split with his father had finally been brought to an end. A formal reconciliation took place in April 1720. Countess Cowper's diary suggests that Walpole approached Caroline in early April to propose that patching up relations would be a good idea. Craggs had been used as an intermediary to Walpole by the king, perhaps because of his previous position in the prince's household. The first suggestion was that although no formal terms would be offered, George must promise to return to live at St James's and that Caroline might get her children back.[49] Walpole persuaded the couple to ignore Lord Cowper's advice to insist on the return of the children but rather to see if it might be achieved. Cowper was more successful in persuading the prince that he would have to return to St James's.[50] The diary also conveys the sense that any reconciliation was part and parcel of a broader political chain of events and both sides entertained hopes that political enemies might be removed as part of the process. Walpole meanwhile claimed that he was using the duchess of Kendal, the king's mistress, as another way of opening up communications.[51] Countess Cowper thought that the king had grown tired of being bossed around by Sunderland and so was willing to contemplate a reconciliation, although she also worried that the prince and princess were being manipulated by Walpole and Townshend in an attempt to regain office.[52] In the middle of all the negotiations Anne fell ill with smallpox so Caroline's desire both to see and be reunited with her children on a more permanent basis increased. George was finally induced to write a note to his father, which was received on 23 April. The king asked his son to meet him in his closet at St James's and a five-minute interview took place in which the prince thanked his father for receiving him and hoped that he would not cause him any trouble for the rest of his life. All that George could remember of his father's response was the repeated comment 'Votre conduite'. Following their brief meeting, George went to visit his daughters

---

[49] *Cowper Diary*, p. 128.

[50] Ibid., p. 129.

[51] Ibid., p. 132.

[52] Ibid., pp. 134–5. One example of this was the way in which the countess thought that the prince had been turned against South Sea stock by Walpole, having previously thought highly of it.

before returning to Leicester House. That he was accompanied by his guards again was a visible indication that the formal breach with his father had been healed.[53] George attended the Chapel Royal with his father on 24 April and the two made their first public appearance together on 27 April when they attended the première of Handel's new opera, *Radamisto*. Handel dedicated the opera to Georg Ludwig (he dedicated *Floridante* to George in 1721). The joint appearance was probably part of a stage-managed reconciliation; at the very least, Handel was sufficiently well connected to the court to ensure that he had a new opera ready for the occasion.[54]

Things did not quite get back to normal between father and son – the king suspected that George had been forced into a reconciliation by Walpole and Townshend. The Whig split was, however, healed. Or rather, a temporary truce was reached whereby each side agreed to live with the other for a little. Walpole and Townshend would be the ultimate victors. Stanhope and Sunderland both became, in a sense, victims of the fallout caused by the collapse of the South Sea bubble. Although Walpole's influence on the scheme that emerged to get the economy back on track following the financial disaster that threatened to drag vast swathes of the elite down has probably been overestimated,[55] he and his brother-in-law-Townshend, were the undoubted political victors of the crisis. George can hardly have shed any tears when Sunderland and his associates became embroiled in allegations of corruption following the collapse in share prices. James Craggs junior died of smallpox on the day that the Commons' report on the crisis appeared and his father also passed away soon afterwards; being unable to argue back, both served as useful scape-goats. Stanhope was taken ill while debating the crisis in the Lords in February 1721 and Sunderland died in 1722, leaving Walpole and Townshend at the top of the political tree.

GEORGE'S HOUSEHOLD AND EXPENDITURE

One effect of Whig reunion was that the number of malcontents wending their way to George's door in the hope of achieving future office reduced dramatically. Indeed, George's political involvement in the early 1720s was minimal compared with the period of the Whig split. How, then, was George spending his time? Some of it was spent with his family – there was almost a second family in the 1720s with William (1721), Mary (1723) and finally Louisa (1724). The name of George's second surviving son is

[53] Ibid., pp. 142–3.

[54] Donald Burrows, *Handel* (Oxford, 1994), pp. 106–10.

[55] See John Carswell, *The South Sea bubble* (Stroud, 2001), building on J.H. Plumb's work (*Sir Robert Walpole* (2 vols, London, 1956–60), i, p. 339) in contrast to the more positive assessment of Walpole's contribution in William Coxe, *Memoirs of the life and administration of Sir Robert Walpole* (3 vols, London, 1798), i, pp. 135–6.

significant, given the fuss that had been caused in 1717 when this had been attempted previously. The elder daughters remained with the king but the younger children lived with their parents, either at Leicester House or at Richmond Lodge, which George and Caroline had purchased from the forfeited estates of the duke of Ormonde in 1719.[56] Richmond was used as a summer residence – Caroline enjoyed the gardens and George could find good sport in the surrounding countryside.

The shape of George's household remained largely the same while he was prince of Wales. His father was not a particular fan of ceremony and the size of the royal household dipped after 1714, although it increased slowly thereafter.[57] George seemed to revel in the ceremonial aspects of his position to a much greater extent than his father so it is unsurprising that he made full use of the resources available to him to set up a royal court in miniature. Understanding how a royal household worked necessitates knowing something about the divisions of responsibility, something about the physical structure of palaces and something about the purpose of courts in the first place.

Neither George nor Caroline had more than a handful of their own German servants whom they brought with them from Hanover so they found themselves slotted into the pre-existing model of how a British royal household worked. By the early eighteenth century, in common with most other European monarchies other than the French, there were a number of posts within the household that were theoretically those of servants but, because they were filled by people of gentle birth, were sinecures. These post-holders received salaries and had to attend court but much of the actual work of keeping the household running was done by others. The court, therefore, was a significant employer across the social spectrum. As a consumer of goods, it had a major impact on the economy of London. Its structures also served to bind together the political elite. The prince and princess drew extensively from the British nobility in the composition of their respective households. Whether by accident or design, this had the effect of reinforcing a sense of identity between the royal couple and their new subjects.[58]

In the royal household there was a division between three basic types of function: the lord chamberlain was responsible for all those servants who had anything to do with the artistic and ceremonial life of the court, the household 'above stairs' as it is sometimes described, while the lord steward dealt with the 'below stairs' servants who managed the culinary and domestic needs of the household. Transportation fell within the remit of the master of horse. Again, such a structure was, in its broad outlines, similar to that in most other European courts.

[56] Colvin et al., *King's works*, p. 218.

[57] Sir John Sainty and R.O. Bucholz, *Officials of the royal household, 1660–1837* (2 vols, London, 1997–8), i, pp. xxii and lxxii.

[58] Gerrard, 'Queens-in-waiting', pp. 147–8.

One can understand who did what by thinking about where in the palace a particular servant belonged. The names and roles of servants had evolved as a means of signifying where physically their major areas of responsibility were. Royal palaces in this period were arranged in such a way as to reinforce and remind subjects of the hierarchical nature of society. Monarchs were clearly at the top of the social pyramid and so access to their presence was, in itself, an indicator of the status of the subject – the closer one could come to the royal presence, the more favoured one was. Palaces were therefore constructed as a series of rooms and just how far one could penetrate through the succession of doors was a signal of one's importance. In the sixteenth century there had been a simple division between a guard, presence and privy chamber. Each division had its own attendants: yeomen of the guard, gentlemen ushers for the presence chamber and gentlemen of the privy chamber. Beyond this suite of rooms, the groom of the stole was responsible for the bedchamber where only the most important of subjects would be admitted.[59]

There was a gradual erosion of exclusivity, however. By the end of Charles I's reign, all courtiers had access to the privy chamber and so a new space was introduced between the privy chamber and the bedchamber – the withdrawing room. In the guise of the drawing room, this had become the main audience room by the eighteenth century. Throughout this slow process, whereby the court gradually encroached upon royal space, leaving only the closet for the king's private business, new layers were simply imposed upon the old; there was no attempt to reform the structure of the household to get rid of superfluous offices. In the early years of Georg Ludwig's reign it was on Caroline's drawing room, rather than the king's, that life at court in St James's centred.[60]

At Michaelmas 1716 George's own household had a secretary and a chancellor plus two legal officers, Spencer Cowper as attorney-general and Lawrence Carter as solicitor-general to deal with administrative matters. The prince's most intimate servants and associates – those of the bedchamber – were managed by the groom of the stole. George had such a figure from the start, whereas his father was only to fill the post in his household in 1719 when he appointed George's political nemesis the earl of Sunderland to that post. Under George's own groom of the stole, the duke of Argyll, there were six peers as gentlemen of the bedchamber and eight grooms of the bedchamber. The latter received £400 a year, while the former collected £600. The six ladies and women of the bedchamber

[59] Court studies has been a huge growth area in recent years. I have drawn on the following in this necessarily brief summary: Sainty and Bucholz, *Officials of the royal household*, i, introduction, Colvin et al., *King's works*, pp. 125–31, Beattie, *English court*, introduction and part I, Smith, *Georgian monarchy*, part III. David Starkey's early work showed the key importance of the groom of the stole as the king's gatekeeper and adviser under the Tudors.
[60] Beattie, *English court*, p. 262.

received £100 a year less than their respective male counterparts. The backstairs pages, of which the prince and princess had four each, were paid £80. The presence pages, whose duties took place within the more public presence chamber rather than the intimate bedchamber, earned only £40. There were gentlemen ushers for the presence chamber who directed the other servants in the public rooms and gentlemen waiters and necessary women who looked after the upkeep of those rooms. Caroline had her own lord chamberlain, the earl of Bridgewater, whose salary of £1,200 was the same as that of the duke of Argyll. Bridgewater's deputy, Thomas Pulteney, on whom most of the work actually fell, took home £300 in salary but had a separate pension of £200. The couple's spiritual needs were overseen by the clerk of the closet, the Reverend John Harris, who received £200.

The household below stairs was supervised by James Craggs junior, the cofferer, who received a salary of £66 supplemented by a pension of £1,250. He oversaw the kitchen, cellar and pantry staff. At this point there were fifteen people employed in the kitchen with salaries ranging from £80 for the master cook down to £10 for the turnspit boys.

George's transportation needs were managed by Richard, Lord Lumley, who was to succeed his father as second earl of Scarbrough in 1721. The prince maintained nine footmen, seven coachmen, seven postillions each with an assistant and five grooms plus assorted others to care for the horses and manage the department. Four equerries and four pages of honour could accompany him on state occasions. Non-equine transport was catered for by two master bargemen with eighteen watermen, or the four chairmen.[61]

The senior bedchamber servants in both George and Caroline's households were, in effect, both companions and clients. They accompanied the prince and princess during their daily lives and were responsible for providing 'body service', that is, taking part in the ceremonial dressing that was widely practised among European royalty. Whereas Georg Ludwig was not dressed formally by his bedchamber servants, George was keen to continue the practice, both as prince of Wales and later as king.[62] Gentlemen and ladies of the bedchamber were the senior of the bedchamber posts, reserved for those of noble birth. The middle-ranking bedchamber group, the grooms and women of the bedchamber, had to do more of the actual dressing, washing, fetching and carrying that close attendance entailed. It was to this group that both Henrietta Howard and her husband belonged in Caroline and Georg Ludwig's household respectively. The final layer of companionate service went to the maids of honour – young women who accompanied the princess

[61] Details derived from BL, Add. MSS 61492, fos 232–7.
[62] Beattie, *English court*, pp. 54–5. For evidence of the practice as king, see Hervey, *Memoirs*, iii, p. 751 where Hervey records a royal conversation from such an occasion in 1737.

and waited upon her. Caroline's household contained a number of maids whose subsequent careers and correspondence were to prove illuminating of court life: Mary Bellenden, Sophia Howe and Molly Lepel.

This snapshot of George and Caroline's household is from the period when they were still resident at St James's. George had the apartments that he occupied there redecorated by Hawksmoor. The demands of the princely household led to thoughts of constructing a new kitchen, specifically for the prince and princess. The kitchens were built in the period 1717–19, but by the time they had been completed the prince and princess had left the palace so the new kitchens on the north-west side were used by the royal household instead.[63]

The structure of the prince's household suggests that he wanted to ensure that he kept up the trappings and appearance of royalty. In this respect George was as keen as any other European royal of the period to make sure that his status was apparent to those around him from the servants he kept and the way in which he travelled about. Further evidence of this can be found from the surviving accounts that detail what exactly he spent his money on. Copies of his accounts as prince of Wales are among the relatively small number of items dealing with George's life that survive in the Royal Archives in Windsor.

Before analyzing what George spent his money on, it is worth considering where exactly his income came from in the first place.[64] The arrangements that were made to fund the prince of Wales after 1714 were different from those that had been in place when there had last been a holder of that office, although elements of the previous regime survived. The prince still had access to funds from lands which he held in his own right as both prince of Wales and, more importantly, from the duchy of Cornwall: in 1716–17, for example, George was to receive nearly £1,100 from his Welsh lands but some £10,100 from the duchy of Cornwall. The bulk of his income, however, derived directly from the Civil List. An act of 1698 had separated the costs of the armed forces and the national debt from the money required to run the royal household, thus creating a separate Civil List for the first time. This was part of the slow process by which a distinction was gradually drawn between the monarch as the sole representative of the state, responsible for all of its functions and obligations, and the notion of the monarch as, in some senses, a private individual whose income and expenditure needed to be differentiated from more general state activity. Emphasis must be placed on the long-term nature of this shift. In addition to the running costs of the royal household, the Civil List also had to cope with the costs of the diplomatic service, domestic

---

[63] Colvin et al., *King's works*, p. 240.

[64] For what follows, see Sainty and Bucholz, *Officials of the royal household*, i, pp. xxxii–xxxviii, Beattie, *English court*, ch. 4 and E.A. Reitan, 'The Civil List in eighteenth-century British politics: parliamentary supremacy versus the independence of the crown', *HJ*, 9 (1966), pp. 318–37.

administration other than that of revenue collection, as well as the upkeep of royal and public buildings and the payment of various pensions. The Civil List was to be funded by a series of designated income streams. The intention was that these would yield £700,000 a year and the arrangements put in place by William were to be continued by Anne. The problem was that this figure was neither based upon accurate estimates of royal expenditure nor guaranteed: if the taxes failed to provide the requisite amount, then debts would build up. Between 1702 and 1710 the claims on the Civil List amounted to some £666,800 annually but the taxes to fund it were yielding only £543,700. The household costs, as distinct from other claims on the list, represented some 40 per cent of the total. By 1714 a deficit had built up on the Civil List and Georg Ludwig was able to secure money in 1715 to pay this off. More importantly, he was also able to ensure that the £700,000 was to be guaranteed – if the income streams failed to deliver the goods, then parliament would vote funds to deliver the remainder.[65] Georg Ludwig thus managed to secure a better deal than his predecessors but the slight sting in the tail was the expectation that £100,000 of this £700,000 would be set aside for the use of the prince of Wales. The Commons also passed a bill which ensured that these funds would be guaranteed to Caroline if George should predecease her.[66] From George's point of view, the 1715 settlement gave him a degree of independence that had been impossible for earlier princes of Wales. George could afford to fund a court that could seriously rival that of his father to an extent that had not previously been the case.

How did George spend his money, then?[67] Much of the expenditure was tied to salaries but even in 1715–16, when George had an additional £70,000 from the exchequer (probably in lieu of payments for 1714–15), he did not live beyond his means and the accounts show a surplus of some £24,000. The year 1715–16 was also unusual in that the prince spent over £150,000. For most of the rest of his period as prince, annual expenditure ranged from £80,000 to £90,000 a year. There are three exceptions to this. In 1717–18, £94,283 was spent but this included £6,858 for the purchase of Leicester House. The year 1719–20 saw expenditure of £93,267, which included £2,759 on alterations at Leicester House. Richmond Lodge had been purchased in 1718–19 but although it cost just £6,000, annual expenditure still came in at £90,241. Within these totals the costs of Caroline's household fluctuated between about £8,000 and £10,500. George found himself in a relatively comfortable financial position. His outgoings only once exceeded the amount that he was guaranteed by the Civil List and, in any case, that was a year in which he had received an additional payment. Any revenues from his income as prince

[65] Sainty and Bucholz, *Officials of the royal household*, i, pp. lxix–lxxii.
[66] *Journals of the House of Commons*, 18, p. 298 (3/9/1715).
[67] The following is based on copies of George's accounts as prince of Wales preserved in the Royal Archives, Windsor, EB/P 4–8.

of Wales went straight into the surplus, as did a certain amount of his Civil List income. The net effect of this consistent living within his means was that by 1727 the surplus had reached £222,500. Further income from the duchy of Cornwall, which George kept after becoming king, meant that even when £226,100 of the surplus was transferred to the king directly in November 1728, there was still a balance of some £20,000 sitting in the accounts in March 1729. George's eldest son, Frederick, was not created prince of Wales and duke of Cornwall until after his arrival in Britain in 1729 so, strictly speaking, there was no reason why George should not continue to draw the revenues until that point.

George's posthumous reputation has tended to be that of someone who was a little mean with his money. The surplus accumulated while prince of Wales might superficially support this view. However, within the detail of his accounts there are plenty of instances to suggest that George was willing to put his hand in his pocket for a good cause. In 1721–2, for example, the prince paid £200 as the bounty for captives in Morocco. Throughout the 1720s, George was a supporter of the Royal Academy of Music, an opera company performing in London, subscribing between £310 and £420 a year. He supported the countess of Schaumburg-Lippe with a pension of £500 per annum throughout the period of the Whig split. The countess was helping with the care of his children but when the split was healed, the pension continued.

Other than a penchant for music and good works, what else do the accounts reveal about George? Unfortunately, there is very little in the way of detail about the monies that were transferred to George's privy purse and what these were spent on; although Caroline usually received some £8,000 in this way, the amount that George received varied from £10,000 to £16,000. At the start of his father's reign, George spent nearly £1,000 on coaches and nearly £1,400 on horses to pull them. He remained strongly interested in equine pursuits and there is no evidence to suggest that his master of horse ever had any problem securing funds.

George's interest in horses was, of course, not unusual for somebody of his upbringing and class. Hunting was a common elite pastime and the skills that it provided were seen as easily transferable to the military arena where the elite would fight as part of cavalry regiments.[68] Although hunting was common throughout Europe, there were some variations in practice and preference. George was a strong advocate of 'par force' hunting in which the quarry was pursued with a pack of hounds, rather than dispatched using weapons. The Hanoverian official court diary recorded that the prince had been out hunting with hounds four times in August 1717.[69] However, while the English gentry were slowly becoming

---

[68] For a general introduction to all matters equine in the period see Peter Edwards, *Horse and man in early modern England* (London, 2007).

[69] As recorded in Ceremonial Buch, 1714–32, NHStA, Dep. 103, IV 323, fo. 23.

more interested in the pursuit of foxes, in part because of the decline in the deer population, George remained resolutely opposed to hunting foxes, regarding it as beneath him.[70] Richmond Lodge provided George with an ideal base for hunting and both George and Caroline enjoyed spending time there; they were there for the summer of 1723 while the king was in Hanover and again in 1725 when Georg Ludwig made another trip back to his native land.[71]

FRIENDS AND FAMILY

Hunting was one pursuit deemed essential for a prince. Another was a certain degree of womanizing. Taking a mistress was a sign of potency and virility and, given the favours that mistresses were likely to receive in return, it was not something that the average prince usually found to be particularly difficult. Attractive women at court were the obvious choices as mistresses and in using this option, as in much else, George was entirely typical of princes of his period. Talk about George's associations with women focused initially on Mary Bellenden, one of his wife's maids of honour. Caroline's maids of honour had a reputation for flirtatiousness. The story that Bishop Burnet had the height of the pews in the Chapel Royal raised, after complaining to Caroline, to ensure that worshippers concentrated on his words and not the maids' beauty is probably not true but it says much about their contemporary reputation.[72]

George's technique for wooing Bellenden seems to have been somewhat unsophisticated. Horace Walpole claimed in his *Reminiscences* that the prince, conscious of Bellenden's well-known shortage of funds, sought to seduce her by ostentatiously counting his cash in her presence.[73] Walpole was a notorious gossip and so caution ought to be exercised in swallowing the story whole – not least because his likely source for it was Henrietta Howard. The subsequent passage suggests that Walpole's purpose in

[70] This is the force of his comments, mocking the duke of Grafton for his desire to go fox hunting on health grounds, as recorded by Hervey in 1735. See Hervey, *Memoirs*, ii, p. 494. For the growing popularity of fox hunting, see Emma Griffin, *Blood sport: hunting in Britain since 1066* (New Haven and London, 2007), ch. 10.

[71] Lady Mary Wortley Montagu recorded details of both trips in her letters. For her involvement, among the beau monde, in a hunting expedition with the prince, see Lady Mary to Lady Mar, August 1725, in Mary Wortley Montagu, *The complete letters of Lady Mary Wortley Montagu*, ed. Robert Halsband (3 vols, Oxford, 1965–7), ii, p. 54.

[72] W.H. Wilkins, *Caroline the illustrious* (2 vols, London, 1901), i, pp. 167–8. Nice as the story is, Wilkins's chronology does not quite work. The higher pews in the Chapel Royal were probably provided around 1700, rather than in 1715, when Burnet requested them of Princess Anne, not Princess Caroline. See Edgar Sheppard, *Memorials of St James's palace* (2 vols, London, 1894), ii, p. 210 which mentions a ballad, possibly by Charles Mordaunt, third earl of Peterborough, on the topic and strongly suggesting the earlier date.

[73] Horace Walpole, *Reminiscences written by Mr Horace Walpole in 1788 for the amusement of Miss Mary and Miss Agnes Berry* (Oxford, 1924), p. 61.

including the tale was to illustrate the extent to which George had pursued a mistress merely because it was something he thought he should be doing and because he wanted to demonstrate his independence from Caroline. Walpole averred that 'so awkwardly did he manage that artifice, that it but demonstrated more clearly the influence of the Queen'. Nevertheless, there is reasonable evidence to suggest that Mary Bellenden was pursued by the prince during 1717 but refused him, not least in letters that Bellenden wrote to Henrietta Howard.[74] Bellenden's resistance seems to have been explained in part by her love for another and by the realization that being a prince's mistress was not necessarily good for her long-term prospects. Subsequently, she secretly married Colonel John Campbell, one of the prince's bedchamber grooms, in 1720. George was apparently angered when he discovered what she had done but had by this point transferred his attentions to Henrietta Howard instead. Howard's latest biographer suggests that it was during the summer of 1718 that the relationship moved beyond mere friendship.[75]

During those summers when the king remained in Britain, the prince was, at least occasionally, to be found accompanying him on official duties. In 1722, George travelled with his father to Salisbury, staying at Hackwood, the seat of the third duke of Bolton, lord lieutenant of Hampshire, before proceeding to Salisbury. There the king and prince attended a service in the cathedral before inspecting two cavalry regiments, two of dragoons and seven of infantry. A strongly anti-Jacobite and anti-popish address was presented to the king, decrying the evils of the Romish religion, before the king and prince dined in public in Salisbury. The king saw fit to release all the debtors from Salisbury gaol, having paid the debts off himself, and did the same for those in the Hampshire county gaol in Winchester. The next stage of the progress took the king to Portsmouth, where he inspected naval ships and was cheered as he stood on the quarterdeck of the *Canterbury*. From Portsmouth the party proceeded to Stansted Park, the seat of the earl of Scarbrough, the prince's master of horse and returned via Chichester and Guildford to Kensington.[76] This mini-progress was similar in length and distance and even route to that which George had been on himself in 1716, although this time the focus was clearly more on the father than the son.

Public appearances of unity were maintained, although some evidently thought that they were little more than a façade. Writing to Henrietta Howard in 1724, Mary Bellenden, now Mrs Campbell, gently chastised her for not coming to visit 'when his Highness goes to visit his dad, which

[74] Borman, *Henrietta Howard*, pp. 99–100. The correspondence can be found in BL, Add. MSS 22627, fos 89–91.

[75] Borman, *Henrietta Howard*, pp. 102–3.

[76] *London Gazette*, 6091, 1–4/9/1722 and Hofjournale, 28/8/1718, NHStA, Dep. 103, IV 323, fo. 94.

he does sometimes, as the Evening Post informs me'.[77] There were some areas in which the king was definitely boss. Georg Ludwig, imbued with a sense of the importance of dynastic politics from an early age as he had been, was keen now that George's own family seemed to be thriving to ensure that appropriate partners were found for all of them as well.

The number of Protestant royal families of requisite status in Europe was relatively small so options were quite limited. The idea was already being floated in the early 1720s that a familial tradition should be continued and that partners for George's elder children, Frederick and Anne, should be found among the Hohenzollern. George's sister, Sophia Dorothea, was married to Frederick William I and their elder children, Wilhelmina (born 1709) and the Crown Prince Frederick (born 1712), were considered good matches for George's offspring. Plans for the continuation of the dynastic union were a feature of the negotiations that led to the signing of the treaty of Charlottenburg in 1723. Sophia Dorothea was a frequent visitor to her father's court in Hanover when the latter visited his Electoral domains and plans for the projected marital alliance sprang from these encounters. These plans were, of course, not shared immediately with George and Caroline because they remained in Britain on all of Georg Ludwig's return visits. Wilhelmina's own account of the travails surrounding the negotiations shows that being the object of such bargains was far from ideal. Remembering the early 1720s, she claimed that she thought it unlikely that she would be allowed to marry her cousin Frederick because all the senior females in his life (his own mother, his grandfather's mistress, the duchess of Kendal, and his grandfather's half-sister, the countess of Darlington) wanted him to be married off to a minor European royal so that they could continue to control him.[78] While this might have been true of Darlington or Kendal, it is difficult to know how Wilhelmina could have thought this of Caroline: she had not seen her son since 1714 and there is little surviving evidence of contact between them after the departure of most of the family from Hanover. Wilhelmina also recalled that she had been inspected several times by Hanoverian matrons to ensure that she was not crooked – the fear being that a misshapen mother might produce misshapen offspring. Her mother sought to counteract this by trying to make Wilhelmina seem as slender as possible so her stays were 'laced so tight, that I became black, and was almost deprived of respiration'.[79] The frustration that Wilhelmina felt about being constantly told what to do and how to behave in an effort to seal the deal are patent in her memoirs.[80]

---

[77] Campbell to Howard, 29/8/1724, [J.W. Croker, ed.], *Letters to and from Henrietta, countess of Suffolk, and her second husband, the Hon. George Berkeley; from 1712–1767* (2 vols, London, 1824), i, p. 175.

[78] Norman Rosenthal, ed., *The misfortunate margravine: the early memoirs of Wilhelmina margravine of Bayreuth* (London, 1970), p. 85.

[79] Ibid., p. 87.

[80] Ibid., pp. 90–2.

Nevertheless, the alliance proved a little more difficult to conclude than her mother hoped. Further attempts were made during Georg Ludwig's visit in 1725 to bring it to a conclusion. Anglo-Prussian friendship was reaffirmed in the treaty of Herrenhausen in September 1725 but the marriage plans were still stalled. In 1726, Prussia was slowly separated from Britain by the Austrians during a period of tension between Georg Ludwig and Charles VI. Georg Ludwig may have intended to reinvigorate talks during his visit to Hanover in the summer of 1727. It was not to be. The king was taken ill en route and arrived at his brother's palace in Osnabrück barely conscious on 20 June. He died there on 22 June 1727.

Chapter 3

POWER AT LAST

George received the news that he had become king from Robert Walpole. The servants accompanying Georg Ludwig on the fateful journey had sealed the gates of Osnabrück following the king's death to ensure that their courier would take the news back to London before it leaked out in any other way. When the messenger reached London three days later, Walpole took it upon himself to convey the news to the new king in person. It being summer, the royal couple had taken up residence at Richmond Lodge. When Walpole arrived, hot from his journey, he discovered that George and Caroline were taking their afternoon nap. Walpole was insistent that they be woken, despite their attendants' reluctance to do this. At last the prince grumpily emerged to be told that he was now king. Asked what he wanted Walpole to do, George replied that he should go to Spencer Compton, the Speaker of the House of Commons. Compton had been treasurer of the prince's household since 1715 and had remained his loyal servant throughout the Whig split and beyond. This was no mean feat as he had managed to remain Speaker during the same period as well.

SHAPING A NEW REGIME

It appeared that Walpole's worst fears were about to be realized. The transition from one monarch to another was usually difficult for the ministers of the previous incumbent. Political logic suggested that the new king would have his own friends whom he would want to reward with office. Moreover, Walpole's rapid reconciliation with Georg Ludwig after 1720 contrasted sharply with Compton's devotion. George's preference for Compton over Walpole during the 1720s had been clear. The prospects for the Townshend–Walpole Whigs did not look particularly rosy. Even some Tories entertained hopes of a return to power.[1]

The account of John, Lord Hervey, court chronicler and gossip, has Walpole proceeding to Chiswick where Compton lived and explaining to him George's obvious desire that he should be his minister. Compton, a little taken aback, indicated to Walpole that his help in the composition of the speech that the new king would have to give to his Privy Council would be much appreciated because Compton had little experience of such

[1] Linda Colley, *In defiance of oligarchy* (Cambridge, 1982), p. 207.

matters.[2] The new king and queen had returned from Richmond to Leicester House where crowds gathered to mark the new reign. As it was now late, the formal ceremony of proclaiming George king was delayed until the next day.

The early days of George's reign illustrated how important the acquisition of power could be for making one attractive and popular. Hervey reported that the corridors of Leicester House that had previously been deserted were now as packed as the floor of the Royal Exchange in the middle of a busy trading day.[3] Walpole, Townshend and the duke of Newcastle who had been chancellor of the exchequer and secretaries of state respectively under Georg Ludwig all felt that their days of power were gone. Compton, as the person reputed to have the king's ear, increasingly found himself the centre of attention, which suggested that the opinion of the political nation was moving in that direction as well.

However, despite the strength of Compton's position, he was unable to retain George's favour. The issue which brought matters to a head was that of money. The new king was anxious for a rapid resolution of the question of his Civil List. Walpole was prepared to steer a generous settlement through the Commons. He proposed that the king be granted £800,000 instead of the £700,000 his father had. An additional £100,000 would be provided for the queen, along with Somerset House and Richmond Lodge – a not unreasonable request, given that proper provision for a consort had not had to be made since the new financial arrangements for funding the monarchy had been set up in the late seventeenth century. From George's point of view, one of the key features of this settlement was that it continued the guarantee of a fixed sum that his father had received in 1715 and it allowed for any excess on the funds designated to fund the Civil List to accrue to it as well. Parliament was, therefore, guaranteeing to make up any deficiency and allowing George to keep the surplus, and all without, despite some plaintive but fruitless oppositional pleas, seeing a set of accounts for royal income and expenditure.[4]

Hervey's *Memoirs*, probably composed at least five years after the events he was describing, attributed Walpole's triumph over his rival to his ability to provide the new king with sufficient funds. Given George's reputation as someone who was careful with his money, the claim has a ring of truth about it. However, Hervey was also keen to stress, along with Walpole's son Horace, that Robert Walpole was able to exercise so much influence because of the hold he had over Caroline. The argument advanced was a relatively common one for the period: that kings might be controlled by their wives or mistresses and so the secret to retaining favour was through these women. Behind every weak throne stood a powerful

[2] Hervey, *Memoirs*, i, pp. 22–5.

[3] Ibid., p. 28.

[4] E.A. Reitan, 'The Civil List in eighteenth-century British politics: parliamentary supremacy versus the independence of the crown', *HJ*, 9 (1966), p. 320.

woman. Walpole himself put the case astutely, if crudely. At dinner with Lord Chesterfield, Walpole was talking about the fact that there no longer seemed to be such a crowd of people around Compton as there had been. Walpole remarked that this was not surprising because Compton 'took the wrong sow by the ear', but he had taken the right.[5] In this case, Walpole was suggesting that he had correctly backed Caroline over Henrietta Howard, realizing that the political influence of the mistress was less than that of the queen.

How far this perception of George being managed by anybody, either wife or mistress, was an accurate representation of affairs is an open question. Reports sent to Frederick William I of Prussia suggested that George was determined to rule himself and reduce the power of the ministers.[6] Both Hervey and Walpole had a huge vested interest in suggesting that their contacts with Caroline provided a patronage route not available to other mortals, just as Compton had probably hoped that his friendship with Henrietta Howard would have been useful politically. More generally, as will become clearer when thinking about the wider political circumstances of George's reign, it suited very neatly the cause of leading Whig politicians like Walpole, the duke of Newcastle, the earl of Hardwicke or Henry Pelham to talk to each other about their skills in directing the king to do what they wanted. The problem comes when historians assume that their accounts of their encounters with the king are taken to be an accurate record of what did happen, as opposed to their aspirations about what could or should occur. While written with much less rhetorical flourish, the notes of Peter King, the lord chancellor, have a much simpler account of why Walpole triumphed over Compton in the battle for power. King attributes Walpole's success to hard work, rather than intrigue. It was Walpole's constant attendance on the king every morning, while Compton was busy in the Commons, that enabled him to win the new monarch's trust. Although Compton was with the king in the afternoons, his credit rapidly diminished.[7]

To suggest that George was not as controlled by Caroline as contemporary politicians and subsequent generations of historians have argued is not to downplay her importance to George. Caroline was undoubtedly a valuable asset to the new king. She had already proved herself to be an adept social hostess. The size of their family indicated a dynastic permanence that had been lacking in recent years. As the first queen consort since the late seventeenth century she had a role to play in redefining what the court was and how it could function in the political and social life of the nation. In this respect, her cultural interests were also useful in projecting the

---

[5] [Philip, second earl of Hardwicke], *Walpoliana* (London, 1781), p. 6.

[6] Johann Gustav Droysen, *Geschichte der Preußischen Politik* (14 vols, Leipzig, 1868–86), Part IV, ii, p. 441.

[7] Peter King, 'Notes on domestic and foreign affairs' in idem, *The life of John Locke: new edition* (2 vols, London, 1830), ii, p. 46.

monarchy's image. As Joanna Marschner has shown, Caroline's artistic patronage was important in creating an 'English genealogy of kingship' for the new dynasty.[8] While Caroline's appreciation of culture may not have been matched by her husband, her skills were complementary to those of the king.

George's approach tended to be more practical. Peter King's impression of the king's early days on the throne is of a monarch very keen to get involved in the nitty-gritty of government, particularly in anything that related to questions of patronage.[9] It is understandable, given the long wait that George had had before taking up the reins of power, that he should be keen to exercise control in those areas which he deemed to be within his prerogative. The ability to make appointments to civil office and within the Church and to hand out military promotions were the most important ways in which monarchical patronage could be dispensed. That said, as Jeremy Black has recently pointed out, there was little sign that members of the aristocratic circle that George had built up as prince of Wales were now to step straight into positions of political influence. Men like the earl of Essex and the earl of Grantham were given profitable sinecures but they were not to become key advisers. Philip, fourth earl of Chesterfield, was the only one of this group whose ambitions stretched beyond that of mere courtier.[10] The relative youth of George's aristocratic associates probably counted against a rapid seizing of the political initiative. Townshend and Walpole were older than the new king, both born in the 1670s, whereas Chesterfield, Grantham and Essex were all younger than George.

CORONATION SPLENDOUR: LONDON AND BEYOND

Struggles for political power were to be characteristic of George's reign but before they could commence properly proprieties had to be observed. The transition from one reign to the next had to be marked ceremonially and publicly. George decided against bringing his father's body back to his new lands and instead allowed him to be laid to rest in his Electoral domains. The body was placed close to that of Sophia in the church within the Leine palace. George was keen that his father's personal effects, sealed as was customary on the late king's death, should be transferred to him; and Fabrice, who had accompanied Georg Ludwig on his final journey, brought some things with him back to London. Meanwhile, a complete inventory was made of those possessions that remained in Hanover.[11]

[8] Joanna Marschner, 'Queen Caroline of Anspach and the European princely museum tradition', in Clarissa Campbell Orr, ed., *Queenship in Britain, 1660–1837* (Manchester, 2002), pp. 130–42 (quotation at p. 133).

[9] King, 'Notes', ii, pp. 47–50.

[10] Jeremy Black, *George II* (Exeter, 2007), pp. 84–5.

[11] Ragnhild Hatton, *George I* (London, 1978), p. 284, NHStA, Dep. 103, 3266.

In London preparations were begun for the coronation of the new king and queen. Responsibility for the organization of the event was divided between the lord chamberlain, who arranged all that happened outside Westminster Abbey, and the earl marshal, who oversaw activities within the abbey. In practice, the dean and chapter of Westminster were also able to exert a fair degree of influence over the shape of events inside the church. The duke of Grafton, as lord chamberlain, oversaw some of the arrangements. However, as the earl marshal was a hereditary office vested in the duke of Norfolk, a Catholic, his role was performed by the earl of Sussex in 1727. Responsibility for the staging and construction of the coronation fell on the Office of Works. George insisted that the event should be appropriately lavish and so more money was spent than on his father's.[12] One of the innovations was to create a raised walkway between Westminster Hall and the abbey so that the crowds that had gathered for the occasion would be better able to view the festivities. Tickets for the event were sold by the earl marshal's office and a scaffold was constructed to enable nearly 1,800 people to get a proper view of proceedings outside the abbey. The festive and commercial atmosphere came through in the provision of boxes that the better off could pay for and the number of stands that were erected around Westminster to allow coffee sellers and the like to ply their trade to the expectant crowds. The abbey itself also got in on the commercial side of things, selling tickets for the area between the west door and the choir.

Both Caroline and George were keen to make a good physical impression. Caroline, in particular, wanted to ensure that she looked her best in all her regal finery. Hervey noted that in addition to her own jewels, valuable as they were, Caroline had borrowed pearls from various other ladies of quality to adorn her head and shoulders, as well as hiring diamonds from jewellers and Jews for her petticoats.[13] The overall effect was impressive, as the coronation portrait by Charles Jervas in the National Portrait Gallery shows. The matching portrait of George gives a similar image of grandeur. One foreign observer of the October day when the event took place noted how remarkable the procession had been – so long that it had taken nearly two hours to go by. In the middle of it, when proceedings had temporarily come to a halt, the aged duchess of Marlborough, wife of the hero of Blenheim, had sought to rest her tired feet by taking a drum from one of the soldiers and using it as a temporary stool.[14]

Inside the abbey things did not go quite according to plan. George Frederick Handel had been commissioned to write new music for the event.

---

[12] Georg Ludwig's coronation expenses were listed at £7,287 compared with £8,720 for George (NA, Works, 21/1). The most expensive Hanoverian coronation by some distance was George IV's attempt to outdo Napoleon. See Roy Strong, *Coronation: a history of kingship and the British monarchy* (London, 2005), p. 372.

[13] Hervey, *Memoirs*, i, p. 66.

[14] César de Saussure, *A foreign view of England in the reigns of George I and George II*, trans. and ed. Madame van Muyden (London, 1902), pp. 239, 257.

The choice of Handel was, in itself, an interesting one. Music for corona- tions had traditionally been composed by the organist of the Chapel Royal. William Croft died in August 1727 and his successor Maurice Greene was not confirmed until preparations were well under way. Handel appears to have been George's choice anyway.[15] Handel's 'Coronation Anthems' were performed for the first time and *Zadok the Priest* has been performed at every coronation since 1727. However, the first performances were not without incident. William Wake, the archbishop of Canterbury, had been conva- lescing at Tunbridge Wells when George became king. The practical arrangements for the liturgical aspects of the coronation may initially have been undertaken by Edmund Gibson, dean of the Chapel Royal. Wake was concerned to have some input, though; after all, he had remained reason- ably faithful to George and Caroline during the period of the Whig split and continued to attend Leicester House in defiance of the king's instruc- tions. Wake had looked into the precedents from previous coronations to construct an order of service.[16] Clear instructions had not been passed on to Handel, however. Orders of service had been printed in advance but manuscript annotations by Wake on a copy of his own order of service indicate that all did not go well. The anthem *I was glad* was 'omitted and no anthem at all sung by the negligence of the choir of Westminster'. The dean of Westminster was sufficiently angered by the choir's general behav- iour to consider sanctioning some of them.[17] Further confusion was to follow. Later in the service, the choir appeared to be singing different anthems – their physical separation on galleries on either side of the abbey adding to the confusion.[18]

After the service, the new king and queen processed to Westminster Hall where they dined in public. César-François de Saussure, a Swiss traveller who left an extensive account of Britain in this period, noted that it was possible to observe the banquet from the gallery. Some of the spectators let down ropes in the hope that the peers below might share some of the royal largesse with them. One area in which George had increased expenditure since the previous coronation was in ensuring that Westminster Hall was properly lit for the occasion. Lady Mary Wortley Montagu, having watched the procession from the comfort of her own home, was able to get to Westminster Hall in good time and observed that nearly everybody there was working hard in their efforts to conceal vanity and gain admira- tion. Some made a better impression than others: the countess of Orkney, William III's former mistress, was looking her age and would have been the largest there, had Lady St John not been present. Wortley Montagu was less than complimentary about both the duchess of Montrose and Lady

[15] Donald Burrows, *Handel and the English Chapel Royal* (Oxford, 2005), pp. 251–5.
[16] Norman Sykes, *William Wake* (2 vols, Cambridge, 1957), ii, pp. 185–8.
[17] David Baldwin, *The Chapel Royal ancient and modern* (London, 1990), p. 224.
[18] Burrows, *Handel and the Chapel Royal*, pp. 259–65.

Portland's choices of outfit.[19] Traditions were maintained. The royal champion entered the hall, mounted and fully armoured, and threw down the gauntlet to the king's enemies before having his health drunk by the new monarchs. After the royal couple and guests had retired Saussure reported that things became a little more chaotic. Anything that remained in the hall was quickly looted by the hungry crowd.[20] For George and Caroline it had been a long day – they had been at Westminster since eight o'clock that morning and the banquet did not end until the evening.[21]

Others had been working hard during the coronation ceremony as well. Bedchamber servants, with their responsibility for ceremonial dress, were kept very busy. Henrietta Howard was anxious in the days prior to the ceremony because traditionally it was at this point that places in the household were confirmed for the new reign. She, in her role of woman of the bedchamber, had shouldered much of the responsibility for the routine organization of the preparations for the coronation, having been asked to do so by the duchess of Dorset, the mistress of the robes. Caroline had left her lodgings around seven o'clock in a sedan chair and had travelled incognito through the park to Westminster, where she was dressed. The clothes had been laid out the night before and guarded overnight. Henrietta Howard had taken the main responsibility for dressing Caroline in what must have been a slightly awkward social situation.[22]

Celebrations for the coronation were not limited to London. Hannah Smith's work has shown how the occasion was used in differing ways by both Whigs and Tories as a means of celebrating their loyalty and confirming their partisan identity. Bells were rung, celebratory poems were composed and recited and wine flowed freely.[23] Even further afield the day was used as a means of reinforcing the dynasty's credibility in Hanover itself.

The ceremonies in Hanover centred around George and Caroline's eldest son, Frederick, the Guelph representative in their homeland. The arrangements in Hanover were co-ordinated by privy councillor von

---

[19] Mary Wortley Montagu to Lady Mar, October 1727, in Mary Wortley Montagu, *The complete letters of Lady Mary Wortley Montagu*, ed. Robert Halsband (3 vols, Oxford, 1965–7), ii, pp. 85–6.

[20] Saussure, *Foreign view*, pp. 261, 263–5.

[21] Strong, *Coronation*, p. 406. Strong entitles his chapter on Georgian coronations 'Insubstantial pageants'. There probably was less immediate spectacle than for some earlier coronations but it is more interesting to note how, in various ways, George managed to adapt his court culture to deal with the pressures of commercial society in Britain and more traditional understandings of princely power in Hanover.

[22] Details from the account that Howard provided for Lady Bute as guidance for the correct procedure for George III's coronation in 1761, reprinted in [J.W. Croker, ed.], *Letters to and from Henrietta, countess of Suffolk, and her second husband, the Hon. George Berkeley; from 1712–1767* (2 vols, London, 1824), ii, pp. 262–4.

[23] Hannah Smith, *Georgian monarchy* (Cambridge, 2006), pp. 142–51, 178.

Hardenberg, who had been with Georg Ludwig on his final journey.[24] His plan was for Frederick to arrive in Hanover from Herrenhausen in the late morning of coronation day. He would receive local notables in the 'Queen of Denmark's' apartments in the Leine palace before greeting the gathered crowds from the balcony. In the *Holzmarkt* immediately in front of the palace, various things would be laid on for the gathered crowd: oxen would be roasted whole and the Hanoverian burghers could drink red wine dispensed from an (English) lion or white from a (Hanoverian) horse. At noon, the first of three salutes would be sounded to indicate that the festivities in the square could begin. Hardenberg had wondered if it would be appropriate to follow English custom and have the church bells rung between noon and one o'clock. Privy councillors von Görtz, von Ilten and von dem Bussche were consulted and agreed to instruct Vice-Chamberlain von Reden to act accordingly. At one o'clock a trumpet fanfare summoned the assembled notables to a banquet, over which Frederick was to preside. In a further effort to ensure that English standards of etiquette were met, it was suggested that Frederick had to be served on this occasion by somebody with at least the rank of marshal. The Hanoverian court composer Venturini premiered some *Tafelmusik* which was to have less lasting impact than Handel's compositions for the festivities in London. At the end of the banquet, Hardenberg had originally envisaged that twenty-four salutes would be fired for the new king, the same number for Caroline, twelve for Frederick and a mere six for Prince William and his sisters. Perhaps with an eye to the ears of the guests, the Privy council reduced this number to six for the new king and queen, four for Frederick and three for his siblings. The day concluded with Frederick observing the illuminations from the palace.

QUESTIONS OF INHERITANCE

Frederick was to remain in Hanover for over a year after the coronation before being summoned to London to take up his responsibilities as prince of Wales. His relations with his parents had not been improved by long separation. If anything, Frederick had become closer to his grandfather, whom he had at least seen on Georg Ludwig's regular return visits to the Electorate. Frederick's future had been part of Georg Ludwig's plans for the dynasty. His marriage was a means by which to further Guelph interests. However, Georg Ludwig's time in Britain had also caused him to give some consideration to the longer-term viability of continuing the personal union of the British and Hanoverian domains. As early as 1716, Georg Ludwig had made discreet enquiries about whether it might be possible to devise an arrangement whereby Britain went to an older son, with Hanover

---

[24] Details from NHStA, Dep. 103, XXIV, 2957 and the entry for 11.22/10/1727 found in NHStA, Dep. 103, IV, 323, fos 199–202.

devolving upon his younger brother. Since George was the only male of his generation, such an arrangement could only happen in the next; that is, Frederick would inherit Britain and his younger brother (as yet unborn in 1716) Hanover. The firm answer that Georg Ludwig initially received from Vienna was that imperial law meant that primogeniture could not be set aside so the elder son could not renounce the claim on Hanover. This period was, of course, one in which relations between father and son were not good. In subsequent discussions among British legal experts under the chairmanship of Lord Chancellor Macclesfield in 1719 doubts were expressed about whether it would be possible to alter the succession law in either territory by an act of Parliament to achieve what Georg Ludwig wanted.[25] Nevertheless, Georg Ludwig seems to have maintained some interest in the idea. Although he signed a codicil confirming his will in 1720, there were subsequent suggestions from George and Caroline that William might be given England while his elder brother inherited Hanover.[26] Copies of Georg Ludwig's will had been lodged both with the imperial court in Vienna and with the senior branch of the Guelph family in Wolfenbüttel.

George must have known about the contents of his father's will, although how much he had discussed it with him is unclear. At the first meeting of the Privy Council after George's accession, Archbishop Wake brought his copy of the will along, assuming that George would open it and read the contents to all of them. Instead, George thanked Wake for bringing the document and pocketed it, unopened. The new king's actions appeared odd to his British advisers but they were unwilling to precipitate a confrontation so early in the new reign. Drögereit speculates that George had received advice from his Hanoverian privy councillors that his father's scheme was unworkable.[27] It is also possible that the new king had heard some account of the earlier British debates in which Georg Ludwig's plans had also been questioned. Removing the copy in London was only the start of George's problems, though. There were two further copies that had to be acquired if the will was to be suppressed entirely. Negotiations with the court in Wolfenbüttel were opened through its representative in London, Count Dehn. The surprise of some of the British ministers at this newly discovered interest in a minor German court can be traced through Peter King's record of the unfolding contacts.[28] George was eventually able to reach an agreement whereby Wolfenbüttel continued to receive

---

[25] Copies of the discussions survive in NHStA, Hann. 92, 70, fos 85–7. There is also a copy in the Royal Archives, Windsor [RA], GEO/52795–803.

[26] Richard Drögereit, 'Das Testament König Georgs I. und die Frage der Personalunion zwischen England und Hannover', *Niedersächsisches Jahrbuch für Landesgeschichte*, 14 (1937), p. 123. Hatton, *George I*, pp. 165–9. King, 'Notes', ii, pp. 15–16 records his discussions with Walpole of this scheme in July 1725.

[27] Ibid., p. 133.

[28] King, 'Notes', ii, pp. 50–4. King was brought into the negotiations in late November on the basis of his legal expertise.

subsidies and the will was returned unopened to him. The return of the Austrian copy was to take much longer. Anglo-Austrian relations had reached a low ebb by 1727 and they were not really to recover until after 1731. It was not until 1737 that the Austrian copy was returned.

However, one of the difficulties about suppressing the will was that some of the likely beneficiaries began to complain. Most prominent among these were Georg Ludwig's daughter, Sophia Dorothea, and his illegitimate daughter by Ehrengard Melusina von der Schulenburg, Petronella Melusina. Sophia Dorothea's claims were only really advanced after the death of her husband, Frederick William I, in 1740. Sophia Dorothea had been involved with complicated situations in relation to wills before. When her mother had died in 1726 both she and George discovered that the payment of certain legacies was dependent on the resolution of disputes between Hanover and Prussia about what was supposed to happen to some of the subsidies that had been paid to her own grandfather, the duke of Celle.[29] The question of Georg Ludwig's will became tied up with another point of contention between the courts of Hanover and Berlin. The Prussians claimed that the Electress Sophia's will had promised that some earrings should go to her daughter, Sophia Charlotte, Georg Ludwig's sister and wife of Frederick I of Prussia. The problem was that Sophia had outlived her daughter and so the codicil of 1696 could not be carried out when she died in 1714. The disagreement was about whether Sophia's intention had been that the jewels should go to the female side of the family or should be preserved on the male side. There was an initial flurry of activity on this issue in 1715 and it was revived again in 1732. In 1740, George wrote to his sister reassuring her that she had not lost anything and subsequently got trustworthy persons to swear an oath to her on this point.[30]

Petronella's claims were pursued by her husband, Philip Dormer Stanhope, fourth earl of Chesterfield. Chesterfield had been a close associate of George while prince of Wales. When Petronella's mother died, the question of what she might have received from her royal lover became mixed up with Petronella's inheritance and Chesterfield threatened legal action against the king to see his wife's claims honoured.[31]

George found himself involved in more than simple disputes about his father's will when it came to dealing with his effects. Georg Ludwig had two Turkish *valets de chambre*, Mehemet and Mustapha who had come into

[29] Wilhelm Havemann, *Geschichte der Lande Braunschweig und Lüneburg* (3 vols, Göttingen, 1853–7), iii, p. 511.

[30] Drögereit, 'Testament', p. 148. Details of the ongoing disputes with Prussia about inheritance issues are detailed in NHStA, Dep. 103, I, 160.

[31] Horace Walpole, *Memoirs of King George II*, ed. John Brooke (3 vols, New Haven, 1985), iii, p. 121 n. 4. Walpole added the note to his discussion of George I's will. The anecdote has a ring of truth about it but, as with much of Walpole's commentary on court life, his sources are opaque.

his service during his campaigns against the Turk in 1686. The pair were trusted implicitly by Georg Ludwig and Mehemet, in particular, had achieved great favour. He was the effective keeper of the king's privy purse in London and had been raised to the rank of an imperial knight in 1716, under the highly appropriate name of von Königstreu (loyal to the king). The two are among the courtiers featured on the painted staircase at Kensington Palace.[32] Mehemet married a wealthy Hanoverian woman and one of his sons was to become a cavalry captain in the Hanoverian army. He died at about the same time as Georg Ludwig and his widow laid claim to a wallet that had been found among the dead king's possessions in his closet in Hanover. The item was marked 'M.M.' and was discovered during the inventory that was drawn up of Georg Ludwig's effects on 2 September 1727 by the court officials Mohr, Patje and Leonhart. Mehemet's widow argued that the wallet, which contained some 1,500 ducats, had been given to her husband during the campaign of 1709 and so should be returned to her. George was unimpressed by this: if such a large sum had really belonged to Mehemet, then surely it would not have been left tucked away in the wallet for all those years? Nevertheless, the widow persisted.

In early 1729 George decided that the easiest way to settle the matter was to allow it to be considered by two Hanoverian judges. The surviving evidence for the case comes partly from the papers of one of the jurists involved which were returned to the royal household when he died in 1799.[33] The jurists appear to have conducted a thorough investigation, interviewing court officials, including Mustapha. The surviving privy purse accounts for 1708 and 1709 were examined to see if there was any trace of the payment having been made. George pointed out that the investigation had revealed that Mehemet appeared to have had various items of furniture in his possession that belonged to the court, rather than Georg Ludwig personally, which should therefore have been returned. George was happy for wigs, silver and crockery that had been in daily use to be divided up among the chamber servants but everything else he considered to be his. Perhaps unsurprisingly, the special commission found in favour of the king. Yet the decision was subsequently referred to the highest Hanoverian appeal court in Celle and the case dragged on until 1735, by which time it was being pursued by Mehemet's sons, as the widow had now died as well. The appeal court eventually confirmed the earlier decision.

SETTLING DOWN: THE POLITICAL CONTEXT

Sorting out his father's affairs was a distraction for George. Keen as he was to ensure that his rights were properly respected, the serious business he

---

[32] Their stories feature in Lucy Worsley, *The courtiers* (London, 2010), pp. 78–81.

[33] NHStA, Dep. 103, XXIV, 1329 (papers of General Auditeur Hotzen). The other material relating to the case is in NHStA, Calenberg Brief [hereafter Cal. Br.] 15, 2684.

had in mind was that of ruling his new lands and exercising power himself.
A new reign required the election of a new parliament. The new House
of Commons contained nearly forty fewer Tory MPs than its predecessor
and the Whig majority seemed assured. A small group of dissident Whigs,
mainly those who had fallen out with Walpole, provided a minor cloud on
the horizon but domestically the new king, buoyed by his exceptionally
generous Civil List, seemed well set.

Foreign affairs were not so rosy.[34] The last few years of Georg Ludwig's
reign had seen relations with the emperor almost reach breaking point.
There had been several areas of disagreement. The emperor's refusal to
acknowledge Georg Ludwig's claim to the duchies of Bremen and Verden,
a series of disputes within the empire between Protestants and Catholics
and the impression that not only was the emperor a far from impartial
judge in these disagreements but that he was also contributing to the
persecution of Protestants had all caused concern. Moreover, relations
had been further soured by worries about the activities of the Ostend
Company and the threat it might pose for the British and Dutch East
India Companies, as well as by a more general sense that the Austrians
were insufficiently grateful for the help the British had provided them in
securing some of their Italian possessions against Spain and the suspicion
that new-found Austrian friendship with Spain was the prelude to an
attack on the other European powers. On the other side the Austrians
were irritated by what they viewed as the impertinence of somebody they
still regarded as a mere Elector, and therefore beneath them in the pecking
order of European royalty, trying to tell them what to do. Although Georg
Ludwig felt that the British thrones meant that he should be treated
differently by the emperor (as more of an equal), the imperial court
persisted in seeing the north German Electors who had acquired royal
titles (the Wettins by election to the Polish thrown, the Guelphs by
succeeding to the British thrones after 1714 and the Hohenzollern by
becoming kings in Prussia in 1701) as subordinates.

Europe had been on the brink of conflict in early 1727 but open war had
been avoided and it was hoped that outstanding disagreements might be
resolved by the Congress of Soissons. Concern with foreign policy was one
of the areas where George expected that his views would be listened to and
taken account of. At the ministerial level the early years of George's reign
were a period of change in foreign affairs. Townshend had previously been
the senior partner in the Townshend–Walpole relationship. As secretary of
state for the northern department he had clear responsibility for foreign
affairs and vastly more experience than the duke of Newcastle, who had
taken over the southern department when Townshend and Walpole had
persuaded Georg Ludwig to part with Lord Carteret, a skilled diplomatist

---

[34] For more detailed accounts of British foreign policy in this period, see Derek McKay
and H.M. Scott, *The rise of the great powers, 1648–1815* (Harlow, 1983), ch. 4 and Andrew C.
Thompson, *Britain, Hanover and the Protestant interest, 1688–1756* (Woodbridge, 2006), chs 2–3.

and therefore more of a threat than his more pliable replacement, in 1724. Townshend's powers were waning. He was ill for long periods in 1727 and 1728 and his absences from court contributed to a loss of influence. Walpole now seemed keen to emerge from his former brother-in-law's shadow (Dolly Walpole, Townshend's second wife had died in 1726) and take a more active interest in foreign affairs.[35] Consequently, there was a lack of clarity about the direction of British policy. Should hostility towards Austria continue? How much reliance should be placed on friendship with France? Was it a good idea to cultivate Spain as a potential counterweight to the power of Austria or France or possibly both? How were relations with other German courts, a matter especially close to the king's heart, to fit in with these broader policy considerations?

Standard accounts of the period have tended to stress the policy differences between Townshend and Walpole as the ultimate reason for Townshend's resignation in 1730, arguing that Townshend's inveterate anti-Austrian attitudes eventually made his demise inevitable. Jeremy Black offers a different perspective, focusing instead on the relationship between Townshend and George and the extent to which Hanoverian concerns became enmeshed with a struggle for power and influence within the administration. The argument, which has considerable plausibility, is that George and Townshend quickly developed a modus vivendi in which Townshend realized that certain areas were non-negotiable and that he would have to bow to royal wishes on them. These included most things to do with Hanover. George continued his father's policy of seeking imperial recognition for the rights of Hanover to Bremen and Verden. He was also concerned to have Hanover's rights in relation to the intervention in neighbouring Mecklenburg respected and was irritated that the emperor seemed to favour Prussia over Hanover in the Mecklenburg dispute.

However, antagonism towards Austria was seen as temporary – once the Austrians saw reason or responded to British coercive measures, then more friendly relations might be restored. What neither George nor Townshend was particularly keen on was a more structural anti-Austrianism, enhanced by alliances and longer-term commitments. In the early years of George's reign this was the issue at the heart of negotiations about whether Britain might enter into a closer relationship with the various Wittelsbach Electors. Members of the Wittelsbach family controlled four Electorates: Bavaria and the Palatinate, as well as the archbishoprics of Trier and Cologne. The Wittelsbach powers were seen, by the French at least, as an important anti-Habsburg bloc within the empire. The hope was that the British might provide peacetime subsidies for the various Wittelsbach powers and support Wittelsbach pretensions on various issues within the empire. While the issue of subsidies was certainly an emotive one, it was probably of greater importance that the arrangements would have put Anglo-Austrian relations on

---

[35] Jeremy Black, 'Fresh light on the fall of Townshend', *HJ*, 29 (1986), pp. 41–64.

a more permanently antagonistic footing. When Townshend eventually decided to resign in 1730 it probably had much to do with his frustration at the constant sniping he had to put up with from Walpole and Newcastle, now trying to develop a more independent profile, and very little to do with a loss in royal confidence. George, it should be noted, did not remove Townshend. The question of the relative balance of power between king and minister, particularly in relation to ministerial appointments, was one that was to be tested on a number of occasions during George's reign. It would be wrong to assume, however, that George was forced to get rid of Townshend by a combination of pressure from Walpole and Newcastle. George wanted to assert the rights of the royal prerogative and the appointment of ministers, especially those who dealt with the crucial area of foreign policy, was not something that he was prepared to cede to others lightly.

PROBLEMATIC RELATIONS

The intermingling of foreign political and dynastic concerns that was characteristic of the period comes into sharp focus when George's relations with Prussia are considered. Georg Ludwig, and his daughter Sophia Dorothea, had been keen to further the notion of a double marriage alliance with the court of Prussia. These plans received a setback with George's accession to the throne and relations with Prussia deteriorated even further in the early years of George's reign. His brother-in-law Frederick William I was not known as the soldier-king for nothing; if anything, he was even more obsessed with everything connected with the military than George himself. One of Frederick William's particular proclivities was to have the tallest soldiers he possibly could. Consequently, he was keen to recruit the vertically gifted into the ranks of the Prussian army, even if they were not necessarily Prussian subjects. The arrest of some Prussian recruiting officers within Hanoverian territory precipitated a notable cooling in relations. The prospect of a marriage alliance seemed to have disappeared entirely.[36]

Neither George nor Frederick William seemed to want the double alliance to take place. In particular, Frederick William was worried that the alliance might damage his relationship with the Austrians. Nevertheless, and despite the recruiting incident, a British soldier cum diplomat, Charles Hotham, was dispatched to Berlin in 1730 in the hope that a political or a dynastic understanding might be reached with Prussia. Hotham was a close associate of George from his time as prince of Wales. Choosing him for this mission was, perhaps, an indication of the personal influence that George could exert in the diplomatic field, although it may also have been related to Frederick William's known preference for soldiers.[37] Hotham's instructions

---

[36] Christopher Clark, *Iron kingdom* (London, 2006), pp. 95–111, Heinrich Schilling, *Der Zwist Preußens und Hannovers 1729/1730* (Halle, 1912).

[37] Du Bourgay to Townshend, Berlin, 2/3/1730 NS, NA, State Papers [hereafter SP], 90/26.

made very clear that he was to insist upon the double aspect of the proposed marriage treaty, despite Frederick William's known reluctance to settle the Prussian crown prince's future domestic arrangements. It was also hoped that the mission might be used to uncover the antics of the powerful pro-Austrian, anti-British faction at the Prussian court. This grouping, centred around the Prussian minister General Friedrich Wilhelm von Grumbkow, and including the Prussian resident in London Benjamin Friedrich von Reichenbach, was seen as deeply antipathetic to British interests. Intercepts of Reichenbach's correspondence with Grumbkow were used to try to illustrate to Frederick William that his intentions were being misrepresented and Hotham tried to work with Kniphausen, who was more sympathetic to British interests, to marginalize Grumbkow and the emperor's minister-plenipotentiary, Count Friedrich Heinrich von Seckendorff. In the event, Frederick William was more worried that his ministers' correspondence was being intercepted and read than about Reichenbach's conduct and, unsurprisingly, the marriage negotiations made little progress.[38] Grumbkow made much of Hotham's emphasis on the marriage alliance, claiming that it was a sign that George was trying to gain control of Prussia.[39] The Prussian queen's continued advocacy of the match did not help much either. It was easy to portray her enthusiasm as deriving from a desire to support the interests of her family, rather than her new country.

Frederick William's mistrust of George's intentions continued beyond the collapse of Hotham's negotiations. When Frederick William's own son, Frederick, tired of the constant verbal and physical abuse meted out to him by his father, decided to run away, he thought that one place where he might ultimately find refuge was with his relations in Britain. Frederick went so far as to share his plans with Guy Dickens, the British chargé d'affaires, and Charles Hotham, even asking whether the British court might be able to pay off some of his debts (the sum 'owing' having been considerably inflated), as well as providing sanctuary.[40] Both indicated that they thought that Frederick's flight was ill advised and was likely to trigger serious repercussions for Anglo-Prussian relations. Frederick ignored the advice and made a break for freedom in August 1730 but was quickly discovered and subsequently interrogated to find out how much British involvement there might have been in his escape plans. His sister and mother were also quizzed to see what they knew. The incident, as Dickens had predicted, did little for relations between the two courts and further soured the relationship between father and son: Frederick was put on trial

---

[38] The ability of successive British ministries to intercept and decipher diplomatic correspondence, with help from the Hanoverian post office, is discussed in Kenneth Ellis, *The post office in the eighteenth century* (Oxford, 1958).

[39] Norman Rosenthal, ed., *The misfortunate margravine: the early memoirs of Wilhelmina Margravine of Bayreuth* (London, 1970), p. 187.

[40] Theodor Schieder, *Frederick the great*, ed. and trans. Sabina Berkeley and H.M. Scott (Harlow, 2000), p. 24.

for desertion and then forced to watch the execution of his friend and accomplice, Lieutenant Katte.

FREDERICK COMES TO LONDON

Poor relations between royal fathers and sons were not uncommon in eighteenth-century Europe, although they were seldom as bad as those between Frederick William and Frederick. Whereas Frederick of Prussia felt stifled by close proximity to his father, unfamiliarity was more of a problem for Frederick of Hanover. In 1728 Frederick had sent a representative to Berlin, Lieutenant Colonel August de la Motte. As de la Motte was a close associate of Frederick who had seemingly enjoyed a productive audience with Frederick William, many put two and two together and made five. It was thought that his mission must be connected to the double marriage negotiations in some way (this was the impression Wilhelmina gave in her memoirs).[41] Frances Vivian has shown, however, by looking through the diplomatic correspondence of the period, that there was something else going on. It seems that Frederick may have been interfering in an attempt to marry Caroline's nephew, the margrave of Ansbach, to Wilhelmina's younger sister.[42] When George learned of his son's actions – how is not quite clear; it might have been the result of intercepts, or a tip-off from either the Ansbach or the Berlin court – he decided that Frederick's meddling had to stop.

Frederick was attending a ball in Hanover in December 1728: a masquerade to celebrate the visit of the count of Schaumburg-Lippe.[43] Subsequent reports, including one picked up by Du Bourgay in Berlin, suggested that during the event Frederick had been taken aside and asked to come to a house in the town where a group of men, sent by his father, explained to him that Frederick must leave Hanover. The group charged with taking Frederick to his parents included the marquis de la Fôret, Lieutenant Colonel de Launey, an officer in the Horse Guards and Friedrich Ernst von Fabrice, who would have been well known to Frederick from his frequent visits to the Electorate with his grandfather. The Hanoverian court diary has a starker account, simply noting that Frederick left Hanover on the day after the ball and that de la Fôret had to sort out the various arrangements around the court, finding keys and checking apartments.

News of Frederick's dramatic journey preceded him, and by the time he reached London tidings of his imminent arrival had spread. The reactions of British newspapers were coloured by their more general attitude towards the king and the administration. Opposition journals, such as the

[41] Rosenthal, ed., *Misfortunate margravine*, p. 139.

[42] Frances Vivian, *A life of Frederick, prince of Wales, 1707–1751: a connoisseur of the arts*, ed. Roger White (Lampeter, 2007), pp. 90–4.

[43] Court Diary entry (3/12/1728), NHStA, Dep. 103, IV, 323, fo. 205v–206r.

Craftsman, chose to emphasize the popular clamour at Frederick's arrival.[44] The official governmental organ, the *London Gazette*, simply reported Frederick's appearance and carried a copy of the complimentary speech that the recorder of London had made to Frederick following his arrival in the capital.[45] Other papers noted that Frederick had started to receive visitors in his own apartments.[46] Those who were suspicious of the government hoped that the arrival of Frederick might precipitate a further bout of conflict within the administration and trigger changes in the ministry. The treatment Frederick received from his parents suggested that this was possible. Frederick was to be housed initially with his younger brothers and sisters. He was quickly invested as prince of Wales in January 1729 and so could start to enjoy the income associated with the title that the king had retained until that point. However, he was not granted the separate establishment of £100,000 that his father had enjoyed as prince of Wales but instead received a monthly allowance of £2,000 from his father's Civil List. Frederick had already accumulated debts of some £100,000 from his time in Hanover so it is perhaps not that surprising that George was unwilling to pump unlimited sums of good money after bad. Frederick's attitude to money was to remain sharply different to that of his father. The king may also have had in mind that Frederick did not at this point have a separate family to support so his financial needs were not as great as George's had been in 1714.

Frederick took up his seat in the House of Lords. Despite the restricted nature of his funds, he began to build up his own household and circle of friends. He found places for some of his grandfather's servants who had been dismissed in 1727,[47] although, given the unusually high number of his own household that George had retained himself in 1727,[48] some of Georg Ludwig's old servants had to be disappointed. The question of Frederick's public role emerged briefly in 1729. George had decided that, after a fifteen-year gap, it was time for him to pay a visit to his Electoral domains and so the issue of what the new prince of Wales would do in his father's absence arose. George opted to leave Caroline in charge of the regency council. Passing over Frederick for that position was seen, not least by him, as a snub. George's decision was also a vote of confidence in his wife. While it would be an exaggeration to speak of a governing partnership, the royal couple were certainly capable of working well together to create an impression of effective rule.

[44] *Country Journal or the Craftsman*, 127, 7/12/1728.
[45] *London Gazette*, 6732, 3–7/12/1728.
[46] *London Evening Post*, 156, 5/12/1728.
[47] Vivian, *Frederick*, p. 95.
[48] R.O. Bucholz, 'Introduction', in Sir John Sainty and R.O. Bucholz, *Officials of the royal household, 1660–1837* (2 vols, London, 1997–8), i, p. lxviii.

RETURN TO HANOVER

George's return to the lands of his birth was to be the first of many. Like his father before him, he found the trip back akin to a homecoming. The visit in 1729 was followed by further visits in 1732, 1735, 1736, 1740, 1741, 1743, 1745, 1748, 1752 and 1755. Given the frequency with which these trips were made, repetition ensured that logistical planning for the summer sojourns became a little predictable. The main constraint on when the royal departure could occur was the end of the parliamentary session, as George was needed then, both to make a valedictory speech from the throne and to sign bills into law. George tended to return to Britain in time to celebrate his birthday in late October. He usually began his journey to Hanover by taking a boat across the North Sea to a convenient port in the United Provinces. Landing there had a number of advantages – it short-ened the journey over land, which tended to be slower than by sea, and it allowed for consultations to take place with Britain's old allies the Dutch. The king might make contact himself, although his anxiety to reach Hanover often meant that while he continued on the road, the accompa-nying British secretary of state would break his journey for a few days of talks before following his master down the road to north Germany.

Over time, the process for sending the royal coach, together with the requisite number of attendants and guards, to meet the royal party ran like a well-oiled machine. The royal party was usually accompanied by a group of ten to twelve riders and food was taken at inns along the route. Although it was sometimes difficult to predict where precisely the royal party would land, their onward journey was worked out in detail: outside Hanoverian territory distances were recorded simply in hours but once the border was crossed the unit of measurement switched to German miles.[49] The hope was that it would be possible to get some of the way on the day that landing took place and the aim was to reach Osnabrück by the evening of the next day. The process became so routine that the Hanoverian lord chamberlain came to have a set of instructions where the names of the appropriate persons could simply be inserted and the docu-ment dated and dispatched. Moving the extensive luggage that the royal household needed, even allowing for everything that was permanently kept in each location, was standardized as well – the royal baggage was to be transported via Holland, and not via either Hamburg or Harburg, even if its subsequent journey to its final destination had, of necessity, to be slower than the monarch's own.[50] Some items had to travel with the monarch, though: the royal bed, for example, accompanied the king to ensure that he did not have to use anybody else's, although George refused

---

[49] NHStA, Dep. 103, XXIV, 2647, fo. 26 for an early example.
[50] NHStA, Dep. 84B, 188, fo. 3.

to wait for the bed to catch up with him in 1732 and set off regardless.[51] According to Horace Walpole, George was scrupulous about maintaining the distinction between his British and Hanoverian properties. Henrietta Howard told Walpole how when George came to the throne he was unable to find a set of golden cutlery that had belonged to Anne. However, George found the items during his first trip to Hanover so ensured that they were returned to Britain.[52]

When George spent the summer in Hanover, he resided primarily in Herrenhausen rather than at the Leine palace, although he was officially received at the Leine palace on his first visit in 1729. Neither all those who accompanied the king nor all the foreign dignitaries who chose to visit him on the continent could be housed at Herrenhausen, though. Consequently the long avenue of lime trees, planted in 1726, that linked Herrenhausen to the town was always busy with traffic before court events. In 1729 George decided that he would use the audience chamber at Herrenhausen for most official functions so the court was instructed to gather at 11a.m. in the antechamber and then to assemble again at 6p.m. in the Gallery for evening events.[53] During the 1729 visit George took the opportunity to travel relatively extensively within his Electoral domains, no doubt to remind his subjects of his continued existence and to make clear that they had not been abandoned by their *Landesvater*. In late July he travelled south, meeting the duke and duchess of Wolfenbüttel en route, and visited the Harz. The mines in the Harz were an important source of revenue for the Electorate. George had the miners march past him and listened to their musical offerings before descending into one of the silver mines, accompanied by de la Fôret. He spent two hours below the ground before coming back to the surface via a second tunnel.[54] In early August, a second progress allowed George to visit the north and east of his domains. He travelled to Hoya, stopping to view the stud farms there on the way, and then proceeded to Stade, and Harburg. At Harburg, George was presented with an address from the English merchants in the neighbouring port of Hamburg. He then inspected troops in Lüneburg before travelling on to the Göhrde.[55] A week or so of hunting at the Göhrde was followed by a few more days' hunting round Celle before George eventually arrived back in Herrenhausen by the end of August. George's travels in 1729 were more extensive than on subsequent visits but they served as a reminder of the continued interest of the Guelphs in the Electorate. Frederick's departure for London in

---

[51] Hans Patze, 'Zwischen London und Hannover. Bemerkungen zum Hofleben in Hannover während des 18. Jahrhunderts', in Peter Berglar, ed., *Staat und Gesellschaft im Zeitalter Goethes* (Cologne and Vienna, 1977), p. 101.

[52] Horace Walpole, *Reminiscences written by Mr Horace Walpole in 1788 for the amusement of Miss Mary and Miss Agnes Berry* (Oxford, 1924), p. 23.

[53] NHStA, Dep. 103, IV, 323, fo. 212.

[54] *London Gazette*, 6797, 19–22/7/1729 and 6799, 26–29/7/1729.

[55] *London Gazette*, 6800, 12–16/8/1729.

December 1728, coupled with the death of Ernst August, bishop of Osnabrück earlier in that year, meant that there was no longer a senior member of the Guelph family permanently resident in the Electorate as there had been since 1714.

The presence of George, therefore, provided, albeit temporarily, a focus for court life in Hanover. His usual practice when in his Electoral domains was to dine in public at midday and in the evening. There was a royal table, a *Marschalltafel* where the *Oberschenk* presided and finally a *Cavalliertafel*, where the duty cavalry captain from the Life Guards presided. Over time, it became clear that George's preference was to choose his own female dinner companions, rather than see who was at court on that day. The men on his table tended to be a mixture of his Hanoverian privy councillors (who were expected to be in daily attendance on the king anyway), visiting diplomats and other men from the court. The lord chamberlain and the senior gentleman of the bedchamber (*Oberkammerherr*), who was in near-permanent attendance on the king, also usually joined the royal party. The latter role was fulfilled by de la Fôret until 1736. Although he was pensioned off in 1738, he formally retained the title until his death in 1751. However, for practical purposes, his role was taken over by Ernst August, count von Bülow, who succeeded to de la Fôret's place in 1751.[56]

Over time, George's activities during his visits to Hanover began to assume a regular pattern as well. On Sundays, George usually heard a sermon from the Anglican chaplain who accompanied him. If the court happened to be in Hanover itself, this took place in the English Chapel. Otherwise either the dining room or the Great Chamber was used if the court was at Herrenhausen. For entertainment there was the possibility of watching theatrical performances, either in the gardens of Herrenhausen or, if the weather did not permit, in the Orangerie or even the Gallery of the palace. If the court was in Hanover, then the theatre within the Leine palace could be used. Performances tended to be held during the day, rather than at night. The king had a troop of French comedians who were responsible for nearly all the theatrical performances.[57]

More elaborate celebrations took the form of balls and masquerades. These were often linked to particular occasions, such as the visit of a foreign prince or to mark George's accession (as occurred in 1735). The gardens at Herrenhausen were ideal for such events. The provision of food was on a lavish scale: the inventory of 1753 for the pastry chef's equipment lists moulds for caramels in the shape of Hercules, Juno and Amor as well

---

[56] Details gleaned from NHStA, Dep. 103, IV, 323 and 324 and Uta Richter-Uhlig, *Hof und Politik unter den Bedingungen der Personalunion zwischen Hannover und England* (Hanover, 1992), pp. 17–34.

[57] Rosenmarie Elisabeth Wallbrecht, *Das Theater des Barockzeitalters an den welfischen Höfen Hannover und Celle* (Hildesheim, 1974), p. 226 lists the name of only one play performed in 1729 but given that the king saw nearly 40 plays during his stay in 1732 (ibid., pp. 226–7) this is almost certainly an underestimate.

as a sphinx mould.[58] The gardens were illuminated and there were also fireworks, using the backdrop of the great fountain or other of the prominent architectural features to convey an image of baroque splendour. This combination of installation and pyrotechnics was a relatively common way to celebrate royal power. Descriptions of the illuminations and their meaning were often published to ensure that the visual message was appropriately received.[59]

Much of George's time was taken up with the business of government but he found ways of relaxing when he had read his daily pile of dispatches and finished his consultations with his British and Hanoverian ministers. Card-playing was a popular recreation for the evenings. Otherwise, George preferred activities that reflected his interest in the military. Hunting featured prominently in most of his trips to Hanover. He made use of the Guelph hunting lodge at the Göhrde or, as in 1740 and 1741, travelled to Linsburg. Some of this 'hunting' was the shooting of previously captured wild animals, although this mainly took place on days out closer to Hanover. The more traditional pursuit on horseback was George's preferred method.[60]

Being in Hanover offered George the opportunity to inspect his Electoral troops and he did this on several of his visits. A different selection of regiments was chosen on each occasion and the reviews took place close to Hanover. The king inspected the troops either on horseback or from an open carriage. He was joined by some of his ministers, including the accompanying British secretary of state, occasional visiting princes and other members of the court. Tents were erected so that the assembled company could take a break from proceedings to find refreshment. In 1729, given the tense state of relations with Prussia, the inspection had a more serious character than in other years. George reviewed troops near Lüneburg. He had also reviewed some of the Hessian troops that had been taken into his pay near Kassel, not least because he thought he might soon have to put them into the field.[61]

The practice of reviewing troops during his stays in Hanover is a reminder that for George these trips were far more important than mere holidays during the summer months. They were genuine opportunities to transact business, particularly of a foreign political nature. The very fact that large numbers of the diplomats accredited to the court of St James's followed the king to Hanover is ample testament to this. The king and his diplomatic negotiating partners had the chance to conduct their discussions

---

[58] NHStA, Dep. 103, XXIV, 2488, fos 29 and 33.

[59] See Eberhard Fähler, *Feuerwerke des Barock* (Stuttgart, 1974) for a general introduction. The technical and cultural aspects of such displays are expertly discussed in Simon Werrett, *Philosophical fireworks* (Chicago, 2010).

[60] NHStA, Dep. 103, IV, 311 and XXIV, 2649.

[61] Richter-Uhlig, *Hof und Politik*, p. 31. The instructions and marching orders for the various reviews for George's reign are preserved in NHStA, Hann. 47, I, 45.

away from the prying eyes of the London press. In this respect, the more
limited nature of the Hanoverian press was a bonus – there was not the
same profusion of newspapers that could be found in London so it was
much easier to control the flow of information, even though some would
inevitably leak out. Reports in the *London Gazette* could give descriptive
accounts of the king's daily social activities but, even if they mentioned the
presence of this or that representative of another power at a particular
occasion, they would rarely elaborate on the purpose of diplomatic
contacts and what had been discussed.[62]

Some people, of course, had to be given more of an idea of what was
on the king's mind. The regency council back in London received regular
dispatches from the secretary of state (and his staff) travelling with the king
and they might, on occasion, be asked for their advice on specific matters.
The full regency council, under Caroline's direction, met regularly to
discuss the correspondence from Hanover (hence meetings tended to be
arranged to coincide with post days, when it was known that there might
be something to talk about). The full council could be a little unwieldy,
and included such figures as the archbishop of Canterbury, so a smaller
grouping evolved to deal with important issues. This group, referred to by
Peter King, among others, as the 'Select Lords', had a number of standard
members – the remaining secretary of state, the first lord of the treasury,
the lord chancellor – but the others involved could alternate, depending
on who was in town and what was to be discussed. Torrington, the first
lord of the admiralty, was a reasonably regular visitor to these meetings,
as was Lord Trevor as lord privy seal. However, figures such as the duke of
Grafton and the earl of Scarbrough, both of whose primary offices (lord
chamberlain and master of horse) were more related to the life of the
court than to politics, were also present on a number of occasions.
This suggests that there still existed a significant degree of overlap
between the court and the wider political world when it came to advising
the king.[63]

SUCCESSION WORRIES AND EUROPEAN INSTABILITY

One of the reasons for the frequency of meetings of the 'Select Lords'
during George's absence in 1729 was not just their fears about what was
happening between Hanover and Prussia but about the broader European
situation. The Congress of Soissons had failed to resolve a number
of outstanding issues, mainly because France's chief minister, Cardinal
Fleury, had made the running from Versailles, leaving the congress a mere

---

[62] For a general discussion of the role of the press in foreign policy in this period, see
Jeremy Black, *British foreign policy in the age of Walpole* (Edinburgh, 1985), ch. 8.
[63] King, 'Notes', ii, pp. 87–113 for his record of the meetings during George's 1729 visit.
The phrase 'Select Lords' occurs on p. 88.

cipher. Consequently, uncertainties persisted about the direction of British policy. An uneasy alliance with France remained. However, France's desire to avoid conflict was slowly diminishing because Louis XV had produced a male heir and therefore the risk of a war of the French succession breaking out was receding as well.

Elsewhere in Europe, though, serious concerns about succession continued. The emperor, Charles VI, was anxious to ensure that his eldest daughter, Maria Theresa, would be able to inherit his Habsburg territories in an undivided form on his death. To that end a 'Pragmatic Sanction' (an agreement to facilitate this) had been formulated. Charles VI was slowly trying to get all the major European powers to agree to it. In Spain, while there was no lack of male heirs, there were still succession-related concerns. Philip V, who had gained the Spanish throne after the death of the last Habsburg king, Charles II, was a Bourbon and many wondered about the sincerity of his renunciation of any claim to the French throne. However, Philip also faced the issue of providing for the children of his second marriage. His pushy second wife, Elizabeth Farnese, was anxious that something should be done for her eldest son Don Carlos. She had her eye on something within the Italian peninsula, although the other powers, concerned to maintain the Utrecht settlement, were less convinced that supporting Spanish pretensions would be wise for the stability of the continent. Hanging over all these considerations was concern about the durability of the Austro-Spanish rapprochement that had occurred in 1725. The fear of other European powers, particularly France and Britain, was that this newly found amity might have longer legs than a simple short-term conjunction. Talk of a marriage between Don Carlos and Maria Theresa did little to allay these fears. Rather, it suggested that there was a prospect that a dynastic bloc comparable to the vast Habsburg territories of the sixteenth century might be recreated. There were two ways in which this fateful combination might be broken: either Austria or Spain could be brought into closer unity with Britain and France. For Cardinal Fleury, despite his misgivings about Elizabeth Farnese, it was clear that the Spanish option was the one to be pursued. The trick that Fleury had to pull off was to bring Britain with him – and there were considerable doubts in London about whether it was wise to follow the French in this respect. Nevertheless, through the summer of 1729, the 'Select Lords' followed the mission of Benjamin Keene, British minister-plenipotentiary, in Spain, while also keeping an eye on Townshend and George's consultations with the Wittelsbach Electors proceeding apace in Hanover.

The physical separation of monarch from most of his ministers was potentially fraught with difficulties. Peter King's notes suggest that there were several occasions on which the 'Select Lords' had to cope with dispatches from Townshend expressing George's reservations about reports he had received from Britain, just as Walpole seems to have used the queen as a means to try to persuade George to act in a manner that he wanted.[64] Walpole also claimed to King that George wrote constantly to Caroline, sending her letters with every post, which gave a detailed account of his actions, 'particularly of his amours, what women he admired and used; and that the Queen, to continue him in a disposition to do what she desired, returned as long letters, and approved even of his amours, and, of the women he used'.[65] Who, precisely, these women were is not known; Henrietta Howard had remained with her mistress, the queen, throughout the period of the king's absence. Indeed, in a letter from the earl of Chesterfield, written in the middle of September 1729, Henrietta had been told that 'by the king's early return, your winter will begin early this year'.[66] Nevertheless, George's visit in 1729 to Hanover was one of his shortest: he was back in London by the end of September and he had to turn his mind to tying up loose diplomatic ends.

Foreign political manoeuvring was to remain high on George's list of priorities for the next couple of years. An agreement was eventually signed with Spain (the treaty of Seville, November 1729) but it would not turn out to be the long-term solution to Britain's foreign political difficulties that some of its advocates had hoped. How important George was in the foreign policy of this period remains somewhat obscure. Traditional accounts have tended to see a struggle between Townshend on the one hand and Walpole and Newcastle on the other with little space for monarchical action. Jeremy Black has suggested on several occasions that George's role in politics needs to be reassessed.[67] In this, Black is probably correct but the evidence is fragmentary. Much of what we know about the discussion of policy and George's views comes through the prism of ministerial correspondence and diplomatic dispatches. George's own voice surfaces only occasionally. That said, politicians or diplomats invoking George's name may have had their own reasons for doing so. One might be that they had particularly privileged access to the king, either directly or via the queen. The very fact that somebody as supposedly all-powerful as Walpole felt it necessary to point out to others, such as Peter King or John, Lord Hervey, that he was able to exert influence over the king suggests that George was still acknowledged to be at the centre of the political action – otherwise why did Walpole not simply do what he wanted without reference to George's views?

---

[64] Ibid., pp. 106–7, 110.

[65] Ibid., p. 111.

[66] Chesterfield to Howard, The Hague, 23/9/1729 in [J.W. Croker, ed.], *Letters to and from Henrietta, countess of Suffolk*, i, p. 368.

[67] Black, 'Fresh light' and idem, 'George II reconsidered. A consideration of George's influence on the control of foreign policy, in the first years of his reign', *Mitteilungen des österreichischen Staatsarchivs*, 35 (1982), pp. 35–56.

PARLIAMENTARY CONCERN AND EUROPEAN DILEMMAS

While the inner workings of decision-making might remain hidden, the effects of foreign policy were easier to see and the parliamentary session of 1729–30 provided a golden opportunity to debate whether recent governmental actions had been the right ones. Two particular areas of concern came through in discussion of the treaty of Seville. Mercantile interests were disheartened that more had not been done to satisfy their grievances, especially those related to the seizure of British ships engaged in trade with south and central America. Other opposition politicians were much more concerned about the Hessian troops that had been taken into British pay. This worry combined older and more recent anxieties. It reflected a general fear of the power of standing armies in peacetime and the damage they could do to the good running of the country that stretched back into the seventeenth century. In some ways, this was a fear to which both Tories and oppositional Whigs could subscribe. Tories could look back to the, in their view, disastrous military rule of Cromwell during the 1650s when parliament had been abandoned in favour of the Major Generals. Whigs, by contrast, associated the standing army with James II's attempt to introduce popery via tyranny. The issue had first been debated extensively in the aftermath of the Nine Years War, when William III had sought to maintain an army in peacetime, arguing that it was necessary for the defence of the country. Ministerial Whigs, while acknowledging that armies might have been a danger in the past, advanced arguments about the ways in which states had changed in the eighteenth century, not least through the transformations in commerce and credit culture, to suggest that it was both safe and expedient to keep up a reasonable force on a permanent basis.[68]

Opposition critiques did not stop there. Some suggested that the employment of the Hessian troops was necessary only because of the disagreements in which George found himself as Elector of Hanover. In this respect, the dispute with Prussia, where the issues at stake seemed a little remote from the British audience, was grist to the opposition's mill. More generally, it was suggested that the entire course of British policy since 1725 had been determined by Hanoverian priorities. It was concern about Austria and anger at the emperor's refusal to acknowledge Hanoverian claims to Bremen and Verden that had led to the collapse of British relations with Austria. Britain would have no need to make alliances with commercial rivals such as Spain, were it not for the anti-Austrian policies of the king and his ministers.

Such claims arguably involved an over-simplification of a complex web of relationships. Ministerial writers, such as Horace Walpole and Stephen

---

[68] For a more detailed articulation of the origins of these competing positions, see J.G.A. Pocock, 'The varieties of Whiggism from Exclusion to Reform', in idem, *Virtue, commerce, and history* (Cambridge, 1985), pp. 230–9.

Poyntz, certainly thought so. (Both had been responsible for the execution of policy in their roles as British representatives at Soissons.) They argued both in parliament and in print that the Hessian forces had brought material advantages to Britain. Their presence had been useful in securing concessions from Spain. Moreover, it was wrong to blame British actions when the real threat to international stability came from the fateful combination of Spain and Austria. Britain needed to look beyond her own shores to prevent the continent being subjected to a new form of universal monarchy in which political dominion would go hand in hand with the spread of Catholicism.[69]

The debates over foreign policy in 1729–30 were characteristic of a broader discussion that would rumble on for much of the eighteenth century (and even beyond).[70] At its heart was the question of what role Britain should play in relation to Europe. Like William III, both George I and George II had extensive experience of European politics prior to their association with Britain and, perhaps unsurprisingly, thought that Britain should play an active role in European politics. This Williamite legacy of continental commitment did much to shape official and ministerial thinking in the early eighteenth century. Ministers realized that it was expedient, to say the least, to pay close attention to royal wishes. On the other side, though, an argument was developing among the politically discontented and discarded that British interests were being sacrificed on the altar of European involvement and that it was much wiser for Britain to adopt a position of minimal continental engagement, relying on the wooden walls of the Royal Navy to defend British interests and using commerce as a means of staying aloof from continental conflicts. Given this context, it is easy to see how the relationship of Britain to Hanover and the seeming preference of the monarch for one of these territories over the other could easily become an emotive issue within political debate. Moreover, fears of foreign influence over British policy could easily be fanned if it were thought that important negotiations were being conducted outside the country by George with little or no reference to his ministers in London. The 1729 trip to Hanover and the reaction to some of the foreign political outcomes that stemmed from it provided an indication in miniature of how these issues would play out on subsequent occasions. This is not to say that opposition concerns missed the point completely – George, as he was to demonstrate more clearly later in his reign, definitely was concerned that Hanover's interests and security should be actively defended. Nevertheless, it is also worth remembering that the rhetoric of Hanoverian priority was so useful for opposition

[69] See Jeremy Black, 'Parliament and foreign policy in the age of Walpole: the case of the Hessians', in idem, ed., *Knights errant and true Englishmen* (Edinburgh, 1989), pp. 41–54 and Thompson, *Britain, Hanover*, pp. 141–9.

[70] The broader discussion is now brilliantly chronicled in Brendan Simms, *Three victories and a defeat* (London, 2007).

politicians that the truth or otherwise of the claim was largely irrelevant to its deployment.

Opposition attacks on the direction of foreign policy were to continue even when, following Townshend's resignation in May 1730, a thawing of relations with Austria took place. Much to the irritation of the French, it became clear that George might be willing to subscribe to the Pragmatic Sanction, subject to reassurances that Maria Theresa's marriage would not cause added instability to the European balance of power and that some of his Electoral concerns would be dealt with properly. A formal acknowledgement of the Pragmatic Sanction, together with a renewed alliance, was completed in the treaty of Vienna, signed in March 1731. Thomas Robinson, the British minister in Vienna, found that in parallel to his own negotiations with the Austrians, Johann Diede zum Fürstenstein was discussing a resolution of George's Electoral concerns. Sufficient progress was made on this front for the Austrians to believe that Hanoverian support for the Pragmatic Sanction would be forthcoming within the empire so they brought it to the Diet of the empire, the Reichstag, in July 1731.[71]

The reconciliation with Austria was sufficiently strong and politically important to survive the strains put on it by the expulsion of his Protestant subjects by the archbishop of Salzburg in the autumn of 1731. At first sight, it might seem paradoxical that what happened in Salzburg had anything to do with relations between George and Charles VI. The context, however, suggested otherwise. As a Protestant Elector, George, along with Frederick William of Prussia, was widely seen as having a special care for the beleaguered Protestants of the empire. This role was reinforced by George's British persona – his claim to the throne rested entirely on his Protestant credentials. The expulsion of the Salzburg Protestants had the potential to reignite confessional conflicts within the empire. This was much more than simply a theoretical possibility. Concerns about Protestant rights had been central to the disputes that had led to a cooling of Anglo-Austrian relations in the early 1720s and fears about the rise of political Catholicism, in the shape of Austro-Spanish friendship, had further fuelled British disquiet after 1725. The emperor's neutrality when it came to confessional issues had frequently been questioned by Protestants and it was easy to blame him if he did little to stop perceived instances of persecution by Catholics against Protestants. Nevertheless, the Salzburg issue, while generating a significant amount of comment in the public sphere, did not result in a withdrawal of either Prussian or Hanoverian support for the passage of the Pragmatic Sanction through the Reichstag in Regensburg. What both powers did gain, however, was new subjects. Many of the expelled Salzburgers found homes in the empty lands of East Prussia where Frederick William was

---

[71] Black, *British foreign policy in the age of Walpole*, pp. 10–11, McKay and Scott, *Rise of the great powers*, pp. 134–7.

keen to increase the population and therefore, as contemporary thinking argued, the strength of the state. Smaller numbers found refuge in Hanoverian territories and some were even transported across to Britain. It was not to be their final destination. They had been recruited by the trustees of a new colony to travel to the New World.[72]

The new colony had been given a royal charter in 1732. James Oglethorpe, its chief proponent, hoped that it might be used to help some of the debtors languishing in English gaols get a new start in life. The charter itself also spoke of the possibilities the development would offer to help those whom religious persecution had forced to flee their native lands. Strategically the lands situated between South Carolina and Florida might also help to shore up the British presence along the eastern seaboard of the American continent and prevent further Spanish expansion northwards. The name of this new colony, after its royal patron, was to be Georgia.

[72] Thompson, *Britain, Hanover*, pp. 149–64.

Chapter 4

A DIVIDED HOUSE?

George's biographers have traditionally lavished attention on the early 1730s. Accounts of his reign invariably have a good deal of detail on life at the court in London from this period – the continuing relationship with Henrietta Howard and its ultimate denouement, the reaction of the royal family to the Excise Crisis of 1733, the frustration of the king at his inability to intervene in the War of the Polish Succession and the breach within the royal family that had not been healed by the time of Caroline's death in 1737. There is, of course, much at this time that is of inherent interest and would hold the attention of any potential biographer. However, there are also much more mundane reasons for the balance of scholarly attention and not least among these is the survival of a seemingly insightful and surprisingly detailed insider account of court life in these years.

COURT COMMENTARY

The memoirs of John, Lord Hervey were first published in a partial edition in the nineteenth century and then in a complete edition by Romney Sedgwick in 1931.[1] It is easy to see why it might be thought that Hervey's account – at nearly a thousand pages – is both comprehensive and invaluable. For Hervey had a key position within the royal household. He was vice-chamberlain and so enjoyed frequent and intimate access to the king and queen. Moreover, as rapidly becomes apparent from the memoirs, Hervey was not only on good terms with Caroline, he also enjoyed excellent relations with Robert Walpole so had an apparently sound source of information about goings-on in the political world outside the court as well. Hervey was, however, a man of distinct views. The memoirs leave little doubt about his opinions and there is a certain air of bitchiness that suffuses the text. When speaking of Caroline's love of learning and of associating with those who valued it, Hervey added that the queen had to limit such activity because 'the king used often to brag

---

[1] Hervey, *Memoirs*. Stephen Taylor and Hannah Smith are currently engaged in a project to produce a modern edition of the memoirs combined with other selections from Hervey's surviving correspondence. The first fruits of this can be found in Hannah Smith and Stephen Taylor, 'Hephaestion and Alexander: Lord Hervey, Frederick, prince of Wales, and the royal favourite in England in the 1730s', *EHR* 124 (2009), pp. 283–312.

of the contempt he had for books and letters; to say how much he hated all that stuff from his infancy; and that he remembered when he was a child he did not hate reading and learning merely as other children do upon account of the confinement, but because he despised it and felt as if he was doing something mean and below him'.[2] On another occasion Hervey, having shortly beforehand noted that he never said anything bad about anyone unless provoked,[3] went on to talk about George's faults: how 'His Majesty's brusqueries to everybody by turns, whoever came near him, his never bestowing any thing from favour, and often even disobliging those on whom he conferred benefits, made him so disagreeable to all his servants, that people could not stand the ridicule even of affecting to love him for fear of being thought his dupes'.[4] Even the most casual of readers of Hervey's memoirs cannot avoid the impression that there was little love lost between him and the king and that his sympathies lay very much with Walpole and Caroline, whom he regarded as far superior in every respect to her husband.

Extreme caution, therefore, needs to be exercised when using Hervey's account as a basis on which to build up an accurate picture of George's personality and proclivities. The effect of hindsight on changing perceptions also needs to be borne in mind. Hervey's account was clearly written with posterity in mind and so he wanted to make the most of the cast of characters available to him. It is probable that the work was begun around 1733 and the bulk of it, probably based on Hervey's journals, focuses on the period 1732 to 1737.[5] The chronological focus relies on more than mere chance. There is a gap for the years 1730 to 1732 where material has deliberately been removed from the manuscript. It has been conjectured that this was because Hervey's account of these years might have caused offence to the royal family. This was the period in which Hervey fell out with Frederick, prince of Wales. Hervey's sexuality was a matter for speculation both at the time and subsequently. He had married Mary Lepell, one of Caroline's maids of honour, in April, although the match was not publicly acknowledged until after Mary had collected her quarterly payment as a maid in October 1720 (maids of honour had to be single). Hervey had a political career as an MP for Bury St Edmunds from 1725 but he went to Italy in 1728 with Stephen Fox, elder brother of Henry Fox and subsequently earl of Ilchester, to recover his health. Hervey seems to have developed an intimate relationship with Fox, judging from their surviving correspondence. However, when Hervey returned to England his eye was caught by Anne Vane, another of Caroline's maids of honour. Vane had previously been linked to William Stanhope, earl of Harrington but she began an affair with Hervey in 1731. Vane had her eyes on a bigger

[2] Hervey, *Memoirs*, i, p. 261.
[3] Ibid., iii, p. 750.
[4] Ibid., p. 751.
[5] Ibid., i, p. lvii.

prize, though, and quickly moved on to Frederick, prince of Wales. As Sedgwick points out, Hervey was probably more annoyed that he had been replaced in Frederick's affections by Vane than that Frederick had replaced him in Vane's.[6] This anger towards Frederick, which is also clear in later passages of the work, was probably most apparent in describing the events of 1730–2 so one of Hervey's relations, to whom the manuscript passed, decided it would be prudent to excise these.[7]

While some use of Hervey is virtually unavoidable for anybody wanting to write about George, it is instructive to compare some of Hervey's judgements in the *Memoirs* with the material found in his contemporary letters. Several of the same concerns emerge. For example, Hervey notes in the *Memoirs* how George tended to hunt on Wednesdays and Saturdays. As Hervey was not as enamoured of the chase, he had been instructed to ride beside Caroline's carriage. Caroline saw this as an opportunity to be entertained by Hervey, whereas Hervey thought it would provide him with an excellent opportunity to press his own views on the queen.[8] Hervey's letters to Stephen Fox also reveal George's obsession with hunting (and Hervey's reluctance to participate). In September 1730, Hervey complained to Fox about the awful weather in which they had been out. Just under a year later, he reported that George had a bad eye so was only using one candle when playing cards but Hervey doubted that this would stop him from hunting (although the king's condition worsened so he did postpone the next day's outing).[9]

Another feature of Hervey's description of court life is his emphasis on how regimented everything was. When describing George's visits to Henrietta Howard's apartments, both when the liaison first began when he was prince of Wales and later as king, Hervey emphasized the regularity of George's attentions.[10] He came at the same hour each day and stayed for the same length of time. George was extremely regular even in his infidelities, and he was keen that every other aspect of court life should accord to a similarly predictable pattern. Writing to Caroline Clayton, one of the women of the bedchamber, in 1733 Hervey noted that 'I will not trouble you with any account of our occupations at Hampton Court. No mill-horses ever went in a more constant, true or a more unchanging circle, so that by the assistance of an almanack for the day of the week and a watch for the hour of the day, you may inform yourself fully, without any

---

[6] Ibid., pp. xxix–xl.

[7] For a more detailed discussion, see Smith and Taylor, 'Hephaestion and Alexander', pp. 283–5 and 299–305. Smith and Taylor also suggest that (p. 284) 'Hervey's homoerotically charged relationship with Frederick' may have led to the textual deletions.

[8] Hervey, *Memoirs*, i, p. 221

[9] Hervey to Fox, Windsor, 9/9/1730, idem to idem, Hampton Court, 27/8/1731 and idem to idem, Hampton Court, 2/9/1731 in Earl of Ilchester, *Lord Hervey and his friends, 1726–38* (London, 1950), pp. 58, 81, 82.

[10] Hervey, *Memoirs*, i, p. 44.

other intelligence but your memory, of every transaction within the verge of the Court.'[11] Mornings were taken up with a mixture of levees, walks and audiences. Twice a week there were drawing rooms. At night the king played cards (either hazard or commerce) and backgammon, while the queen preferred quadrille.

There remain notes of impatience in the letters, such as the comment during the duke of Lorraine's visit in 1731 that he 'was entertained on Saturday with a bad pack of hounds and yesterday with a bad play',[12] yet there are also occasions when Hervey seems to have had a more indulgent attitude towards his royal master. Hervey's recurrent poor health comes across clearly in his letters. He informed Fox in November 1731 that he felt so awful after the duke of Newcastle and Frederick's balls – a complaint he instructively described as 'like drunkenness' – that he had been unable to perform his duties properly in the drawing room and had left the king to be 'lighted out' by whomever he could find. As he was a consummate courtier, failure to perform ceremonial duties seems to have weighed heavily upon him.[13] Earlier in the year, Hervey had collapsed in Caroline's drawing room and had been helped into her bedchamber by Walpole, Lord Scarbrough and Charles Churchill. Hervey noted that 'the King assisted with more goodness than his general good-breeding alone would have exacted, and has sent here perpetually'.[14]

The *Memoirs* therefore provide an instructive account into some aspects of court life but not others. Hervey was good on gossip and personal relationships, partly because he seems to have enjoyed sharing with both Walpole and Caroline. He was a much less reliable guide when it came to political, particularly foreign political, issues. In these cases, as will become evident, he tended to swallow Walpole's spin uncritically and regurgitate it without further thought.

THE EXCISE CRISIS

However, George and Caroline valued Hervey as a source of news about what was going on outside the palace walls. In this respect, Hervey came into his own during the Excise Crisis of 1733. As an MP, Hervey was able to provide the king and queen with accounts of the unravelling of the scheme that Walpole had hoped would boost government revenues considerably. Following Townshend's departure in 1730, Walpole was left as the most senior minister. Improved relations with Austria seemed to reduce the prospect of armed conflict so Walpole sought to minimize the tax burden on the landed classes, who made up most of parliament, by

---

[11] Hervey to Clayton, Hampton Court, 31/7/1733 in Ilchester, *Lord Hervey*, p. 169.
[12] Hervey to Fox, Hampton Court, 19/10/1731 ibid., p. 103.
[13] Idem to idem, St James's, 27/11/1731 ibid., p. 114.
[14] Idem to idem, St James's, 11/1/1731 ibid., p. 67.

keeping the Land Tax low. He was also able to discharge the Hessian forces, thus removing another plank of the opposition critique of ministerial policy.

Reducing the Land Tax was not without its problems. Walpole realized that he would have to make up the lost revenue from somewhere. Indirect taxes seemed to offer the answer. As they were invisible at the point of sale, they were potentially more palatable. However, an effective state apparatus was required to collect them. Recent research has shown that most of the growth of the British state in the early eighteenth century, in terms of personnel, was in Customs and Excise officers, whose chief task was the collection of such indirect taxes.[15] Having floated the idea of reimposing a Salt Duty in 1732, Walpole's major proposal of the 1733 session was to introduce a Tobacco Excise Bill. He had originally intended to introduce a similar measure for wine as well but his opponents' claims that a general excise scheme was intended were as untrue as they were incendiary.

The outlines of Walpole's scheme were both simple and sensible. Following the legislation that had already been introduced in 1723 to deal with tea, chocolate and coffee, Walpole proposed that instead of customs duties being paid on tobacco when it entered the country, all imports should be placed in bonded warehouses and not released until the appropriate excise duties had been paid. The aim was to crack down on smuggling and fraud, as many of the opponents of the scheme quickly realized.[16] Merchants' opposition to the scheme was easy to understand – they were the prime beneficiaries of the status quo. However, Walpole had also managed to alienate the independent country gentlemen in the Commons who he had assumed would be strong supporters of the scheme due to their desire to keep the Land Tax as low as possible. What Walpole had failed to grasp was that the spectre of expanded intervention by an increased number of excisemen was just as worrying for this group.

On 14 March, when the Excise Bill was debated in the Commons, Hervey was kept very busy. He had to send frequent notes back to St James's to keep the king informed of the progress of the debate and, when he returned to the palace, he was questioned until long into the night about how the debate had gone and even on the appearance of various MPs.[17] George does not seem to have been particularly happy about opposition to the Bill. Hervey's view was that the reasons behind this were twofold: Walpole had convinced him that it might bring in more money for the Civil List and therefore opposition to it was anti-monarchical. In the king's view, opposition leaders had reached new heights of insolence. When Hervey reminded George of how strong the opposition had seemed

---

[15] John Brewer, *The sinews of power* (London, 1989), ch. 3.

[16] For a succinct summary of the history and structure of the excise scheme, see Michael Jubb, 'Economic policy and economic development', in Jeremy Black, ed., *Britain in the age of Walpole* (Basingstoke, 1984), pp. 136–42.

[17] Hervey, *Memoirs*, i, pp. 148–9.

in 1730, the king replied that this was early in the reign when there was still an element of ministerial struggle. Now that he had given his clear backing to Walpole, all opposition should evaporate.[18]

Yet for all Hervey's seeming confidence that George would do the right thing and back Walpole, there remained elements of doubt. Both Hervey and Henry Pelham were assiduous in their attendance on the king during the period from mid-March to mid-April when the Bill was under discussion in parliament. They had good reason to be wary. The opposition were making the most of the opportunity to cause trouble. Chesterfield, the earl of Stair and the duke of Bolton had come out against the scheme and other prominent members of the household, including Lord Clinton and Lord Scarbrough, followed. George's support for Walpole seemed to waver. Moves to punish some of the rebels by dismissing them from office prompted the threat of counter-resignation from Wilmington, Dorset and Scarbrough, and George paused. As Paul Langford points out, almost regardless of what the king thought personally, the perception that Walpole's hold on the closet was weakening was damaging enough.[19] As the weeks went by, ministerial majorities declined. The low point was reached when a motion to hear the petition of the City of London against the Bill was defeated by just seventeen votes on 10 April. The next day it became clear that Walpole had decided to drop the Bill.

The king's reactions to the crisis led Hervey to opine that George's original intention had been 'to have all his ministers in the nature of clerks, not to give advice, but to receive orders; and proposed, what by experiment he found impracticable, to receive applications and distribute favours through no principal channel, but to hear from all quarters, and employ indifferently in their several callings those who by their station would come under the denomination of ministers'.[20] In Hervey's view, this situation had been avoided because Caroline had persuaded George that Walpole was, in fact, the best 'principal channel' for patronage requests. Hervey's claim that Walpole had managed to monopolize the levers of patronage is debatable but, in many ways, Hervey's assumption about what a minister was there for is more interesting. Ministers were not just there to follow instructions: one of their main jobs was to act as oil in the cogs of patronage. A strong sense of the 'king's government' remained in place so perhaps it is not altogether surprising that George was quick to leap to the conclusion that opposition to his ministers' measures was opposition to him. The notion of 'His Majesty's loyal opposition' was still nascent and George would probably have viewed the formulation as a contradiction in terms. His actions in the aftermath of the crisis certainly suggested so.

[18] Ibid., pp. 150–1.
[19] Paul Langford, *The excise crisis* (Oxford, 1975), pp. 83–5.
[20] Hervey, *Memoirs*, i, p. 152.

George now took decisive action. It was this, as much as anything, that secured Walpole's position and enabled him to recover it following his defeat over the excise.[21] On 13 April Chesterfield and Clinton were dismissed from their court offices as lord steward and lord of the bedchamber. Cobham, Stair and Bolton subsequently lost their places when they staged a further rebellion by backing calls in the Lords for an enquiry into the South Sea Company in June.[22] Their punishment included being deprived of the colonelcy of their respective regiments – Cobham and Bolton's deprivation was immediate; Stair's came as a result of further disobedience in 1734. The king was determined to ensure that insubordination did not go unpunished, even if the offence had not been committed in a military context. George's actions eventually served as a clear signal that Walpole still had his backing but the crisis had been a shock to the system. It was also a reminder of the extent to which royal favour was crucial and that courtiers looked to George to take a lead. When what he wanted was uncertain or if he hesitated, ministries could find themselves in difficulties.

WAR IN POLAND

The rumbles of the Excise Crisis had barely died down when George was faced with another difficult set of decisions, although this time they related to external, rather than internal, affairs.[23] Augustus II of Saxony-Poland, known as the Strong and fabled for the number of his illegitimate children, had died in early 1733. As so often in the eighteenth century, the succession to a crown was to provoke a conflict. In the case of Poland-Lithuania the likelihood of disagreement over the fate of succession was higher than in other places because the throne was elective so disputes could arise even without the failure of the male line, which tended to be the trigger elsewhere. The fate of the Polish crown was to become an episode within a broader set of international tensions. On the one hand, Augustus's son, another Augustus, was pressing his own claims to be elected in the place of his father. He could count on Austrian support for his candidature, as he was married to the Archduchess Maria Josepha, the daughter of Charles VI's older brother. Austrian support did come at a price, though: Augustus had to support the Pragmatic Sanction (and therefore renounce any claim that his wife might have to the Habsburg inheritance). The Russians were also happy to keep a member of the Wettin dynasty on the Polish throne. On the other hand, Louis XV was keen to support the claims of Stanislaw Leszczynski. Leszczynski had

---

[21] Langford, *Excise crisis*, pp. 96–7.
[22] Ibid., pp. 99–100.
[23] I have written about this at greater length in Andrew C. Thompson, *Britain, Hanover and the Protestant interest, 1688–1756* (Woodbridge, 2006), ch. 6.

already held the throne briefly himself when Augustus II had been removed during the Great Northern War by Swedish pressure. From the French point of view, however, the fact that he was Louis XV's father-in-law was more important.

The election to the crown was made by the Polish nobility. The rhetoric of the desire for a free and fair election was enunciated by all sides, just as large purses were opened to ensure that advocates of freeness and fairness were adequately compensated for their trouble. In September 1733 Leszczynski was elected. The Russians responded by invading Poland and conflict escalated from there. Instead of bothering to march an army all the way to Poland, the French attacked two imperial fortresses on the Rhine. The Austrians therefore wanted to mobilize allies in response to the French threat. They tried to persuade the empire to declare war on France, with the hope that an imperial army could defend the fatherland. They also thought that the terms of the recently signed treaty of Vienna (1731) meant that Britain and the United Provinces were bound to come to their aid too.

The situation presented George with difficulties. On two different fronts, as Elector of Hanover and king of Great Britain, he was being asked to enter into conflict over the Polish throne. Hervey thought that George was especially anxious to get involved both because he constantly craved military adventure and because, as a good subject of the emperor, he felt it was his duty as an Elector to do so.[24] The second comment, in particular, illustrates the limits of Hervey's political knowledge – George was more than happy to express his views very forcefully to the emperor, especially when he felt that his own rights had been infringed, and so his participation in wars on the emperor's behalf was only ever likely to be on terms that were advantageous to him. Nevertheless, Hervey portrayed Walpole as the critical brake on the king's activities that prevented Britain from being dragged into a conflict that was largely irrelevant to British interests. Hervey was also opposed to British intervention, although he was modest enough to admit that Walpole's contributions had been more significant in 'persuading' the king.[25]

What Hervey failed to appreciate was something that was crystal clear to George. Given how keen Charles VI was for George to become involved in the conflict, there was a deal to be done. The diplomatic instructions issued to British representatives in Poland in the early days of the conflict stressed the need for circumspection.[26] Caution remained the watchword through much of 1733. In a German context, George remained anxious that sending troops to help the emperor might weaken

[24] Hervey, *Memoirs*, ii, p. 340.

[25] Ibid., i, p. 227.

[26] Harrington to Woodward, Whitehall, 9/3/1733, most secret, Lewis Walpole Library, Farmington, Connecticut [hereafter LWL], Charles Hanbury Williams papers [hereafter CHW papers], vol. 3, p. 270.

Hanover's defences. This was more than simple paranoia, as relations with Prussia remained difficult because of disagreement about leadership of the imperial intervention in Mecklenburg and the disposition of Prussian and Hanoverian forces in the duchy.[27] Additionally, George used the emperor's desire for troops to extract concessions about the conditions prevailing for Protestants within the empire. It was only after the emperor had agreed that various Protestant complaints would be considered in any peace settlement at the end of the war in a declaration made in March 1734 that George was prepared to commit his Hanoverian troops.

George successfully used his diplomatic leverage in a German context. In a British one, rather different options were available but the path that George pursued showed an equal desire to extract maximum diplomatic advantage from the situation. In 1734 he sought the mantle of mediator between the warring factions. Robert Walpole's brother, Horace, was dispatched to the United Provinces to see if the combined efforts of the maritime powers could help settle Europe's differences. British pretensions in this regard were ultimately to prove fruitless. Although Cardinal Fleury hinted that he might be willing to accept British mediation, he continued to keep his own lines of communication open with the Austrians. It was by this means that a settlement was at last reached and so George was unable to portray himself as the arbiter of Europe. Nevertheless, there is good evidence to suggest that George's diplomatic skills were considerably better than the monochrome picture of the frustrated fighter, given to us by Hervey, might suggest.

PERSONALITY AND PATRONAGE

Hervey's portrait of Walpole's centrality to the decision-making process raises an interesting question about the extent to which it was possible for the ministerial tail to wag the royal dog. Hervey's views on this point were definite: George, despite all his numerous protestations to the contrary, was constantly being pulled in one direction or another by those around him. Early in the *Memoirs* Hervey reported that George had remarked that Charles I had been governed by his wife, Charles II by his whores, James II by his priests, William III by his men, Anne by her favourite women and his father by anybody who could get at him, adding that George himself was blissfully unaware of the extent to which he was being directed by Caroline. Hervey was not sure whether the story was true or not, which suggests that he was not present at the alleged utterance. His further comment that the tale had the ring of truth about it and was generally believed tells us something about perception, as does the verse, supposedly in circulation at the time, that Hervey included:

---

[27] For the importance of Mecklenburg, see Mitchell D. Allen, 'The Anglo-Hanoverian connection, 1727–1760', unpublished Ph.D. dissertation, University of Boston, 2000, pp. 78–9.

You may strut, dapper George, but twill all be in vain;
We know tis Queen Caroline, not you, that reign –
You govern no more than Don Philip of Spain.
Then if you would have us fall down and adore you,
Lock up your fat spouse, as your dad did before you.[28]

The problem was that, for all Walpole's tough talk about how he could twist the king round his little finger, it is difficult to find occasions when he was able to force George to do something he was clearly against.

There were several areas which George regarded as intrinsic to his prerogative and he was very unwilling to give up any control in them. Foreign policy was one of these. Patronage, both military and ecclesiastical, was another. When a bill was introduced in the February 1734 session to make commissions in the army life appointments and to prevent the king from removing colonels without parliamentary approval, George was quick to act. Noble supporters of the bill, like Stair, were deprived of their regiments. The duke of Marlborough, who was prevailed upon to introduce the Bill in the Lords, was roundly condemned by George: Marlborough was the son of George's old antagonist Sunderland so George's dislike is not that surprising. The motion was defeated soundly, with several speakers condemning it as an unwarranted encroachment on the royal prerogative. Oppositional impertinence received what George regarded as its just reward. Such actions might be misinterpreted as evidence of despotic tendencies, especially when seen through the lens of those obsessed by the perils of a standing army. However, it can also be argued that George's own interest in military patronage had a generally positive effect on the quality of the British officer corps. George was anxious to ensure that, as far as was practicable, commissions could not simply be sold and that to some extent those gaining promotion did so on the basis of basic military competence as opposed to simple aristocratic birth.[29] From the perspective of Whig aristocrats, George's actions in this area, as elsewhere, might be perceived as meddling. Looking at the bigger picture, however, reveals a slightly different, and more nuanced, view. George's emphasis on ability as a basis for promotion and his interest in promoting good military practice through inspections and reviews meant that his impact on the British army was generally positive and promoted consolidation. This was especially important in the early years of his reign when the army's active service was limited.[30]

If military matters were dear to George's heart, he did take an interest in ecclesiastical affairs as well. The reason for this was probably related more to a desire to defend his rights than to a burning personal faith. It is

[28] Hervey, *Memoirs*, i, p. 69.
[29] Anthony Bruce, *The purchase system in the British army, 1660–1871* (London, 1980), pp. 26–30.
[30] James Hayes, 'The royal house of Hanover and the British army, 1714–60', *Bulletin of the John Rylands Library*, 40 (1957–8), pp. 328–57.

difficult to discern what George's religious convictions were. He had been happy to attend the Chapel Royal after his arrival in Britain in 1714 and there was no suggestion that he was especially exercised by having to abandon the Lutheranism of his upbringing. He regularly attended divine service throughout his life, but would make the preacher wait if had something more important to do.[31] His Protestantism was of a largely conventional variety. He was not above poking gentle fun at clerical pretensions.[32] As in other aspects of his life, he could express strong views about those he did and, more importantly, did not like. Yet he was also concerned about the importance of preserving good order in both church and state and his desire to defend Protestant interests, at home and abroad, went beyond simple political expediency.

Both George's Lutheran childhood and his more recently acquired Anglicanism had prepared the king for his role as supreme governor. His interest in ecclesiastical patronage was not perhaps as extensive as Caroline's,[33] but, as Stephen Taylor has shown elsewhere,[34] the king had distinct views when it came to the disposal of higher church offices. Although George might complain that he had to bow to ministerial pressure, there were a number of occasions in the 1740s and 1750s when he was able to get his own way, particularly in filling a series of vacancies in 1757 at a time when the political scene more generally was in turmoil. His influence seems to have increased after Caroline's death, perhaps an indication that while she lived he had been happy to leave such matters to her. Yet, while the court was still an important site for religious debate and the exercise of ecclesiastical patronage, it was no longer the only means by which clerical careers could be advanced. Although serving as a royal chaplain at St James's or accompanying the king as chaplain on a visit to Hanover had previously been seen as a certain route for preferment, this was no longer the case.[35] Here, as elsewhere, the court's monopoly as the sole centre of patronage was broken but it retained an importance, nevertheless.

[31] See p. 88 above and p. 292, n.6 below.

[32] See p. 115 below.

[33] Stephen Taylor, 'Queen Caroline and the church', in Stephen Taylor, Richard Connors, and Clyve Jones, eds, *Hanoverian Britain and empire: essays in memory of Philip Lawson* (Woodbridge, 1998), p. 101.

[34] Stephen Taylor, ' "The Fac Totum in Ecclesiastic Affairs"? The duke of Newcastle and the crown's ecclesiastical patronage', *Albion*, 24 (1992), pp. 422–9.

[35] On the decline of the court as 'the essential prerequisite for the highest offices' of the church, see Stephen Taylor, 'The clergy at the courts of George I and George II', in Michael Schaich, ed., *Monarchy and religion: the transformation of royal culture in eighteenth-century Europe* (Oxford, 2007), pp. 129–51 (quotation p. 151). For the prospect of advancement because of attendance at Hanover see George's remark to John Thomas, later bishop of Salisbury, in 1740: 'Doctor, you are out of luck, there is no bishop died since we have been here; but as the deanery of Peterborough is become vacant, I will give you that, till I can do something better for you' (Jakob Friedrich Bielfeld, *Letters of Baron Bielfeld translated from the German by Mr Hooper* (4 vols, London, 1768–70), iii, p. 223).

CHANGES AT COURT

The court remained crucial to the king's social world. George's domestic arrangements were to undergo several major transformations in the middle of the 1730s. His relationship with Henrietta Howard continued, though it had reached the stage of comfortable familiarity rather than great passion. Howard herself had been able to do something to improve her position and was now a little less dependent than she had been on her court appointment. She had gained a formal separation from Charles Howard in 1728. Yet Charles's brother thought enough of her to leave her a bequest in his will; his brother, whose profligate ways were well known, was deliberately excluded. Charles Howard did at least gain something from his brother's death. He became ninth earl of Suffolk. Henrietta benefited from his changed status as well. As countess of Suffolk, she was now of too high a social standing to continue as a woman of the bedchamber. She had either to be promoted within the household or resign from court life altogether. In some ways, the latter option might have been her preferred one. She had purchased land at Marble Hill in 1724 and the small inheritance from her brother-in-law, together with her own money, would have allowed her to complete her building projects free from the unchanging labour and toil that attendance at court entailed. However, Henrietta was to be promoted instead. She became the mistress of the robes, the most senior position in Caroline's household and so was able simultaneously to increase her salary and reduce her workload. Her estranged husband's death in September 1733 gave her the prospect of yet more freedom. She was close to several members of the political opposition: the earl of Chesterfield was a friend and she was becoming increasingly attached to George Berkeley, an MP who had gone over to the opposition following the dismissal of his elder brother as first lord of the admiralty in 1727. It was these associations that would contribute in part to Henrietta's downfall. In the autumn of 1734 she did something she had not done for a long time and took a holiday in Bath. While there, rumours began to circulate that she had been spending too much time with George's known opponents. On her return to court George's cold reaction to her suggested that all was not well. Henrietta sought to resign her post and, following a difficult interview with Caroline, left the court for good in November 1734. Although rumours of political intrigue cannot have helped her reputation, it was clear that the king had also grown increasingly tired of her company.[36]

Henrietta Howard's departure was not the only change that George's court witnessed in 1734. Lord Scarbrough had been a loyal servant of George throughout his time as prince of Wales but he resigned his post as

---

[36] Tracy Borman, *Henrietta Howard* (London, 2007), chs 11–13, Lucy Worsley, *The courtiers* (London, 2010), ch. 6.

master of horse in 1734, having become a little too close to opposition politicians for his own liking.[37] The other departure was arguably even closer to George. His daughter Anne married William IV, stadholder of Friesland and great hope of the Orangist cause in the United Provinces. The wedding had originally been intended to take place in November 1733. When William had arrived in London just before the marriage his future father-in-law had not been particularly welcoming. William's arrival was not marked by a salute from the cannon in the Tower and he travelled round the streets of London with little in the way of ceremony, having been provided with only a single coach by the king.[38]

Hervey believed that George wanted to indicate to William that it was only by marrying his daughter that William became somebody worth taking seriously. Hervey's jibe contained an element of truth. William's position in the United Provinces was far from commanding. He had added the stadholderships of Groningen and Gelderland to his hereditary title but there was little prospect, despite what had been claimed during the negotiations over the marriage treaty, that he would gain any more power and influence in the key provinces of Holland and Zeeland. Marriage into the British royal family would do much to enhance his status but the benefits for Britain were less tangible. The Dutch had been a key ally of the British in recent struggles with the French so there was a certain popularity to the match but George was well aware that the political clout of his daughter's new husband had significantly diminished since the zenith of Orange power in the late seventeenth century.

William's appearance and health were far from perfect. He suffered from curvature of the spine and his right shoulder was noticeably hunched. Caroline was so interested in the extent of the deformity that she had dispatched Hervey to Somerset House on the night of William's arrival to get a first-hand account of his physical state. Hervey reported that William was no Adonis and his body was 'as bad as possible' but that his 'countenance was far from disagreeable'.[39] Shortly before the wedding, William was taken ill during a thanksgiving service in the Dutch Church in London. The wedding was therefore postponed to allow him to recover.[40] William was eventually allowed to move from the damp riverside quarters of Somerset House (the palace had been unoccupied since the death of Catherine of Braganza) to the better air of Kensington, and he ultimately went to take the waters at Bath.

By March 1734 William had recovered sufficiently for the marriage to proceed. The wedding took place in the French Chapel at St James's, which

---

[37] Hervey, *Memoirs*, i, pp. 247–50.
[38] Ibid., pp. 230–1.
[39] Ibid., p. 231.
[40] Veronica Baker-Smith, *Royal discord: the family of George II* (London, 2008), p. 64.

was lavishly decorated by William Kent for the occasion.[41] George, despite his family's worries, behaved well throughout. Anne's other relations were not as good at disguising their emotions. Her mother and sisters wept through the ceremony with concern for her fate, leaving Hervey to remark that it had more of 'the mournful pomp of a sacrifice than the joyful celebration of a marriage'.[42] Frederick was miffed that his younger sister was marrying before him and made his feelings known. Nevertheless, William looked dashing in a suit of gold brocade and the wedding party were serenaded with the first performance of Handel's 'This is the day that the Lord has made' [HWV 262]. Anne had paraphrased the text of Psalm 45 herself. Her support for Handel was well known and the composer chose to mark the occasion of her wedding with the première of his serenata *Parnasso in Festa* on the night before the wedding.[43]

After the service the newly-weds feasted on turbot, mutton in blood, roast beef, veal, chicken ragout, soup, capons, boiled potatoes, boiled ham and chicken and cauliflower. The second course had partridge, quail, squab, pheasant, woodcock, tartlets and jellies, marrow puddings, asparagus, smelts, oysters, Dutch beef, stewed peas and a Dutch pastry delicacy – *vlaai*.[44] The assembled company proceeded to observe the happy couple during the bedding ceremony, where it was impossible to ignore William's crooked back. Caroline subsequently wondered to Hervey how she could have entrusted her daughter to such a monster. Showing an unusual degree of tact, Hervey responded that married couples soon grew so used to each other's bodies that they were no longer struck by those things that others continued to regard as especially beautiful or strange.[45]

William and Anne remained in London for some time after the wedding. For about six weeks the new couple were at the centre of court life and the London social scene. George rapidly tired of William's popularity. Hervey reported that William's appearance at theatres would be greeted with shouts of joy and rapturous cheering, while the king had to settle for muted applause. Something similar happened when they travelled around London – the crowds loved William but were markedly less enthusiastic

---

[41] The French Chapel was the building now usually known as the Queen's Chapel. It had been built to allow for Catholic worship by two Stuart queens, Henrietta Maria and Catherine of Braganza, but was used by French and Dutch Protestants during Anne's reign. Confusingly, it was known in the nineteenth century as the German Chapel as the French and German Protestant congregations swapped chapels in 1781. The fact that it was not in regular use meant that the extra decorations and galleries for the wedding could simply be left in place when the event was postponed. See Howard Colvin et al., *The history of the king's works: volume V, 1660–1782* (London, 1976), pp. 244–54 and Donald Burrows, *Handel and the English Chapel Royal* (Oxford, 2005), pp. 331–2.

[42] Hervey, *Memoirs*, i, p. 271.

[43] Donald Burrows, *Handel* (Oxford, 1994), pp. 178–9.

[44] Baker-Smith, *Royal discord*, pp. 66–7.

[45] Hervey, *Memoirs*, i, pp. 271–2.

about the monarch.[46] This seeming popularity may have been tactical, rather than deep-felt. As a prince of Orange, William was easy to associate with an apparently better past. Nostalgia could be a powerful rallying cry for the politically discontented. Nevertheless, such a strong demonstration of popular indifference cannot have done much for George's temper or ego.

FURTHER FAMILY CONFLICT

George's familial problems did not stop there. The tensions between the king and his eldest son were mounting as well. Trouble was manifesting itself in several ways. The discontented politicians who had disagreed with Walpole about the Excise Crisis and lost their places as a result had begun to beat a path to Frederick's door, reviving a pattern of political behaviour that the king was only too familiar with from his own time as prince of Wales. A degree of cultural competition had also begun. George had been a reasonably consistent supporter of Handel's musical career for a while: he had regularly subscribed to the Royal Academy of Music in the 1720s. In the early 1730s, however, Handel found himself in competition with a new outfit. The Opera of the Nobility had begun to perform in Lincoln's Inn Fields in late 1733, while Handel initially remained at the King's Theatre in the Haymarket. However, by the start of the 1734–5 season, when his agreement with the King's Theatre had run its course, Handel was replaced in the Haymarket by the Opera of the Nobility and had to remove his own Italian opera to the new Theatre Royal, Covent Garden.[47] George was persuaded to indicate his support for Handel by subscribing to a box for the season. Anne, whose musical proclivities were well known, may have been instrumental in this.

The operatic competition had a political element as well. The Opera of the Nobility was increasingly the place where opposition politicians could be found. Although Frederick patronized both Handel and his new rivals at first, it was difficult to avoid the sense that Frederick was engaged, whether consciously or not, in a cultural and political popularity contest with his father. This competition may have had some beneficial effects for cultural diversity in London, but it was not necessarily welcomed by the likes of Handel. Handel remembered that the last father–son feud in 1717–20 had effectively ended Italian opera in London for a period because the antagonism of the rival courts had caused the patronage necessary to sustain a commercial opera company to evaporate. Handel had survived only because James Brydges, earl of Carnarvon and subsequently duke of Chandos, had offered him support.[48] Carnarvon was able to do this because he had been paymaster of the forces abroad during the War of the

---

[46] Ibid., p. 282.
[47] Burrows, *Handel*, ch. 8.
[48] Ibid., pp. 78–81.

Spanish Succession. Like the post of treasurer of the navy, this office was one of the most potentially lucrative of government posts because it was considered perfectly normal for all monies to be passed through the office-holder's personal accounts. Consequently, the paymaster could invest balances and keep the interest for himself.

Frederick's purchase of Carlton House in March 1733 offered the chance for the prince of Wales to give physical embodiment to the notion of a rival court.[49] Its location was close to, but separate from, St James's. Frederick's major grievances could be reduced to two, interrelated, complaints: that he had not been properly provided for financially and that he still did not have a wife. He believed that a solution to the latter would lead to an increase in the former. Frederick's allowance was still only £24,000 a year. He had not yet gone into open opposition to his father – advisers like George Bubb Dodington, George Lyttelton and Chesterfield thought it would be unwise to mount an open parliamentary campaign at this point. Other political malcontents saw Frederick as a potential saviour. Tories continued to hope that their seemingly permanent political exclusion might be reversed under a new monarch and so saw Frederick as somebody to be cultivated, even if their advances were not reciprocated.

Anne's marriage provoked a formal request from Frederick that moves be made to end his single status.[50] The king did very little about this in 1734. Anne had returned to London while her husband was fighting in the War of the Polish Succession. She had not immediately warmed to life in the United Provinces and used William's absence to return to the bosom of her family. Her stay proved to be controversial. She believed herself to be pregnant and was anxious to stay in London for the birth of what she hoped would be a male heir. William, and his Orangist supporters, was far from happy about the idea. To reinforce the claim for Orange political pre-eminence in the United Provinces it was vital that the next generation should be born at home, preferably in The Hague. Caroline realized that it would be impolitic in the extreme for Anne to remain in London. Anne tried hard to prolong her visit to Britain, using her husband's inability to leave the front in Germany and then the potential harm that she could do to the unborn child if she risked a crossing of the North Sea in rough autumn weather to delay her departure. She was finally ordered by William to take the shortest route across the Channel via Calais. Even then, she tried to prevaricate, claiming she could not travel from Harwich to Dover without coming via London (the Gravesend ferry being considered inappropriate). Her father, concerned to bring matters to a swift conclusion, allowed her coach to come through London but only on the

[49] For Frederick's works on Carlton House, see Frances Vivian, *A life of Frederick, prince of Wales, 1707–1751: a connoisseur of the arts*, ed. Roger White (Lampeter, 2007), pp. 140–9.
[50] Hervey, *Memoirs*, i, pp. 298–9.

condition that it did not stop, and Anne eventually found her way back to the continent. George was unimpressed by the fuss and the potential for political embarrassment that Anne had created. Anne was not actually pregnant but her behaviour had longer-term consequences. Future requests for visits to London were denied and George, anxious not to upset republican sentiments in the United Provinces, was wary of visiting his daughter during his regular journeys to the Netherlands en route to Hanover.[51]

A HANOVERIAN SUMMER AND ITS CONSEQUENCES

George returned to Hanover in 1735, eager to see if he could do anything to further his ambitions as an arbiter in the Polish conflict. He was to be disappointed in this regard, just as he was during a similar trip in the following year. There were, however, to be important familial changes that stemmed from the trip. At a dynastic level George used the visit to settle upon Augusta of Saxe-Gotha as a suitable bride for Frederick.[52] Augusta came from an even less prominent princely family than William. Nevertheless, she impressed George, when he interviewed her, with her respect for him and her general affability. She did not seem the sort of person who would further inflame Frederick's wilder side and she might even have a calming influence on him. Augusta's family were more than happy to see her marrying into one of Europe's leading Protestant ruling houses, although her mother seemed a little naïve in her belief that Augusta would not need to learn English because, after more than two decades of Hanoverian rule, she was sure that everybody in Britain would now be speaking German.

The second alteration was more personal to George, although its consequences were equally enduring. At some point during the 1735 trip George began a relationship with Amalie Sophie Marianne von Wallmoden. Born in 1704, Wallmoden came from the upper strata of Hanoverian society and her family had already enjoyed several intimate connections with the Guelphs. It is likely that her grandmother, Maria von Meysenbug, had been Georg Ludwig's close companion and possibly mistress in the 1670s.[53] Wallmoden's father's correspondence with George's uncle, Ernst August, has been seen by some as suggestive of a more than platonic relationship. George seems to have entered into his new relationship with gusto. His regular correspondence with Caroline was said by Hervey to include minute details of the new relationship – what Wallmoden looked like, what she did, where they went, what George had bought for her and how much it had all cost.[54] On his eventual return to London, George

[51] Baker-Smith, *Royal discord*, pp. 75–6.
[52] Hervey, *Memoirs*, ii, p. 474.
[53] Ragnhild Hatton, *George I* (London, 1978), p. 36.
[54] Hervey, *Memoirs*, ii, pp. 457–8.

continued to talk frequently about the delights of his time in Hanover and forced Caroline and Hervey to look at pictures of various scenes of Hanoverian court life, while George regaled them with further details of his adventures with Wallmoden.[55] Such was the strength of George's passion for his new mistress that he was reluctant to leave Hanover to go back to London as normal to celebrate his birthday – he did not depart until the start of November, whereas he had made his return journey in late September on his previous two visits.

George just managed to arrive back in London in time for his birthday. However, the return to Britain had done little for his mood. Hervey attributed some of George's anger to the speed on his home-coming and the impact this had on his health.[56] The journey back was faster than in 1732 when it had taken a fortnight but George had also managed it in five days in 1729. Whether his health complaints were due to the haste of his travel is debatable. He was feverish for several weeks and he suffered a bad attack of piles which would have done little to calm his mood. Irritation at his enforced return to Britain and absence from Wallmoden also played a part. Hervey claimed that George's bad temper was felt by everybody at court. George was said to have remarked to Lady Sundon shortly after getting back that whereas in Hanover he could reward those who had done their duty to him, in Britain he had to reward rascals and 'buy them not to cut his throat'. His view of the British was of a nation of king-killers and republicans.[57]

One particular incident highlighted the difference in outlook between Hervey and the king. Given how late George's return was, he was only able to spend a couple of days in Kensington before returning to St James's for his birthday and to spend the winter in London (George's birthday was traditionally the point at which the court moved back to St James's). In his absence Caroline had done some rummaging and discovered some Leonardo and Holbein sketchbooks in an old desk. She had also moved some of the paintings in the drawing room around. The king was not happy with the changes and insisted that his old favourites be restored. Hervey had the temerity to enquire whether the king really wanted the Van Dyck picture of Charles I's children removed and replaced with George's preferred 'Fat Venus' only to be told, 'I like my fat Venus much better than anything you have given me instead of her'.[58] Remarks like this, nearly all culled from Hervey, have been used to create an impression of George as an ignorant philistine with no appreciation of

[55] Ibid., p. 528.

[56] Ibid., pp. 484–5.

[57] Ibid., p. 486.

[58] Ibid., p. 489. Possible candidates for George's preferred picture are Giovanni Cariani's *Venus in a landscape* (*c.* 1530–5) which was presented to Charles I (RCIN 402912. Images from the Royal Collection can be accessed at www.royalcollection.org.uk/eGallery) and Giorgio Vasari, *Venus and Cupid* (*c.* 1543) which had been acquired by Caroline for the Royal Collection (RCIN 405486).

art. There is little doubt that he was not as concerned with collecting as either his son or grandson. However, he did show some appreciation for art when it intersected with his other interests – he liked small martial equestrian portraits, for example.[59] Moreover, he seems to have been a person of reasonably fixed opinions. He knew what he liked and did not have much time for others' views. Had his tastes coincided with Hervey's, he would probably have been fêted as a great aesthete. That they did not, does not, of itself, make him a bore.

The king's mood improved little during the winter of 1735–6. Hervey was particularly reproachful of his treatment of Caroline, noting that she was constantly reproved and contradicted by the king.[60] Hervey was well placed to observe George's fits of temper. Henrietta Howard's departure meant that George had to alter his evening routine a little. The time he had previously spent in her apartments on the evenings that he was not at the opera or playing cards, he now spent with his daughters. Having tried their patience and talked 'a little bawdy' to Lady Deloraine, governess to Mary and Louisa, George would return to the queen's apartments and converse with her. Hervey was often present on these occasions, perhaps because Caroline found it easier to cope with George's discourses if somebody else was present.

Hervey gave the impression that he was willing to give as good as he got in verbal exchanges with George, especially if he could draw his ire away from Caroline. He recounted a long tirade of George's about Bishop Hoadly, the Low Church cleric and one of Hervey's friends, in which George complained about Hoadly's careful timing of a controversial book on the sacraments. The king claimed that Hoadly had waited until he had secured promotion to the see of Winchester before venturing into print on whether the sacraments should be used as tests of civil obedience. George's reported remark that for somebody who had famously preached during the Bangorian controversy that 'the kingdom of Christ is not of this world', thus calling into question the legitimacy of civil government of the church, Hoadly's desire to keep his £6,000–£7,000 a year was a touch hypocritical displayed a wit with which the king is seldom credited. However, coping with him in such moods seems to have been trying, to say the least.[61] It should be noted, however, that other court insiders took a slightly different view of George and Caroline's relationship during this period. Lady Irwin, writing to her father, the third earl of Carlisle, in early February 1736 noted that George had been quite ill and in bed for much

[59] Oliver Millar, *The Tudor, Stuart and early Georgian pictures in the collection of Her Majesty the Queen* (2 vols, London, 1963), i, pp. 26–8.

[60] Hervey, *Memoirs*, ii, p. 496.

[61] Ibid., pp. 498–503. It is worth recalling that Hervey's account of this episode began with George remarking that his poor health had put him in a bad humour.

of the last week but that Caroline had not appeared in public and had attended him 'in the most careful and affectionate manner'.[62]

Frederick, meanwhile, had been maintaining a relatively low profile, attending court infrequently. A message was sent to him on 4 February, just as George was beginning to feel better, to ascertain whether he would accept Augusta as his bride. Frederick replied that he consented to his father's choice. Preparations for the marriage duly commenced. One crucial constraint was the timing of the event. George appeared anxious to return to Hanover as soon as the parliamentary session was ended. It was unusual for him to visit in consecutive years but the birth of a son to Wallmoden in the spring of 1736 may have influenced his decision. Augusta landed at Greenwich in late April. Lady Irwin had already been appointed to Augusta's household as a lady of the bedchamber and she accompanied Augusta on her journey from The Hague. She reported to her father that Frederick had been to visit his new bride soon after her arrival and had supped in public with her.[63] Augusta faced a similar problem to William: George was reluctant to honour her with much ceremonial prior to the marriage. Frederick had shown Augusta some of the sites of London from his barge in the short space of time between her arrival and the wedding. On the day of the event itself, Augusta was conveyed from Greenwich to St James's. When brought into the royal presence, Augusta prostrated herself, which Hervey felt probably helped endear her to George, who set store by such marks of his status. Before the ceremony Frederick's sisters dined with him and his betrothed. The meal was not without incident as Frederick insisted that his sisters should sit on stools, rather than armchairs, and should not be waited on by servants on bended knee. No doubt such niceties might have impressed Augusta as a mark of Frederick's importance but his family refused to do anything differently from their usual practice so the sisters had the stools removed and their armchairs brought in.

The wedding, performed by the bishop of London, was grand but not quite on the scale of Anne's nuptials. There was little time to prepare the Chapel Royal between Easter communion on 25 April and the wedding on 27 April. Augusta was led up the aisle by William, duke of Cumberland. Handel had composed an anthem for the occasion, 'Sing unto God, ye kingdoms of the earth' (HWV 263), although its first performance was not, as often happened with Handel's royal compositions, as good as he might have hoped.[64] After the ceremony, the bride and groom received George and Caroline's blessing before they all sat down to supper. The final act was the

[62] Irwin to third earl of Carlisle, 5/2/1736, HMC, *Fifteenth report, Appendix, part VI. The manuscripts of the earl of Carlisle* (London, 1897), p. 159.

[63] Irwin to third earl of Carlisle, Greenwich, 26/4/1736, ibid., p. 170.

[64] It was described as 'wretchedly sung' by Egmont in his diary (R.A. Roberts, ed., *Diary of Viscount Percival afterwards first earl of Egmont* (HMC, 3 vols, London, 1920–3), ii, p. 264).

bedding ceremony. Hervey's only comment on this was that Frederick's nightcap was taller than a grenadier's cap. He also noted that the next morning Augusta looked so refreshed that she must have slept very soundly. Caroline was amused by Frederick's attire and reported to Anne that George had behaved well throughout. Handel's opera *Atalanta* was completed about this time and its final scene of Mercury conveying the blessing of the gods on Meleagro and Atalanta's nuptials made it timely. Frederick was not present at the first performance, preferring to attend a play instead, but he did order a command performance in November 1736.[65]

ABSENCE AND OPPOSITION

The wedding safely completed, George made haste to travel to Hanover. In the king's absence, Caroline spent some time at Richmond before settling into Kensington for the summer. Frederick was not particularly enamoured of life at Kensington. He tried to spend as much time as possible in London. Many of his grievances remained unresolved. His allowance had been increased – from £24,000 to £50,000 a year – but it was still not as large as that which his father had enjoyed nor as secure. No jointure had been settled on Augusta and Frederick still lacked a political role, although his circle of oppositional friends was growing. Augusta was slowly becoming accustomed to her new life. She rapidly learned English although it was more difficult for her to assimilate in other areas. As a devout Lutheran she had scruples about taking communion in the Church of England and even preferred to attend the Lutheran Chapel at St James's than join the rest of the family in the Chapel Royal. Firm words from Caroline, prompted by Walpole, about the political inexpediency of this approach eventually had the desired effect.[66]

George, meanwhile, was enjoying his Hanoverian summer. He was glad to be reunited with Wallmoden. Hervey reported an incident where a ladder was discovered outside Wallmoden's window with a man lurking in her garden but George seemed either to accept her innocent explanation for it all or take it on the chin.[67] The 1736 visit was a little unusual in that George was not accompanied by either of his secretaries of state but instead by Sir Robert's brother, the diplomat and MP Horatio (or Horace) Walpole. Harrington, who had accompanied the king on his previous two visits, was supposedly too ill to travel, although royal dislike and ministerial divisions provide a more likely explanation. Walpole found himself in a difficult position. George was keen to make progress on a number of the outstanding disputes within the empire, particularly those over the

---

[65] Hervey, *Memoirs*, ii, pp. 550–3, Vivian, *Frederick*, pp. 203–7, Burrows, *Handel and the Chapel Royal*, pp. 340–4, Baker-Smith, *Royal discord*, pp. 82–3, Burrows, *Handel*, pp. 188–9, Winton Dean, *Handel's Operas, 1726–1741* (Woodbridge, 2006), pp. 343–4.

[66] Hervey, *Memoirs*, ii, pp. 560–1.

[67] Ibid., p. 558.

succession to the Rhine duchies of Jülich and Berg and over East Friesland. He was also still keeping a close eye on developments in Mecklenburg, although it had now been superseded as a potential point of friction with Prussia by the other disputes. All these problems involved a complicated set of intersecting interests. The United Provinces, Prussia and France all had their axes to grind and the emperor was anxious not to do anything that might endanger the negotiations that aimed to bring the War of the Polish Succession to a conclusion. George was able to place himself at the centre of a web of diplomatic exchanges and made full use of both British and Hanoverian figures to pursue his own interests and ends. He was also anxious to disrupt a potential alliance between France and the Baltic powers. Horace Walpole was not privy to all these discussions and so struggled to keep abreast of them, as did the ministers in London.[68]

Much of George's diplomatic efforts during the summer of 1736 were lost on those back in London. For simple souls who viewed royal absence as unnecessary and British meddling in continental affairs as unhelpful the 1736 trip was grist to an oppositional mill. Not only was the king gone for longer than on any of his previous visits, but Frederick was an ostentatious and apparently popular presence around London. Breaking with his previous practice, George delayed his departure from Hanover until well past his birthday, celebrating in some style with a banquet, ball and fireworks at Herrenhausen instead, and finally left on 18 December. Popular discontent at George's sojourn in Hanover had an economic dimension. London tradesmen were angered that the lack of a birthday celebration had harmed their business because the number of people coming up to town had fallen.[69] This is one of a number of indications that the court was still an important economic force even within a burgeoning commercial society. Other aspects of popular disquiet took the form of witty broadsides and prints. Hervey reported that a paper had been posted on the Royal Exchange stating that 'it is reported that his Hanoverian Majesty designs to visit his British dominions for three months in the spring'. Another was a spoof lost and found advertisement, stating that a man of St James's parish had left his wife and six children and offering a reward of 4s 6d for any intelligence as to his whereabouts. The reward would not be increased as nobody judged him 'to deserve a crown'.[70]

George's return was delayed further by adverse weather conditions in the North Sea. The flotilla of ships carrying George and his entourage was caught in a violent storm. Some of the ships made it across but

---

[68] Uta Richter-Uhlig, *Hof und Politik unter den Bedingungen der Personalunion zwischen Hannover und England* (Hanover, 1992), pp. 122–36. The lengthy legal proceedings surrounding the disputes in East Friesland and Mecklenburg form the central subject matter of Michael Hughes, *Law and politics in eighteenth-century Germany* (Woodbridge, 1988).

[69] Hervey, *Memoirs*, ii, p. 609.

[70] Ibid., p. 610.

George's was forced back to the Dutch coast. Although Caroline feared that George had been lost at sea, news of his survival eventually filtered through to London. The winds and the state of Sir Charles Wager's health, who, as first lord of the admiralty, had taken personal command of the king's yacht, kept George stuck in Hellevoetsluis for nearly a month. Even Hervey was forced to admit that the tenderness of the exchanges between Caroline and George, when it became clear that the king, as had been feared, had not drowned, was a sign of the genuine affection that existed between them.[71]

FREDERICK AND THE OPPOSITION

Frederick had enhanced his own popularity during his father's absence. When a large fire broke out in the Inner Temple in early January 1737, he visited the scene and encouraged those fighting the fire, as well as providing some financial assistance.[72] However, Frederick's popular appeal was not the only reason that George had to be wary of him in the early months of 1737. Frederick's financial difficulties were becoming acute. He was living well beyond his means and his creditors were growing impatient. One partial solution to his problems would be to secure an increase in his income and so he began to make more active moves to petition parliament to revisit the issue.

To achieve success Frederick needed to build a parliamentary coalition sufficient to overturn a ministerial majority or to reduce it so much as to make concessions politic. Lobbying therefore began in earnest. Other members of the royal family looked on with an increasing degree of disquiet. Walpole tried appealing to various members of Frederick's household. Lord Scarbrough was dispatched to see Frederick directly and warn him of the potential harm of his actions for the Hanoverian succession. It was claimed that disagreements among the royal family helped nobody but the Jacobites. Yet Frederick remained resolute that £100,000 a year was nothing more than he deserved. Some blamed his stubbornness on his friends and advisers – Hervey singled out the earl of Chesterfield and the dukes of Marlborough and Bedford together with Richard Grenville, George Lyttelton and William Pitt (collectively known as the 'Cobham Cubs', after Grenville's uncle Viscount Cobham, who had supported their oppositional parliamentary careers).[73] Reports of George's recurrent ill health may also have contributed to a sense among Frederick's supporters that this was a winnable fight.

Walpole gradually realized that he was unlikely to be able to prevent a motion about the prince's allowance being debated in the Commons. Nevertheless, he tried one last time to head Frederick off. On 21 February

[71] Ibid., p. 641.
[72] *Daily Gazetteer*, 478, 6/1/1737.
[73] Hervey, *Memoirs*, iii, p. 667.

the cabinet council, consisting of Lord Hardwicke, the newly appointed lord chancellor, along with the lord president, lord steward, lord chamberlain, the dukes of Richmond, Newcastle and Argyll, the earls of Pembroke and Scarbrough and Lord Harrington visited Frederick with a settlement offer. Walpole, whom Frederick was known to dislike, quietly absented himself from the party. Their message expressed George's regret that his sojourn abroad had rendered him unable to settle Augusta's jointure but he now proposed to do so. Frederick was also offered security of his current allowance for life, with payments becoming quarterly rather than monthly. Frederick politely replied that he was grateful for the offer but the matter was now out of his hands.[74]

In the Commons, William Pulteney proposed that Frederick's allowance be increased and a few days later Lord Carteret made a similar proposal in the Lords. On both occasions the result of the division was a victory for the ministry and a defeat for Frederick. The Commons majority was small, though – a mere thirty votes. It was rumoured that Frederick would have won, had all those who had promised their support to him given it. However, a sufficiently large group of Tories, perhaps wishing to stay aloof from a Hanoverian quarrel or perhaps unwilling to support Pulteney's claims of general loyalty to the royal family even in the context of a specific dispute, abstained, which meant that Walpole survived. The majority in the Lords was larger but it was easier to whip in the Scottish peers and the Episcopal bench so ministerial defeats in the Lords were much easier to avoid, provided clear signals of royal intentions were forthcoming.

Frederick had now entered a period of open parliamentary opposition to his father. The stage was set for a further confrontation and, in a haunting repetition of the events of 1717, it was ostensibly triggered by a child. Frederick had been cagey about Augusta's health for some while. At the end of the parliamentary session George had removed himself to Richmond for the summer, while Frederick and Augusta had gone to nearby Kew. Early in July Frederick informed Caroline that Augusta was pregnant but when Caroline asked Augusta at their next meeting when the child was due, Augusta responded that she did not know. All further enquiries on the subject met with a similar response. Frederick had determined that his child would be born in London, against the known wishes of his parents.

On 31 July Augusta went into labour, having dined in public with the king and queen earlier in the day.[75] Frederick promptly had her bundled into a coach to get her to London. Her waters had broken before they left Hampton Court (where the court had moved earlier in the month). Augusta was thrown around, no doubt in considerable pain, as the coach galloped at full tilt for St James's. Little had been done in the way of

---

[74] Ibid., pp. 673–4.
[75] Hervey was a witness to much of the aftermath of the incident and received a fuller account of earlier events from Frederick via Caroline. See ibid., pp. 756–64.

preparations for her arrival so tablecloths substituted for sheets. Shortly after her arrival in St James's, Augusta gave birth to a daughter. Frederick was aware that there were certain rules governing the birth of royal children, particularly that the birth must be witnessed by members of the Privy Council. He had been wise enough to ensure that some were present, having summoned Lord Wilmington from his home in Chiswick and Lord Godolphin from his house near St James's. Somehow news of Frederick's hasty departure from Hampton Court had not reached his parents, who had already gone to bed when news of the princess's labour arrived via a courier. Their immediate response was to go and see what had happened for themselves. Caroline rose and dressed and set out for St James's with Hervey, Grafton, Lord Essex, who was George's current lord of the bedchamber in waiting, and the Princesses Caroline and Amelia together with their attendants. Caroline inspected the new princess and subsequently declared herself satisfied that Frederick had not engaged in some subterfuge to pass another's child off as his own – the new princess was too small and ugly to make that possibility seem likely, despite Caroline's suspicions of her son.

Frederick's parents were unimpressed by his behaviour and the potential dangers to which he had exposed their unborn grandchild. They found themselves in a difficult position. Their preference for their younger son William over Frederick was widely reported, even to the extent that some talked of moves to prefer William in the succession over his brother. Walpole and Hervey were anxious that nothing be done that would further encourage popular support for Frederick. George was, however, unwilling to compromise in a situation where he felt his honour had been slighted and where he had been misled by his eldest son. Despite Frederick's apologetic letters to his parents which attempted to explain and justify his actions, tempers remained frayed. It had been made clear to him that he would not be welcome at court and Frederick expressed his disappointment at this, as well as his surprise that his parents should have taken his behaviour so badly. He reiterated his hope that his parents, together with Augusta's mother, would stand as godparents to his daughter.[76]

George and Caroline finally agreed to act as godparents. The baptism was performed at the end of August with proxies representing the king and queen. However, George's irritation with Frederick had not really subsided in the interim. He had fixed on the issue of whether Frederick had misled him about Augusta's likely due date (the new princess had been named after her mother). Despite Frederick's apologetic professions, his actions belied his claims of deference to his parents' will. Hervey drafted a declaration outlining George's complaints against his son. Following some

---

[76] The exchanges between Frederick and his parents are preserved in the Royal Archives, Windsor under RA GEO/52809–23. The French originals are accompanied by English translations. The letter quoted is Frederick to George, St James's, 4/8/1737, RA GEO/52813.

alterations by Walpole and Hervey this was submitted to cabinet council and then taken to Frederick by the dukes of Grafton and Richmond, accompanied by Lord Pembroke.[77] The message expressed indignation at the affront to George's honour and irritation at the way in which Frederick had concealed his plans. He was banned from St James's, although George did leave Augusta in the care of her mother for the present but reserved the right to take her back under his direct care at some future point.

The quarrel quickly found its way into the public eye. Frederick's household decamped to Kew. The king had made clear that those who attended his son should not also attend him. Just as in the earlier Whig split, families found themselves with divided loyalties, although the pull of George's court was always going to be strong. Lady Irwin told her father of the departure of the Ladies Effingham and Torrington from Frederick's household because of their husbands' desire to remain in favour with the king. Irwin thought that her father, or perhaps Lord Scarbrough, might be a good person to mend the breach, details of which were now circulating widely.[78] Some efforts had been made to keep matters under wraps – Sir Benjamin Keene, the British extraordinary envoy in Madrid, was sent copies of some of the exchanges between George and Frederick but was told specifically not to spread these any further and that they were not being shared widely.[79] Copies of the correspondence between George and his son still found their way into print in the *Gentleman's Magazine*.[80]

CAROLINE'S DEATH

The year of familial troubles for George was to take one final, dramatic turn. On 9 November 1737 Caroline was inspecting her new library, built to a design by William Kent, on the west side of St James's Palace overlooking the park.[81] During the visit, she was taken ill with severe pain in her lower abdomen.[82] Her indisposition caused George to consider cancelling the drawing room but Caroline stoically insisted that she was feeling a little better. She survived the drawing room and was reprimanded by the king for ignoring the duchess of Norfolk. She then retired to bed. Hervey found her there later in the evening. Knowing that Hervey's valetudinarian tendencies made him a good source of information on all matters medicinal, Caroline enquired what he would take in these circumstances. Hervey named various patent remedies that he had found helpful for stomach complaints in the past and these were duly fetched.

[77] For Hervey's draft see *Memoirs*, iii, pp. 807–8. The message as sent is reprinted ibid., pp. 814–15. There is another copy at RA GEO/52808.

[78] Irwin to third earl of Carlisle, 11/10/1737, HMC, *Carlisle*, pp. 186–7.

[79] Courand to Keene, Hampton Court, 12/9/1737 OS, BL, Add. MSS 32795, fos 350–2.

[80] *Gentleman's Magazine*, 7 (1737), pp. 639, 677–82.

[81] Colvin et al., *King's works*, p. 242.

[82] The following is based on Hervey's extensive account of Caroline's last days. Hervey, *Memoirs*, iii, pp. 877–915.

The round of blooding and induced vomiting that represented the height of mid-eighteenth-century medical sophistication continued with no noticeable improvements in the patient's condition. Caroline had become convinced that this would be her final illness and confided such to her daughter Caroline, who was herself attempting to recover from a bout of rheumatism. Caroline's conviction of her imminent demise rested on the fact that she had a ruptured hernia in her navel area of which she had first become aware after her final pregnancy with Louisa. George knew of the condition but Caroline only let on that this might be the cause of her problems after she had been ill for several days. After the royal surgeons became aware of this possible explanation, Caroline not actually having been examined before this point, they advised that an operation be attempted in which an incision was made to try to push the gut back into the body. The chances of such a procedure succeeding were limited but the attempt was made nevertheless.

Throughout her illness Caroline was surrounded by members of her family. George was with her constantly, sleeping on couches or even the floor to ensure that he would be close at hand, should her condition change. George's presence in her bedchamber, however, made it difficult for Caroline to sleep for any length of time. The Princesses Caroline and Amelia and the duke of Cumberland were also frequent visitors to their mother's bedside. During a more lucid period, Caroline left what amounted to final instructions for her children. She entrusted the education of Mary and Louisa to Caroline, warning her to take account of their differing temperaments. William was reminded of his familial duties but also told to do nothing against his brother, except surpass him in merit.[83]

Frederick was notable by his absence during Caroline's last days. On hearing that his mother was ill, he had sent a message, via a third party, to the court enquiring whether he might come and visit. George's answer had been a decisive negative and Caroline agreed that she had no desire to see Frederick, even at this stage. Concern about Frederick went beyond his mere presence. Caroline was anxious to discover what would happen to the property at Richmond that had been given to her as part of her jointure. Both she and George were relieved to discover that it would pass to George for his lifetime before it went to Frederick. George was also angered to discover that members of Frederick's household had taken to visiting the queen's apartments regularly to see if they could gather snippets of intelligence. Anne was kept informed of her mother's illness but her sisters took care that their letters to her were constructed in such a way as to ensure that Anne could not use them as an excuse to travel to London. After the difficulty George had had in persuading her to return to her husband and new lands on her last visit, he was anxious to avoid a repeat performance.

[83] Ibid., p. 895.

Caroline also seems to have been concerned for George's future well-being. She was keen that George should marry again. George was not particularly happy with the suggestion, responding amidst his tears, 'non – j'aurai des maîtresses'. Caroline's succinct reply was 'ah mon Dieu! Cela n'empêche pas'.[84] George's behaviour was a little erratic. He expressed tenderness for Caroline and his gratitude for having had her as a wife but Hervey noted that even when complimenting her, he could not resist talking about himself – how he too had been brave, particularly when faced with the storm on his last crossing back from Hanover, how he deserved such an excellent wife. Princess Amelia told Hervey that she had taken to pretending to be asleep so she did not have to listen to her father endlessly talking about himself.[85] The strain of a protracted illness where there was little that could be done to relieve Caroline's suffering is clear from Hervey's account.

Caroline died on 20 November 1737. There was some controversy about her behaviour in her last days. The lack of reconciliation with her son and the absence of a priest caused comment. In the end, the archbishop of Canterbury was summoned and he prayed with Caroline night and day. The next demand was that Caroline should take the sacrament but this was not to be fulfilled. Her last reported word was, however, 'pray'. Contemporary newspaper reports focused on the fact that Caroline had died a good death. Mary Selwyn, one of Caroline's women of the bedchamber, made much of this in a letter to Hannah Lowther, a former maid of honour to Mary and Anne, although this may have reflected a desire to create the public impression of a pious end. Selwyn also noted that Caroline had instructed the king to look after all her servants and that George had honoured this request, as well as taking on approximately £13,000 worth of pensions that Caroline paid out.[86]

The effect of Caroline's death on George was marked. Even Hervey was forced to admit that his grief indicated a 'tenderness of which the world thought him utterly incapable' and served to raise his popularity.[87] George oversaw the arrangements for Caroline's funeral with great care, assisted by a special committee of the Privy Council. Organizing a royal funeral was a considerable undertaking, even in an era when, as Michael Schaich has shown, these were increasingly private rather than state occasions.[88] The lord chamberlain and the lord steward, for example, had to ensure that sufficient mourning had been ordered to enable all the necessary household officials to be kitted out in black. They were also responsible for seeing that props such as a black chair for the chief mourner were

---

[84] Ibid., p. 896.

[85] Ibid., pp. 912–13.

[86] Mary Selwyn to Hannah Lowther, 29/11/1737, RA GEO/52824.

[87] Hervey, *Memoirs*, iii, p. 916.

[88] Michael Schaich, 'The funerals of the British monarchy', in idem, ed., *Monarchy and religion*, pp. 421–50.

provided.[89] Mourning was a serious business. News of a royal death invariably triggered a run on black material.[90]

The funeral took place on the evening of 17 December in Westminster Abbey. The date was not widely publicized perhaps because of the ceremony's theoretically private nature. Caroline's body had been moved from St James's in the early morning and lay in state in the Prince's Chamber of the House of Lords prior to the funeral. George did not attend, having already made his final farewells at a private service. Amelia performed the duties of chief mourner, supported by a long procession of court dignitaries. George had ordered that a new vault be prepared in the abbey's Henry VII Chapel and that the side of the coffin should be removable so that when he was laid to rest himself, their remains could mingle. As with so many royal events in this period, Handel composed an anthem for the occasion, which was performed after the burial service: 'The ways of Zion do mourn' [HWV 264]. George attended a rehearsal of the music incognito in the French Chapel on 14 December – at nearly fifty minutes, it was a substantial work. Precedent was not broken in another respect. Reports of the performance itself were mixed.[91] Despite the grand accounts of the ceremony that appeared in the official press,[92] some felt that it left something to be desired. Opposition papers, such as the *Country Journal* or *Old Common Sense*, noted that because the funeral had begun earlier than expected, the crowds were not particularly large.[93] Thomas Wilson, a royal chaplain and prebend of the abbey, noted in his diary that the funeral 'was not managed with the Decency one would have wished. A great deal of confusion in marshalling the procession.'[94] Others regretted the effects that the mourning would have. One of the countess of Denbigh's correspondents noted how sorry he was for the long period of mourning, not just because of the death of the queen, but because now 'the Lyon coat must lie by a great while; I have never wore it. I have another apprehension about me, which is that, since it's necessary to mourn so very strictly out of the kingdom, when I come to London perhaps I may be ordered to black my face, who can tell.'[95] Lady Irwin had already told her father that,

---

[89] NA, LC 2/24.

[90] See Paul S. Fritz, 'The trade in death: the royal funerals in England, 1685–1830', *Eighteenth-century studies*, 15 (1982), pp. 291–316 for a broader view of the social and economic impact of royal death.

[91] Burrows, *Handel and the Chapel Royal*, pp. 362–5, Roberts, ed., *Egmont diary*, ii, p. 454. Handel wanted to adapt his anthem to an Italian text for use at a benefit concert in 1738 (Burrows, *Handel and the Chapel Royal*, p. 381) but was prevented from doing so by George. A reconstructed version of the Italian anthem was given its première performance in May 2009.

[92] *London Gazette*, 7660, 20–24/12/1737 is the basis for most other accounts.

[93] *Old Common Sense*, 47, 24/12/1737, *Country Journal*, 598, 24/12/1737.

[94] C.L.S Linnell, ed., *The diaries of Thomas Wilson, D.D.* (London, 1964), p. 219.

[95] J. Stanhope to countess of Denbigh, Paris, 16/12/1737, HMC, *Report on the manuscripts of the earl of Denbigh, preserved at Newnham Paddox, Warwickshire* (London, 1911), p. 225.

despite the general order that peers' coaches should be put into mourning, she did not think that it would be universally obeyed within London, so there was little point in doing it in the country.[96]

All this mattered little to George. He had lost his wife and companion of more than three decades. Her social skills had been valuable in establishing the couple in Britain after 1714, as had her committed Protestantism. As first princess of Wales and then as queen consort, she had helped in a revival of court life, complementing George's brusque manner with an ability to say the right thing. Her contribution to securing the Protestant succession and establishing the Hanoverians in St James's had been significant. Consequently, the king's grief was profound and prolonged. George declined to take the sacrament, as was his custom, on Christmas Day and instead ordered the preacher, the dean of Exeter, to make his late wife and not the birth of Christ the subject of his sermon. When Egmont, the indefatigable diarist of 1730s' political life, attended court in early January 1738 he was able to speak to the king but noted that George 'stayed not two minutes out, and had grief fixed on his face'.[97] One chapter in his personal life had closed. Whether Caroline's death was to have political consequences as well remained to be seen.

[96] Lady Irwin to third earl of Carlisle, 3/12/1737, HMC, *Carlisle*, p. 190.
[97] Roberts, ed., *Egmont diary*, ii, pp. 458–9.

Chapter 5

CHALLENGES AND CONFLICTS

Caroline's death left a significant gap at the heart of George's court. Yet speculation quickly grew about who would succeed to Caroline's position of supposed influence over the king. Hervey reported that Newcastle and Grafton wondered whether Princess Amelia would now fill that role but Walpole responded with characteristic directness that George was unlikely to commit incest so instead it would be necessary to consider either Countess Wallmoden or Lady Deloraine.[1] Lady Mary Deloraine had become George's mistress some time during the summer of 1737, although he does not seem to have been particularly enthused by her, noting that she stank rather too frequently of Spanish wine.[2]

'J'AURAI DES MAÎTRESSES'

The idea that Wallmoden might come over from Hanover to reside permanently in Britain had been mentioned, even before Caroline's death. However, from the political perspective, Walpole felt that her presence was now even more critical, to offer some sort of comfort to the king. George was still clearly upset, having struggled to make his speech at the state opening of parliament in 1738 and even finding it difficult to maintain his composure at official court functions.[3] Wallmoden arrived in London in June 1738 and moved into the apartments previously occupied by Henrietta Howard. She was naturalized in February 1740 and created countess of Yarmouth in March. Her husband divorced her in the summer of that year.

Wallmoden's position at court was not an easy one. Dislike of George's apparent preference for all things Germanic had been growing for several years so the installation of a German as the king's *maîtresse en titre* was unlikely to be popular. In addition, Wallmoden was very much an outsider. She did not

---

[1] *Memoirs*, iii, pp. 918–19.

[2] Ibid., p. 919. Deloraine had enjoyed a typical courtly career. She had been a maid of honour to Caroline prior to her marriage. Her first husband, Henry Scott, earl of Deloraine, was a gentleman of the bedchamber to George. After her husband's death, Deloraine became governess to the Princesses Mary and Louisa and was, after some negotiation, allowed to remarry in 1734.

[3] R. A. Roberts, ed., *Diary of Viscount Percival afterwards first earl of Egmont* (HMC, 3 vols, London, 1920–3), ii, p. 461, Veronica Baker-Smith, *Royal discord: the family of George II* (London, 2008), pp. 96–7. The expressions of condolence by the Lords and Commons are reprinted in *Gentleman's Magazine*, 8 (1738), pp. 50–1.

have ready access to the networks of friendship, mutual interdependence and association that made up much of court life. Nevertheless, those who observed her during her first months in Britain noted that she seemed able to carry herself appropriately and that she was evidently used to attending court and was well versed in how to behave once there.[4]

Lady Deloraine was considered by some to be more conventionally attractive than Wallmoden but George was reluctant to invest much effort in getting this relationship to work. He was happy to spend a certain amount of time with Deloraine but did little more. In some ways, the period immediately after Caroline's death was a relatively stable one for the king. He continued in his regular habits of court life, with the predictable round of drawing rooms and levees, although being in mourning meant that he did not attend public performances at the theatre. He stayed away from the theatre throughout 1738 and only returned in January 1739 to see *Henry V*. Even then, he did not see plays or operas with quite the frequency that he had when Caroline was alive.[5] Now well into his fifties, he was unlikely to want to do much to change things from the way that he liked them. His relations with Frederick remained frosty but the 1738 parliamentary session contained little of the heat of the year before, at least over Frederick's allowance. Such tranquillity was to prove temporary, however.

The murmurings were already becoming noticeable in 1738. The one significant moment of dissent in the 1738 session had been when a petition was introduced on 3 March by merchants demanding that the ministry do more about Spanish depredations. The case of Robert Jenkins, an officer in the merchant navy, who had lost part of his ear when his ship was boarded by the Spanish in April 1731, became a focus for agitation. Jenkins was ordered to appear in the Commons to display his injury but he did not ultimately attend. Nevertheless, his plight roused sufficient attention to ensure that his name was to become indelibly associated with the conflict – the War of Jenkins' Ear.

CONFLICT WITH SPAIN IN THE AMERICAS

Complaints about the way in which British ships had been treated in the Americas were hardly new, as the Jenkins case illustrates. They had rumbled on at varying levels of intensity since the treaty of Utrecht in 1713. What was becoming increasingly important was how those in power dealt with them.[6] Sir Benjamin Keene had been labouring hard in Madrid for a considerable time in an effort to reach a negotiated settlement of outstanding grievances.

---

[4] A. Windham to Charles, third Viscount Townshend, 22/6/1738, HMC, *Eleventh report, Appendix, part IV. The manuscripts of the marquess Townshend* (London, 1887), p. 356.

[5] Harry William Pedicord, '*By their majesties command': the house of Hanover at the London theatres, 1714–1800* (London, 1991), p. 14.

[6] For an excellent introduction to the diplomacy of this period, see Philip Woodfine, *Britannia's glories* (Woodbridge, 1998).

Part of the problem was that British complainants had a fine line to tread. Theoretically, British trade with the Spanish Americas was limited by the terms of the Asiento agreement that granted unlimited trade in slaves but restricted other economic activity to a relatively low yearly limit. British vessels were trading much more than the terms of the agreement allowed but were then complaining when the Spanish navy attempted to enforce the original terms by boarding ships and confiscating cargoes. A split was slowly emerging in London between the more pacific views of Walpole, who was keen to avoid a break with Spain, and Newcastle, who was coming round to the view that Spanish activities had reached such a level that some form of punishment would have to be inflicted if Britain wanted to preserve its international reputation.

From the king's point of view, any ratcheting up of foreign political tensions was only likely to benefit his influence. Despite Walpole's long service at the heart of British government, foreign policy remained an area where he lacked confidence, relying on those around him to offer advice and direction. This meant that his brother Horace and Newcastle and Harrington, as secretaries of state, enjoyed an enhanced role in consideration of foreign affairs but George wanted to exercise his own skills in this area as well.

The feeling that the government was not doing enough to support distressed British mariners manifested itself in several ways. On the one hand, much was made in the popular press of the inappropriate ways in which captured British sailors were treated – they had been deprived of proper English food, like roast beef, and had to make do with foreign fare instead. On the other hand, it was increasingly the case that public space in London, in particular, was becoming a stronghold of patriot feeling. Mention of George being berated in public by angry subjects on this issue suggested both that the king remained relatively visible within the capital and that it was an issue capable of arousing significant public passions.[7]

The patriot case boiled down to something very similar to earlier complaints about the direction of British foreign policy. Britain's position within Europe was in decline and the ministry had not done enough about it. The solution, portrayed as both cheap and easy, was a greater concentration on trade and maritime enterprises, at the expense of involvement in the affairs of the continent. Frederick was, in some ways, a convenient figurehead for such a campaign. Boy patriots, such as William Pitt, spoke up for it in the Commons. Frederick's own position improved in May 1738 when Augusta gave birth to a male heir, quickly christened George because of fears that he might not survive. The successful performance of his dynastic duties both enhanced Frederick's reputation and gave him increased political leverage.[8]

---

[7] Ibid., pp. 129–30.

[8] Brendan Simms, *Three victories and a defeat* (London, 2007), pp. 256–9, Frances Vivian, *A life of Frederick, prince of Wales, 1707–1751: a connoisseur of the arts*, ed. Roger White (Lampeter, 2007), p. 275.

The problem from the ministry's point of view was that war with Spain could not be divorced from a wider set of concerns about European politics. How easy it was going to be to negotiate a settlement with Elizabeth Farnese, Philip V's ambitious second wife, was an open question. But other issues played a role too. Not only was it feared that an open conflict with Spain might drive France into Spain's arms but relations with other European powers were also tense. From George's perspective, Frederick William of Prussia was a constant irritation. His unwillingness to resolve disputes over the succession in Jülich and Berg in a manner acceptable to George, that is by supporting George's candidate as opposed to his own, was frustrating. Further afield, conflict between the Habsburgs and the Turks threatened the balance of power in south-eastern Europe. The more general worry was about the ongoing tensions between France and Austria. Fleury's attitude remained ambiguous but it was feared that his more pacific inclinations were slowly being turned towards a more hawkish outlook by such figures as Germain Louis Chauvelin, marquis de Grosbois and foreign minister.

Nevertheless, despite ministerial attempts to look at the bigger picture, pressure to deal with the Spanish issue mounted during 1738. When the new parliamentary session opened in February 1739, George had to make a speech from the throne that opened with how mindful he was of the suffering of his subjects in America.[9] The context for George's observation was the Convention of Prado, signed in the previous month. The convention was a final attempt to regulate disagreements without the resort to open conflict. The grand total of each side's claims against the other was added up and agreement reached that Spain 'owed' a sum of £27,000 to settle the disputes. The question of where the border between the new British colony of Georgia and Spanish Florida should run was to be investigated by a commission.

Popular pressure, as expressed by city merchants, was sceptical about Prado. It seemed like too little too late. Ministerial spokesmen continued to push the line that war with Spain was not advisable at the present juncture, given the precarious nature of the European situation, but their pleas fell largely on deaf ears. A scramble to shore up Britain's alliances with continental powers followed. Denmark was the first power to be paid a subsidy to avoid its agreeing to a French alliance. There was even talk of George's desire for a renewed friendship with Austria, although whether Austria would be willing to ally with a power that it felt had betrayed it during the War of the Polish Succession was unknown.[10] Moreover, for all George's vaunted ambitions to act as Europe's arbitrator, it had been Fleury and France who had stepped in to calm things down between Charles VI and the Ottomans and not him. What was becoming apparent to both George and his ministers was that the relative isolation

---

[9] Cobbett, *Parliamentary History*, x, col. 874.
[10] Newcastle to Waldegrave, Whitehall, 5/1/1739 OS, private and particular, BL, Add. MSS 32800, fo. 33.

of their diplomatic position in the later 1730s was going to cause problems in the context of a deteriorating European situation. George clearly wanted to keep abreast of everything that was going on, instructing Keene to send his dispatches from Spain directly to London, rather than via Paris, to ensure that he was informed sooner about events. However, wherever he and British ministers looked for allies, the cupboard seemed bare. Even Britain's traditional allies, the Dutch, were proving obdurate. In some ways, Anne's marriage to William had done little to help British influence in the United Provinces because George had now to be extremely careful that his actions were not perceived to be overtly partisan in advancing the claims of his daughter and son-in-law to increased political influence.[11]

The convention did not lead to a resolution in quite the way that its signatories had hoped. The Spanish had assumed that the British would withdraw Haddock's squadron from the Mediterranean but Newcastle was now reluctant to do so, following his exposure to a blast of pro-navy argument in the aftermath of the convention. Without the naval withdrawal, the Spanish refused to pay and so a stalemate was reached. War eventually broke out in September 1739. The early news from the naval campaigns seemed promising. Admiral Vernon was able to capture Porto Bello in Panama in November 1739. As the headquarters of many of the Spanish coastguard ships that had been so systematically harassing British vessels, it was an important symbolic victory, if nothing else. News of Vernon's triumph reached London in March 1740 and prompted an upsurge of enthusiasm for navalist thinking and Vernon was fêted as a national hero: he was granted the freedom of the City of London and his exploits were commemorated in a wide range of media.[12] One lasting monument to this wave of pro-navy sentiment was Thomas Arne's 'Rule Britannia', taken from his masque *Alfred* and first performed for Frederick at his new residence of Cliveden in the summer of 1740.

EUROPEAN UNCERTAINTIES

European concerns could not be ignored, however. British ministers remained ever watchful of what France might do, given the conflict in the Americas. The fear was that the opportunity of using the Jacobites to disrupt British plans during wartime would be too tempting to miss. Despite Fleury's reassurances that France was behaving itself, it was known that Spain was putting out feelers to the exiled Jacobite court. Moreover, Fleury was an old man in his late eighties and what the

---

[11] Simms, *Three victories*, pp. 266–73, Newcastle to Keene, Whitehall, 20/3/1739, BL, Add. MSS 32800, fo. 227.

[12] Woodfine, *Britannia's glories*, pp. 207–8. For a detailed discussion of Vernon, see Kathleen Wilson, 'Empire, trade and popular politics in mid-Hanoverian England: the case of Admiral Vernon', *Past and Present*, 121 (1988), pp. 74–109.

direction of French policy might be if he were to be replaced by a more aggressive minister was unknown.[13]

The European situation was brought into sharp focus in 1740 by a series of royal deaths. The first of these was of Frederick William I of Prussia in May. A change in Prussia's ruler seemed initially to offer a welcome opportunity for an improvement in Anglo-Prussian relations. George thought that his nephew, Frederick, would probably be more open to diplomatic advances than his father had been. It was hoped the generational gap would help. Georg Ludwig had always found it easier to deal with Frederick William than George had and the part played by being the senior partner in the relationship was probably important. As early as 1734, when Frederick William's ill health had suggested that he might not be long for this world, George had left instructions in Hanover about how important it would be to dispatch a representative to Berlin in the event of Frederick William's demise.[14]

Gerlach Adolf von Münchhausen was chosen to undertake the mission when the time finally came. Münchhausen had enjoyed a steady rise through the ranks of the Hanoverian ministry during the 1730s, where he had been responsible for educational and ecclesiastical affairs, but he had some previous diplomatic experience, having represented Hanover at the Reichstag in Regensburg in the 1720s and he evidently enjoyed George's favour. Münchhausen's first impression of the new Prussian monarch was telling. He viewed Frederick as being more cultured than his father and more inclined to value literature. His indifference to religion was already apparent. This was problematic because one of the cards that Münchhausen had hoped to play was to convince Frederick that improved Prusso-Hanoverian relations would be of incalculable benefit to the Protestant cause within the empire. Finally, Münchhausen believed that Frederick would reintroduce some, but not all, of the court etiquette that Frederick William's soldierly disposition had deemed unnecessary.[15] Münchhausen sought to persuade Frederick that France posed the greatest danger to Prussian interests and that alliance with George was the best way to prevent the growth of French power. It was feared that Frederick was already negotiating with France so action was necessary to neutralize his efforts. While Frederick was willing to listen to his uncle's entreaties, he was also sure that he had to steer his own course and was reluctant to ally with Britain without concessions on the Rhine duchies and East Friesland disputes. Nevertheless, Frederick also intended to keep his options open for as long as possible and so, having met Münchhausen on a few occasions,

---

[13] Derek McKay and H.M. Scott, *The rise of the great powers, 1648–1815* (Harlow, 1983), pp. 159–62.

[14] F. Frensdorff, 'G.A. von Münchhausens Berichte über seine Mission nach Berlin im Juni 1740', *Abhandlungen der Königlichen Gesellschaft der Wissenschaften zu Göttingen. Philologisch-Historische Klasse*, neue Folge 8,2 (1904), p. 11.

[15] Ibid., pp. 37–40.

he dispatched his own diplomats to Herrenhausen to visit George who had decided to spend the summer in Hanover.

ANOTHER DYNASTIC MARRIAGE

In such a tense European situation, it was understandable that George should want to travel to Hanover in 1740. His summer visits offered excellent opportunities for the personal contacts and negotiations that George continued to favour when it came to diplomacy. Before his departure, however, George had concluded a marriage alliance for his penultimate daughter that he hoped would have a broader political significance as well. Mary was to be married to Friedrich, the heir of William of Hessen-Kassel. Hessen-Kassel was one of a number of middle-ranking German states whose regiments were available for hire to the highest bidder and George had already made use of this source of men in the late 1720s. William had been a reasonably staunch ally of George but relations were complicated by the fact that William's elder brother was Frederick I, king of Sweden and William was merely his regent in Hessen-Kassel and so had to defer to him in many respects. Sweden's traditional closeness to France meant that there was a risk that Hessian regiments might find their way into French hands and George had offered to take some of them into British pay in January 1740 precisely to avoid this outcome.[16] The hope was that a dynastic union might offer an added level of protection against this eventuality.

The circumstances of Mary's marriage were a little unusual. At first George had welcomed the idea that the wedding would be celebrated in Kassel but had second thoughts about the propriety of sending his unmarried daughter out into the world. He was also anxious that everything should be settled before his departure for Hanover. The solution to the problem seemed to be a proxy marriage. Unfortunately, there were few post-Reformation precedents for such a procedure and neither the clergy nor the lawyers who were consulted seemed happy about this way of proceeding. Nevertheless, the forceful expression by George of his desire for everything to be sorted out quickly, regardless of objections, led to a ceremony being performed in the Chapel Royal in St James's with Mary's brother, the duke of Cumberland, standing proxy for her husband. Mary's marriage was also marked by a performance of Handel's music. On this occasion Handel did not produce an original work but instead brought together a selection of movements that he had already used in the wedding anthems for her elder sister and brother.[17]

---

[16] The scheme is mentioned in Newcastle to Waldegrave, Whitehall, 22/1/1740, most secret, BL, Add. MSS 32802, fo. 28.

[17] Hervey, *Memoirs*, iii, pp. 929–31, Donald Burrows, *Handel and the English Chapel Royal* (Oxford, 2005), p. 355.

Travelling in a party of five coaches, Mary departed for Kassel, where her sister Anne was among those waiting to greet her.[18] Celebrations of the marriage in Kassel included the performance of a traditional German torch dance on one day, followed by a ball with traditional English dances on the next. The festivities went on for several weeks but her new husband's heavy drinking was already giving Mary pause for thought and she was reluctant to see her sister and brother-in-law depart.[19] The marriage treaty that had been signed in St James's prior to Mary's departure had set her dowry at 40,000 Reichstalers, although it also specified that 8,000 Reichstalers must be available each year for her own use. Mary had formally renounced all claims to George's German lands, so long as the male line survived. It was also agreed that she would content herself with the monies settled on her by the treaty or by George's will and not ask for additional income in the future. George was clearly keen to ensure that he was not pressurized into supporting his Hessen-Kassel relatives in the years to come.[20]

George was accompanied on his 1740 trip by Harrington as secretary of state and there were other important courtiers among his entourage. Wallmoden, by now countess of Yarmouth travelled with the king, as did the dukes of Richmond, Grafton and Manchester, as well as Countess Albemarle and Countess Cowper. As always, George was also accompanied by the Hanoverian privy councillor charged with looking after his affairs as head of the *Deutsche Kanzlei* in London. The visit in 1740 was the first trip back to Germany for Ernst von Steinberg who had replaced Johann Philipp von Hattorf, following the latter's death in 1737. Steinberg may have achieved his summons to London through the power of personal connection – he was married to Wallmoden's sister.

The quest for potential allies on the continent loomed large in the negotiations that summer. Although the Danes had agreed to a subsidy arrangement, their troops would be taken into French service as soon as the three-year British deal ran out so there were questions about whether, in these circumstances, it was worth continuing the agreement. Mary's marriage, by contrast, had helped in securing 6,000 Hessians, should the situation demand it. Following Münchhausen's mission to Berlin, negotiations were continued at Hanover by Frederick's representative, Friedrich Sebastian, Count Truchsess von Waldburg.[21] Harrington kept his colleagues back in London informed of progress. Following Caroline's death it had been

---

[18] For details of the arrangements for Mary's journey, including the provision that her coach should be of a higher quality than those of the others in her party, see NHStA, Dep. 103, IV, 227, fo. 72 and NHStA, Dep. 103, XXIV, 2648.

[19] Baker-Smith, *Royal discord*, pp. 105–6.

[20] Marriage treaty, St James's, 8/5/1740 OS, NHStA, Dep. 84 A, 51.

[21] Truchsess von Waldburg, like the diplomats whom Frederick chose to announce his accession to the Kaiser and Louis XV, was also a colonel in the Prussian army (Johann Gustav Droysen, *Geschichte der Preußischen Politik* (14 vols, Leipzig, 1868–86), Part V: vol. i, p. 66).

necessary to make some changes to the composition of the regency. The king wanted the potential Prussian alliance to be considered by 'those Lords, that are usually consulted upon Affairs of Secrecy and Importance'.[22] The group in question probably consisted of Newcastle himself, as the other secretary of state, Lord Chancellor Hardwicke, Lord President Wilmington (the ennobled Spencer Compton) and Robert Walpole.[23] When necessary, it could be supplemented by other figures, such as the first lord of the admiralty.

The exchanges between Harrington and his colleagues in London during the summer of 1740 capture particularly well the problems and possibilities of George's personal approach to diplomacy. Asked for their view on the proposed alliance with Prussia, it was difficult for those away from the nitty-gritty of negotiation to say more than it would depend on the terms involved. Newcastle wondered whether other traditional allies, such as the Dutch, had been consulted and how far an alliance with Prussia might affect relations with Austria, which had traditionally been the foundation of all British efforts to contain the power of France.[24] However, in relation to the technicalities of any potential agreement with Prussia, including a resolution of the outstanding issues of the Rhine duchies and East Friesland, the ministers in London had to confess their ignorance of the precise ins and outs of these disputes and deferred to George when it came to resolving them.[25] The ministers in London were, therefore, in an extremely difficult position. They were almost entirely reliant for their information on Harrington. They could do little more than rehearse general foreign political principles, such as the desirability of including the Dutch, and agreements were generally forwarded to them for rubber-stamping. Ministers were still, in a very real sense, servants of the crown in the area of foreign policy. They could advise but not decide. Put another way, George had the whip hand. There were, however, some constraints on his freedom of action. He had to remain aware of the limits of political acceptability. The outcome of some of his subsequent visits to Hanover suggested that this could be problematic. On this occasion, the instinct of those in London that Frederick was probably stringing out the negotiations to see what he could get proved largely accurate.[26] This was not, however, an insight unique to those away from the centre of diplomatic activity. George felt it too but wanted to ensure that every effort had been made before abandoning hope of an alliance.

[22] Harrington to Newcastle, Hanover, 27/7/1740 NS, private, NA, SP 43/25, fo. 294r.

[23] This is the group mentioned in Newcastle to Harrington, Whitehall, 3/7/1740 OS, private, NA, SP 43/27 fo. 26 who met to discuss how best to respond to Frederick William's death.

[24] Newcastle to Harrington, Newcastle House, 25/7/1740 OS, private, ibid., fos 122–3.

[25] Stone to Harrington, Whitehall, 22/8/1740 OS, private, ibid., fos 170–2.

[26] Hardwicke to Newcastle, Wimpole, 30/8/1740 OS, BL, Add. MSS 32694, fo. 537v.

GEORGE IN HANOVER: THE ELECTOR IN HIS ELEMENT

One thing that the Prussian negotiations in 1740 did leave behind was a description of what life at George's court in Hanover was like. Baron Jakob Friedrich Bielfeld accompanied Truchsess on his mission and subsequently published some of his letters from the period in a French work of 1763 which was later translated into English.[27] Writing to another Prussian courtier, Baron Pöllnitz, Bielfeld noted, as many other observers of George's court had done already, that courtly activities followed a regular pattern. The king rotated those with whom he ate on a predictable basis. On two evenings a week the French comedians performed. Other nights were devoted to cards in the gallery. As a visiting diplomat, Bielfeld had to make the journey twice a day from Hanover out to Herrenhausen along the dusty road beneath the lime trees. He found the gardens at Herrenhausen superb rather than pleasing and also thought that the great fountain was a little out of proportion. Nevertheless, he was impressed by the garden theatre and enjoyed the productions he saw there. Interestingly, Bielfeld noted that, despite the similarity of court life from day to day, there was still sufficient to keep him occupied.[28] He was less impressed by the interiors of the apartments at the palace.[29]

Bielfeld also left descriptions of George and Wallmoden, probably based on his observations of them during his stay. Wallmoden was not described as a great beauty but her overall appearance was pleasing, even if she inclined towards the large. Her wit and conversation were considered to be particular assets and her attachment to George was viewed as personal, rather than because of his title. Bielfeld's evidence for his last claim was that there was little sign of her building up her own fortunes or those of her family by abusing her position as favourite and she did not seem to interfere in the business of government. That said, she was constantly by the king's side, was always one of his party for games of ombre and sat next to him at theatrical performances in an armchair, while others had to sit further back.[30]

When describing George, Bielfeld noted that it was difficult to avoid being dazzled by royalty. Nevertheless, his words provided a reasonable picture of what the king was like in late middle age. George was not especially tall but he had fine legs and always liked to show off his Garter decorations. He stood straight and had clearly cultivated a regal pose over long years. His eyes were set back a little in his head and Bielfeld thought his mouth slightly too large. He always appeared in a well dressed wig, although his temples suggested that he was greying. He was described as a

---

[27] Jakob Friedrich Bielfeld, *Letters of Baron Bielfeld translated from the German by Mr Hooper* (4 vols, London, 1768–70).

[28] Ibid., iii, pp. 201–2.

[29] Ibid., p. 207.

[30] Ibid., pp. 211–16.

man of sense and integrity and his knowledge of government was singled out as unusually impressive. He was keen on systems, both in his views of government and in his life more generally. After rising early, the king read the newspapers regularly before saying his prayers privately. He then read his dispatches and letters and called in his ministers. While firm in his resolutions, he could be severe in his resentments. He was also inclined to push the boundaries of economy to the limit.[31]

Bielfeld's letters show that George was not spending all his time in the summer of 1740 engaged in negotiations. There was, as had become customary, a review of troops. George was also visited by several of his daughters. Anne travelled to Hanover to see her father, eager as ever to see what help he might be able to give in her ongoing quest to increase her husband's profile within the United Provinces. Her hopes of finding him in a more relaxed mood at his summer retreat proved ill-founded because the king refused to discuss political matters seriously with his daughter. Instead, George used the visit, along with that of Mary and her new husband, as an excuse for holding a series of festivities lasting several days. There were illuminations in the Herrenhausen gardens and a masque in the opera house in Hanover. George appeared in Turkish dress, accompanied by Sultana Wallmoden. Mary dressed up as a rural nymph. Anne added to the general mood of celebration with her expert harpsichord playing and subtle singing.[32]

CONFLICT OVER THE HABSBURG SUCCESSION

George had left Hanover by the time he heard news of the other deaths that were to alter fundamentally the European situation. The emperor Charles VI and Tsarina Anna Ivanova died within a few days of each other in late October 1740. The importance of the first death was immediately clear. Austrian policy had been orientated towards this moment for the best part of two decades. As noted earlier, the Pragmatic Sanction was the device that Charles VI had hoped would ensure that his eldest daughter, Maria Theresa, succeeded him in his Habsburg lands. The guarantees of other European powers that they would adhere to this arrangement had been actively sought in the years prior to 1740. On the face of it, Austrian efforts had been largely successful as all the major powers had agreed to accept the Pragmatic Sanction by the time of Charles VI's death. Whether these promises would be honoured in practice was an entirely different matter, however.

The vultures rapidly began to circle around the Habsburg inheritance. The Electors of Bavaria and Saxony were both married to Habsburg archduchesses, Maria Theresa's elder cousins, and so felt that their wives'

[31] Ibid., iv, pp. 9–13.
[32] Ibid., iii, pp. 235–8, Baker-Smith, *Royal discord*, p. 108.

claims could not be ignored, previous promises to the contrary notwith-standing. Frederick II of Prussia also thought that the double deaths created an opportunity for him. The Hohenzollerns had traditionally enjoyed a healthy respect for Russian power and were reluctant to do anything to anger their eastern neighbour. However, Anna Ivanova's successor was a child – Ivan VI – so Frederick calculated that Russia would be unlikely to be able to intervene to stop what he now proposed. One of the results of Frederick William's emphasis on the importance of the mili-tary and his eschewal of the expensive trappings of baroque monarchy was that Prussia had a large army, a full war chest and no debt. Frederick's target in 1740 was the mineral-rich Habsburg province of Silesia. Not only would taking Silesia add to Prussian prestige, but pre-emptive action would prevent it falling into Saxon hands, thus avoiding the possibility that Augustus III could consolidate his Saxon and Polish lands into a more viable territorial unit. The Prussian invasion of Silesia, successfully completed in a matter of weeks, sent shockwaves throughout Europe. Frederick's actions were seen by many as a naked land grab. The minimal efforts he made to justify his actions on the basis of legal claims were very much an afterthought. Charles VI's carefully constructed set of signatures had not proved sufficient to prevent a major conflict.[33]

From George's perspective, Frederick's actions were worrying in several respects. The invasion of Silesia was likely to disrupt the equilibrium within the empire that he considered crucial to the general balance of power in Europe. His first reaction to Charles VI's death had been to make enquiries of other (usually friendly) German courts as to what might be done to ensure that the Habsburg inheritance was preserved.[34] George was angered by what he viewed as his nephew's eye to the main chance. This may have been the product of frustration but Frederick's aggressive stance served to revive fears about the potential threat that Prussia posed to Hanoverian security. The early months of 1741 saw George engaged in a series of nego-tiations to build a coalition to counter Frederick and support Maria Theresa. An alliance of Hanover, Saxony, Austria, the United Provinces and perhaps even Russia was envisaged. The Danish and Hessian troops that George had taken into his pay could be used and Frederick would be taught a lesson. The vehemence of George's response was a reflection of the incredulity which Frederick's actions had provoked. George seems to have taken a very personal approach to the negotiations and left little to his British ministers.[35]

---

[33] The literature on Frederick's campaigns is understandably large. For succinct introduc-tions, with excellent guides to further reading, see Dennis E. Showalter, *The wars of Frederick the Great* (Harlow, 1996), M.S. Anderson, *The war of the Austrian succession, 1740–1748* (Harlow, 1995), H.M. Scott, *The birth of a great power system 1740–1815* (Harlow, 2006), chs 2–4 and Christopher Clark, *Iron kingdom* (London, 2006), ch. 7.

[34] Uriel Dann, *Hanover and Great Britain, 1740–1760* (Leicester, 1991), p. 23. Dann's account of George's diplomacy in the 1740s and 1750s is admirably thorough but I place less explanatory weight on George's desire for Hanoverian territorial expansion.

[35] Ibid., pp. 27–8.

Events again intervened, though, to force George's hand. Despite talk of an aggressive stance towards Prussia, other options were kept open. George tried to use both British and Hanoverian diplomats to gain concessions from Frederick in exchange for Hanoverian and British neutrality. Hanoverian claims to Hildesheim and permanent control of Osnabrück were at the top of the list but it went even further. George's willingness to negotiate with both sides partly reflected his constant hope that he might be able to make gains if he could portray himself as the mediator but it was also a product of fear of the likely French reaction to the unfolding of events in central Europe. The British were already worried about whether France would find an excuse for intervening in the ongoing conflict with Spain. How the French would react to Charles VI's death was to prove crucial.

PROTECTING THE ELECTORATE

The prospect of French intervention meant that all previous calculations had to be reassessed. The impetus behind France's more aggressive stance lay with Charles Fouquet, duc de Belle-Isle. Belle-Isle began his campaign for French action in January 1741, arguing that instead of upholding the Pragmatic Sanction, France should support the candidacy of Charles Albert of Bavaria for the imperial throne. Belle-Isle was dispatched to the empire and was able to build up a group of Electors willing to back Charles Albert. The three ecclesiastical Electors signed up to the Wittelsbach camp quite quickly. More importantly, Belle-Isle's contacts with Frederick led to the latter signing an alliance with France in June 1741. Frederick was angry that Maria Theresa, despite the Austrian defeat at Mollwitz in April 1741, refused to accept Prussia's seizure of Silesia as a done deal. The growing division of Europe into two distinct armed camps meant that George was going to have to make a decision about which side to back. The French thought he would uphold the claims of the Pragmatic Sanction. The moment of decision was delayed for a time, though. Attempts were made to persuade the Austrians that some concessions to the Prussians would be in order and to suggest to Frederick that Maria Theresa was open to compromise. The aim was to win both powers for an anti-French alliance.

Given the ever more complex sets of negotiations that George was engaged in and monitoring, his decision to make another trip back to Hanover in 1741 was understandable. Part of the difficulty that George faced in the summer of 1741 was how to negotiate the labyrinth of constraints under which he was operating. On the British side, parliament had voted a subsidy of £300,000 at the end of April 1741 that was designed to support Maria Theresa and to uphold the Pragmatic Sanction. Perhaps because of her status as a female victim, perhaps out of a genuine desire to maintain a traditional pro-Austrian, anti-French policy, there seemed to be a certain amount of public support for moves to defend the Pragmatic Sanction. At the same time the arrival in the empire of a French army of some 40,000 commanded by the marquis de Maillebois in September 1741 served to focus George's mind on the extent of the threat to Hanover.[36]

George had dispatched Friedrich Karl von Hardenberg to Paris in late August 1741 to see if an arrangement could be reached to head off the threat posed by Maillebois' army in Westphalia. The febrile atmosphere of rumour and negotiation had already taken its toll on George's health. There was talk of 'sacrificing his own life', rather than living to see the ruin of Hanover that he now thought was 'inevitable'.[37] Harrington, who was again accompanying the king, informed Newcastle at the beginning of August that George had already begun to wonder aloud whether any additional support might be forthcoming from Britain to defend Hanover, although he realized that such aid was unlikely.[38] The deteriorating Anglo-Hanoverian position was apparent from Harrington's observation a few weeks later that it was unlikely that anything could now be done to stop the French advance. Interestingly, Harrington speculated that France's aim was not actually to attack Hanover but to ensure that George stood aside and did not intervene in France's attempt to destroy Austrian power completely. In these circumstances, Harrington felt it would be best if George beat a hasty retreat to London so as 'not to remain in the middle of Germany, an idle Spectator of the ruin of it, and of the House of Austria without being able to give any assistance to either'.[39] Harrington claimed that George had not reacted too badly when he had put this view to him.[40]

The full extent of George's diplomatic activities, particularly Hardenberg's mission to France, does not seem to have been vouchsafed either to the British ministers in London or even, in its entirety, to the Hanoverian Privy Council.[41] Hardenberg had been instructed to inform Fleury that George, while tempted to support the candidacy of Maria Theresa's husband, Francis Stephen of Lorraine, for the imperial title, had not finally made up his mind and that he might be willing to consider supporting a French candidate. More importantly, though, Hardenberg had to defuse the immediate threat to Hanover's security. It was this that led to the signature on 12 October 1741 of the Neustadt Protocol. In what was, effectively, a neutrality agreement, George stated that he would not

[36] Ibid., pp. 29–35, Anderson, *War of the Austrian succession*, pp. 77–9, Scott, *Birth of a great power system*, pp. 54–5.

[37] Paul Vaucher, *Robert Walpole et la politique de Fleury (1731–1742)* (Paris, 1924), pp. 397–8. Harrington to Newcastle, Hanover, 2/8/1741 NS, private, BL, Add. MSS 32697, fo. 341r.

[38] Harrington to Newcastle, Hanover, 2/8/1741 NS, private, BL, Add. MSS 32697, fo. 340r.

[39] Idem to idem, Hanover, 30/8/1741 NS, ibid., fo. 434.

[40] Ibid., fo. 435r.

[41] Dann, *Hanover*, pp. 35–40, Mitchell D. Allen, 'The Anglo-Hanoverian connection, 1727–1760', unpublished Ph.D. dissertation, University of Boston, 2000, pp. 120–5, H.M. Scott, 'Hanover in mid-eighteenth-century Franco-British geopolitics', in Brendan Simms and Torsten Riotte, eds, *The Hanoverian dimension in British history, 1714–1837* (Cambridge, 2007), pp. 284–5.

support Maria Theresa in his Electoral capacity, that he would cease any thought of offensive action against France's Prussian allies and that he would back the candidacy of Charles Albert in the forthcoming imperial election.

On the face of it, George had caved in to French pressure, anxious to defend his Electoral domains from invasion. His British ministers initially expressed dissatisfaction at the apparent abandonment of Maria Theresa. They had already resolved, having discussed Harrington's correspondence, that there was nothing that the British parliament could do to aid in the defence of Hanover but expressed irritation that support for Maria Theresa seemed to have fallen by the wayside because of Hanoverian concerns.[42] As Newcastle remarked to Harrington, 'what Lewis the 14th did but aim at, with a most victorious army during the first part of his Reign, Lewis the 15th will bring about, and accomplish, perhaps without striking a Stroke'.[43] This was sent before the Neustadt Protocol had been signed but rumours of a neutrality agreement were clearly widespread. During September and early October 1741 British ministers were worried about whether the agreement would oblige Britain to remain neutral or would simply be an Electoral affair. Harrington was at pains to point out that it was the latter. Yet the overwhelming sense from Newcastle's correspondence in this period, even allowing for his penchant for melodrama, was of rising panic about the lack of information flowing from Hanover and how the British ministers would be able to explain and justify George's actions. Early in the crisis, Newcastle had opined to Hardwicke that even if the ministers in London recommended neutrality for the Electorate, it would not matter that much because 'the king, if he has a mind to do it, & can do it, will do it, without us'.[44]

THE CONSEQUENCES OF NEUTRALITY

Newcastle and his fellow ministers spent much of the autumn of 1741 explaining to other powers that the commitments that George had entered into had been entirely in his Electoral capacity. In addition to problems abroad, there were increased rumblings at home. An election was to be held in 1741. Since the last election in 1734, defections to the opposition had eroded the administration's majority. Yet the results revealed further losses. A majority of 42 had more than halved to 19. The shift appears more dramatic when it is remembered that there had been less than 100 contested elections. Although not all the opposition gains were made from contested polls, the swing to the opposition had been marked in Cornwall,

---

[42] Newcastle's 'Considerations upon Lord Harrington's letters', 24/8/1741 OS, BL, Add. MSS 32967, fos 452–5.

[43] Newcastle to Harrington, Claremont, 18/9/1741 OS, very secret, BL, Add. MSS 32698, fo. 36.

[44] Newcastle to Hardwicke, Claremont, 19/7/1741 OS, BL, Add. MSS 35407, fo. 44v.

a county with a disproportionate number of seats and where Frederick, as duke of Cornwall, could exert significant electoral influence. Ministerial losses were also apparent in Scotland where the duke of Argyll, who had also gone into opposition, played a similar role.[45]

One thing of which George and his ministers could be certain was that the new parliamentary session would bring criticism of British foreign policy. The war with Spain was not going well. Following his efforts at Porto Bello, Vernon had argued that the war in Spanish America needed to be pursued more vigorously and that an expedition against Cartagena on the coast of what is now Colombia would be a suitable next step. Vernon led a substantial fleet, backed by a large number of troops, in an amphibious assault during March and April 1741. Ultimately it turned out to be fruitless. Disease had a much more significant impact on Vernon's forces than Spanish arms but the result was the same. News of Vernon's defeat had reached London by June. The apparent misconduct of the Spanish war was linked by opposition writers to events in Germany through the claim that Admiral Haddock had been instructed to allow a Spanish force to land unopposed in Italy for fear that the French might otherwise attack Hanover. All in all, the situation was a sorry one. As in the debates about George's foreign political actions in the late 1720s and early 1730s, the issue of continental involvement versus a naval strategy loomed large.[46]

Parliamentary pressure on the ministry increased as the session progressed. There was a lengthy debate on the conduct of the war on 21 January 1742 when the ministerial majority was a mere three votes.[47] Walpole hoped to reach an accommodation with Frederick by persuading George to increase his allowance to the desired £100,000 but Frederick stood firm and refused to call off his MPs until Walpole had been dismissed. Walpole had been able to stave off opposition calls to have papers relating to recent foreign policy transactions presented to the Commons but he was less successful when it came to dealing with petitions. In cases of disputed elections, aggrieved parties could petition the Commons to consider the case and who triumphed in these struggles was usually a good signal of the direction in which the political wind was blowing. Walpole and his supporters had hoped that the consideration of the petitions would raise their majority to much more workable proportions. Instead, it became clear that confidence was ebbing away from Walpole.

Walpole resigned in February 1742, having been created earl of Orford. George's reaction to Walpole's departure was reported to have been a

---

[45] Romney Sedgwick, *The House of Commons, 1715–1754* (2 vols, London, 1970), i, pp. 46–7.

[46] Simms, *Three victories*, pp. 284–6. For a more detailed discussion of the opposition case, see Kathleen Wilson, *A sense of the people* (Cambridge, 1995), pp. 140–65.

[47] Cobbett, *Parliamentary history*, xii, cols 331–73.

tearful one.[48] Walpole's elevation to the peerage was a sign that George retained a degree of confidence and trust in his erstwhile minister. Rebuilding a workable administration proved difficult. As J.B. Owen noted in what is still the most comprehensive survey of the politics of the period, the reconstruction of events is rendered more obscure by the gaps in the papers of two of the principal players, Newcastle and Hardwicke.[49] George's initial strategy was to put out feelers to some members of the opposition, in the hope that he could divide and rule. Pulteney and Carteret were singled out for approaches. George was later to claim to Pulteney that he had been selected over Argyll because he knew that Pulteney wanted only to remove Walpole whereas the latter's ambitions were much more extensive.[50] The complex series of discussions between administration and opposition resulted in some shuffling of offices and a sense of betrayal among the rank and file of opposition MPs. Wilmington was to replace Walpole as first lord of the treasury. Harrington took up Wilmington's former office as lord president and Carteret entered the administration as secretary of state in Harrington's place. Pulteney faced accusations from Argyll and others that he had abandoned their cause and that he should have pressed harder to create a truly 'broad-bottomed' administration – one that was comprehensive and non-partisan.

Walpole's departure had already drawn some of the sting of opposition complaints and had enabled the king to reinforce his position. A reconciliation of sorts was achieved between George and Frederick. Frederick's allowance was to be increased by another £50,000 a year, although there would be no retrospectiveness and Frederick's hopes of his other debts being covered by parliamentary funds remained unfulfilled. The crucial concession extracted from Frederick was that he, and his associates, would not pursue a witch-hunt against Walpole, so talk of investigations and impeachment was quickly dropped. Buoyed by the addition of Frederick's MPs, the administration could adopt a more sanguine attitude towards opposition pressure in the Commons. Negotiations continued about the reconstruction of the administration but George now felt able to stand strong on the allocation of some of the minor places. An attempt by members of the opposition to make their acceptance of places on the admiralty board conditional on more places being made available for their, mainly Tory, associates was forcefully rejected by George at the beginning of March. He struck Sir John Hynde Cotton, a known Jacobite sympathizer, from the list. In the Commons the next day, angry opposition MPs tried to pass a motion calling for a secret committee to enquire into Walpole's administration during the previous twenty years (thus incorporating all the foreign policy transactions

---

[48] William Coxe, *Memoirs of the life and administration of Sir Robert Walpole* (3 vols, London, 1798), iii, p. 593.
[49] J.B. Owen, *The rise of the Pelhams* (London, 1957), p. 88.
[50] Ibid., p. 92.

since the treaty of Hanover in 1725, the usual starting point for opposition critique). The motion was defeated by the narrowest of margins but was the basis of a ministerial revival. For the rest of the session the Old Corps Whigs (the followers of Walpole and Newcastle) were able with Carteret, Pulteney and the prince of Wales's supporters to head off further opposition attacks.[51]

The events of early 1742 have often been portrayed as marking a defeat for George. He had, largely against his will, been forced to dispose of a minister whom he still trusted and find places for (some of) those whom he disliked. The episode slots neatly into an account of eighteenth-century British politics that sees a slow but inevitable triumph of the power of the Commons over that of the king. It was also the first of several instances in the later years of his reign when George wondered aloud who was actually in charge, leading to the oft repeated description of George as a 'king in toils'.[52] Certainly, there were reports while events were running their course of George commenting on his perceived impotence. In the immediate aftermath of Walpole's resignation, Sir Dudley Ryder reported that talk of the negotiations between the rival political factions had 'put the King into great fright. He asked [the] Earl of Orford whether he was to be King any longer or not, and cried.'[53] However, George's occasional, and undoubtedly sincerely felt, outbursts of frustration should not be seen as either entirely objective or even indicative of his own views in his calmer moments. Although Walpole had gone, George had neither had to admit significant numbers of the opposition into positions of power nor submit to all his son's demands. He was still able to rely on the fact that there was a deep ambivalence even among opposition MPs about forcing him to do anything against his will because of the continuing ambiguities of where opposition stopped and lese-majesty began. Harrington had been reasonably quiescent when it came to George's Hanoverian schemes, and there was little reason to suppose that his replacement Carteret would be any less accommodating, not least because George's previous experience of British (and Hanoverian) ministers had been that they found it almost impossible to resist his will when it came to foreign policy.

PRAGMATIC INTERVENTION

While the results of George's diplomacy had been working themselves out on the domestic stage, events on the continent had moved on.[54] Maria Theresa had been hard pressed in the second half of 1741 with a

[51] Ibid., pp. 96–101.

[52] J.D. Griffith Davies, *A king in toils* (London, 1938) is a classic statement of this view; as Davies remarks (p. vi), George was dominated by others throughout his life, first his father, then Caroline and Walpole and finally Carteret and the Pelhams.

[53] Harrowby MS quoted by Sedgwick, *Commons*, i, p. 51.

[54] For a more extensive account of continental events in this period, see Anderson, *War of the Austrian succession*, pp. 80–96.

Franco-Bavarian army marching towards Vienna and Frederick remaining firmly ensconced in Silesia. Yet, partly because of the British-mediated Convention of Klein-Schellendorf, Austria was not entirely surrounded. Frederick agreed to a cessation of hostilities in Silesia, provided that the fortress of Neisse surrendered. Accepting Prussian occupation of Silesia at this point was little more than recognizing the realities of the situation from Maria Theresa's point of view. The convention released some troops for use elsewhere and the immediate danger to the survival of the Habsburg monarchy passed. Nevertheless, Charles Albert of Bavaria was elected Emperor in January 1742, Münchhausen casting the Hanoverian vote for him on George's behalf. George, ever keen to ensure that precedent was observed, made it clear that he wanted Münchhausen's entourage to be equivalent to that which his father had sent to Frankfurt for the last election in 1711. Hanoverian representation should be both dignified and economical.[55] Yet even while the election was taking place Habsburg forces under Count Khevenhuller were pushing the Bavarians back first from Austria itself and then as far as Munich. Frederick showed the inconstancy for which he was to become notorious and agreed terms with Maria Theresa in July 1742,[56] again with the help of mediation from the earl of Hyndford, George's representative in Berlin, that left him in control of Silesia but ensured his withdrawal from the wider conflict. Faced with Frederick's apparent disappearance from the conflict, the French army in Bohemia was in retreat by the end of 1742.

The stage was therefore set for further intervention by George in continental affairs. Carteret, despite his recent conversion from the opposition and its concomitant emphasis on naval war, was quick to talk the language of the balance of power and the necessity of preserving Austria as a bulwark to prevent Europe being dominated by France, a language that was characteristic of the Whigs in power for much of the first half of the eighteenth century.[57] Fortunately, and not entirely coincidentally, such views generally chimed well with George's own and so it was possible for Carteret and George to co-operate, despite the fact that Carteret's emphasis on 'keeping the Elector an Englishman' might ostensibly seem to imply that a conflict of views was likely.[58]

The first signs of a new commitment to intervention were visible in military deployments. There had been talk during 1741 of sending a British army to the continent under General Wade to be used in the Low Countries to defend the Barrier fortresses. Nothing had come of this then,

[55] George to Reden, St James's, 16.27/1/1741, NHStA, Dep. 103, XXIV, 2118, fo. 6.

[56] The treaty of Berlin confirmed terms agreed in the previous month at Breslau. See also, Anderson, *War of the Austrian succession*, pp. 101–11.

[57] On importance of balance of power thinking, see Simms, *Three victories*, pp. 1–5 and Andrew C. Thompson, *Britain, Hanover and the Protestant interest, 1688–1756* (Woodbridge, 2006), ch. 1.

[58] Quoted by Dann, *Hanover*, p. 45.

not least because of the intervening crisis over Hanoverian neutrality, but the plans were revived in 1742.[59] Now Carteret proposed that a body of Hanoverian forces, paid for by Britain, should be added to the British contingent.[60] This arrangement was not widely publicized at the time. Nevertheless, George was able to get rather good terms for the employment of his German troops. His royal self paid his Electoral self recruiting money for an army that was already in existence and the force of nearly 16,000 that was to join British forces contained a large proportion of (more expensive) cavalry regiments.[61] A Hanoverian force, under General Pontpietin, was on its way to join the British forces commanded by Lord Stair, newly reconciled to the administration, by the middle of September 1742.

The switch to a more active stance in relation to the conflicts of the continent was not without its problems. One was how to justify the use of Hanoverian troops in action against France, given the previous neutrality agreement. Here George was able to fudge things slightly, claiming that the troops were now serving him in his British rather than his Hanoverian capacity, but this was little more than a technicality. Another was what the troops would be used for, given the changing nature of the war. Prussian withdrawal had enabled Maria Theresa to move more forces against the French army in Bohemia, which had, in turn, prompted Louis XV to send Maillebois's army to the same area to offer support. The French move prompted talk of the need to send what had become known as the 'Pragmatic army', due to its ostensible purpose of upholding the Pragmatic Sanction, into the empire. Stair, the army's commander, disagreed. He had plans for a direct invasion of France and pleaded his case in London, only to be turned down, having enjoyed some initial support from Carteret and the king.[62]

Stair's other difficulties related to his relationship with Pontpietin.[63] Although Stair believed that he had command of the entire army, including the Hanoverians, Pontpietin believed that he was obliged merely to consult Stair fully and that he would still receive orders directly from George. As 1742 progressed, frustrations grew on all sides. The king wanted to see action and had to be persuaded by his British ministers not to take personal command of the army. The Dutch and the Austrians still wanted the Pragmatic army to winter in the empire, not least so it could be shown that the Hanoverians, despite reports to the contrary, were willing to serve in Germany. Newcastle was to claim later that he had pressed strongly throughout the period for the army to move but that the

[59] For a detailed discussion of the earlier efforts, see Wolfgang Handrick, *Die pragmatische Armee 1741 bis 1743* (Munich, 1991), pt I.

[60] Ibid., pp. 97–113.

[61] Gert Brauer, *Die hannoversch-englischen Subsidienverträge, 1702–1748* (Aalen, 1962), p. 131.

[62] Handrick, *Die pragmatische Armee*, pp. 127–42.

[63] Dann, *Hanover*, pp. 50–1.

king had refused because of his worries about putting his Hanoverian soldiers at risk late in the campaign season. There may have been an element of truth to this, although there is also a strong sense of Newcastle retrospectively trying to justify his own conduct,[64] but it was more probable that George was under pressure from his Hanoverian ministers to exercise extreme caution in doing anything that might expose the Electorate to a renewed danger of attack, either from France or Prussia.[65]

The army was eventually marched into the empire but its inactivity was the subject of parliamentary complaint in the interim. Although George's new ministry had managed to garner an increased degree of parliamentary support, some elements of the opposition remained unreconciled. William Pitt had not followed Frederick's other supporters back to the court and he was a vocal critic of the seeming Hanoverian priorities of the administration.[66] Nevertheless, there was little of the anxiety that had characterized the previous session. The year 1743 seemed to offer better prospects for George and his ministers.

George's impatience to involve himself more in the conflict finally got the better of him in May 1743 when he departed for Hanover again. He was accompanied by his second son, William, duke of Cumberland. Frederick was left behind. Whether he was a frustrated soldier, like his father, is unclear but his younger brother benefited from the principle of the 'heir and the spare' and was therefore freer to pursue his own interests, without the additional burdens imposed by perpetuating the dynasty. George did not depart to join his army immediately. He went out hunting with Cumberland on 1 June before leaving to join the Pragmatic army on the 16th. He travelled via Kassel and rendezvoused with his troops close to Mainz. He had a personal retinue of about twenty servants and was also accompanied by his Hanoverian master of horse, Karl Friedrich von Peterswald. Once with the army, George ate in public on the days in the run-up to what was to be his only battle of the campaign at Dettingen.[67]

The logistics of a king going to war were complicated. Franz Johann von Reden, the lord chamberlain, took responsibility for ensuring that the necessary arrangements were made. His notes show that seven separate dishes would have to be prepared for the king for his meals, even while he was travelling, and that he would dine with a group of at least eight others. Even on campaign, there would be an additional table of knights, just as there was when George dined in Herrenhausen. Reden initially thought that this might be for as many as twelve people but subsequently reduced the figure to eight. Silver and table linen could be taken from Hanover but pewter would have to be acquired en route, perhaps in Frankfurt. A group

---

[64] Owen, *Pelhams*, pp. 136–7 notes the dating but does not draw any conclusions from it.

[65] Dann, *Hanover*, p. 53.

[66] For a more balanced assessment of Pitt's attitudes to Hanover, see Brendan Simms, 'Pitt and Hanover', in Simms and Riotte, eds, *Hanoverian dimension*, pp. 28–57.

[67] NHStA, Dep. 103, IV, 324, fos 86–93.

of five kitchen staff would attend to the king's culinary needs, carrying their kit with them on mules.[68] The royal coach required six horses, a further twelve were needed for the two other coaches in the party, two for the wardrobe wagon and ten for the escorting grenadiers, including the royal trumpeter.[69] A British description of George's retinue as it left for war mentioned 662 horses, 13 Berlin coaches, 35 wagons and 54 carts.[70] Courtly etiquette was to be preserved, regardless of the surroundings.

George's only chance to put his armchair generalship into practice came on 27 June 1743. The Pragmatic army had advanced along the north bank of the Main as far as Aschaffenburg, where George was billeted in the castle. However, the army's supply lines had been cut so the decision was taken to fall back to Hanau. Marshal Noailles had moved some of his troops across the Main behind the Pragmatic army and the road back to Hanau was blocked by a force of some 23,000 under the duke of Gramont. Gramont had ranged his forces between the river and a narrow gap of wooded hills so the only option for George and his troops was a frontal assault. The official British account of the battle described George as leading the British infantry on the right wing, sword in hand, throughout.[71] After several hours of heavy fighting, Gramont pushed the French household cavalry forward, followed by several infantry regiments. The French attack enjoyed some initial success in pushing back the allied line but it ran out of steam and, following an allied counterattack, the French, now robbed of artillery cover, were forced back. The road to Hanau now open, the Pragmatic army pushed forward. It was to be the last occasion on which a reigning British monarch took personal command of his troops in battle.

Subsequent generations have been keen to ascribe victory at Dettingen to George – most accounts agree that the French seemed to have suffered more casualties. Nevertheless, as Sebastian Küster points out in an exhaustive study of reactions to the battle, the first news to reach Paris was of a French victory.[72] This says much about the generally indecisive nature of many eighteenth-century armed confrontations. In wars in which battles were often the result of a failure to manoeuvre sufficiently effectively and campaigns were frequently fought to gain advantages at the negotiating

[68] Reden's notes, 6/6/1743, NHStA, Dep. 103, XXIV, 2652, fos 2–4.

[69] Reden to Partz, 7/6/1743, ibid., fo. 16.

[70] 'For his Majesty's equipage and his Servants attending him to the Army, as they began their march on the 27 May/7 June 1743 from Utrecht', BL, Add. MSS 32700, fo. 154. As Utrecht is listed as the place of departure, this strongly suggests that these horses and vehicles were used by members of George's British retinue, such as the duke of Richmond, rather than the king personally. See Richmond to Newcastle, Utrecht, 27/5–7/6/1743, Timothy J. McCann, ed., *The correspondence of the dukes of Richmond and Newcastle, 1724–1750* (Lewes, 1984), p. 98.

[71] *London Gazette*, 8236, 28/6–2/7/1743.

[72] Sebastian Küster, *Vier Monarchien – Vier Öffentlichkeiten: Kommunikation um die Schlacht bei Dettingen* (Münster, 2004), pp. 248–9.

table, rather than to destroy opponents completely, George's big military moment could easily be portrayed as the classic case of winning the battle but not the war. Stair, ever anxious to make his views known, argued that the French should be pursued but George, partly because of the caution expressed by the Austrian commander, Wilhelm Reinhard von Neipperg, refused.

Carteret, who had nervously observed the battle from his coach,[73] promptly began negotiations in an effort to capitalize on George's perceived military success. George himself remained close by to keep an eye on proceedings, although he was also determined to make the most of his opportunity to command. Lieutenant Colonel Charles Russell, who was in the 1st Regiment of Foot Guards and consequently in a good position to observe the monarch, left some reports of George's activities in the field. In the aftermath of Dettingen, while still camped at Hanau, the king appeared in uniform consistently, arriving booted at his levee around ten in the morning. He then talked to grandees and perhaps spent some time with Carteret before dining at noon. He tended to dine with German officers and then slept in the afternoon before reappearing for the evening when he might play cards or converse. Russell, like other British officers, noted the apparent partiality of the king for German officers and men, although he was guarded in his comments because of his awareness that letters from the army, particularly those directed to St James's, were routinely opened.[74]

Carteret's negotiating partner was Prince William, regent of Hessen-Kassel, the new father-in-law of George's daughter, Mary. George's son-in-law, Prince Friedrich of Hessen-Kassel, was an officer in the Pragmatic army. Prince William was representing the interests of the new emperor, Charles VII, whose Bavarian homeland was now largely occupied by Maria Theresa's forces. The outline of the deal was that, in exchange for disavowing the French and his claims to the Habsburg inheritance, Charles VII would have his Bavarian lands returned to him, perhaps even enhanced by the addition of some secularized ecclesiastical territories in the south-west of the empire. At the same time, further subsidies would go to Maria Theresa and Habsburg fortunes would be restored. The twin approaches, to the emperor via the 'treaty' (it was ultimately not signed) of Hanau and to Maria Theresa via the treaty of Worms, both aimed to bolster British efforts to confine France and keep a balance of power within Europe.[75]

The names of the prospective agreements reflected the physical progress of the Pragmatic army. It advanced down the Rhine during the summer of 1743, reaching Speyer in the middle of September. George

---

[73] Lieutenant Colonel Charles Russell to his wife, Hanau, 19/6/1743 OS, HMC, *Report on the manuscripts of Mrs Frankland-Russell-Astley of Chequers Court, Bucks* (London, 1900), p. 252.

[74] Lt Col. Charles Russell to his wife, Hanau camp, 23/7/1743 OS, ibid., p. 273.

[75] Dann, *Hanover*, pp. 54–5, Anderson, *War of the Austrian succession*, pp. 117–27.

continued to enjoy his commanding position. He personally led one of the columns on the march from Worms to Speyer in September 1743. There were advantages to having a royal leader. George was accompanied by his mule-train which was well stocked with cold provisions. When he called a halt, both the king and those around him could take advantage of this repast.[76]

Unfortunately, Carteret and George's alliance plans quickly ran into difficulties. The first was that Maria Theresa, despite her desperate need for funds, was reluctant to return Bavaria without the restoration of Silesia as a quid pro quo and also disliked being simply a pawn in British moves against France. The failure to appreciate that other powers might have priorities other than containing France was a besetting weakness of British central European policy in the latter part of George's reign. Secondly, the lack of inclusion of other parties directly in Carteret's discussions caused acrimonious exchanges. Frederick the Great was particularly annoyed that he had not been included and William of Hessen-Kassel, reaching the view that Carteret was not sincere, left Hanau in a strop. Such was his anger that the Hessian subsidy treaty was not renewed in 1744 and Hessen-Kassel's troops were put at the service of the emperor. Thirdly, the ministers back in London were jumpy about Carteret's negotiations. Their experiences in 1740 and 1741 had made them wary of schemes devised by the king and the secretary of state which offered apparent advantages to Hanover and cost Britain money. Moreover, there was also the worry that Hanoverian concerns might lead to Maria Theresa losing out again, just as she had in 1741.[77] Even while Carteret was negotiating, Newcastle was protesting to Orford that Carteret and the king had set out with the sole objective of appearing 'a good German; and to prefer the Welfare of the Germanick Body, to all other Considerations'.[78] Mixed up with the Old Corps' desire to defend the balance of power was a more immediate worry that Carteret was pressing the claims of the newly created earl of Bath to succeed Wilmington as first lord of the treasury, following the latter's death in early July. The Old Corps had their own preferred candidate, Newcastle's brother, Henry Pelham and believed that Carteret had already agreed to advance Pelham to Wilmington's place.[79] In the end, George plumped for Pelham. He maintained a vestigial dislike of Bath but the cause of the Old Corps was also helped by the presence of the duke of Richmond, master of horse, with the king.[80]

---

[76] Lt Col. Charles Russell to his wife, Speyer camp, 17/9/1743 OS, HMC, *Frankland-Russell-Astley*, p. 290.

[77] This comes through strongly in Newcastle to Hardwicke, Claremont, 24/10/1743 OS, private, BL, Add. MSS 32701, fos 202–3.

[78] Newcastle to Orford, Newcastle House, 22/7/1743 OS, BL, Add. MSS 32700, fo. 315v.

[79] Owen, *Pelhams*, pp. 159–60.

[80] See the various exchanges between Newcastle and Richmond for July and August 1743 in McCann, ed., *Correspondence of the dukes of Richmond and Newcastle*, pp. 101–19.

If some of George and Carteret's diplomacy was directed towards broadly European ends in the summer of 1743, other aspects of it had a more personal and dynastic nature. The marriage of George's youngest daughter, Louisa, to Crown Prince Frederick of Denmark was tied into a complex set of calculations about the future of the Baltic. Unlikely as it may sound, one of the main reasons behind this marriage was concern about the future of the Swedish crown. Queen Ulrike Eleonora's death in November 1741 had made the question of the future of the Swedish succession an urgent one. She was childless. Her husband, Frederick, was from Hessen-Kassel, so one possibility was that either Frederick's younger brother, William, or William's son, Friedrich, might be an appropriate candidate. Friedrich was George's son-in-law so it was thought that he might favour this option. Russia, on the other hand, was not keen on the Hessen-Kassel candidacy and wanted to promote the interests of the house of Holstein-Gottorp to which Tsarina Elizabeth was closely related. Another option was that a French-backed member of the house of Zweibrücken, a branch of the Wittelsbach family, might succeed. A final option was for a Danish candidate. The complex nature of the competition for the Swedish throne, which was also connected to attempts to resolve an ongoing conflict between Russia and Sweden, meant that the various parties were anxious to win support from external allies such as France, Britain and Russia. Carteret, on the other hand, was keen to gain influence at the Danish court, if only to avoid the French gaining the upper hand there, so Louisa's portrait was sent to a trusted Danish noble to exhibit before the royal family in the hope that it would find favour with them. The crown prince was suitably impressed and persuaded his parents to agree to a match. The only condition imposed by the Danes was that the British would not oppose Frederick's candidature for the Swedish crown. Carteret was happy to go along with this, although his understanding of 'not oppose' did not preclude continuing moves to help other candidates. After haggling over the size of the dowry, agreement was reached before Carteret departed to join the Pragmatic army, although a formal treaty was not signed until after Dettingen.[81]

The marriage took place at Hanover following George and Cumberland's return from campaigning. George had issued orders from his camp in Speyer to ensure that Louisa's journey was as straightforward as possible.[82] Louisa's sister Mary was present despite having recently given birth. The ceremony was, again, conducted by proxy so Cumberland stepped in once more to perform the role of groom. The proposal that he should marry Frederick of Denmark's sister, another Louisa, had faltered because of the likely costs and Cumberland's demands for an adequate allowance to be provided for his

[81] This paragraph is based upon Richard Lodge, 'The treaty of Abo and the Swedish succession', *EHR*, 43 (1928), pp. 540–71. I am indebted to Clarissa Campbell Orr for drawing it to my attention.

[82] George II to Fôret, Speyer, 30/9/1743, NHStA, Dep. 103, IV, 249, fo. 64.

establishment. The wedding took place in the church within the Leine palace. The walls were richly decorated with tapestries depicting the history of the Guelphs and the altar was pushed back to create more space within the choir. Louisa's arrival was marked by cannon fire and the guns were also discharged at the beginning of the *Te Deum* and on her departure from the church. During the post-wedding festivities, a torch dance featured among the celebrations.[83]

AFTER DETTINGEN

George returned to Britain, following the adventures of the summer, in November 1743. The shine of the victory at Dettingen had already begun to wear off. News of the victory had been celebrated extensively within Britain. Bells had been rung and thanksgiving sermons preached. Yet as the summer wore on, and the Pragmatic army remained largely inactive, the mood began to shift. Opposition journals, such as the *Craftsman*, began to question Carteret's continuing negotiations and cavil at the lack of progress. The approach of the parliamentary session also brought a growth in discussion in both periodicals and pamphlets. Reports that George had shown an unacceptable degree of favouritism towards his Hanoverian troops began to circulate. These were fuelled, in part, by discontent in the upper ranks of the British command. Both Stair and Richmond were to voice their dissatisfaction.[84] Stair went so far as to resign his command because he felt that the wrong strategy was being pursued.[85] Richmond, with his close connections to the Pelhams, was wary of Carteret's intentions and kept his friends in London well informed of the toings and froings.

By the time George returned from Hanover, reaction to his military exploits had divided into two neat camps. On the one hand, there were those keen to play up the king's personal bravery, linking it to his previous

---

[83] Court Diary, NHStA, Dep. 103, IV, 324, fos 94–5; C. E. von Malortie, *Beiträge zur Geschichte des Braunschweig-Lüneburgischen Hauses und Hofes* (6 vols, Hanover, 1860–72), ii, pp. 39–54; Georg Schnath (with contributions from Rudolf Hillebrecht and Helmut Plath), *Das Leineschloss: Kloster, Fürstensitz, Landtagsgebäude* (Hanover, 1962), pp. 97–8.

[84] Richmond to Newcastle, 24/6.5/7/1743, 29/6.10/7/1743, in McCann, ed., *Correspondence of the dukes of Richmond and Newcastle*, pp. 101–4 for complaints about George's partiality for his Hanoverian troops. It should be noted that Richmond's letters also reveal his irritation both that George had brought his Hanoverian vice-master of horse with him and his dissatisfaction that Richmond had not been given overall control of the king's stable, particularly galling given Richmond's superior status. The fact that François de la Croix de Fréchapelle, son of George's former Hanoverian master of horse, seemingly neglected his duties did little to improve Richmond's opinion of him.

[85] Stair's resignation memorial, detailing his dissatisfaction with the conduct of the campaign, first found its way into print in an appendix to some editions of *A true dialogue between Thomas Jones, a trooper, late return'd from Germany and John Smith, a serjeant in the First Regiment of Foot Guards* (London, 1743). It also appeared as *The memorial of the E—— of S——* (London, 1743).

adventures at Oudenarde. This could be seen in a variety of media, including popular ballads, cartoons and celebratory sermons. The official aspects of commemoration found a focus in Handel's Dettingen *Te Deum*, and were mixed into the celebrations to mark the king's sixtieth birthday. Handel had begun composition of the piece after the publication of the thanksgiving prayer that was to be read at services on 17 July to mark the victory. The scale of the work suggested that Handel hoped it might be performed at an official thanksgiving service, similar to the one that had taken place in 1713 to mark the peace of Utrecht and for which Handel had also composed a *Te Deum*. This was not to be. Instead the work was first performed in the slightly cramped surroundings of the Chapel Royal in late November on the second Sunday after George's return from Hanover (the first Sunday was the anniversary of Caroline's death so deemed inappropriate for such an event).[86]

On the other hand, there was a growing, and increasingly vocal, group of writers who wanted to question the whole basis of the connection between Britain and Hanover.[87] Arguments about the strategic vulnerability of Hanover were wrapped up in a broader critique of a foreign policy whose priorities were continental, rather than colonial. Unsurprisingly, the king came in for a certain amount of personal criticism in these works. At a specific level, his conduct during the Dettingen campaign was criticised. His alleged favouritism towards his Hanoverian troops was mentioned frequently. The view that he had ensured that the Hanoverians were placed towards the rear of the line of battle, and thus were less susceptible to casualties than the British regiments, was cited as evidence of this. George's attire on the day of the battle also came in for criticism. He had worn a yellow Hanoverian sash, which was taken to be indicative of where his priorities lay. In neither case did the charges really stand up – reports of the line of battle showed that Hanoverian troops had been as involved in the action and the wide variety of contemporary estimates made it almost impossible to judge whether casualties had been inflicted disproportionately on one national group within the Pragmatic army as opposed to another.[88] George's dress was not a deliberate snub but a recollection of the garb he wore on his only other major military adventure at Oudenarde.[89] Even so, in a subsequent portrait of George leading his troops at Dettingen by John Wootton, there is no sign of a yellow sash.

[86] Küster, *Vier Monarchien*, pp. 396–7 and ch. 10 *passim*, Bob Harris, *Politics and the nation* (Oxford, 2002), pp. 111–12, Donald Burrows, *Handel and the English Chapel Royal* (Oxford, 2005), pp. 385–90.

[87] Bob Harris, 'Hanover and the public sphere', in Simms and Riotte, eds, *Hanoverian dimension*, pp. 196–7 and G.C. Gibbs, 'English attitudes towards Hanover and the Hanoverian succession in the first half of the eighteenth century', in A.M. Birke and K. Kluxen, eds, *England und Hannover / England and Hanover* (Munich, 1986), pp. 33–5.

[88] Küster, *Vier Monarchien*, p. 56. Something that is often overlooked, although not by Küster, is that the largest contingent within the Pragmatic army was Habsburg.

[89] Dann, *Hanover*, p. 53.

However, to gripe about the inaccuracies of the anti-Hanoverian case in the pamphlet debates of 1743 and 1744 is to miss the point. Or rather, it is important to recognize that there was such dissatisfaction with the Hanoverian link and its consequences that people were prepared to believe that such stories might be true – that the British lion really was being made subject to the Hanoverian horse, as a contemporary cartoon had it. There was also, it should be noted, a spectrum of opinion. The Pelhams were not that unhappy to see Carteret portrayed as the 'Hanoverian troop minister'. Attacks on him, and his foreign policy, served only to increase their political leverage and importance to George. It was also expedient to blame the failure to follow up the victory at Dettingen on Carteret's diplomacy – for while the Pelhams may privately have been frustrated by their distance from the negotiations, in the face of a rising tide of anti-Hanoverianism, it was useful to be able to shift responsibility to other quarters publicly.

There was a more serious side to opposition writing, however. Chesterfield, in particular, had turned himself into the cheerleader for anti-Hanoverian sentiment. *The case of the Hanover forces* was a violent attack both on the wasted opportunities and ongoing corruption associated with Walpolean politics and on the dangers of sacrificing British interests abroad in favour of other territories, such as Hanover.[90] Like some of the pamphlets that the ministry published to defend its actions, it enjoyed a wide circulation.[91] The financial costs and seemingly small return of George's actions in 1743 provided a perfect opportunity for opponents of the ministry to cause trouble in parliament. To defend themselves against the possible charge of disloyalty, opposition writers could employ the rhetoric of acting in the true interests of Britain and thus playing up their own patriotism while implicitly undermining that of ministerial writers. Chesterfield was to publish two further justifications of his original pamphlet, responding to attacks by writers such as Horace Walpole who claimed that his work was both libellous and an attack on the king.[92] The furore in the public sphere continued throughout the parliamentary session of 1743–4 with pamphlets being published both for and against.[93]

The difficulty that the Pelhams or Old Corps Whigs faced was how they could outmanoeuvre Carteret and reduce his influence on the king

---

[90] [Edmund Waller and Philip Dormer Stanhope], *The case of the Hanover forces in the pay of Great Britain, impartially and freely examined: with some seasonable reflections on the present conjuncture of affairs* (London, 1743).

[91] Harris, 'Hanover and the public sphere', p. 186. Viscount Perceval's pro-ministerial *Faction Detected, by the evidence of Facts* (London, 1743) went through several editions in 1743. Although close to the prince of Wales, Perceval was happy to support continental intervention at this stage.

[92] [Horace Walpole], *The interest of Great Britain steadily pursued* (London, 1743), p. 3.

[93] Harris, *Politics and the nation*, pp. 42–3. For a detailed discussion of the relevant pamphlet literature on both sides, see Nick Harding, *Hanover and the British empire, 1700–1837* (Woodbridge, 2007), pp. 119–32.

without at the same time appearing to be little more than populist mouth-pieces for opposition attacks on 'Hanoverian politics'. As Owen pointed out many years ago, the extent to which Orford realized that this was an issue of management, as opposed to straight coercion, is an indication of the extent to which George still enjoyed considerable freedom of action. George would have to be won round to the Pelhams' point of view. If he could be weaned away from Carteret, there was less risk that Carteret would be able to sustain a non-Whig administration by turning to the Tories for support instead.[94] Newcastle's correspondence from this period contains various hints about how he thought that George might be best managed.

In one sense, the hurly-burly of parliamentary politics made little difference to the king's outlook. Certainly, there were discussions among ministers about how the apparently Hanoverian proclivities of their monarch could best be defended, particularly when it came to the neces-sity of spending British funds to keep Hanoverian troops in food and forage. However, George's ministers were able to carry the vote in the Commons on the retention of Hanoverian troops, albeit with a slightly reduced majority since the last comparable vote on Hanoverian troops in 1742.[95] It cannot have been entirely coincidental, though, that George chose to revisit the question of the continuation of the personal union between Britain and Hanover at this juncture. The Hanoverian Privy Council's response to George's request for them to think about the future viability of the personal union argued that there were several advantages that the union brought.[96] In essence, these boiled down to strategic benefits. Having a European outpost was valuable for the construction of solid anti-French alliances, which the Hanoverian ministers thought were at the heart of British policy. In that case, there was a similarity of interest between Hanoverian attempts to support the Habsburgs and a British desire to have a strong Empire as a bulwark against the advance of France. A sense of common Protestantism was also invoked. Additionally, the Hanoverian ministers doubted whether it would be possible for George to break the union. The legal qualms over whether the two territories could be separated if it involved the renunciation of Frederick's rights over one or the other, something which had already surfaced in the debates

[94] Owen, *Pelhams*, pp. 188–90. For a broader discussion of George's latent power, even in seeming political crisis, see J.B. Owen, 'George II reconsidered', in A. Whiteman, J.S. Bromley and P.G.M. Dickson, eds, *Statesmen, scholars and merchants* (Oxford, 1973), pp. 113–34.

[95] Sedgwick, *House of Commons*, i, p. 55 and Owen, *Pelhams*, pp. 207–9.

[96] Hanoverian Privy Council to George II, 7/2/1744, NHStA, Hann. 92, 70. There are reasonable discussions of the contents in Allen, 'Anglo-Hanoverian connection', pp. 161–4 and Harding, *Hanover*, pp. 132–5. For the broader perspective on debates over the contin-uation of the union utilizing material destroyed in the Second World War, see Richard Drögereit, 'Das Testament Georgs I. und die Frage der Personalunion zwischen England und Hannover', *Niedersächsisches Jahrbuch für Landesgeschichte*, 14 (1937), pp. 94–199.

about the suppression of Georg Ludwig's will, were also mentioned. George therefore decided to leave the issue alone, although he was to return to it when another European crisis again brought the question of the interrelationship of his two territories to the fore in the last years of his reign.

STRUGGLES FOR POWER AND INFLUENCE

If the domestic situation within Britain was a cause of irritation and exasperation to the king, the outlook on the European continent gave George considerably more pause for thought in the early months of 1744.[97] One difficulty was that other European monarchs were unwilling to play the roles that George had allotted to them and happily join together in a coalition against France. Another, though, was that it was becoming clear that Carteret and the king's diplomatic efforts in the aftermath of Dettingen were unravelling fast. The particular cause for concern was the treaty of Worms, signed in September 1743 but whose terms became widely known following its publication in Dutch newspapers in February 1744. What bothered Frederick was that the contracting parties (George, Maria Theresa and Charles Emmanuel III of Sardinia) had made mention of various previous treaties as being the basis for the borders of their respective lands but did not mention the agreements of Breslau/Berlin that had initially brought conflict between Frederick and Maria Theresa to a conclusion. Frederick's concern, entirely justified as it happens, was that Maria Theresa refused to accept the loss of Silesia. Maria Theresa's recent alliance with Saxony, at first an opponent of her succession, heightened Frederick's fears. The result was that Frederick renewed his attempts to gain French support for a further campaign against Maria Theresa, with the aim of extracting further guarantees of his possession of Silesia from her.

The results of his diplomacy, aided by a switch to a more interventionist attitude at the French court following the dismissal of the cautious foreign minister Amelot, were to be seen in the Union of Frankfurt, created in May 1744. The union, which consisted of Frederick, the emperor (still a Wittelsbach), the Elector Palatine and the landgrave of Hessen-Kassel was supposed to be for the defence of the empire and its liberty but Frederick made very clear that its members felt betrayed by Carteret's actions of the previous year. From George's perspective, the inclusion of Hessen-Kassel in the grouping was particularly galling as William had been both a long-term ally and was now dynastically connected to George as well. The chain of events that would result in Frederick's invasion of Bohemia in August 1744 had been set in motion.

George's difficulties were compounded by the increasingly aggressive stance of France. In late 1743 Louis XV had started to talk seriously about

---

[97] For what follows, see Dann, *Hanover*, pp. 57–62 and Anderson, *War of the Austrian succession*, pp. 122–36.

invading Britain and had sought the co-operation of his uncle, Philip V of Spain. These moves met with the active support of the exiled Jacobite court, keen to use any twist or turn of the international situation to gain foreign aid for an invasion to recover the British thrones. An invasion was planned to coincide with a French declaration of war against Britain and Hanover in early 1744. As it was, the French force assembled under the Marshal de Saxe, illegitimate son of Augustus II of Saxony, at Dunkirk embarked only for a storm to disperse both the transports and the covering French naval squadron. Plans for the invasion were temporarily abandoned and Saxe's army dispatched to the Austrian Netherlands but the French declared war nevertheless. The conflict was, if anything, broadening and deepening and the prospects of a rapid conclusion, which had seemed very real in the summer of 1743, diminished daily. The invasion of the Austrian Netherlands prompted further questions about George's foreign policy. Would the Dutch finally agree to enter the conflict and declare war on France, rather than simply supplying some auxiliary troops to Maria Theresa? What would the Pragmatic army now do?

George was again convinced that the only way in which a co-ordinated strategy could be pursued was if he resumed personal command of the army. After the trials and tribulations of the previous summer, the Old Corps Whigs were anxious to avoid this outcome at almost any cost. Newcastle and Pelham were also keen that relations with the Dutch should be put on a surer footing. Given the escalation of the conflict, they wanted firm commitments about the number of men that the Dutch would be prepared to put into the field. Despite Carteret's opposition, Newcastle persuaded the king to press the Dutch, which he duly did.[98] Pressure was applied to George from other directions as well. George's proposals for a subsidy for Saxony in case of further Prussian aggression ran into a brick wall with the Old Corps. Newcastle reported that the king had given way with relatively good grace, although he had gloomily predicted that they would all repent of it, when it was too late. It was also apparent that relations between the Old Corps and Carteret were worsening. Newcastle told Hardwicke that they needed to formulate a strategy because he feared that Carteret was growing tired of being outvoted by Pelham, Harrington, Hardwicke and himself and that one side or the other must take over the major role in the administration.[99] A few weeks later Hardwicke was able to report that Newcastle's resistance to George's departure for the continent had yielded results. Hardwicke had seen Carteret just as the latter was leaving the closet. Carteret had whispered that the plans for a visit to the continent were now off. This had prompted Hardwicke to ask George about his projected trip and he was told that it had been abandoned. George also accused the Old Corps of wanting him to stay at home because they hoped to break Carteret's influence and seize power for

[98] Owen, *Pelhams*, pp. 224–5.
[99] Newcastle to Hardwicke, Newcastle House, 6/6/1744 OS, BL, Add. MSS 35408, fo. 21.

themselves. He claimed Hardwicke sought to confine him, to which Hardwicke responded that all he, and his friends, desired was to be a true servant of His Majesty.[100] Although George had reluctantly acceded to Old Corps advice, this did nothing to prevent him complaining about the conduct of the war. Gossip circulated that he was far from happy with the timidity of Field Marshal Wade and believed that Stair would have done a better job. Stair, incidentally, was also complaining about the quality of the generals in the Low Countries.[101]

Frederick's invasion of Bohemia in August 1744 did little to improve relations between George and his ministers. As Frederick had decided to ignore Saxony's neutral status and march his troops by the most direct way to attack Maria Theresa, George's first reaction was one of irritated self-vindication. It is unlikely that the approval of a proposed British subsidy for Saxony earlier in the summer would have made a real difference but it reinforced George's view that his command of foreign affairs was more acute than the Pelhams'. The Pelhams, on the other hand, retorted that Frederick's actions were the result of the ineptness of Carteret's diplomacy and the ministerial crisis escalated yet again.

It was not only Frederick's military moves that were causing problems. His minister in London, Andrié, was in contact with several of the leading opposition figures, as the earl of Marchmont's diary for the period reveals. Andrié's various conversations with the opposition leaders provided some interesting insights into George's character, as well as indicating the depth of anti-Hanoverian feeling among this group. George apparently remarked that he was unsure why his journeys to Hanover were so unpopular with 'the people here' (meaning the opposition leaders in the Lords) for 'they went all out of town to their country-seats; but it was unjust, for Hanover was his country-seat, and he had no other'. In Andrié's version of the encounter as recorded by Marchmont, George went on to say that a separation of Hanover from England might be achieved by some sort of negotiation but that he was unhappy with 'Hanover lawyers' who had prevented him from reaching a proper accommodation with Frederick over some outstanding issues over Silesia, Osnabrück and East Friesland.[102] Given that George had raised the issue of the separation of Britain and Hanover earlier in the year, there is a ring of truth about the account, despite the slightly tortuous path through which it was transmitted. Andrié also complained that George had, in a break from strict diplomatic etiquette, turned his back on him. He had been incensed enough to report the king's behaviour to Carteret and Harrington but they had both said that it was 'a weakness in the king' and that Andrié should continue to attend court. Frederick, however, on hearing

---

[100] Hardwicke to Newcastle, Powis House, 24/6/1744 OS, BL, Add. MSS 32703, fos 156–7.

[101] Diary of earl of Marchmont, 4/8/1744 and 7/8/1744 in G.H. Rose, ed., *A Selection from the papers of the earls of Marchmont* (3 vols, London, 1831), i, pp. 8–10.

[102] Ibid., 2/10/1744, p. 53.

Andrié's report, had decided to give Hyndford, the British extraordinary envoy and plenipotentiary accredited to his court, the same treatment.[103] George's behaviour, known, in court parlance, as 'rumping', was characteristic of the way in which he did very little to disguise his feelings about a particular individual.[104]

Andrié's talks with the opposition and the publication of several works attacking the ministry's conduct since the Hanau negotiations were a signal that the parliamentary session was approaching again. The Old Corps, worried about what it would bring, now began a concerted campaign to remove Carteret. Newcastle had been concerned in late August that the king should be shown that he could not go on with both Carteret and the Old Corps and that a choice had to be made.[105] By mid-September, Newcastle wanted the Old Corps to meet to agree a collective strategy that would lead either to Carteret's departure or their own.[106] An ultimatum was subsequently issued to the king. Either an immediate arrangement was to be reached with the Dutch, which would not be possible without the dismissal of Earl Granville (as Carteret had become following his mother's death in mid-October), or the Old Corps would feel obliged to leave themselves. George protested, arguing that he ought to be able to determine who his ministers were. Newcastle had to agree with this but responded that if the ministers thought a policy wrong, then they were at liberty to resign, rather than execute it.[107]

In a final throw, George tried to separate Harrington, who had been a loyal servant during the Hanoverian journeys of 1740 and 1741 and had only recently become intimate with Newcastle, Pelham and Hardwicke, from the other Old Corps leaders. In an audience with the king, subsequently reported to Hardwicke by Newcastle,[108] Harrington had to endure a lengthy tirade, beginning with the king's irritation that the speech from the throne had not yet been completed by his ministers. George then complained about the measures that he would probably be asked to support. In response to Harrington's enquiry as to whether George might continue to support Granville, the king angrily answered that this was impossible, as Newcastle had poisoned both the Lords and Commons against him. He supposed that Harrington must have Granville's office instead and go to the United Provinces to concert something with the

[103] Ibid., 4/9/1744, p. 39.

[104] George's habit of turning his back was so common that a number of the opposition lords like Stair and Chesterfield had formed a 'Beef Rump Club' to signal their collective disfavour in the aftermath of the Excise Crisis. The king was not amused to learn of its existence. See entry for 11/3/1734 in R.A. Roberts, ed., *Diary of Viscount Percival afterwards first earl of Egmont* (HMC, 3 vols, London, 1920–3), ii, p. 53.

[105] Newcastle to Pelham, 25/8/1744 OS, BL, Add. MSS 35408, fo. 39.

[106] Newcastle to Hardwicke, Newcastle House, 14/9/1744 OS, ibid., fo. 54

[107] Idem to idem, Newcastle House, 19/11/1744 OS, ibid., fo. 95

[108] Idem to idem, Newcastle House, 16/11/1744 OS, ibid., fos 90–1.

Dutch. Harrington, no doubt repeating the agreed Old Corps line, inter-jected that things were not so simple and that it was necessary that George showed public confidence in his ministers. This prompted George to complain again about the measures he was being asked to support: 'How could he support Measures, that he thought so wrong? That the view was to abandon our Allies; and put a shameful End to the war, as was done in 1712: that the pretext was the Dutch not furnishing their Quotas, which would end now, as it did then, in making a dishonourable Peace.'[109]

The subsequent flattery of Harrington was what convinced Newcastle that this was part of a conscious attempt to detach him from the Old Corps. His letter concluded with a reminder to Hardwicke of the neces-sity of crafting an appropriate speech and the observation that 'the Abandoning our Allies, as was done in 1712, is the King's sole Topic; and I find, our best friends think (and particularly the Bishop of Salisbury) that care must be taken to guard against that'.[110] George's historical sense here is interesting. The reference to 1712 recalled the British withdrawal from the Grand Alliance while Bolingbroke (still an active figure in British poli-tics in 1744) was negotiating with France. The duke of Ormonde's forces had left Eugene of Savoy's army. The remaining members of the alliance, which included the Dutch, Habsburgs and Hanover, had subsequently suffered a heavy defeat at the battle of Denain. In one sense, George was simply expressing a fear that Carteret's departure might lead to Britain abandoning Maria Theresa, ironic given that the Old Corps had been among her staunchest supporters. Yet there were also other resonances – the fear of Tory influences on the ministry and the impact that this might have on foreign policy and George's propensity to use history when inter-preting the world around him.

Even under this intense pressure, George still tried to cling on a little longer to save Granville.[111] For once, Prince Frederick, another admirer of Granville, found himself in agreement with his father and also made some efforts to support him. George tried to get Orford to come to London to help him. Pelham, who had known nothing of the approach, urged Orford to stay in the country but, when pressed, Orford told George that he would probably have to accept that Granville's position was untenable.[112] Just before the start of the parliamentary session Granville finally resigned.

George was angered and disappointed that he had been forced, as he viewed it, to part with Granville. As in 1742, the loss of parliamentary confidence appears to have been a crucial component in Granville's depar-ture. Yet, if the lesson was supposed to be that parliament could now dictate to the king who his ministers should be, then George proceeded to ignore it.

[109] Ibid., fos 90v–91r.
[110] Ibid., fo. 91v.
[111] Owen, *Pelhams*, pp. 236–8.
[112] For some of the relevant letters, see Coxe, *Walpole*, iii, pp. 601–6.

1 George with his mother and sister, prior to his parents' divorce in 1694. His relationship with his mother has been a field for fertile, but ultimately unconvincing, psychological speculation.

GEORGIVS AVGVSTVS *Prince of Hanover: Grandson to y eld* I *[illustrious] Princess Sophia [Dutches] [Dowager] Daughter t [o] Elizabeth Queen of Bohemia, Sister t [o] King Charles First, Declared t [o] Succeed to y Crown of England & [c.] by y latter Act for settling the Succession in to [the] Protestant Line*

2 An engraving of George as electoral prince of Hanover. It was produced as part of a propaganda effort by the Whigs, in the aftermath of the Act of Settlement, to indicate the importance of the Protestant succession. The text highlights his claims to the throne and his Protestantism.

3 The Hanoverian claim to the British thrones came through the Electress Sophia, granddaughter of James I and VI. She enjoyed a close relationship with her grandson, George, and encouraged him to master the English language.

The most Illustrious Princess Sophia Electrice Dowager of Brunswick, Successor to y Crown of England &c. after her Majesty Queen Ann & her Royal Issue.

4 A formal portrait of George as prince of Wales. Unlike his father, George seemed to enjoy the formality and ceremony of court life.

5 Henrietta Howard, countess of Suffolk, George's mistress, depicted around 1720, dressed for a ball at court.

6 George in his coronation regalia in 1727.

7 Caroline dressed for her 1727 coronation. She was very concerned to appear at her best, borrowing jewels for her robes to give an impression of splendour.

8 George's father, Georg Ludwig, portrayed in a relatively simple style. Prior to obtaining the British thrones, he had enjoyed considerable success as a military commander, both against the Turks and the French. George longed to emulate his father's success but had relatively few opportunities to do so.

9 An image of uncharacteristic family harmony. Frederick, prince of Wales, sits at the front playing the bass viol, while his sister Anne plays the harpsichord. Caroline plays the lute and Amelia sits reading. Kew Palace can be seen in the background.

10 George's moment of military glory at the battle of Dettingen (1743). He is pictured with his son, the duke of Cumberland, and the fourth earl of Holdernesse, who was later to become a secretary of state. George's supposed preference for his Hanoverian troops during the course of the campaign provoked a public outcry. Wootton tactfully omits any suggestion that George had worn a yellow Hanoverian sash during the battle by painting him in a blue sash.

11 This seemingly innocuous depiction of the Hanoverian countryside has a deeper political meaning. Rotating it reveals an image of George, underlying his supposed preference for his German territories.

12 A further anti-Hanoverian image. A Hanoverian soldier hides behind the tree and is accused of cowardice by a passing English officer. In the centre, the English Lion is being dominated by the white Hanoverian horse, depicted with a sash and a Khevenhüller hat.

13 A very literal rendition of George's distaste for some of his administrations. In the period of ministerial instability between 1742 and 1746, various combinations of ministers were tried. Here, Newcastle and Pelham try to persuade George to swallow Sir John Hynde Cotton, a rotund Tory, in an attempt to form a broad-bottomed ministry.

14 William, duke of Cumberland, in military uniform, complete with his garter star. David Morier, the Swiss painter of the image, had won Cumberland's patronage with his detailed and accurate renditions of military life. Cumberland himself won a considerable reputation as a soldier and commander, although his relations with his father deteriorated when he was forced to sign a neutrality agreement for Hanover at Kloster Zeven in 1757 during the Seven Years War.

15 Amalie Sophie Marianne von Wallmoden, countess of Yarmouth and George's mistress. George's visits to Hanover in 1735 and 1736 were partly driven by a desire to see her. She moved to London after Caroline's death and occupied the apartments previously used by Henrietta Howard.

16 George's daughter Mary. Her marriage to Friedrich of Hessen-Kassel helped to secure Hessian troops to defend the king's German domains. However, her domestic life was unhappy and George intervened to help secure her future after her husband's conversion to Catholicism.

17 George's youngest daughter Louisa. Her marriage into the Danish royal house was for dynastic purposes. Like her mother, Caroline, she died as a result of complications related to a hernia.

18 A depiction of the Protestant succession. At the top, Georg Ludwig presides over the Hanoverian royal house. George and Caroline are pictured beneath him, followed by Frederick, Augusta and their children at the bottom. The importance of the dynasty's Protestantism is emphasised by the crushed figure of the pope to the right of Caroline.

19 George was a frequent visitor to his Hanoverian domains. This image illustrates some of the detrimental effects of George's absence on London's economy. Trade is being carried in a coffin and the coffee houses are empty because the court is not in town. Although George's visit to Hanover in 1750 was not as long as some of his previous sojourns, it is a reminder of the continued economic importance of the court.

20 George, even at the end of his reign, was still seen as crucial to good government. Here he sits trying to restore liberty and justice, while Newcastle, dressed as the ass, and Fox, look on.

21 George in later life, in an image that is regarded as a particularly good likeness. It was not completed until after his death.

GEORGIO SECUNDO
Patrono suo, optime merenti,
Semper venerando:
Quod clementi Populo,
Justissime, humanissime,
In Pace, et in Bello,
Feliciter Imperavit:
Quod Academiam Cantabrigiensem
Fovit, auxit, ornavit:
HANC STATUAM,
Æternum, faxit Deus, Monumentum
Grati Animi in Regem,
Pietatis in Patriam,
Amoris in Academiam,
Suis Sumptibus poni Jussit
THOMAS HOLLES
DUX DE NEWCASTLE
ACADEMIÆ CANCELLARIUS
A. D. MDCCLXVI

22 George dressed in Roman garb. The statue now stands in the entrance hall to the
Cambridge University library. It was presented to the university by the duke of
Newcastle, in grateful recognition of the services rendered both to him and the
university by the king.

Chapter 6

REBELLION AND REVIVAL

Granville's departure created as many problems as it solved. The country still had to be governed, an administration formed and, perhaps most importantly, the war prosecuted. The Old Corps hoped that, given time, they could consolidate their influence within the closet and form a workable majority in the Commons. The prospects for the latter seemed reasonable. Granville's friends were likely to be strong supporters of the war. What was needed was to bring in some members of the opposition to shore things up – something not beyond the bounds of possibility. Influence in the closet would prove to be another matter. Whereas there had been an acceptance, albeit grudging, in 1742 by George that Walpole had to go, the anger at Granville's departure was still fresh and was slow to dissipate. Moreover, George made it perfectly clear that he would happily ditch the Old Corps as soon as an opportunity arose.

NEW MINISTRY

The Old Corps leaders had to work hard to persuade the king that Chesterfield, after his prominent role in the recent anti-Hanoverian campaigns, should be shown any favour at all. George reluctantly agreed to make him lord lieutenant of Ireland – a post that was unlikely to require frequent personal contact. Chesterfield was also entrusted with the task of travelling to the United Provinces in an effort to spur the Dutch into greater action. Hardwicke reported to Newcastle at the start of 1745 that he had attended a levee, along with Grafton, Tweeddale, Chesterfield and Cholmondeley. The king had spoken only to Hardwicke and his displeasure at seeing Chesterfield was evident.[1] Chesterfield's own audience with the king prior to his departure for The Hague also left little doubt about George's feelings towards him. Elsewhere, a few Tories were given places – Lord Gower as privy seal, replacing Cholmondeley whom the king particularly liked, and Sir John Hynde Cotton as treasurer of the chamber. The apparent broadening of the basis of the administration to encompass figures from the opposition led to the epithet 'broad bottom' being attached to it – the size of some of its members, including Cotton, making this doubly appropriate. Of the leading opposition figures, only

---

[1] Hardwicke to Newcastle, Powis House, 5/1/1745 OS, BL, Add. MSS 32704, fo. 3.

William Pitt was left without a place. He had been suggested as a possible candidate for the secretaryship of war but George had been firmly opposed, perhaps because of Pitt's known anti-Hanoverian views, perhaps because of the difficulties of finding an appropriate compensatory post for Sir William Yonge, the incumbent, or even because Pitt himself wanted to stay out of office to keep his populist credentials intact.[2]

George had undoubtedly suffered a setback. To be forced to part with two favoured ministers in a relatively short space of time suggested that his power was not as uncontested as he might have thought. Nevertheless, the fact that the Pelhams still placed such emphasis on winning his confidence via the closet shows how central he remained to the political process. Hardwicke had a long audience with George in early January 1745 in which he tried to persuade the king to offer more visible signals of his support for the Old Corps. George listened to much of Hardwicke's oration in sullen silence, occasionally interrupting to complain how he had been forced to part with Carteret. However, he retained sufficient humour to respond to one of Hardwicke's pleas for greater support for his servants with the comment that 'ministers are kings in this country'.[3]

Many of the major opposition figures had been brought inside the tent so, perhaps unsurprisingly, the 1745 parliamentary session turned out to be relatively peaceful. The number of troops to be employed in the Low Countries was increased without too much difficulty but the question of subsidies for Britain's allies provoked more debate. Britain's subsidy contract with Hanover had lapsed at the end of 1744. Removing Hanoverian troops from British pay was probably popular but it was not entirely practicable in the context of the combined war effort. Consequently, negotiations had been conducted between British, Hanoverian and Austrian representatives to secure a larger subsidy for Maria Theresa but with the understanding that this would be used to employ the Hanoverian troops that Britain had previously been funding. When the matter of the increased subsidy came before the Commons, it was stated that it was destined for paying Hanoverian troops so that they would still be paid for by the British taxpayer, albeit indirectly. Nevertheless, Pitt had overcome his earlier objections and the debate on the issue was not nearly as violent as it had been in previous years.[4]

THE CONTINENTAL CAMPAIGNS OF 1745

Part of the argument for the increased commitment of funds and troops was that it was likely to bring about a speedy end to the war. However, the continental situation was altered again, this time by the death of

---

[2] J.B. Owen, *The rise of the Pelhams* (London, 1957), pp. 248–9.
[3] Hardwicke's notes on his audience, 5/1/1745, BL, Add. MSS 35870, fos 87–91 (quotation fo. 90v).
[4] Uriel Dann, *Hanover and Great Britain, 1740–1760* (Leicester, 1991), pp. 61–2.

Charles VII in January 1745.[5] Britain and Hanover had signed a defensive alliance with Saxony and Austria earlier in the month, designed to uphold the Pragmatic Sanction. Charles VII's death gave further cause to believe that the older system of the empire might be restored: with a Habsburg back on the imperial throne, the general situation would improve. Certainly the coalition ranged against Maria Theresa began to look less secure. Max Joseph of Bavaria rapidly moved to end his conflict with Austria, promising his vote for Maria Theresa's husband Francis Stephen in the forthcoming imperial election in exchange for the evacuation of Habsburg troops from his territories. George's Hanoverian ministers were ecstatic, even hoping that a general humbling of Frederick might be part of this process. Frederick, they argued, had shown bad faith by breaking the treaty of Breslau, which had brought the first Silesian war to an end in June 1742, so George need not feel bound by his promise to allow Frederick to keep Silesia. The king needed little encouragement in this regard and when Frederick, through his representative in London, Andrié, raised the possibility of British mediation shortly after Charles VII's death, he met with a distinctly cool response.[6] Newcastle, meanwhile, was already worrying, rightly as it happened, about whether the temptation for revenge on Prussia might not be too great for his royal master. Newcastle hoped that Austrian power might be restored without too much damage being inflicted on Frederick and he urged Hardwicke that the Old Corps needed to construct an agreed position with regard to the latest foreign political twists because 'if we can agree among ourselves, the King will be governed by Us'.[7] Part of Newcastle's concern arose from his impression that George favoured a Saxon emperor over the candidature of Francis Stephen of Lorraine; he shared his worries with Chesterfield in February 1745, noting that George seemed reluctant to have anybody interfere in matters related to the imperial election.[8] It is unlikely that George ever seriously contemplated anything other than a restoration of the Habsburgs but his desire to keep his British ministers away from imperial affairs, where he considered himself to have a much greater competence, was entirely characteristic.

While the pressure on Frederick seemed to be increasing in Germany, his French allies were faring rather better in the Low Countries. Led by Marshal de Saxe, the illegitimate half-brother of the Saxon Elector, Augustus III, French forces had laid siege to Tournai. The Pragmatic army, now commanded by Cumberland, determined to raise the siege and forced battle with Saxe at Fontenoy, a little to the east of Tournai. Despite

---

[5] M.S. Anderson, *The war of the Austrian succession, 1740–1748* (Harlow, 1995), pp. 140–9.

[6] Dann, *Hanover*, pp. 67–8.

[7] Newcastle to Hardwicke, Newcastle House, 26/1/1745 OS, BL, Add. MSS 35408, fos 120–2 (quotation fo. 122v).

[8] Newcastle to Chesterfield, Newcastle House, 22/2/1745 OS, BL, Add. MSS 32804, fos 227–31.

the heroic efforts of Cumberland to keep his troops together in the face of withering artillery and musket fire, he was unable to break through the French lines and had to retreat. His troops had sustained heavy casualties but they had, at least, remained in good order throughout. Cumberland was less impressed with the conduct of some of his allies, particularly the Dutch. Their cavalry had been largely ineffective and had left the field in a disorderly manner. Cumberland wrote a pointed letter to his sister, highlighting how heavy the British and Hanoverian losses had been.[9] Cumberland himself was widely praised for his courage and the care that he had shown for his men. His appointment as captain-general, the first person to hold that title since Marlborough, seemed justified. However, Fontenoy had still been a defeat and it had opened the Low Countries for Saxe's army. A number of other Flemish towns fell to Saxe thereafter.

George was in Hanover again over the summer of 1745. Hopes of punishing Frederick, despite the objections of the British ministers, diminished with Frederick's victory over a Saxon and Austrian army at Hohenfriedburg in early June. In the light of the revival in Prussian fortunes, George's aims turned from punishment to conciliation. Harrington spent his time in Hanover in a series of negotiations which led to a convention, signed at the end of August, with Prussia. There was a mutual guarantee of George and Frederick's respective territories, thus enabling George to believe that Hanover's security had been strengthened. George agreed to mediate with Maria Theresa in an effort to get her to agree to a permanent peace on the basis of Prussian retention of Silesia. Frederick promised not to vote against Francis Stephen in the forthcoming imperial election.

Maria Theresa, who knew nothing of the negotiations, was less than pleased to discover that George and his ministers wanted to bounce her into giving up her claims to Silesia. Her reluctance to back down was enhanced by the successful election of her husband as emperor in September. Represented, as at the previous election, by Münchhausen, George cast his vote for Francis Stephen and, for once, Frederick kept his word – his representative left Frankfurt on the day before the election so was not present when it took place. Meanwhile, Frederick continued to push back his Habsburg and Saxon opponents in the field. The final straw came at Kesselsdorf in December when Leopold of Anhalt-Dessau delivered the blow that led to both Saxony and Maria Theresa coming to terms. In the treaty of Dresden, signed on Christmas Day 1745, Frederick acknowledged the Pragmatic Sanction, accepted Francis Stephen as emperor but was confirmed in possession of Silesia and Glatz. The changed military situation also put paid to several independent diplomatic initiatives that George had been pursuing since the Convention of Hanover.[10]

---

[9] Reed Browning, *The war of the Austrian succession* (Stroud, 1993), pp. 206–13, Veronica Baker-Smith, *Royal discord: the family of George II* (London, 2008), p. 123.

[10] Details can be found in Ernst Borkowsky, *Die Englische Friedensvermittlung im Jahre 1745* (Berlin, 1884).

THE JACOBITE REBELLION

George's mind had been on other things during the autumn. He had been summoned back from Hanover by the news that he was facing a full-scale challenge to his authority at home.[11] Charles Edward, the eldest grandson of James II, had landed in Scotland with a small group of supporters in late July. By the middle of August, when he raised his standard at Glenfinnan, he had been able to gather together a force of perhaps 1,000 men to begin his attempt to recover the throne he believed was rightfully his father's. The ministers in London, worried by the news reaching them from Scotland, wrote urgently to George to ask him to return to Britain at once. They also hoped that Cumberland, and significant numbers of British troops, would be withdrawn from Flanders to deal with the domestic situation.[12] The clauses in treaties with the United Provinces which guaranteed the reciprocal provision of troops in cases of invasion were put into effect. The initial hope was that a force under Sir John Cope would be able to deal with the rebels but Cope failed to engage them and diverted his troops to Inverness, leaving the way clear for Charles Edward and his forces to take Edinburgh, which they did in the middle of September. News of Edinburgh's capture brought Cope and his army dashing back and his forces met those of Charles Edward at Prestonpans where they were overwhelmed by the rebels.[13]

The loss at Prestonpans and the capture of the Scottish capital served to concentrate minds in London. Cumberland and his troops were now recalled from Flanders. In the interim another force under Field Marshal George Wade was sent north to intercept the rebels. Charles Edward left Edinburgh and marched south, managing to evade Wade, who had reached Newcastle, by taking a route that allowed him to capture Carlisle instead.[14] Back in London, George was keen to put on a display of family unity. The celebrations for his birthday were lavish as usual. The whole family appeared together to create the impression of solidarity. Frederick had just become a father again and had organized an extravagant christening party for which he had arranged a cake of Carlisle castle to be prepared. Guests were given the option of throwing sugarplums at it. Other members of the royal family were less than impressed by such carryings-on.[15]

Despite the apparent success of the Jacobite enterprise, there were some signs of loyalist sentiment. Thomas Arne's new setting of 'God save

---

[11] For extended accounts of the rebellion, see W.A. Speck, *The butcher: the duke of Cumberland and the suppression of the '45* (Oxford, 1981) and Christopher Duffy, *The '45* (London, 2003).

[12] Speck, *Butcher*, pp. 27–30.

[13] Duffy, *'45*, pp. 11–24.

[14] Ibid., ch. 8.

[15] Baker-Smith, *Royal discord*, p. 127.

our noble king', which was to become the national anthem, was growing popular in the capital's musical circles, perhaps suggesting that enthusiasm for the Stuart cause was not as widespread as Charles Edward had hoped.

A second force was dispatched from London, this time under Sir John Ligonier, to intercept the advancing Jacobites. Sir John's ill health led to his replacement as commander by the more youthful Cumberland, who at twenty-four was a year younger than Charles Edward. Charles Edward had, in the interim, taken both Manchester and Preston. Cumberland faced a dilemma. He was unsure which route Charles Edward would now take. A feint by Lord George Murray persuaded him that Charles Edward intended to try to link up with Welsh Jacobites so he moved his troops accordingly. Charles Edward had, in fact, moved his troops to Derby, meaning that he had got between Cumberland and London. Cumberland quickly realized that he had been misled and made plans to move his troops to intercept Charles Edward before he reached London, while simultaneously warning the ministers to move those regular troops stationed around the capital to Finchley, in case the Young Pretender should evade him.[16] The size and quality of the forces at the king's disposal meant that the danger to London was probably minimal, despite the panic with which the news of Charles Edward's arrival at Derby was greeted. Nevertheless, the Young Pretender's decision to halt his advance at Derby had left open a fertile field for counterfactual speculation.[17]

Once it became clear that Charles Edward had decided to turn around, Cumberland was keen to press on in pursuit of the retreating rebels. He urged Wade to do the same, although the slowness with which Wade moved soon rendered his efforts futile. Cumberland's pursuit was briefly interrupted when he received word from his father that news of a potential French invasion meant that he should withdraw his troops back to London, but George quickly changed his mind and Cumberland was allowed to continue after Charles Edward. He was able to catch up with the Jacobite rearguard near Penrith on 18 December, the last engagement between two armies on English soil. Honours were reasonably even – Cumberland had not been able to reach the main Jacobite army but he had forced some of them to stand and fight. Cumberland next raised the siege of Carlisle and then returned to London to be on hand in case of a French invasion.[18]

Charles Edward continued his retreat into Scotland but was able to engage the forces of General Henry Hawley near Falkirk in the middle of January 1746 and came away victorious. News of another setback prompted George to send Cumberland back to Scotland and he had arrived at Edinburgh by the end of January. He held court in Holyrood as

[16] Speck, *Butcher*, pp. 85–92.

[17] Duffy, *'45*, pp. 300–13 is particularly judicious on this point.

[18] Speck, *Butcher*, pp. 97–102.

a symbolic reminder of the restoration of his father's authority before beginning the further pursuit of Charles Edward. The Jacobites had been engaged in a fairly ineffectual siege of Stirling but had abandoned this by the time that Cumberland began to move north. His first reaction to the news of a further Jacobite retreat was to write to the ministers in London to tell them that the rebellion was, in effect, at an end.[19] Of course, rebel leaders and their estates would have to be seized but the main danger had passed. This news was to prompt a political crisis in London but in relation to the rebellion itself, Cumberland's confidence was to prove misplaced.

The final fling for the Jacobites came with the capture of Inverness from forces under the command of the earl of Loudoun. Cumberland altered his plans. He established his winter headquarters at Aberdeen and waited for the weather to improve to enable him to deal a final blow to the rebellion. Time in Aberdeen allowed Cumberland to give some thought to how he might deal with the rebels. He began to talk in terms of 'military executions', although Scottish lawyers were worried about whether this overstepped legal limits. The advice coming from London suggested that Cumberland could use any measures he deemed necessary. Cumberland had also evolved new tactics to deal with the charges of the Highlanders wielding their axes and broadswords. His troops were drilled in a move that involved them pointing their bayonets to the right, rather than straight ahead, to reach through the exposed side of their opponents.[20]

Cumberland had been joined by Hessian troops under the command of his brother-in-law Friedrich but Friedrich was somewhat reluctant to get involved. He was not especially committed to the cause for which he was fighting and was anxious not to endanger his forces, one of his father's greatest assets, too much. Relations with his brother-in-law were strained. The capture of a Hessian hussar led to an exchange of letters between Friedrich and Lord George Murray about the basis on which Friedrich proposed to conduct his campaign in Scotland and whether such European norms as frequent prisoner exchanges would apply. Cumberland was furious at the attempt by the Jacobites to turn themselves from rebels into belligerents. Friedrich also seems to have associated with several Jacobite sympathizers during his time in Scotland, perhaps because he was already contemplating a conversion to Catholicism.[21]

As spring came, Cumberland moved on Inverness, reaching Nairn on 14 April. By this stage, Charles Edward had little choice but to stand and fight. He was running short of both men, who had gradually drifted away as the army had retreated north, and funds. A French ship carrying money to the rebels had been intercepted so the situation was becoming critical.

[19] Ibid., pp. 112–14.
[20] Ibid., pp. 121–30.
[21] Duffy, '45, pp. 127–8, 470, 530.

Charles Edward attempted a surprise attack on Cumberland's army, assuming that as 15 April was Cumberland's birthday, an assault carried out in the early hours of the 16th would find his troops in no fit state to resist. The overnight march was a failure and the Jacobites retreated dejected. Cumberland, by contrast, had rewarded his troops with a birthday tot of brandy but had then roused them early.[22] The whole army was ready to meet the Jacobites at Culloden in good order. The ensuing encounter quickly turned into a rout.[23] Jacobite forces were decimated by Cumberland's artillery and then by grapeshot. Where Charles Edward's forces were able to get close enough to Cumberland's lines to engage in hand to hand combat, the training in bayonet technique came into its own. The Jacobites were heavily outnumbered anyway and suffered serious casualties. From a force of perhaps 5,000, the casualty rate was above 70 per cent. No quarter was given and the wounded were left to die. The fact that they were seen as rebels, that they had reportedly not offered quarter at Prestonpans and that Cumberland claimed the next day that the Jacobites had been ordered not to offer quarter themselves at Culloden were used to justify the slaughter.

Cumberland was to spend the next few months in 'pacifying' the Highlands.[24] The actions of his troops were undoubtedly on the severe side. Those found still to be bearing arms were summarily executed, although those who surrendered were treated more leniently. Charles Edward evaded capture and eventually made his way back to the exiled Stuart court in Rome. Many of his followers were not so fortunate. The presence of Cumberland's army allowed local scores to be settled. Rebels, real or perceived, were exposed to a scorched earth policy with houses burnt and possessions seized. It was this, as much as his behaviour at Culloden, that led to the nickname that Cumberland was to carry with him for the rest of his life: the Butcher. Nevertheless, when Cumberland finally left the Highlands and returned to London in late July 1746 he was welcomed as a hero. A general thanksgiving service was celebrated in English and Welsh churches at the start of October. Handel had, once more, composed music to mark the occasion and 'British William' was hailed for 'scouring rebellion and baffling proud France'.[25] The libretto of *Judas Maccabaeus*, composed in the summer of 1746 but not performed until the following year, was dedicated to Cumberland. Burrows argues that, although not directly influenced by the Scottish campaign, it did provide a means to channel public sentiment about Cumberland's victories, as well as complimenting the victor.[26] The tough

---

[22] Speck, *Butcher*, pp. 133–5.

[23] Duffy, *'45*, ch. 20, Speck, *Butcher*, ch. 6.

[24] Duffy, *'45*, pp. 527–34.

[25] Händel-Werke-Verzeichnis [HWV] 228 (Occasional Songs), no. 9. The text by John Lockman was first performed at Vauxhall Gardens.

[26] Donald Burrows, *Handel* (Oxford, 1994), pp. 290–1.

line that Cumberland had begun in the Highlands was continued after his departure and much blame was subsequently apportioned to him for it.

MORE MINISTERIAL DIFFICULTIES

The London political world to which Cumberland returned had been further shaken in his absence. The Old Corps Whigs had grumbled to each other throughout much of 1745 about the continued favour that Granville seemed to enjoy with George. Although no longer formally in power, Granville retained an influence in the closet that was difficult to ignore. Through the early months of 1745, Newcastle reported various occasions to both his brother and Hardwicke when he had been faced with an angry monarch and demands for Granville's return.[27] The extreme sensitivity that Newcastle felt about this is evident in Harrington's report from Hanover in late July 1745 that George had not complained much about his British ministers recently and he had only mentioned Granville once.[28] Despite Harrington's reassurances, George's absences in Hanover were never good for Newcastle's political equilibrium. He was willing to see opposition to his designs almost everywhere at the best of times – Hardwicke had to play an almost constant mediatory role between Newcastle and Pelham – but the inability to talk to George regularly served only to heighten his sense of impotence and his fears that policy was drifting along in directions that he disliked. His experiences with Harrington and Carteret during George's recent visits to the continent had made him doubly suspicious of what his brother secretary was doing. The situation at home was little better. Bath, Stair and Tweeddale were constantly opposing the Pelhams on the regency council, suggesting, for example, that the rebellion was not nearly as serious as Newcastle had believed it to be.

George was not best pleased that he had been forced to return to Britain earlier than planned. His anger focused, not unnaturally, on the Pelhams and there is some evidence that he began to think more actively about doing something to rid himself of his apparent dependence on them. His views on the Old Corps had not changed as he continued to make clear to them. The fact that not just Newcastle but Henry Pelham, usually less prone to hysterical over-reaction than his brother, also noted the difficulty of their meetings with the king in the closet is evidence of the seriousness of the Pelhams' plight. George had two options for forming an alternative administration. One was to turn to Bath and Granville. The other was to see if Harrington might be persuaded to ditch his erstwhile allies and organize an administration on his own account. Harrington

---

[27] Owen, *Pelhams*, pp. 275–6.
[28] Harrington to Newcastle, Hanover, 26/7/1745 NS, private, BL, Add. MSS 32704, fo. 476v.

refused to co-operate but George's clear animosity to the Pelhams remained. Chesterfield had been urging Newcastle for some time to take a stand but the seriousness of the rebellion meant that a confrontation was postponed, if only temporarily.[29]

The rebellion served to focus minds during the parliamentary session which began in mid-October. George, aware perhaps of the difficulty of managing the Commons, moderated his tone towards the Pelhams. Nevertheless, he was still willing to make his views known when he felt that something of pressing concern was being debated. One of the responses to the crisis in Scotland had been a proposal from the duke of Bedford that the nobility might raise their own regiments and, when they were about half complete, the government take over the costs of them. As a means of raising troops, the plan had some merits but the devil was in the detail. Bedford wanted the regiment's proprietor to be able to pick his own officers: some might come from the regular army but some might simply be members of the local gentry. This proposal sparked fears that it would become an easy means by which nobles could help their friends and relations gain rank without having to go through the formal, and more regulated, mechanisms of gaining a commission. A portion of those in the Commons with military connections put forward an address to require that only those with commissions in the regular army were granted rank. George was very much in favour of this and let it be known. The resulting Commons vote revealed a majority of only two against this amendment. The Pelhams promptly put pressure on George to change his views, which he did, grudgingly, and the proposal was defeated with a larger majority when it was raised again.[30]

Matters came to a head in early February 1746. George remained resistant to any accommodation with Pitt. The Pelhams, however, thought that it was worth negotiating with him, in an effort to build up their strength in the Commons. The king once more made tentative approaches to Bath about the possibility of a rival administration. Bath, basking in his newly found favour, told Harrington that George would never accept Pitt as secretary at war. Stung by yet another overt display of disapprobation and conscious that Cumberland's reports that the Scottish situation was now under control would probably lead to the re-emergence of open warfare in the closet, Harrington, Hardwicke, Newcastle and Pelham gathered at Hardwicke's on 9 February to plot their next move. The scheme they determined upon was that of collective resignation. Harrington and Newcastle met George to resign their seals on 10 February, blaming Bath's growing influence.[31] The day after saw Pelham and Bedford follow suit. Chesterfield made clear his support for the walk-out. Hardwicke indicated

[29] Owen, *Pelhams*, pp. 279–82.

[30] Ibid., pp. 287–8 and Speck, *Butcher*, pp. 72–4.

[31] Newcastle to Chesterfield, Newcastle House, 10/2/1746 OS, BL, Add. MSS 32706, fo. 136.

that he would retire at the end of the legal term. A number of others indicated a willingness to support the Old Corps over the king, seemingly without much in the way of prior collusion.

George turned to Granville and Bath, perhaps more in dogged hope than really believing that they would be able to form a stable administration. They could not, despite Bath suggesting that the prince of Wales might be able to bring in sufficient Tories to make the administration viable. That was a bridge too far for George. He had been too indoctrinated with the Whig view that most Tories were closet Jacobites to entertain the idea of a Tory administration seriously. Additionally, the prospect of having to rely on his son's intervention was hardly an appealing one. The City made its feelings about the political disruption abundantly clear. There was a run on the Bank and a loan of £3 million that was to be advanced to cope with the costs of the war evaporated.[32]

Of the three ministerial crises that George had endured in the last four years, being forced to bring back the Pelhams was probably the most frustrating and humiliating. The Pelhams set conditions upon their return. They wanted to have guarantees that George would show his favour and confidence in them publicly. One way of doing this was to be through the disposal of the vacancies in the knighthood of the Garter to appropriate individuals; another was that any remaining supporters of Granville and Bath were to be removed from office. Pitt would have to be found office and George had to support the Pelhams when it came to foreign policy. Some of these demands were met but George managed to assert himself in other areas. He continued to refuse Pitt's appointment as secretary at war and Pitt received instead a well-paid but not particularly important post as vice-treasurer of Ireland. The king was also able to resist attempts to remove members of his household. The Finch brothers, Edward and William, sons of the Hanover Tory, the earl of Nottingham, retained their posts at George's insistence.[33] Both were diplomats cum MPs who had risen through Granville's patronage, although they wisely switched allegiance to the Pelhams after 1746.[34]

POLITICAL ACCOMMODATION AT LAST?

After the trials and tribulations of the early months of 1746, it might have been expected that the period of high political instability would continue: the Pelhams were still the Pelhams, after all. George seems, however, grudgingly, to have reached an accommodation with them that at least

[32] Owen, *Pelhams*, pp. 294–7, Reed Browning, *The duke of Newcastle* (New Haven and London, 1975), pp. 133–4.

[33] Newcastle to Chesterfield, Newcastle House, 15/2/1746 OS, private, BL, Add. MSS 32706, fo. 172r.

[34] For Edward Finch's earlier diplomatic career, see Andrew C. Thompson, *Britain, Hanover and the Protestant interest, 1688–1756* (Woodbridge, 2006), pp. 103–7.

allowed for a viable working relationship. The reasons behind this change of heart were several. George may well have realized that there were occasions on which he needed to beat a tactical retreat. His disputes with the Old Corps had been conducted on the basis that they wanted open displays of royal favour precisely because they still believed that this was a necessary condition of a stable administration. The Pelhams were not ideologically opposed to the exercise of prerogative powers. Rather, like all contemporary politicians, they wanted to ensure that it was exercised for their benefit. Thus, the strings of patronage were still a powerful means both of binding politicians to the court and of emphasizing the continuing centrality of the monarch. It might almost be said that George's seemingly endless battles with politicians over the previous few years had given him a better sense of what was and, more significantly, what was not achievable, leading to an increase in his political and tactical savvy.

Owen places much emphasis on the importance of having a single figure who was both 'Minister for the King in the House of Commons' and 'Minister for the House of Commons in the closet'. Walpole had been the last figure to hold both roles and Henry Pelham was to emerge as the next after the crisis of February 1746.[35] There is something to this, although even in Owen's careful formulation there is still a sense of the incipient supremacy of the Commons over all other branches of government that was to be the keystone of nineteenth-century Whig accounts. What was probably more important for George was not finding a Commons manager with whom he could do business but the discovery that Newcastle's foreign political aims and his own were not necessarily that different.

Newcastle's reasonably constant refrain since the start of the war had been that not enough was being done to help Maria Theresa and that all British efforts should be concentrated against France. In this context, Frederick's Prussia was a distraction on a number of levels. Frederick continually refused to play the role allotted to him within British foreign political thinking as a potentially useful ally against France.[36] His irritating habit of quickly shifting sides made him difficult to assimilate into a system and the threat that Prussia posed to Hanover had a complicating effect on all of George's calculations because of his understandable concern for the security of his German, as well as his British, territories. Newcastle had bemoaned the diverting impact of 'Hanoverian measures' on a number of occasions and had been perfectly happy to take advantage of the upsurge of anti-Hanoverian sentiment to marginalize Granville. The treaty of Dresden had, however, altered the situation considerably. With Prussia again out of the war, George's fears for Hanover's security diminished and Newcastle's pro-Austrian stance became closer to the king's own.

[35] Owen, *Pelhams*, p. 298.
[36] The problems that Frederick's advent on the European scene posed for Britain are explored at greater length in Thompson, *Britain, Hanover*, pp. 193–9.

Leaving aside the Jacobite rebellion, the military situation elsewhere in the war had been mixed. While still in Hanover in the summer of 1745, George had received the good news that a naval expedition under Commodore Peter Warren had succeeded in capturing the French fortress of Louisburg at Cape Breton in Nova Scotia. Although there had been a small number of British regular troops involved, much of the force had been made up of militia forces, recruited from Britain's North American colonies. The impetus for the attack came largely from the governor of Massachusetts, William Shirley, who was concerned about the threat that the French presence posed to the Newfoundland cod banks. The victory, which Shirley subsequently hoped might prove to be the stepping stone for further British intervention with more regular troops in Canada, was hugely popular with the British public. It also enhanced the reputation of those involved – Warren was promoted rear-admiral and Shirley became the colonel of a British regiment to be recruited in the colonies.[37] The conflict in North America was known there, although not elsewhere, as 'King George's war' which is ironic because its successes were of little interest to the king.

Elsewhere there was less reason for optimism. Although Prussia's withdrawal from the war left open the possibility of a greater concentration of British and Hanoverian forces on the conflict in the Low Countries, there were other difficulties. One was that the United Provinces remained nominally neutral. Dutch troops were involved in defence of the Barrier fortresses but otherwise their direct military contribution was slight. Disputes over the command of what had originally been the Pragmatic army continued, as did the concerns of Newcastle and Pelham that the British taxpayer was not getting value for money, particularly from the Austrian troops that were being employed using British subsidies. Additionally, the Marshal de Saxe was enjoying considerable success. Brussels fell in February 1746 and Mons was taken by the French in July. The British desire to defend the Barrier fortresses did not seem to be shared by their erstwhile allies and thoughts in London slowly began to turn towards the desirability of a negotiated settlement.[38]

The timing of any settlement was always going to be difficult and it would prove to be a further cause of tension within the administration in London. The French put out some tentative feelers about a peace deal in the spring of 1746. The merits of making an immediate peace, following an approach from the marquis d'Argenson, the French foreign minister, were strongly argued for by Harrington, with some support from Chesterfield and Robert Trevor, whose service in the United Provinces made them highly sceptical about the prospect of any real support being forthcoming from the Dutch. Newcastle, Hardwicke and Pelham argued

---

[37] Brendan Simms, *Three victories and a defeat* (London, 2007), pp. 344–5.
[38] Anderson, *War of the Austrian succession*, pp. 156–8.

that a continuation of the war efforts was essential.[39] How far this new bellicose pose was a product of an Old Corps desire to retain favour in the closet is uncertain. George's opinions on the matter had been made abundantly clear to Newcastle and Harrington, however. Newcastle reported to Hardwicke that he and Harrington had engaged in an extensive discussion with George about what to do. The tone of Newcastle's report could not have been more different from his relatively recent descriptions of royal behaviour. Gone are the complaints of rudeness and ill temper. Instead, on this occasion, Newcastle noted the 'great Decency' with which George had behaved. Crucially, this good conduct was coupled with strong support for Newcastle's views, despite Harrington's protests that if peace were not made now, then the Dutch would go ahead and negotiate a separate settlement, once more leaving Hanover exposed to the risk of French invasion. Even the invocation of a threat to Hanoverian security failed to move the king.[40]

In addition to concerns about the European situation, the summer of 1746 provided George with a delicate case of whether to make use of prerogative powers at home. The aftermath of the Jacobite rising had to be dealt with. George had to consider several appeals for clemency from those condemned to death for their participation in the rebellion. Arthur Elphinstone, sixth Lord Balmerino, William Boyd, fourth earl of Kilmarnock and George Mackenzie, third earl of Cromarty had all been put on trial. As peers, they were tried for treason before the House of Lords in late July 1746. The results of the trial were guilty verdicts in all cases, with the death sentence passed. Newcastle had kept the king informed of the unfolding of proceedings, writing to George as soon as the verdict was known. George, as he did so often, simply returned Newcastle's note with his own comments on the bottom, remarking that he was 'very glad this tedious affair is over, and every thing, that is done, to shew humanity, without preventing justice is proper'.[41] Appeals for mercy were subsequently lodged, as well as requests that the executions might be deferred, even if they were not abandoned. Cromarty was saved – his wife and various other magnates intervened successfully on his behalf. The other two, however, were executed. George resisted any attempt to postpone the executions, writing to Newcastle to confirm his agreement with Hardwicke's position: 'whenever criminals are reprieved, it allways looks like a hardship when they are executed afterwards, and every one of them will try as they can to gain as much time as is possible'.[42]

[39] The differences between the two groups are highlighted in Newcastle to Poyntz, Newcastle House, 23/5/1746 OS, BL, Add. MSS 32707, fo. 237.

[40] Newcastle to Hardwicke, Newcastle House, 21/5/1746 OS, BL, Add. MSS 35408, fo. 224.

[41] Newcastle to George, Whitehall, 1/8/1746, BL, Add. MSS 32708, fos 1–2. Newcastle's note carries the additional designation 'Friday, 3 pm'.

[42] George's note on the rebel lords' petition, no date [but late July/early August 1746], BL, Add. MSS 32707, fo. 492v.

The war in the Low Countries continued to go badly in the summer of 1746. Chesterfield and Harrington were still pressing for peace and Henry Pelham, aware of the growing costs of the war and the increasing size of the national debt, now seemed keener on a settlement. Various peace plans had been floated but George's irritation with these moves seemed to focus increasingly on Harrington. It was reported by Chesterfield that George had been particularly irked that Harrington had flung down his seals when he had resigned in February. George, who had raised Harrington to the peerage, considered this sort of behaviour extremely ungrateful.[43] Harrington himself was feeling ever more marginalized. He suspected that although he was secretary for the northern department and consequently responsible for relations with the United Provinces, Newcastle was carrying on a correspondence with the earl of Sandwich, George's representative in The Hague. Newcastle was doing so, although it was not uncommon for secretaries, especially those with pretensions to be the senior of the two, to maintain contacts with a broad range of diplomats both within and without their provinces. Harrington raised the matter with the king in an audience in late October. George responded that Newcastle was within his rights to conduct correspondence with foreign courts through whatever channel he chose. Harrington felt piqued and offered his resignation, which the king accepted with alacrity.[44]

The question of who should replace Harrington was an interesting one. The Old Corps feared that, despite the growing signs of confidence they had received, George would turn back to Granville when presented with an opportunity like this. Instead, Newcastle was pleasantly surprised to discover during his audience with the king immediately after Harrington's resignation that George thought that Chesterfield might make a reasonable successor to Harrington. Chesterfield's relationship with George had gone through its ups and downs over the years, from loyal household servant as prince of Wales through opposition in the 1730s, disputes over his wife's inheritance to cheerleader for anti-Hanoverianism in the early 1740s. Chesterfield had even commented to the earl of Marchmont that George's failure to rid himself of the Pelhams had led him to resolve to meddle little and leave the important decisions to the ministers because he was incapable of making them himself. He had also suggested that George was only in favour of the war when things seemed to be going well; as soon as somebody indicated that the war was ruining the country, his attitude changed.[45] Despite Chesterfield's confidence in his ability to mould George, his appointment did not proceed until he had offered certain

---

[43] G.H. Rose, ed., *A selection from the papers of the earls of Marchmont* (3 vols, London, 1831), i, pp. 182–3.

[44] Ibid., p. 184.

[45] Ibid., p. 181.

assurances about his willingness to abandon his pacifism in favour of the active prosecution of the war that the king wanted.[46]

From the Pelhamite perspective, 1746 had been a year of successful consolidation. George, on the other hand, had had a more difficult few months. His attempts to bring Granville and Bath back into government had failed and he had been forced to turn back to the Pelhams. Newcastle's shift towards his foreign political views was helpful but the military situation remained worrying. Both at home and abroad, it would remain troubling into the next year.

PROSECUTING THE WAR AND PRESSURE FOR PEACE

Domestically, 1747 marked a return to form. The relative quiescence of the prince of Wales came to an end with signals that Frederick was once more thinking about gathering a formed parliamentary opposition. Frederick made advances to the Tories in the hope that some arrangement could be made. The reversionary interest was back in business and an air of almost normality had returned to politics. As Henry Pelham remarked to Dudley Ryder in March 1747, reporting Frederick's own comments, 'there was no way for the Prince of Wales to make a figure here but in war or by opposition. He, being precluded from the former, would use the latter.'[47]

Although the composition of Frederick's new opposition did not have the stellar qualities of its previous incarnation in the late 1730s, it was considered sufficiently worrying to require action on the ministry's part. The expedient that was used was to dissolve parliament at the end of 1747 and hold a general election before the prince had had the opportunity to organize properly. The tactic seemed to work. Once all the dust had settled, the administration secured 351 seats to 92 for opposition Whigs and 115 Tories. The election featured fewer contests than in 1741 – indeed, there were only 62 contested seats, the lowest number of any election in the period – suggesting an opposition unwilling or, more probably, unprepared to take on the government.[48] Even in Cornwall, where Frederick might have suspected that his interest would be strongest, a total of 27 opposition MPs from the previous parliament fell to a mere 19.[49]

The calling of an early election had, however, been one of the few points of agreement between Newcastle and his brother in early 1747. Foreign policy continued to divide them, with Newcastle's reinvigorated attachment to continental involvement in stark contrast to the fiscal concerns of his brother. The Dutch remained as reluctant to commit

[46] Owen, *Pelhams*, p. 305.

[47] Quoted in Romney Sedgwick, *The House of Commons, 1715–1754* (2 vols, London, 1970), i, p. 57.

[48] Figures ibid., p. 57. Owen, *Pelhams*, p. 317 gives a slightly lower figure for the number of ministerial MPs, based on material in the Newcastle papers.

[49] Owen, *Pelhams*, p. 315.

forces as before. However, they found themselves with little choice in the matter as Saxe, now raised to the rank of 'Marshal General of the King's camps and armies',[50] proceeded to wreak havoc in the Low Countries. Saxe invaded the United Provinces and quickly took most of Dutch Flanders. He had wanted to do so after his successes of the previous year but d'Argenson's hopes of an early peace had frustrated the plan. His actions now did much to bring the war to a speedy conclusion.[51]

Saxe's advances into the United Provinces awoke the Dutch from their apathy. Their anger, as it had in 1672 when Louis XIV had invaded, was turned against the patrician republican elite. Tough times called for a real leader and in the ensuing panic, the Grand Pensionary, chief minister of Holland and Zeeland, turned to the Orange family for help. Within a matter of weeks, William found himself elected admiral and captain-general, as well as becoming Stadtholder of all seven of the provinces that made up the country. Anne travelled with her husband to Amsterdam, although they had to make the journey by land because the yacht that William's home province of Friesland had given them as a wedding gift had been reclaimed in an effort to cut costs.[52] Despite George's careful policy of trying to ensure that there was little overt interference in Dutch politics, he clearly viewed the accession of his daughter's husband to the post of Stadtholder as beneficial for British interests. When popular unrest had first manifested itself in Zeeland in April 1747, a British naval squadron had been rapidly dispatched to the Scheldt to support what was to become a populist Orange coup. George's support was not uncondi-tional, though. He was anxious to ensure that his son-in-law was aware of George's system and war aims.[53]

Despite the Dutch revolution, the military situation remained discour-aging. Saxe was not forced back and he continued to harry the Barrier fortresses. He defeated an allied army commanded by Cumberland at Laufeldt in July 1747. French casualties were heavy and the reports of the conduct of the British and even the Hanoverian troops were generally favourable.[54] Blame, however, fell on the Dutch. Unsurprisingly, the conduct of their troops was denounced in the British press. Yet even Cumberland was moved to write that they seemed to be of limited value.[55] Although Cumberland was able to prevent Saxe from seizing Maastricht in the aftermath of his defeat, other fortress-towns succumbed to the

[50] The title had been used on two previous occasions: in the last months of the life of Louis XIV's commander the maréchal de Villars and for Henri, viscomte de Turenne (Anderson, *War of the Austrian succession*, p. 171).

[51] Ibid., p. 172.

[52] Baker-Smith, *Royal discord*, p.145.

[53] Newcastle to Sandwich, Newcastle House, 28/4/1747 OS, private, BL, Add. MSS 32807, fo. 142v.

[54] Simms, *Three victories*, p. 348.

[55] Baker-Smith, *Royal discord*, pp. 146–7.

advancing French. The key centre of Bergen-op-Zoom fell in September.
When Cumberland visited his sister and brother-in-law in The Hague in
the autumn of 1747 he made his thoughts on the quality of Dutch troops
extremely clear, causing Anne to be embarrassed and her husband to
engage in long justifications of his conduct.

The deteriorating military situation was causing further strain on
the relationships between George's ministers in London. Despite his reassurances that he was willing to back the war, Chesterfield, along with
Pelham, was arguing forcefully for making peace because he did not
believe that the resources could be found for another campaign. Newcastle
thought that things were not as bad as Chesterfield claimed and favoured
taking advantage of every opportunity to plan and prepare for the next
campaign season. Hardwicke, treading a fine line between the two groups,
was keen that a reasonable set of peace proposals should be drafted while
simultaneously continuing the preparations for war.[56]

Part of the problem for George and his ministers was that Saxe's military successes were slowly but surely enhancing France's bargaining power
and diminishing their own. Louis XV, who had observed some of Saxe's
battles during the campaigns in the Low Countries, was not particularly
interested in retaining control of Flanders. What did matter, though, was
what he could exchange Flanders for at the negotiating table. The British
had one more card to play. Negotiations had already been under way in St
Petersburg to try to engage Russia as a source of auxiliary troops, paid for
as always by British gold, to tip the balance in the conflict. Agreement was
eventually reached, first for Russian troops to be used in eastern Europe to
remind Frederick of the inadvisability of making any moves against
Hanover and then, in November 1747, for Russian troops to be used in
western Europe. It was too little too late. By the time the Russians had
started their ponderous march westwards, the Dutch were on the point of
collapse and serious negotiations to bring the war to an end began.[57]

Negotiations had been ongoing at various points since October 1746
between Britain and France in the Dutch town of Breda but these
were now transferred to Aachen and resumed with renewed intensity.
Sandwich, who represented British interests, found that the only settlement to which the French were prepared to agree was one based on the
mutual restitution of conquests between Britain and France, so Louisburg
was returned to France, although the British regained Madras. From the
strategic point of view, Louis XV had agreed to evacuate the Low
Countries, deemed by both ministers and king to be crucial to British security, but the return of Louisburg angered 'blue water' pamphleteers who
felt that Britain's destiny lay elsewhere.[58]

---

[56] Newcastle to Cumberland, Newcastle House, 12/9/1747 OS, BL, Add. MSS 35409,
fos 105–10.
[57] Anderson, *War of the Austrian succession*, pp. 175–7.
[58] Simms, *Three victories*, pp. 350–4.

MANAGING THE KING?

One of the other casualties of the final months of the war was Chesterfield. His health had not been good when he accepted the seals in October 1746 and the struggles with Newcastle over the conduct of the war had taken a significant mental and physical toll. By early 1748 he had had enough and resigned on 10 February. He had the dubious pleasure of learning of the complete collapse of Dutch resistance, which he had long predicted, shortly after his departure from office. Chesterfield was able to observe the king at close quarters during his period as secretary of state and was later to write a character of the king, giving his considered views on George.[59] However, the contemporary comments captured by Hugh Hume Campbell, third earl of Marchmont, in his diary are also of interest.

Marchmont had an audience with the king himself in September 1747 as part of his attempts to remind the king that he had been a strong supporter of Cumberland's recent measures to 'pacify' Scotland in the aftermath of the rebellion. Marchmont had found George in taciturn mood and came away from the meeting somewhat nonplussed.[60] When he described his recent experience to Chesterfield, the latter remarked that Marchmont should not take the king's behaviour too much to heart. George, Chesterfield explained, had no real sentimental attachments to anybody and he 'went on with his ministers, because he saw they had the superiority; that if he liked anybody, it was Lord Granville, who carried on his business agreeable to his views, and in the manner he liked; but that he had no support. He said, the King was resolved to be quiet, and that he was an old man, and did not care how he left things to him, who was to succeed him.'[61] Chesterfield also remarked that it was difficult to get any business done on 'public days' (those when George held drawing rooms) because the king was anxious not to be kept from the assembled company where he assiduously spoke to all those women that he knew.[62] He also claimed that George was overly dependent on first impressions when it came to assessing character.[63]

Whilst the king may have fulfilled his obligations to court ritual with his habitual thoroughness, Marchmont recorded the frustrations of some of his other ministers, like Chesterfield, in their dealings with him. Yet Newcastle was reporting to Hardwicke how much easier he now found the king. Part of the reason for this may have related to Pelham's reported complaint that Newcastle always avoided asking the difficult questions in

---

[59] There is a MS version of these in the British Library (BL Stowe 308, fos 3–5). They were published in *Characters of eminent persons* (London, 1777). See pp. 291–2 for a full discussion of Chesterfield's character.

[60] Rose, ed., *Marchmont papers*, i, p. 189. The date of entry is 1/9/1747.

[61] Ibid., p. 197.

[62] Ibid., p. 198.

[63] Ibid., p. 225.

the closet, leaving his brother to deal with them instead.[64] Marchmont's diary also bears witness to the continuing worries of the Old Corps that George was still under Granville's sway in some way. Edward Finch, who it will be recalled had managed to retain his household place following the ministerial crisis of 1746, was singled out as the conduit by which Granville's views were transmitted to the monarch. The method is also noteworthy. As a courtier, Finch was frequently involved in George's card games during the evening and, once they were both out, there were plenty of opportunities for the two of them to gossip and cabal in the corners of the room.[65] This highlights both Old Corps worries about the ability to control the king and the continuing importance of the court as a venue for the conduct of politics. The distinction between courtiers and politicians remained blurred.

A final aspect of Marchmont's diary reinforces this point. On a few occasions Marchmont reported Lady Yarmouth's views and opinions. Once she was simply the agent for the transmission of the king's own views, letting it be known that George really did think that he had no power, reinforcing the impression of him being a prisoner of the whims of his ministers.[66] This perception could, of course, be useful to a number of interested parties, including the king himself. From the point of view of a minister, like Chesterfield, Newcastle or Walpole, to suggest that the king was open to influence, either directly in the closet or through his wife or mistress, was to create an impression of their own power and importance over and against that of the king. It enhanced their credentials within the patronage system, making them more sought after as patrons and interme-diaries. From the king's perspective, letting all and sundry know how trapped he felt might be a useful tool if he ever did want to engineer a change of administration, as well as setting down the parameters within which he would expect any alternative set of ministers to operate. Lady Yarmouth's own position as a potential conduit to George herself was also served by reporting such royal complaints.

Yet even Lady Yarmouth's influence was not without its limits. Marchmont also recorded that the countess seemed to be able to exert a moderating influence on George in some respects, but not in others. When George was angry with Frederick, Lady Yarmouth apparently spoke up for him, urging George not to go too far. The king responded that 'she was always speaking for that puppy' but paid some attention to her views. Talking of the dangers posed to Hanover by the continuation of the war was another matter. George refused to listen to her and became irritated with her for raising it.[67] Marchmont was probably interested in the last anecdote

[64] Ibid., p. 219.
[65] Ibid., p. 224.
[66] Ibid.
[67] Ibid., p. 275.

because it seemed to confirm the popular view that George was always much more concerned about Hanoverian affairs than British. The king's irritation may have been related to the perceived unwarranted interference in Electoral affairs. He may also have suspected that Lady Yarmouth had been influenced by a British minister, who hoped that placing Hanoverian security at the forefront of discussions about the continuation of hostilities might win George round to a more pacific viewpoint.

The difficulties of 'managing' George, as the Pelhams would have seen it, were manifested again when it came to finding a suitable replacement for Chesterfield as secretary of state. Newcastle suggested to Sandwich that he was a possible candidate, although how seriously this was meant is an open question, given Sandwich's youth.[68] Newcastle may have favoured him for his potential pliability but he told Sandwich that, despite support from Cumberland and himself, it would be better to have some-body with less warlike inclinations if the coalition of old and new Whigs was to be kept together. Instead, Newcastle sought Sandwich's advice as to how best to keep on good terms with Sandwich's patron, John Russell, fourth duke of Bedford.[69] Sandwich and Bedford had both come into the ministry following Granville's departure. Bedford had become first lord of the admiralty, although much of the daily administration had fallen on Sandwich's desk as his deputy. Bedford was ultimately to be given the post of southern secretary, with Newcastle swapping to the northern post vacated by Chesterfield. However, Newcastle continued to cultivate Sandwich as a useful diplomatic contact. He was quick to warn Sandwich of the importance of keeping open a direct channel of communication with him and his instructions on how this should be achieved show the close interest that George took in the routine management of foreign affairs. If Sandwich had any point or observation that he wanted to keep for Newcastle's eyes only, then it had to be included in a separate letter because 'the King very often asks me, if I have any private letters from you, and sometimes, there are many things, that I would willingly shew, and am prevented by one, or two Points flung in, which would be more properly put in a Letter by Themselves'.[70]

PEACE

Newcastle was to remain a little unsure of his new colleague: Bedford's temper could make him difficult to deal with, but when he had calmed

[68] In fairness to Newcastle's sincerity, it should be noted that Bedford also professed the view that Sandwich was a reasonable candidate for the secretaryship but was simply unacceptable at the moment. Bedford to Sandwich, 12/2/1748, Lord John Russell, intro, to *Correspondence of John, fourth duke of Bedford with an introduction by Lord John Russell* (3 vols, London, 1842–6), i, p. 323.

[69] Newcastle to Sandwich, Newcastle House, 12/2/1748 OS, private, BL, Add. MSS 32811, fos 213–14.

[70] Idem to idem, Newcastle House, 19/2/1748 OS, private, ibid., fo. 239r.

down it was often easier to make him see reason. Newcastle also felt that maintaining good relations with the duchess of Bedford would be important. The process of peacemaking threw up difficulties of various sorts along the way. The main issue in relation to the king was where he would want to spend the summer. George's last trip to Hanover had been three years ago and Newcastle and Hardwicke began to get jittery about the consequences of his desire to travel abroad again. At the start of April Hardwicke reported that he had seen George in the closet and found him to be annoyed by various things. Interestingly, though, Hardwicke noted that although George interposed on several occasions, he mainly listened to Hardwicke's views and his anger was not as passionate or violent as had often been the case. Nor had the king given any indication that he would definitely travel to Hanover.[71]

By the end of April, Newcastle was writing to Hardwicke apologizing for not having had the chance to have a private conversation with him when they had last seen each other. Newcastle was keen to convey the substance of his recent audience, in which the king had made clear that he would be going to Hanover. Newcastle had thought it best not to demur and had actually been rather pleased when George had indicated that Newcastle should stay in London because he 'could direct things more as He liked'.[72] The problem with this was that, given their previous experience of George's willingness to intervene personally in diplomacy when abroad and the difficulties of controlling the secretary who travelled with the king, Newcastle thought it would be much better if he travelled with George instead. There were also more immediate fears. Negotiations for the peace settlement might be derailed if George decided to meddle, and Bedford might use the chance of a summer with the king to promote his own position at the expense of the Pelhams. For all these reasons, Newcastle worked hard to convince George that he should have the honour of accompanying him, to which the king eventually agreed. Newcastle could not, however, depart as soon as George wanted so Newcastle's private secretary Andrew Stone, who was also an under-secretary of state, was given the task of travelling with the king and managing things for Newcastle until he could make the journey himself.[73]

George left London after the end of the parliamentary session in May. A set of preliminaries for peace had already been agreed at Aachen, allowing for a ceasefire six weeks after they had been signed. The delayed cessation of hostilities allowed the French to take Maastricht, reinforcing their superiority in the Low Countries. George stopped very briefly on his way to visit Anne and William. Despite the difficulties that the United Provinces had faced politically and militarily in recent months, they were

[71] Hardwicke to Newcastle, Powis House, 2/4/1748 OS, BL, Add. MSS 32714, fo. 420.
[72] Newcastle to Hardwicke, Newcastle House, 30/4/1748 OS, BL, Add. MSS 35409, fo. 159r.
[73] Browning, *Newcastle*, pp. 151–2.

rejoicing in the birth of a son, who, it was hoped, would ensure the survival of the Orange dynasty. Anne had lost a number of children already and republican critics were quick to cast doubt on the child's paternity. Nevertheless, Anne devoted considerable attention to William Jr, even taking the unusual step for a person of her rank of feeding him herself.[74] Charles Bentinck told Newcastle that George had met the princess royal in the street and had engaged William in a twenty-minute conversation in Utrecht before pressing on because he was, as always, anxious to complete the journey.[75]

Following his arrival in Hanover, George decided to inspect his Hanoverian troops and summoned nearly 9,000 for that purpose. As so often happened, George's arrival in the Electorate triggered a series of visits from local princes and members of his family. His daughter Mary joined him for the summer, as did her father-in-law, Prince William of Hessen-Kassel.[76] Cumberland hoped to join his father but the demands of over-seeing the army in the Low Countries kept him busy for much of George's visit. Newcastle journeyed to Hanover with his wife, stopping for consultations in the United Provinces as he did so. A mere twenty-four years after becoming a secretary of state with responsibility for foreign affairs he was making his first trip outside Britain. Andrew Stone reported his safe arrival in Hanover to Hardwicke at the start of July, noting that his master had found it necessary to make the journey out to Herrenhausen sooner than he had expected after his dinner because the court hours were earlier in the Electorate than in London. Stone was mildly irritated that Newcastle's baggage, which had been sent by sea to Bremen rather than following a land route, had not yet arrived because it contained all the duke's plate as well as, more importantly, a spare trunk of clothes for Stone.[77]

Amidst the ongoing deliberations at Aachen, Newcastle and the king also had to consider relations with Prussia and Austria. Early in 1748, Henry Legge, an MP associated with Bedford and member of the admiralty board, had been selected to undertake a mission to Frederick.[78] Newcastle had chosen him partly because he thought that Bedford and Sandwich would approve. The original hope had been that Frederick might be persuaded to put pressure on France to conclude a peace treaty but the various delays caused by Chesterfield's departure, a trip to The

[74] Baker-Smith, *Royal discord*, p. 148.

[75] Bentinck to Newcastle, The Hague, 4/6/1748 NS, BL, Add. MSS 32812, fo. 238. Charles was the younger brother of William Bentinck. The pair were advisers to the Orange family and were sons of William III's minister Hans Willem Bentinck, first earl of Portland by his second wife. When their half-brother had inherited the English title and estates in 1709, they had returned to the United Provinces.

[76] NHStA, Dep. 103, IV, 324, fos 137–8.

[77] Stone to Hardwicke, Hanover, 9/7/1748 NS, BL, Add. MSS 35409, fo. 175.

[78] For a detailed discussion of the mission, see Richard Lodge, 'The mission of Henry Legge to Berlin, 1748', *Transactions of the Royal Historical Society*, 4th series, 14 (1931), pp. 1–38.

Hague to persuade the Dutch to guarantee Frederick's possession of Silesia, an interlude in Aachen to discover from Sandwich the areas in which Prussian pressure might be useful and a stop in Hanover to discuss the situation with Münchhausen meant that the preliminaries were signed shortly after Legge finally reached Berlin.

Legge's desire to incorporate Prussia into Britain's system of alliances was one that was shared in certain quarters in London but such an agreement, in Newcastle's view, could not come at the expense of sacrificing relations with Austria. Newcastle showed, perhaps unwittingly, a greater degree of diplomatic insight than Legge in this respect. His concern was that Frederick was trying to split Britain from Austria and in this he was probably right.[79] Legge's mission had, in any case, provoked Maria Theresa's anger. Not only did Britain seem to be negotiating a separate deal with France but the hand of friendship had also been extended to the house of Habsburg's arch-enemy. Frederick had, however, tried to entice his uncle into an agreement by offering support for his pretensions to incorporate the bishoprics of Osnabrück and Hildesheim into Hanover. Backing for Hanoverian claims to Osnabrück was particularly attractive. The right to appoint alternate bishops of Osnabrück had been one of the few gains that the Guelphs had made in 1648 (it had been the foundation from which George's grandfather had built up his branch of the family) but permanent incorporation would mean that George could provide lands for Cumberland, for example, in his own right. Newcastle's suspicions of Frederick's intentions were shared by Münchhausen. Legge found himself blamed for exceeding his authority in talking to Frederick about Hanoverian matters and sidelined politically. It cannot have helped his cause that it was rumoured that he had remarked that George's arrival in Hanover had spoilt the prospects of a successful negotiation with Berlin.[80]

MARKING VICTORY

One of the chief fruits of George's 1748 visit to Hanover was the friendship that was to develop between Newcastle and Gerlach Adolf von Münchhausen, the leading minister of the Electorate. As Uriel Dann has argued,[81] the two were temperamentally similar but also shared a political outlook that valued the importance of maintaining the existing system of alliances, especially the combination of George with the Habsburgs, and saw in this the means to restore stability to European politics. Beyond the personal rapport that the two built up during their summer encounters, a more permanent structural link was put in place between them in the

[79] See the concerns expressed in Newcastle to Robinson, Hanover, 16/7/1748 NS, private, BL, Add. MSS 32813, fo. 33v.

[80] Sedgwick, *House of Commons*, ii, p. 207, William Coxe, *Memoirs of the administration of the Right Honourable Henry Pelham* (2 vols, London, 1829), i, pp. 445–8.

[81] Dann, *Hanover*, p. 73.

aftermath of the visit. Ernst von Steinberg, the countess of Yarmouth's brother-in-law, who had taken responsibility for directing the Hanoverian chancery in London since 1737, decided that he wished to remain in Hanover after returning with George on this trip. He was replaced by Münchhausen's younger brother, Philipp, whose presence in London served to reinforce ties of friendship and co-operation.

Newcastle's experiences in 1748 gave him a sense of what George was like when he was in his 'country seat'. The recreational opportunities were something that Newcastle may have needed more encouragement than most to take advantage of.[82] Shortly after his arrival, George visited Hanover to inspect the new building works that were taking place in the town.[83] George used his 1748 visit to engage in an extensive tour of his Electoral domains. He visited Göttingen and saw the university there, named after himself. The 'Georgia Augusta' was, with some justification, also known as the 'Gerlacho Adolpho' in recognition of the significant role that Münchhausen had played in its foundation during the 1730s. Newcastle accompanied the king on this trip and was awarded an honorary degree by the university for his trouble. The students commemorated the royal visit by the production of a volume of panegyric material which George decided to present to the university library, along with various other volumes. Newcastle also added to the library's collections.[84] The visit had been orchestrated by Münchhausen and the Festschrift produced to mark the occasion strongly suggests that there was a propagandistic element to the visit.[85] The publication had been put together by Johann Lorenz Mosheim, one of the university's most eminent professors of theology and its first chancellor.[86] Mosheim wanted to portray George in a manner familiar from other iconographic descriptions. Emphasis was placed both on his Protestant credentials and on his hard-working attitude. In addition to the written propaganda, designed to boost George's reputation, Mosheim included descriptions of the visual means that had

---

[82] Writing to Newcastle when he transferred to the northern secretaryship in 1748, Charles Hanbury Williams told Newcastle that while the new job would make him very busy, 'don't entirely neglect yourself; Five days shalt thou labour hard, but the sixth & seventh (for I would have your Grace avail yourself of the Jewish as well as the Xtian Sabbath) Thou shalt rest at Claremont, and, if possible, do no manner of work' (Hanbury Williams to Newcastle, Dresden, 13/3/1748 NS, separate, BL, Add. MSS 32811, fo. 334v).

[83] General Evening Post, 2300, 18/6/1748.

[84] London Evening Post, 3241, 9/8/1748.

[85] Thomas Biskup, 'The university of Göttingen', in Brendan Simms and Torsten Riotte, eds, The Hanoverian dimension in British history, 1714–1837 (Cambridge, 2007), pp. 135–6.

[86] Johann Lorenz Mosheim, Beschreibung der grossen und denckwürdigen Feyer die bey der allerhöchsten Anwesenheit des allerdurchlauchtigsten, grossmächtigsten Fürsten und Herren, Herren Georg des Andern, Königes von Grossbritannien, Frankreich und Irrland, Beschützers des Glaubens, Herzoges zu Braunschweig-Lüneburg, des Heil. Röm. Reiches Ertzschatzmeisters und Churfürsten, auf deroselben Georg Augustus hohen Schule in der Stadt Göttingen im Jahr 1748. am ersten Tages des Augustmonates begangen ward (Göttingen, 1749). The very length of the title shows the extreme deference with which George was regarded by his Hanoverian subjects. Mosheim was a prolific theologian and church historian, some of whose works were translated into English.

been used to portray George in the best possible light. Two triumphal arches had been erected. One proclaimed the way in which German liberties had been preserved by the Dettingen victory. Another ascribed the preservation of the balance of power to George's astute political interventions.[87] The second theme, in particular, had featured prominently in Hanoverian accounts of the value of the personal union.[88] Münchhausen had defended the value of the connection between Britain and Hanover in similar terms.[89] Given Newcastle's presence on this visit, the thrust of the display was unlikely to have been coincidental.

Other aspects of the trip had a less didactic purpose. George took the opportunity to return to the Göhrde to indulge his passion for hunting. After the hunting trip in September, he made a short tour of the duchy of Lauenburg to the north-east of Hamburg which his father had acquired in 1702.[90] Newcastle joined Lady Yarmouth and various of George's Hanoverian courtiers for the hunting trip.[91] Back in Herrenhausen, George was able to wander in the gardens, and attended performances by his French comedians. Although the precise details of the plays performed are not known,[92] plans for the seating arrangements at some of the productions do survive. One depicts a plan of the stalls with George next to the countess of Yarmouth who is seated next to Ernst August, count von Bülow and then Newcastle. Count von Bülow was in almost constant attendance on George during his Hanoverian visits. He was a gentleman of the bedchamber and was to succeed formally to the title of senior gentleman (*Oberkammerherr*) in 1751. The other plan shows the arrangement of boxes, probably at the opera house. The two boxes in the centre were reserved for the king. Closest to the stage were boxes for the Austrian and Russian ministers on one side and for the Polish and Prussian on the other. A box for the Dutch minister was on the right of the king's, and boxes for various Hanoverian officials from both the administration and the court filled the remaining spaces.[93] Newcastle also witnessed the extensive celebrations that took place to mark both the anniversary of George's coronation and his birthday.[94] Initial reports had suggested that George would be back in London in time for his birthday but a combination of diplomatic activity and a degree of reluctance to return meant that he did not leave the Electorate until towards the end of November.

---

[87] Ibid., pp. 14–20.
[88] Thompson, *Britain, Hanover*, pp. 34–6.
[89] Dann, *Hanover*, p. 133.
[90] NHStA, Dep. 103, IV, 228, fos 14–15.
[91] Ibid., IV, 311, fo. 4r.
[92] For details of known productions in the period, see Rosenmarie Elisabeth Wallbrecht, *Das Theater des Barockzeitalters an den welfischen Höfen Hannover und Celle* (Hildesheim, 1974), pp. 218–29.
[93] NHStA, Dep. 103, IV, 300, fos 78 and 82.
[94] Ibid., IV, 324, fo. 137r.

Awareness of how George spent his summers was sketchy. Newspaper reports in 1748 were full of talk about when the treaty of Aachen would finally be signed.[95] The details of the king's movements were recorded, such as the journey to Lauenburg, as well as where Cumberland or Newcastle happened to be.[96] There were also rumours of various sorts floating around about the plans of George and his entourage. One report suggested that a marriage between Cumberland and a Prussian princess was imminent, as part of a treaty to support the Protestant interest.[97] Another that 'a Lady of great Distinction, at Hanover, will not return to England any more, but reside there for life'.[98] The obvious candidate for this rather opaque reference was Lady Yarmouth. Others speculated on when the king might return, using the possible recall of parliament or an increase in activity in tidying up at St James's Palace as possible indicators.[99] When the king eventually returned, the peace treaty had finally been signed at Aachen and the papers were full of analyses of its consequences.

The official celebrations to mark the conclusion of the peace were extremely elaborate. They were designed to be visually spectacular with fireworks and were accompanied by music, composed by Handel, which remains popular to this day. The event is therefore of interest in its own right but it has also been taken by some, notably John Brewer, as exemplifying the problems that court culture had run into by the middle of the eighteenth century.[100] The celebrations took some time to prepare. The treaty had been signed by Britain, France and the United Provinces in the middle of October but it took just over a month to get Spain, the Habsburgs and Sardinia to put pen to the paper of the final agreement. The British festivities did not take place, however, until April 1749.[101] Construction of the venue for the display in Green Park had begun in November 1748. The centrepiece was a temple, constructed of wood and canvas but painted to look like stone, of considerable size. It was over 100 feet high and nearly 150 feet long. There were additional pavilions on each side. Both the royal arms and other pictures were displayed along the top of the edifice. There were statues of the gods – Diana, Jupiter, Apollo and Ceres on the frontage with Mercury and Minerva at either end – together with representations of the sun and a statue of George giving peace to Britain and reviving commerce, as well as representations of the four cardinal virtues

---

[95] For example, *Whitehall Evening Post or London Intelligencer*, 410, 24/9/1748.

[96] *General Evening Post*, 2339, 15/9/1748 and 2315, 21/7/1748. The latter also suggested that George had invited his family to Hanover to celebrate the imminent conclusion of a peace treaty and scotched the rumour that the bishop of Osnabrück was dead, for whose title Cumberland was deemed to be an obvious candidate.

[97] *General Evening Post*, 2335, 6/9/1748.

[98] *Whitehall Evening Post or London Intelligencer*, 412, 29/9/1748.

[99] *General Evening Post*, 2343, 24/9/1748.

[100] John Brewer, *The pleasures of the imagination* (London, 1997), pp. 25–8.

[101] There is an excellent description of the fireworks in *Gentleman's Magazine*, 19 (April 1749), pp. 185–7.

together with Liberty, Plenty and Peace and images of the kings of Britain, France and Spain embracing. Latin inscriptions attested to the king's love of peace and his role in restoring stability to Europe.

Something of the size of the event is indicated by the fact that the arrangements for coaches delivering spectators were published in the press. Access was to be via Horse Guards and then coaches had to leave via Buckingham House. All other wheeled traffic was banned in the park for the duration.[102] Others also took advantage, erecting viewing platforms and advertising their availability.[103] Some of the wall around the park near Piccadilly was pulled down to ease access. There were warnings that the event would provide a great opportunity for thieves, with so many out, so servants should be left to guard properties.[104]

In the preparation of the celebrations there had been some dispute about the role that music would play in relation to fireworks. George had initially been somewhat sceptical about having music at all. However he had been persuaded by John, second duke of Montagu, his master of the great wardrobe as well as of ordnance, that Handel's proposed orchestration would be suitably martial and pleasing to the king's ear. The promise of some military instrumentation had not been enough, though. George had expressed the desire to have no violins. Consequently, Montagu became worried by reports that Handel was planning to reduce the number of trumpets and French horns from sixteen to twelve because, as he was sure that Handel was unwilling to get rid of the strings altogether, it would be more difficult to disguise the orchestral nature of the piece if the brass section was cut.[105] Handel, by contrast, was concerned that an unbalanced orchestration would reduce the opportunities for future performances.[106] George's ultimate reaction to the first performance is unknown.

The display itself was not without incident. George, together with members of his family and leading nobles including the dukes of Bedford, Montagu and Richmond, observed proceedings from Caroline's new library in St James's, overlooking Green Park. Frederick and his family chose to watch from the duke of Middlesex's Arlington Street house. The royal party walked down to observe the machinery for setting off the fireworks at around 7 p.m. The musicians performed during George's inspection of the equipment. The display proper required darkness so it

[102] *London Gazette*, 4514, 18–22/4/1749.

[103] For example, the advertisement for 'Piddock's Buildings for seeing the Fireworks' which made much of the fact that coaches could deliver their guests to the venue throughout the evening. See *London Evening Post*, 3351, 22/4/1749.

[104] *General Advertiser*, 4527, 26/4/1749.

[105] Montagu to Charles Frederick, 28/3/1749 in Otto Deutsch, *Handel: a documentary biography* (London, 1955), p. 661. Charles Frederick was 'Comptroller of his Majesty's fireworks as well as for War as for triumph' and later became surveyor-general of the ordnance office.

[106] Christopher Hogwood, *Handel: Water Music and Music for the Royal Fireworks* (Cambridge, 2005), p. 84.

did not begin until 8.30. An opening rocket was fired, followed by the discharging of 101 cannon, strategically placed on Constitution Hill. Fireworks were then let off for a considerable length of time because it was nearly an hour later that one accidentally set fire to the north pavilion. Prompt action by those in charge ensured that several arches were quickly cut away to prevent the fire spreading to the main edifice. Jean-Nicholas Servandoni, who had designed displays for the French court before agreeing to orchestrate this display, was so concerned to ensure that his creation was not completely destroyed that he assaulted another royal official who got in his way as he was dashing to help. The incident did damage the overall effect, as some of the major pieces could not be ignited because of the fire. In spite of this setback, the length of time that the central sun blazed forth (nearly a minute) was regarded as particularly impressive. After the fireworks were over, the remains of the temple were illuminated until the early hours of the morning. The royal party withdrew shortly after midnight.

Thus described, it is difficult to see, other than the problem with the fire, why the event might have been regarded as a failure. Brewer's central point is that the value of the royal spectacle had been undermined by the fact that there had been a sneak preview of parts of it a few days before. Jonathan Tyers, the entrepreneurial owner of Vauxhall Gardens, had been approached by Montagu to help with the provision of various illuminations (large back-lit images used to create atmosphere) and with the lighting for the event. The royal household did not have the necessary resources, at least in London, to do all this itself and so called on Tyers. Tyers, ever the businessman, made clear that his help came at a price: he demanded the right to stage a rehearsal of Handel's music for the event in Vauxhall Gardens. Handel was at first sceptical about the idea but George ordered Handel to comply with Tyers's request.[107] Tyers duly staged the rehearsal on 21 April and it was reported to have been a great success – he even charged 2s 6d for admission as opposed to his usual shilling. Some reports opined that the audience was as large as 12,000, although recent research suggests that this figure is over-inflated.[108]

Brewer sees the contrast between the mismanagement of Green Park and the slick capitalism of Vauxhall Gardens as emblematic of a broader shift: from the court as the centre of cultural power to the more diffuse setting of the metropolis. In broad terms, Brewer is probably right but his views need to be qualified in certain key respects. First, there is the question of audience. There were far more people in Green Park than paid for the privilege of attending at Vauxhall. Secondly, and more importantly, the contrast between traditional courtly culture and the thrusting

---

[107] See Montagu to Charles Frederick, 9/4/1749 in Deutsch, *Handel*, p. 663.

[108] David Hunter, 'Rode the 12,000? Counting coaches, people, and errors en route to the rehearsal of Handel's *Music for the Royal Fireworks* at Spring Gardens, Vauxhall in 1749', *London Journal* (forthcoming). I am grateful to Dr Hunter for sharing his findings with me.

modernity of commercial capitalism can be overdone.[109] The ways in which people sought to sell views of the event at Green Park, just as they did when it came to other royal events like coronations, show that a simple dichotomy does not capture everything. This impression is reinforced from two rather different directions.

The celebrations in Green Park were but one part of the official commemorations to mark the Peace of Aachen. On 25 April George, along with Frederick, Cumberland and Princess Amelia, had heard a thanksgiving sermon preached by Archdeacon John Denne in the Chapel Royal. Handel composed music for this service as well.[110] Robert Drummond, the bishop of St Asaph who was to end his career as archbishop of York, preached before the House of Lords, and John Conybeare, soon to become bishop of Bristol, preached before the Commons. The court celebrated the peace in a variety of ways. Elsewhere in the country elements of the courtly commemorations were replicated. There were firework displays in Holt, Hull, Plymouth and Stockton to name but a few, although those in Newcastle had to be cancelled due to an outbreak of a cattle disease.[111] These took place both because fireworks were a traditional means of celebrating but also because they were emulating what was happening in Green Park, as is clear from the accounts that royal arms and statues of peace were part of the displays.[112]

The other way in which the interface between commerce and the court worked was that the courtly connection might be used as part of the selling point of a particular event. Soon after the Green Park display had taken place, a notice appeared offering music and entertainment in Cuper's Gardens which promised 'to conclude every evening with an exact representation, in miniature, of the magnificent edifice, with its proper Ornaments, viz Emblematical Figures, Transparencies, &c and the Fireworks to imitate, as near as possible, the Royal ones, exhibited (on Account of the Peace) in Green Park'.[113] The proprietor also promised to make every effort to keep out undesirable persons (something about which there had been complaints in Vauxhall Gardens). There was, in other words, a market for the social exclusivity offered by a vision of court life. Emulation was, quite literally, the sincerest form of flattery. In this context, the court and the emergent commercial sphere can be seen as both more

---

[109] Ibid., pp. 6–8 suggests that claims about the new social inclusivity of the Vauxhall audience, as contrasted with that in Green Park, are particularly misleading.

[110] Donald Burrows, *Handel and the English Chapel Royal* (Oxford, 2005), pp. 411–15.

[111] *Whitehall Evening Post*, 499 and 500, 29/4/1749 and 2/5/1749 and *London Evening Post*, 3356, 4/5/1749.

[112] The broader meanings and importance of firework displays are discussed in Simon Werrett, *Philosophical fireworks* (Chicago, 2010) and I have benefited greatly from discussions with Dr Werrett.

[113] *General Advertiser*, 4531, 1/5/1749.

interconnected and more interdependent than might initially appear. What George had managed to achieve, perhaps unconsciously, was an amalgam of courtly life and consumerism. The commemorations of the Peace of Aachen neatly encapsulate how court ritual could be successfully exploited commercially. George's public appearances in 1748 also illustrated his ability to adapt himself to his audience. The London public of Green Park was more amorphous and anonymous than the more socially exclusive public that he had encountered on his visit to Göttingen. Sometimes George could revel in his role as the *Landesvater* – a baroque prince and the 'alpha and omega' of the Hanoverian public sphere – whereas in London he had to be more aware of constitutional, commercial and cultural constraints on his behaviour.[114] For much of his reign he was able to bridge this expectation gap with little difficulty but the tensions between the two aspects of his rule were to become increasingly pronounced in the last years of his reign.

[114] The 'alpha and omega' phrase comes from Sebastian Küster, *Vier Monarchien – Vier Öffentlichkeiten: Kommunikation um die Schlacht bei Dettingen* (Münster, 2004), p. 191.

Chapter 7

COMPLICATIONS AND CONTROVERSIES

George's political position in the aftermath of the Peace of Aachen was complicated. Although a peace deal had been signed, it felt more like a cessation of hostilities than an enduring settlement. Maria Theresa was anxious that the loss of Silesia should not become permanent. The threat of further conflict between Britain and France over extra-European possessions had abated but remained unresolved. Within Britain, the Old Corps Whigs seemed able to maintain a reasonable hold on both the administration and the Commons. Yet Frederick was once again starting to make trouble so it was uncertain how long the parliamentary peace would last. There was an overwhelming sense of relief that a costly war had been brought to an end; as with most eighteenth-century British wars, the national debt had increased considerably during its course, nearly doubling from just under £47 million to just over £76 million.[1]

ALLIANCES AND SUBSIDIES: EUROPEAN ENTANGLEMENTS?

Despite the costs of the war, Newcastle was keen to ensure that Britain's foreign political commitments and spending were not scaled back too far, even in peacetime. His insistence on continuing to spend money on foreign subsidies angered those, including his brother, who wanted to reap the peace dividend. Nevertheless, there were sound reasons for Newcastle's position. He had come to appreciate the importance that George attached to his foreign political powers and he also realized that the king had distinct views on how best to achieve security for his British and Hanoverian domains. The way in which it was thought that this could be done was by strengthening the demoralized Habsburgs.[2] What was needed following the aftermath of the War of the Austrian Succession was an imperial revival – not outside Europe but within it. A sense of balance and stability needed to be restored to central Europe to allow the Holy Roman Empire to continue to function properly. This was vital not just for the peace of that part of Europe but also because the empire was seen as

---

[1] John Brewer, *The sinews of power* (London, 1989), p. 30.
[2] Newcastle to Cumberland, Hanover, 6/11/1748, BL, Add. MSS 35410, fo. 62 reporting his recent conversations with George.

a crucial geopolitical prop, along with the Barrier fortresses in the Low Countries, to British security.[3]

George's Hanoverian ministers also did their bit to nudge Newcastle and the king in the direction of rebuilding relations with Austria. The ties of friendship created by Newcastle's 1748 visit to Hanover were to prove important for establishing a solid working relationship between the British and Hanoverian components of George's domains over the next few years, although friends were not all that Newcastle had acquired in Hanover; he wanted to get hold of some of the Rhenish wine he had sampled while there on his return to England and requested that August Wilhelm von Wangenheim, one of George's senior Hanoverian courtiers, send some over for him.[4] Politically speaking, it was contacts with Münchhausen that opened up new possibilities. It was Münchhausen's intervention that helped persuade Newcastle (and then helped Newcastle persuade Pelham) that it was worth paying the final instalment of £100,000 in February 1749 that the Habsburgs wanted to complete the subsidies owed to them.[5] Münchhausen contended that it was not worth risking the friendship of Maria Theresa over such a (relatively) small sum of money. The intervention in February reiterated a number of themes that Münchhausen had addressed at the end of the previous year. In December 1748 he had sent Newcastle a memorandum highlighting the persistent dangers that France posed to Great Britain and calling for support for the Habsburgs to remain a crucial part of British attempts to contain French power. Showing an awareness of the constraints under which George had to operate within Britain, Münchhausen also argued that parliament would be unlikely to accept changes to the system of alliances if this meant abandonment of Austria.[6]

The issue of Austrian subsidies was the first of several occasions when the wisdom or otherwise of British investment in the continental powers was debated in the next few years. Faced with the scepticism of Hardwicke and Pelham, Newcastle was forced to articulate his foreign political vision. He thought that a strong navy was a vital part of British security, going so far as to urge his colleagues to ensure that the number of sailors was kept at a reasonable level after the war, not least because he feared that the French were rearming.[7] However, a purely naval strategy was not going to be enough. The point that Newcastle was to make repeatedly was that, in order to be effective, a naval policy had to work in tandem with a system

---

[3] Brendan Simms, *Three victories and a defeat* (London, 2007), pp. 356–7. This is a theme that Professor Simms examines in greater detail and over a longer time period in his new book, *Battle for Europe: geopolitics 1453–2009* (Penguin, 2011).

[4] Newcastle to Wangenheim, Newcastle House, 10/2/1749 BL, Add. MSS 32816, fo. 100.

[5] Uriel Dann, *Hanover and Great Britain, 1740–1760* (Leicester, 1991), p. 81.

[6] Memorandum, included in Münchhausen's letter, 8/12/1748, BL, Add. MSS 32815, fo. 249.

[7] Newcastle to Bedford, Hanover, 23/10/1748 NS, BL, Add. MSS 35410, fos 29–30.

of continental connections. If, as he argued to Hardwicke, France were to perceive that either alliances were being abandoned or that the navy was not being properly supported, this would encourage them to break the peace. If both policies were pursued, then the prospect of renewed conflict was reduced significantly.[8]

Newcastle's favoured continental alliance partners were clear. Despite their shortcomings towards the end of the last war, the Dutch, particularly in their new Orangist incarnation, were vital to any system of alliances, as was Maria Theresa. These would be the powers, together with the British, that could stop either Prussia or France from disrupting European stability again. On the question of whether subsidies should be used to win powers, such as Denmark, away from France, Newcastle expressed himself ever more forcefully. There was a need to balance sound economic prudence against ill-judged parsimony when it came to subsidizing continental powers. While there was a risk that there might be those, such as some of the minor German princes who put their troops out to hire to the highest bidder, who might accept British gold now but accept more French gold later, the careful negotiation of treaties and selection of partners could (and should) minimize this risk. Newcastle reiterated his support for the navy but argued that a navy 'unsupported with even the Appearance of a Force, upon the Continent, will be of little Use. It will provoke; but not effectually prevent. It may, indeed, be more easily carried here, as co-inciding with the Notion of the Tories; But it will end, in a few years, in nothing. France will out doe us, by Sea; when they have nothing to fear, by land; And they can have nothing to fear there, if we can have nothing to oppose them.'[9]

Newcastle's reasoned advocacy of a mixed strategy showed an awareness of the differing constituencies to whom he had to appeal. Navalist rhetoric played well, as Newcastle's remark to Hardwicke suggested, in the Commons. Most importantly, though, a consistent appreciation of the weight that George attached to his involvement in the broad scheme of European affairs meant that colonial affairs remained subordinate – a means by which the commercial wealth necessary to support a larger strategy could be obtained. George's own views on priorities were straight-forward. When the newly appointed head of the board of trade, the earl of Halifax, tried to argue that his position, with the key role he had to play in colonial management, meant that he should have the right to attend the meetings of the king's chief ministers, his request was declined.[10]

Much more to George's taste were the efforts that Newcastle began in 1749, and was to pursue for several years thereafter, to shore up Maria Theresa's position. The scheme Newcastle had in mind was to push for an

[8] Newcastle to Hardwicke, Hanover, 10/11/1748, ibid., fo. 70.
[9] Newcastle to Hardwicke, Claremont, 2/9/1749, ibid., fos 140–54 (quotation fo. 153v).
[10] Simms, *Three victories*, p. 360.

early election of the King of the Romans. Within the Holy Roman Empire, both the imperial title and that of King of the Romans, which was reserved for the emperor's putative successor, were elective. Newcastle's idea was to have Maria Theresa and Francis Stephen's eldest son, the Archduke Joseph, elected, thus diminishing the likelihood of the imperial title again passing outside the Habsburg family, as it had done in the early 1740s.[11]

To put the scheme into practice, it would be necessary to secure a few more votes within the Electoral college. Those of Hanover, Bohemia, Trier and Mainz were already assured. Attention therefore turned to Cologne, the Palatinate, Bavaria, Saxony and Prussia. It was unlikely that these Electors would be willing to support the scheme without additional material inducement. As the United Provinces had already opened negotiations with Cologne over various other matters, it was here that Newcastle turned first. By the end of 1749, he had managed to secure a subsidy for Cologne and an agreement was signed in early 1750. The question of where to go next was difficult. Since the scheme sought to enhance Habsburg power and thus check French advances, it was unlikely that France's allies would be willing to consider an approach. This ruled out the Palatinate and Prussia. An approach to Saxony was possible but liable to complications because of Saxon debts to Hanover. Given the difficulties that paying for Hanoverian troops had caused during the 1740s, Newcastle was anxious to avoid creating the impression that any subsidy agreement was little more than a sham and a way of diverting British funds to Hanover by covert means. This left Bavaria as the only option. Newcastle was eventually able to secure a deal with Bavaria. However, the terms offered were better than those given to Cologne, prompting the latter to threaten to renege on the agreement unless a better offer was forthcoming. This threw a monumental spanner into the works. Newcastle had waited to share news of his election scheme plan with Maria Theresa until negotiations were well under way. The initial Austrian response had been somewhat noncommittal. They were not averse to strengthening their own position with the empire but they did not want to do so in a way that damaged relations with other powers or was perceived to be simply helping the British with their own foreign policy agenda. Cologne's decision to push for a reopening of negotiations led to the Austrians postponing calling an election in September 1750.

Newcastle had been overseeing the ongoing negotiations from Hanover, as he had used the king's visit in the summer of 1750 to travel to the continent to ensure that he could keep abreast of developments. News of the

---

[11] On the origins of the scheme, see D.B. Horn, 'The origins of the proposed election of the King of the Romans, 1748–50', *EHR*, 42 (1927), pp. 361–70 and Reed Browning, 'The Duke of Newcastle and the Imperial Election plan, 1749–1754', *Journal of British Studies*, 7 (1967–8), pp. 28–47. The scheme is also discussed in Andrew C. Thompson, *Britain, Hanover and the Protestant interest* (Woodbridge, 2006), pp. 208–13.

postponement of the election was a blow but not, as yet, fatal to his plans. He soldiered on with his negotiations, turning his attention now to Saxony. By September 1751 an agreement on a Saxon subsidy had been reached. Cologne had by this stage defected to France, much in the manner that Hardwicke and Pelham had feared would happen, so the Saxon agreement took on greater importance. Yet even here, success was more apparent than real. The complexities of imperial law and custom were such as to vex even the most seasoned of observers. Early in the negotiations, Prussia had complained that an election now would be premature and contravened important imperial precedents. These complaints had been dismissed by reference to previous instances of Prussian support for exactly what Newcastle was now trying to achieve. The Saxon case was more complicated. Count Brühl, who had negotiated the agreement on behalf of Augustus III, had ensured that the final agreement was subject to the laws and constitutions of the empire. This seemingly innocuous phrase had significant implications. It meant that any election would be subject to the approval not just of the Electoral college but also of the college of princes.[12] The practical prospect of the election taking place was rapidly diminishing. This did not stop Newcastle, though. He attempted to win Austrian support for a formal election in 1752. The Austrians had shifted from acquiescence to hostility. They demanded that Newcastle secure not a simple majority of the Electoral college but unanimity instead.

Although Münchhausen had at first displayed enthusiasm for the project, by 1752 this was waning. One consistent feature of Münchhausen's approach had been his desire to ensure that various grievances about the treatment of Protestants within Habsburg lands were addressed as part of a quid pro quo for George's support for the election scheme. Almost regardless of his personal religious inclinations, George's position as a north German Protestant Elector virtually compelled him to take a stand when it came to the fate of his co-religionists within the empire. A sense of shared Protestantism could also be useful for dealing with the conflicts that arose between British and Hanoverian interests.[13]

The imperial election scheme and its failure illustrated several lessons. On the one hand, it served as a reminder that Habsburg policy could not necessarily be moulded that easily to fit in with British requirements. On the other, it was a further indication of the importance that trips to Hanover had for the shaping of British diplomacy in the period. Most of the notable times of activity on the project coincided with Newcastle's three visits to the continent between 1748 and 1752. In contrast to earlier instances, when British ministers had fought hard to dissuade George from such frequent returns to the Electorate, Newcastle's desire to make his

---

[12] Simms, *Three victories*, pp. 374–5.
[13] For a much fuller analysis of this point, see Thompson, *Britain, Hanover*, ch. 1.

foreign political mark seems to have made him more open to the king's itinerancy. Newcastle was so keen to return to Hanover that he even sent Wangenheim a detailed set of instructions in early 1750 on how his quarters in Hanover should be improved before his next visit.[14]

THE COURT IN HANOVER

From George's point of view, his visits in both 1750 and 1752 followed the pattern that had been established by his previous sojourns in the Electorate. There were military parades and inspections. He spent time hunting at the Göhrde on both occasions with an entourage that included Hanoverian courtiers, as well as the occasional visiting diplomat.[15] In 1750, time was also spent hunting at Hallerbrücke. Newcastle noted the king's enthusiasm for the pursuit of wild boar – apparently, the only British members of the hunting party prepared to pursue boar enthusiastically were those from Yorkshire.[16] There were performances by the French comedians in the evenings, as well as several large balls, complete with fireworks and illuminations. Visitors made their way to Hanover to visit the king. Some of the diplomats and ministers attached to the court in St James's crossed the Channel with the royal party, while others were dispatched specially from their respective courts. It was also an opportunity for George to see British diplomats stationed abroad for himself so it was not uncommon for those resident in Dresden, Vienna, Berlin or other German courts to spend some of the summer in the Electorate, briefing George in person about the situation on the ground. Other visitors included George's daughter Mary and his son-in-law, Friedrich of Hessen-Kassel. Both visited, although separately, in 1750 and 1752.[17]

Keeping a court running without a continual royal presence was no mean feat. The court in Hanover was unusual in the mid-eighteenth century in that, after Frederick's departure in 1728, there were long periods when there was a gap at the centre of court life because there was no member of the ruling family present on whom attention could be focused. Nevertheless, some sort of courtly life continued, even if it lacked the glamour and intensity of the pre-1714 period. There were certain fixed points in the week. Although Frederick had held court every day when he lived in Hanover, there was a necessary reduction in official occasions thereafter. On Sundays, however, members of the court would gather in one of the reception rooms in the Leine palace and bow to a picture of George, held upright on a chair. The assembled company would chat quietly to each other for an hour or so, behaving in the modest manner that would be expected if the monarch had actually been present, before

---

[14] BL, Add. MSS 32820, fo. 111.
[15] NHStA, Dep. 103, IV, 311, fo. 4 and *London Gazette*, 8987, 8–11/9/1750.
[16] Newcastle to Pelham, Hanover, 16/10/1750 NS, BL, Add. MSS 32723, fo. 110.
[17] NHStA, Dep. 103, IV, 324, fos 138–62.

proceeding to dine in the palace's hall. Service was conducted as if George were there in person. The costs of keeping these tables, which were reportedly good places to eat, were met by George. Afterwards, the ladies would occupy themselves with sewing or, more probably, join the men in the various sorts of card games and gambling that were characteristic of eighteenth-century court life.[18]

Such a level of court activity in Hanover, even in George's absence, had to be paid for. The surviving files in Hanover allow the partial reconstruction of the complexity and costs of keeping the Hanoverian court going. In its structure, it was not particularly different from any other European court of the period. There were members of the household who performed largely ceremonial tasks, such as waiting on and accompanying the monarch, and then there was a much larger body of servants who ensured that the court could continue to function. An account of the costs of various court offices, unfortunately undated but certainly from George's reign, includes a list of nearly 300 people who received payments from the court.[19] The weekly bill was reckoned to be just over 500 Reichstalers.[20] Allowances came in various kinds, though. George was also obliged to provide his servants with a variety of accessories necessary for them to perform their jobs. A list from 1752 of the requirements of the court's liveried servants included 214 individuals for whom the court had to purchase a uniform. In the case of the first group listed, the pages, there was information on the sizes needed for each item, as well as a detailed list of how much gold braid, which buttons and what stockings would be required.[21] When it came to cost, the total involved was 13,840 Reichstalers, with the most expensive component of the livery being the hats.[22] In addition to clothing, at various points in the 1750s there were requests for the Electoral treasury to supply sufficient silver to enable new trumpets to be cast for the court trumpeters.[23] Other accounts give a slightly different impression of outgoings. A list of salaries, livery money and pensions from the early 1750s gives figures of 103,831 Reichstalers for 1751 and 120,758 Reichstalers for 1753 respectively. Here some of the palace guards were included, yet the total number of people involved was still between 250 and 300. The major difference between the 1753 and 1751 figures was the inclusion of nearly 14,000 Reichstalers for paying hunt officials in 1753 who had presumably been overlooked in 1751.[24] In 1743,

---

[18] Joachim Lampe, *Aristokratie, Hofadel und Staatspatriziat in Kurhannover* (2 vols, Göttingen, 1963), i, pp. 135–7.

[19] NHStA, Dep. 103, XXIV, 250. The document is signed by von Reden as *Oberhofmarschall* which dates it to 1735–58. Given the references to various pay increases in the 1740s, it probably comes from the latter part of that timeframe.

[20] Ibid., fo. 5. An approximate exchange rate would be 6 Reichstalers to the pound.

[21] NHStA, Dep. 103, XXIV, 541, fo. 1.

[22] Ibid., fo. 15v.

[23] NHStA, Dep. 103, XXIV, 1557.

[24] NHStA, Dep. 103, XXIV, 3551.

99,983 Reichstalers had been spent.[25] By way of comparison, the *Staatskalendar* listed about 450 officials associated with the civil administration, as opposed to about 250 attached to the court in this period.

The court infrastructure included a dairy farm and a menagerie. A complete list of the occupants of the menagerie does not survive but the management of both farm and menagerie was not without its problems. Concerns about the running of the farm led to the appointment of a new administrator in 1739 who was instructed to look after the royal funds well and ensure that he lived a sober life.[26] Care had also to be taken with animal food coming to the menagerie from the royal kitchens to ensure it reached its intended recipients and was not misappropriated by other servants. All animal deaths had to be recorded and reported.

Most jobs at court had detailed job descriptions. Changes had to be approved by the king in London. The new order for the court pages in 1735 described both their duties and how they were to be educated. Scriptural study and church attendance made up a significant part of the pages' week. They were to acquire more secular skills as well, such as basic literacy and numeracy, and the accomplishments that would make them good courtiers, like the ability to dance properly and perform music. All this had to be fitted around their more formal duties.[27]

The supply of food and drink for any court was a complicated business. As George was providing sustenance for courts in both London and Hanover simultaneously, it is not entirely surprising that he made use of some of the game caught on his Hanoverian estates to provide food for his German court directly. A complete list of game receipts does not survive but in the winter of 1736 to 1737, some twenty animals, including three deer, found their way to the kitchens of the Leine palace and this number was to rise a little in subsequent years. Supply was, however, subject to significant variation. The winter of 1739 to 1740 was harsh so von Reden urged George to make a contribution towards the costs of game hunted around Celle to allow those who had caught it to buy fodder for their horses.[28]

The court cellar was a source of considerable temptation. Royal absence might lead potential miscreants to think that pilfering would go undetected. If anything, the opposite seems to have been the case. An audit in 1728 revealed a number of discrepancies and moves were made to improve the security arrangements to ensure that stock levels were maintained. However, a further investigation in 1732 led to the *Hofweinschenk*, Herr Keim, losing his job. There were doubts about whether the correct wine had been produced during the visit of the duke of Lorraine, Maria

[25] Ibid., XXIV, 3552.

[26] George to von Reden, St James's, 9–20/3/1739, NHStA, Dep. 103, XXIV, 1717.

[27] NHStA, Dep. 103, XXIV, 1914. The instructions were signed by von Reden on 23 November 1735.

[28] Ibid., 2225, fos 2 and 51–2.

Theresa's future husband. Other incidents were taken into consideration and Keim was dismissed. The vigilant oversight may well have been the product of George's general interest in running a tight financial ship. The contents of the cellar suggest that he did not scrimp on quality. There was a wide selection of burgundies, Rhône and Moselle wines, as well as champagne. The only notable difference from the cellars in London was the absence of fortified wine of various sorts from Iberia ('sack') and claret.[29]

In terms of the material culture of the court, inventories were kept of everything from spoons to valuable works of art. This attention to detail was both necessary, given the need to keep track of where everything was in an institution as large as the court, and a reflection of George's obsession with order. Horace Walpole noted a tale from Henrietta Howard describing how George had seen a set of gold cutlery which had belonged to Anne when he first came to Britain in 1714 and had been slightly perturbed when he could not find it among his father's effects in London when he acceded to the throne himself. When he travelled back to Hanover in 1729, he had discovered the items there and had consequently returned the set to London, in order to ensure that there was a proper separation between what rightfully belonged to each portion of his domains.[30] The accuracy of the incident is less relevant than what it reveals about the meticulousness of George's character, although it has an air of truth about it.

Following his father's death, George asked for detailed inventories to be made of the jewellery and other valuables in Hanover so that he would know the whereabouts of anything connected with his Electoral inheritance.[31] In Hanover lists were kept of dinner services in both silver and less precious materials. New 21-piece services had been purchased in both 1750 and 1752, suggesting that renewals and replacements tended to coincide with royal visits and the periods of highest use.[32] The court in Hanover also had several fine porcelain services. An inventory of 1740 gave pride of place to a Japanese example but also included one from Dresden where the production of the Meissen factory was slowly decreasing reliance on the Far East for fine pottery. Many of the items in the service were cups of different sorts – for chocolate, warm wine, tea and coffee – reflecting the use they were put to on large court occasions when these drinks were routinely offered to guests.[33] The products of George's English domains

---

[29] Ibid., 2281. Contrast the consumption details from London in the 1730s and 1740s in NA, Lord Steward's department [hereafter LS] 13/269.

[30] Horace Walpole, *Reminiscences written by Mr Horace Walpole in 1788 for the amusement of Miss Mary and Miss Agnes Berry* (Oxford, 1924), p. 23.

[31] NHStA, Dep. 103, XXIV, 3266: III contains the inventory and instructions to construct it.

[32] Ibid., 2488, fos 1–3.

[33] Ibid., 2616.

were not entirely ignored in Hanover. The king had a reasonable collection of English pewter.[34]

What the walls of the Leine palace and Herrenhausen looked like in George's later years can be deduced from the picture inventory compiled in 1754. The inventory lists 1,117 pictures by room in each of the palaces. The vast majority (994) were in the Leine palace with the rest being kept at Herrenhausen. Most works are listed by subject, rather than by artist. There are a few exceptions. There was an original Van Dyck in the Presence Chamber in the Leine palace and a Rubens *Madonna and Child* in a closet close to the royal bedchamber. The former is interesting, given Hervey's record of George's anger at the replacement of one of his beloved Renaissance 'Fat Venus' pictures with Van Dyck's *Children of Charles I* during his Hanoverian sojourn in 1736.[35] The royal bedchamber contained pictures of George's paternal grandparents, the goddess Diana, various heraldic devices and coats of arms and a portrait of the countess of Yarmouth. Although George would only have slept in the room occasionally because most of his time during his Hanoverian trips was spent at Herrenhausen, the choice of paintings suggests more than a simply random selection. Genealogy was one of his obsessions. His continued closeness to the countess of Yarmouth explains her presence and his admiration for his grandmother, in particular, had been apparent since his youth. The absence of depictions of either his father or his eldest son might be reflective of the strained relations that he enjoyed with both. Elsewhere the inventory shows that there was an extensive collection of European royalty scattered throughout the palace. Most of George's Tudor and Stuart relations were to be found somewhere and Louis XIV was placed in the royal closet. The plan for one of the largest rooms in Herrenhausen reveals a visual depiction of the history of the dynasty. Large portraits of the Winter King and Queen were flanked by various members of the Guelphs, including George and Caroline together on the north wall, as well as a painting of George's mother, which shows that the art works had been rearranged since George's accession as his father would have been unlikely to have displayed a picture of his estranged and disgraced spouse.[36] The index to the inventory has some interesting features too. There was a genealogical index, perhaps reflecting George's known proclivities. A separate alphabetical index shows that there were twelve pictures of Georg Ludwig and Ernst August, thirteen of Sophia and nine of George himself in the collection. Caroline was the

---

[34] Ibid., 2617.

[35] Hervey, *Memoirs*, ii, pp. 488–9.

[36] Very few portraits of Sophia Dorothea survive. Lionel Cust claims that Georg Ludwig gave explicit instructions for images of her to be collected and destroyed. Lionel Cust, 'On a portrait of Sophia Dorothea of Zell', *Burlington Magazine for Connoisseurs*, vol. xix, no. 101 (August 1911), pp. 301–2.

subject of seven pictures, Frederick, prince of Wales of four and Lady Yarmouth featured only once.[37]

In terms of the costs of running the court in Hanover, George seems to have been kept relatively well informed of the level of outgoings. He signed off the quarterly accounts, although it is not clear whether these were sent to London or whether he signed them in bulk on one of his Hanoverian trips. Overall the accounts show, not surprisingly, that George's visits to Hanover did cause a spike in costs but the decline in court expenditure after 1760 was more gradual than rapid.[38] Indeed, the fact that livery costs remained reasonably constant between the 1750s and the 1760s suggests that George III's reign did not lead to an immediate diminution in the size of the court establishment in Hanover.[39] It is also worth noting that, in contrast to some other European states, there was already a clear division in Hanover between the costs of running the court and those associated with general civil administration and that each was handled by a different group of people: privy councillors did not automatically have a role to play in the day-to-day running of the court.[40] This differentiation of roles was already apparent by George's reign, though its origins may have been earlier. It reflected rather neatly, and perhaps not coincidentally, the situation in Britain with its increasingly clear separation between the Civil List and the national debt.

In Britain, George was a relatively modest royal builder and there is little evidence of extensive new building work in Hanover. Serious repairs had to be made to the Leine palace following a fire in 1741, although the area affected housed the judicial and financial administration for the Electorate, rather than more courtly functions.[41] George's only other major innovation seems to have been installing mirrors on the walls of the Gallery at Herrenhausen.[42] Upkeep and maintenance of the palaces and gardens in Hanover consumed the majority of the budget. With the exception of the theatres, where George's presence definitely did lead to more being spent on repairs and improvements (1,391 Reichstalers in 1750 compared with a mere 124 in 1754), there is little pattern to the expenditure. Overall, the average spending by decade, as listed in the accounts, was less after 1760 than it was before on buildings. In relation to the gardens, the trend was also downward. Nearly a third of the garden budget went on the upkeep of the fountain and waterworks at

---

37 NHStA, Dep. 103, XXIV, 2587.

38 Ibid., 3547–50.

39 Ibid., 3550.

40 This point is emphasized in Cornelia Roolfs, *Der hannoversche Hof von 1814 bis 1866* (Hanover, 2005), p. 30.

41 Georg Schnath (with contributions from Rudolf Hillebrecht and Helmut Plath), *Das Leineschloss: Kloster, Fürstensitz, Landtagsgebäude* (Hanover, 1962), pp. 94–7.

42 Udo von Alvensleben and Hans Reuther, *Herrenhausen: Die Sommerresidenz der Welfen* (Hanover, 1966), p. 41.

Herrenhausen.[43] The engine had been installed by an English engineer, Joseph Andrews, between 1718 and 1720 and the fountain was considered particularly excellent, attracting visitors from across north Germany.[44] George expanded the range of plants in the garden and was keen to keep the standards of care up, not least because he was a frequent user of the gardens for relaxation and for bigger entertainments during his visits. Special houses were constructed to grow pineapples in 1743 and 1757.[45]

Despite George's desire to keep his Hanoverian and British court affairs largely separate, there are a few instances of crossovers. William Kent had carried out a number of projects for the crown, including the designs for Merlin's Cave and the Hermitage in Richmond Park for Caroline.[46] Kent was also commissioned to design objects for George's Hanoverian palaces. Ellenor Alcorn has suggested that the designs that Kent executed for some chandeliers and girandoles were part of a broader scheme of internal refurbishment that George planned for his Hanoverian palaces in the 1730s. He had purchased a large group of silver furniture in 1731 and commissioning the pieces from Kent was the next contribution he made to the silver inventory of his Electoral domains.[47] The newly executed chandeliers were almost certainly hung in the Presence Chamber of the Leine palace where they were part of the large display of court silver used as part of the celebrations to mark Louisa's proxy marriage in 1743.

Overall, the study of George's court in Hanover suggests a more varied engagement with courtly culture than a simple narrative of decline. In many ways, the most interesting feature of George's use of the court in Hanover was his ability to adapt to the circumstances in which he found himself. In Britain, the pressures of an expanding commercial society in London were moving the court away from its previous position of centrality. It was now merely at the centre, rather than being the centre, of national life.[48] Yet in Hanover George participated in a court life that differed very little from that of many of his fellow European rulers. This might suggest, as George's unkind British critics often did, that the king's instincts and preferences were for a continental-style European absolutism and that he understood imperfectly the constitutional role he had to perform in Britain. Such accusations serve only to confuse rather than illuminate. George certainly expressed his frustration on various occasions with the fact that his British ministers felt that they could, as he saw it,

---

[43] NHStA, Dep. 103, XXIV, 3632.

[44] Alvensleben and Reuther, *Herrenhausen*, p. 70.

[45] Ibid., p. 75.

[46] H.M. Colvin, J. Mordaunt Crook, Kerry Downes and John Newman, *The history of the king's works: volume V, 1660–1782* (London, 1976), pp. 221–4.

[47] Ellenor M. Alcorn, ' "A chandelier for the King", William Kent, George II, and Hanover', *Burlington Magazine*, vol. cxxxix, no. 1126 (January 1997), pp. 40–3.

[48] Clarissa Campbell Orr, 'New perspectives of Hanoverian Britain', *HJ*, 52 (2009), p. 516 citing R.O. Bucholz.

dictate to him on matters of policy or ministerial selection. Yet it would be a mistake to think that British monarchical culture had diverged so far from its European counterparts as to make the crown completely subservient to its ministers. Instead George found himself having to perform a delicate constitutional balancing act. He could push his powers only so far in Britain. He was constrained in several ways. His foreign political decisions needed to be paid for and here he had to ensure that parliament was willing to vote the necessary funds; so management, rather than command, was the order of the day. Similarly, the separation of the public administration from that of the court meant that his ability to build and use culture for monarchical display was limited by access to funds. George managed to adapt, though. He made use of royal patronage to associate himself with cultural activity without having to pick up the entire bill. His court, arguably, was facing up to the challenges posed by commerce. In Hanover he could afford to be more expansive but his natural inclination to ensure that he got a good deal meant that his spending was not excessive. Nevertheless, he was able to use the resources available to him to project an image of grandeur and majesty.

COURT POLITICS AND RIVALRIES

George's travels between Britain and Hanover had other effects. On the straightforwardly political level, attendance on the king during his Hanoverian journeys was both a signal of favour and an opportunity to expand influence. Mention has been made already of the use to which Newcastle put his journeys with the king, in terms of pushing the imperial election scheme in the period 1748 to 1752. The middle one of these journeys, that of 1750, was important for domestic political reasons as well. Newcastle had grown increasingly frustrated with his fellow secretary, the duke of Bedford. Bedford's faults were several. When it came to policy, from an early stage Bedford had expressed disquiet about a foreign political strategy based on subsidies. His close associate Sandwich was equally sceptical and, at least when Newcastle was away, Pelham had suggested that he was not unsympathetic to their views either.[49] Given that both Bedford and Sandwich had been closely linked with naval administration at times in the 1740s, their reluctance to fund continental armies was, perhaps, understandable but it was nevertheless irritating for Newcastle, who felt that his position as senior secretary was being challenged by their reluctance to toe an Old Corps line. Bedford had also shown himself to be a less assiduous secretary than Newcastle. He preferred to spend time at Woburn rather than hang around in the capital to transact political

---

[49] Pelham to Bedford, Greenwich Park, 7/8/1748, Lord John Russell, introduction to *Correspondence of John, fourth duke of Bedford with an introduction by Lord John Russell* (3 vols, London, 1842–6), i, p. 437.

business. He missed meetings and George had noticed that his attention to detail was imperfect. However, the king was also rather taken with the respect that Bedford showed in the closet when he did deign to visit London so any attempt to remove him would have to proceed with circumspection.[50]

Such care was made even more necessary by the political allies that Bedford had cultivated. His status as a major landowner of itself gave him a significant degree of political power, and this was enhanced by his growing association with members of the royal family. Cumberland and his sister Amelia had allied themselves with Bedford. The precise motives of the royal brother and sister are unclear. Amelia may have been dissatisfied by the influence which she perceived that the countess of Yarmouth held over her father, having hoped that she might have been able to exercise power herself.[51] Cumberland may have felt that not enough was being done to guard against the likelihood of a future European conflict, although Bedford would seem to be an unlikely ally for somebody holding these views. Nevertheless, the set of emergent political alignments was increasingly complex because the Bedford group found itself opposed both by the Old Corps Whigs and by the revitalized political opposition that centred round the prince of Wales. Newcastle, by contrast, was drawing closer to Lady Yarmouth, in the hope that she might be able to use her influence to persuade George that it was necessary to part with Bedford. His attendance on George at Hanover in the summer of 1750 offered the perfect opportunity for him to push this plan. Slowly Newcastle's efforts began to bear fruit. George became more aware of Bedford's indolence. In addition, the death of the duke of Richmond, master of horse, in August 1750 created a vacancy into which Bedford could be moved when the time came.[52] Nevertheless, Newcastle was not able to do enough to get George to dismiss Bedford yet. He was also a little displeased by the king's willingness to appropriate the Election scheme as his own.

Bedford's eventual fall in 1751 did owe something to the shifting fortunes of court politics, however. Although the prince of Wales had moved back to a position of more direct parliamentary opposition to his father in 1747, it was not until two years later that his faction began to gain much in the way of momentum. It was helped by a dislike of what was perceived as Cumberland's excessive militarism. Cumberland had proposed, in his role as captain-general, that military discipline be tightened in various respects. Frederick disliked the influence that Cumberland had on those half-pay

---

[50] Reed Browning, *The duke of Newcastle* (New Haven and London, 1975), pp. 167–8.

[51] E. H. Chalus, 'Amelia, Princess (1711–1786)', *Oxford Dictionary of National Biography*, Oxford University Press, September 2004; online edn, January 2008 [http://www.oxforddnb.com/view/article/62471, accessed 7 September 2009].

[52] Browning, *Newcastle*, pp. 169–70.

officers who were also MPs so, together with his new adviser the second earl of Egmont, he set about blackening his brother's name. Egmont also began to devise plans for how the ministry would be reconstructed when the prince replaced his father. As well as working out which of the prince's followers would gain which office, there were also plans to repeal some of the innovations in military law that Cumberland had backed, which would reduce the right of placemen to sit in the Commons, and hence Cumberland's natural constituency of support. Cumberland was also to be removed from his military posts.[53]

Such planning for the next reign reflected the prevailing political realities. George was now becoming an old man. In 1749, when Egmont was drawing up his plans, the king was only a year younger than his own father had been when he died in 1727. Frederick's rivalry with his brother had several components. He remained frustrated that William had been able to take advantage of the military opportunities which he felt had been denied to him. He resented the favour their father bestowed on his brother and he also feared that Cumberland harboured political ambitions of his own. The smear campaign that was directed against him was brutal. It reached its height with the publication in early 1751 of an anonymous broadside entitled *Constitutional queries*. This played on traditional British fears about the power of a standing army in peacetime, suggesting that Cumberland was a latter-day Cromwell, but went further in implying that Cumberland had ambitions to seize the throne for himself, comparing him to Richard III.[54] The precise authorship of this attack was unclear, although Egmont was blamed. The tract was deemed sufficiently incendiary to warrant burning by the public hangman.

Newcastle, faced with opposition from Bedford and Cumberland, and conscious of George's advancing years, had made tentative approaches in the latter part of 1750 to Frederick's court. Egmont, who is the principal source for the sketchy information on this unusual turn of events, noted that Newcastle had been driven to such measures by Cumberland's opposition to his subsidy projects.[55] Newcastle's willingness to establish contacts with Frederick was a sign of his political pragmatism but it was also a signal of how complicated the political situation had become. Newcastle was effectively George's chief minister, so it was unsurprising that his relations with Frederick had not been particularly good in recent years. They had been soured considerably by Frederick's attempt to get himself elected chancellor of the university of Cambridge. Frederick had first made

[53] Romney Sedgwick, *The House of Commons, 1715–1754* (2 vols, London, 1970) i, pp. 57–8 and A.N. Newman, 'Leicester House politics, 1748–1751', *EHR*, 76 (1961), pp. 580–5.

[54] The earl of Ilchester (G.S.H. Fox-Strangways), *Henry Fox, first Lord Holland* (2 vols, London, 1920), i, pp. 161–2.

[55] Aubrey Newman, ed., 'Leicester House politics, 1750–60, from the papers of John, second earl of Egmont', *Camden Miscellany XXIII*, Camden 4th series, 7 (1969), p. 193.

signals that he coveted the post in 1747. Newcastle, as high steward, had felt that when the duke of Somerset eventually died, thus creating a vacancy, he was in the prime position to succeed as chancellor. News of Frederick's plans led Newcastle to secure a declaration from George that he hoped the university would not choose a member of his family as the next chancellor without his specific approval. Frederick declined to pursue his candidacy and Newcastle was duly elected in December 1748.[56] Consequently, Newcastle's courting of Frederick was not going to be straightforward, although Frederick, despite the 'blue water' rhetoric of many of his supporters, did have an active interest in supporting a continentalist foreign policy.[57]

FREDERICK'S DEATH AND ITS CONSEQUENCES

Bedford's removal was eventually achieved but Frederick did not play, at least directly, the part that Newcastle might have hoped. For all the talk among Frederick's supporters about the necessity of planning for a new start in the next reign, it was to be their patron who first departed the scene. Frederick had been at Kew, supervising work he was having done there, when he was taken ill in March 1751 with a cold. It is unlikely that the illness was simply the result of spending time outside in the damp, although Egmont was quick to jump to this conclusion.[58] Following standard medical practice of the day, Frederick's blood was drawn. It was hoped that he would make a full recovery and he did seem to revive a little over the next few days. He was expressing considerably more interest in the state of his father's health than willingness to discuss his own. Despite his wife's injunctions to rest and recover at home, Frederick was determined to attend his father's drawing room and to go to parliament to witness the bills being passed into law at the end of the session. The king had reportedly been indisposed himself recently, and Frederick was keen to assess the state of his father's health personally. Reports were circulating that although the king was now up and about again, his condition was more serious than it appeared.[59] Frederick did attend the Lords where his supporters made several mocking references to the state of the king's health and Frederick reassured Egmont that evening that everything was ready, should his father die. It was reported that Frederick was definitely

---

[56] Browning, *Newcastle*, pp. 170–1.

[57] Newman, ed., 'Leicester House politics', p. 194. For a discussion of Frederick's continuing attachment to his Hanoverian heritage, see Andrew C. Thompson, 'Frederick and Hanover', unpublished paper given at 'Politics and patronage: a tercentenary colloquium for Frederick, prince of Wales', held at History of Parliament, London, April 2007.

[58] Newman, ed., 'Leicester House politics', p. 195.

[59] Ibid., pp. 195–6, Robin Eagles, ' "No more to be said"? Reactions to the death of Frederick Lewis, prince of Wales', *Historical Research*, 80 (2007), p. 348.

on the mend. Frederick's optimism proved ill-founded. On the evening of 20 March, having received the all-clear from his doctors, Frederick was seized with a coughing fit at home in Leicester House and collapsed and died.[60]

The precise cause of Frederick's death was difficult to determine. The autopsy suggested that his lungs had been seriously weakened. He had previously suffered from pleurisy and probably contracted pneumonia as well. His death was popularly blamed on an injury caused by being hit by a ball while playing sport a few years before. George was informed of his son's death by Lord North, who dashed to court to interrupt the king's card game with the news. Horace Walpole was later to suggest in a typically gossipy letter that George had been largely unmoved by the news, commenting that he had thought his son was recovering. Frederick's supporters felt that George, Cumberland and Amelia were 'indecently merry' at court.[61] However, George, despite the animus he had felt towards Frederick at various times in his life, was sufficiently moved to weep when visiting Augusta a few days later so he was clearly affected in some way by the loss of his heir.[62]

In London, plans proceeded for Frederick's funeral. Some members of his household, particularly George Bubb Dodington, felt that the provisions made were insufficiently grand. The absence of commissioned music was noticeable, as was the lack of participation by any of Frederick's family. George had been ill and had not even attended his wife's funeral in 1737 so his absence was perhaps explicable. Cumberland's decision to stay away suggested a more deep-felt hostility. Yet, for all Dodington's complaints, the amount spent on the occasion was very much in line with comparable royal funerals of the period. Nearly £2,400 was expended on Frederick's funeral, compared with some £1,200 for his sister Caroline in 1757 and £2,950 for his father in 1760.[63] In terms of official mourning, Frederick also seems to have received his due. The initial length of mourning in Hanover was set at three months but this was subsequently extended to six, although the second three months were lesser, rather than full, mourning.[64] As in 1737 at Caroline's death, the Hanoverian court was very keen to ensure that what they did was in line with what was happening in London, in terms of clothing and the curtailing of official court activities.[65]

Frederick's death created an interesting political situation. His erstwhile followers had to decide what to do next. Frederick's eldest son, George, was not yet of age and so the chances of continuing in formed opposition

---

[60] Newman, ed., 'Leicester House politics', p. 198.

[61] Ibid., p. 207.

[62] Eagles, 'No more to be said', p. 350.

[63] Ibid., pp. 356–60.

[64] NHStA, Dep. 103, XXIV, 3270.

[65] Ibid., 3269 contains details of the requests for advice on how to behave in 1737.

were minimal. Given that there had been little love lost between Frederick and Cumberland, it was unlikely that they would transfer their loyalties to their former patron's younger brother so many adopted the only course left open to them and sought a reconciliation with the king and the Pelhams. Augusta led the way in this. However, George's recent illness and age meant that thought had to be given to the arrangements that would have to be put in place if he were to die while his grandson was still a minor. A regency of some sort was needed. George's thoughts had turned initially to Cumberland as the ideal regent but he was persuaded by a combination of Pelhamite pressure and Augusta's remonstrances that this was ill advised. Some of the mud that had recently been thrown at Cumberland's reputation had stuck. Worries were expressed about his militaristic tendencies.[66] After some heated debate, a compromise was reached.[67] The Regency Bill made Augusta regent for her eldest son but she was to be advised by a council with Cumberland as its head. The composition of the council included the major officers of state and the original proposal also left the king with the option of appointing a number of extra individuals himself; it was eventually decided that he would have the power to nominate four. A two-thirds majority would be needed for major decisions, such as declaring war, dissolving parliament or making new appointments. Five members had to be present to make the council quorate and no alterations could be made to the succession or the acts that secured the religious settlements in Scotland and England.[68]

The reunion of Leicester House with the court left Bedford dangerously exposed to Pelhamite attack. With the collapse of formed opposition, Pelham felt that removing Bedford, and thus creating another potential centre for political trouble, had become less risky. He had finally come around to George and Newcastle's view about Bedford's disruptive impact on the smooth running of the administration, having experienced Bedford's opposition to some of his own measures. George remained, however, reluctant to push Bedford out. Consequently, the Pelhams devised a stratagem to achieve this end. It was agreed that George would dismiss Bedford's protégé, Sandwich, from his post as first lord of the admiralty. It was hoped that Bedford would find this an intolerable slight on his own position and follow Sandwich out of office.[69] Events unfolded exactly as the Pelhams had hoped. Sandwich was dismissed on 13 June 1751 and Bedford's resignation followed a day later. His departure was not entirely quiet, though. He claimed to the king that the Pelhams had turned against him simply because of his friendship with Cumberland. George's

---

[66] Newman, ed., 'Leicester House politics', pp. 200–1.

[67] For the discussion in the Commons, see Cobbett, *Parliamentary History*, xiv, cols 1002–47.

[68] Undated regency proposals [1751], RA, Georgian Archive [GEO]/52937–40.

[69] Browning, *Newcastle*, p. 173.

distaste at the way in which a further change in his administration had
been achieved is perhaps reflected in reports that he was cold towards
Newcastle for some time afterwards and Newcastle had to exert his talents
as a courtier to win the king round.[70]

Bedford was replaced by Robert D'Arcy, fourth earl of Holdernesse.
Holdernesse had a number of advantages. He had been appointed a lord
of the bedchamber in 1741 and had been present at Dettingen with
George. He had subsequently held diplomatic postings in Venice and,
latterly, the United Provinces. He enjoyed royal favour but he was also,
from Newcastle's point of view, young enough (he was in his early thirties)
to be susceptible to the influence of an older and more senior colleague.
Newcastle clearly envisaged a subordinate, not to say subservient, role for
the new secretary. The reshuffle of offices also created a gap as lord president of the council. The new appointee was Granville. Given his previous
record of animosity towards the Pelhams, his return to high office might
seem surprising but he had retained George's favour so the choice met
with royal approval. Moreover, Newcastle's political journey since the
middle of the 1740s had taken him closer to George's views on the importance of an interventionist foreign policy. Granville's record suggested that
he would be a strong supporter of such moves and a useful counterweight
to the caution of Hardwicke and Pelham.

Frederick's death seems to have prompted George to think about his
own mortality. He signed a new version of his will, dealing primarily with
his German dominions, on 3 April 1751.[71] An earlier will survives from
1732.[72] This had been altered in various ways, mainly by the addition of
two codicils that had provided for Cumberland. The first, in 1740, had left
a sum of just over 1.1 million Reichstalers for Cumberland's use after
George's death. The source of the funds was bonds of various kinds that
George held from the prince of Orange and the duke of Schaumberg-
Lippe. Cumberland had no say in how the funds were managed during
George's lifetime but he knew that they had been designated for his future
use.[73] A modification was made to this in 1746 to include additional silver
for Cumberland, as well as some lands in Osnabrück. Cumberland, in
return, agreed to pay George's English legacies.[74] The 1751 will, like its
predecessor, began with the claim that George was following his grandfather's good example in providing for those of his children who would not

[70] Rigby to Bedford, 26/6/1751, Russell, intro., *Bedford correspondence*, ii, p. 96; Browning,
Newcastle, p. 174.

[71] George's will, 3.14/4/1751, RA, GEO/52921–31. Clauses in the will are identified
thus: §N.

[72] George's will, 25/8/1732, RA GEO/52777.

[73] Cumberland's acknowledgement (10/6/1743) of George's 1740 codicil, RA GEO/
52850–4.

[74] Cumberland's further acknowledgement, Kensington (1.12/8/1746), RA GEO/
52880–5.

be specifically inheriting dominions. There was probably an element of grandfatherly piety, as well as tradition. Frederick had also commended his own grandfather's example to his children in his instructions for his son and heir in 1749.[75] Invocation of George's paternal grandfather was slightly double-edged, though. It had been Ernst August who had caused a significant rift between Georg Ludwig and the majority of his younger brothers by his insistence on the implementation of primogeniture. This meant that, other than Georg Ludwig, they all found themselves at the mercy of their father's largesse, with their prospect of inheriting territories eliminated.

Nevertheless, the king's will clearly set out George's intentions on how his family should be provided for in the future. He asked to be buried next to Caroline and he named his grandson, Prince George, or his heir, as the sole successor to his German dominions (§§1 and 2). The prospect of dividing his German and British dominions was therefore ruled out, despite the discussions that had taken place in the 1740s. Cumberland was now to be provided with an inheritance from George's Hanoverian funds. The capital sum of 3.3 million Reichstalers was to be settled on him. From this, he, and any of his heirs from an appropriate marriage, could take 3 per cent for their own use (§3). The capital could be used for the purchase of territories and lands proximate to George's German territories if the opportunity arose but otherwise it was to be preserved (§4). Cumberland could dispose of his portion to any of his future offspring as he saw fit, subject to the condition that they were from a suitable marriage (§5). Cumberland was also made responsible for the care and upkeep of his sisters. George's German successors were excused from this task, unless Cumberland's line failed (§§6 and 7). In that case, the funds set aside for Cumberland were to be returned but the responsibility for caring for Cumberland's sisters would pass with them as well. George's successors were urged to deal with marriage portions in the traditional way (§8). That said, it was unlikely that either of George's unmarried daughters, Amelia and Caroline, would marry as they were already well into middle age. Each of George's daughters was to receive 40,000 Reichstalers from the privy purse (presumably the German one, given the currency in which the legacy was denominated). Should any of George's daughters predecease him then the legacy was to be divided equally among the survivors. In the unfortunate circumstances that they all did, then the legacy was void (§§9 and 10).

Having provided for his family, George was concerned to ensure that the Electorate would be governed properly. His Electoral successor, Prince George, was to have all the king's jewels (§11). Should the prince still be a minor when the king died, then Cumberland was to act on his behalf in Hanover and was to be given an additional 100,000 Reichstalers to help him.

[75] Hervey, *Memoirs*, i, pp. xxxiv–xxxv.

In contrast to the complicated arrangements that had to be made in Britain to accommodate the competing claims of Augusta and Cumberland, the situation in Hanover was regulated by royal fiat. If a regency became necessary, there should be two Germans of ministerial rank in London to assist Cumberland (§12). This would be a return to the situation that had prevailed in the first years of the Hanoverian succession when both Andreas Gottlieb von Bernstorff and Hans Kaspar von Bothmer had been present in London to advise Georg Ludwig. Bernstorff's decision to remain in Hanover in 1720 had halved the Hanoverian ministerial presence in London. Cumberland was also reminded of the importance of getting advice from the Hanoverian Privy Council when it came to making decisions about the Electorate. In keeping with George's strict view about the separation of the various component parts of his domains, there was an injunction that no German cash should be remitted to Britain and that no Englishman should ever be set over his German dominions as a 'Stattholder, or Governor' (§13). Whether, given the complaints of the patriot opposition, George saw the irony of this is unclear. The will concluded with a blessing for his family (§14) and information about where copies of the will were to be found (§15). One was to be lodged with the Privy Council in Hanover, another with the Electorate's highest court in Celle and the third was to be kept in London. The document was witnessed by Philipp von Münchhausen and five other officials from the *Deutsche Kanzlei*.

It did not take long for further modifications to be made to the will. A codicil of the same date gave further details of the legacies for George's daughters.[76] An additional 25,000 Reichstalers was to be given to George's unmarried daughters and 100,000 Reichstalers was set aside for the countess of Yarmouth. Those Hanoverian privy councillors employed in secret affairs were given 10,000 Reichstalers and there was 3,000 Reichstalers each for George's privy secretaries and 1,000 Reichstalers for the clerks of the privy chancery. Little more than a week later, even more alterations were made.[77] Most of the provisions of the previous will were confirmed except that George now wanted to make detailed provision for the disposal of some of his personal effects. The rings given to him by his wife were to go to his unmarried daughters, along with the miniatures of George and his wife produced by Christian Friedrich Zincke. The other pictures by Zincke in the same box as those of the king and queen were also to go to Amelia and Caroline. The jewels in the other strongboxes were to go to Cumberland. Finally, George asked that his body be placed in the same coffin as that of the queen.

Frederick's death had prompted George to put his family affairs in order and the timeliness of his actions was to be reinforced by other developments in 1751. His daughter Anne's husband, William IV of the United

[76] Codicil to George's will, 3.14/4/1751, RA GEO/52933.
[77] Addition to George's will, 11/4/1751 OS, RA GEO/52936.

Provinces, had enjoyed indifferent health for some time. The news that George was making regency arrangements within Britain prompted William's adviser, Charles Bentinck, to travel to London in June 1751 to study them for himself.[78] Given that William's heir was only three, it seemed a wise precaution and so it was to prove. William's health deteriorated over the summer. He spent some time at the spa in Aachen, putting his faith in rest and the waters, but on his return to the United Provinces he suffered a stroke and died in October 1751. The regency arrangements that were put in place mirrored the British proposals closely. Anne was to become governor and guardian of the United Provinces on behalf of her son, although she still had to battle with the delicate balance of forces between her and the States-General and the governments of the individual provinces.

George was to suffer a further loss before the end of the year. His youngest daughter, Louisa, queen of Denmark, developed a pregnancy-related hernia and her doctors decided that an operation was in order. Just as in her mother's case, surgical intervention was ineffective and Louisa died of complications in December 1751. In his memoirs of George's reign, Horace Walpole recorded him as commenting that 1751 had been a 'fatal year to my family! I lost my eldest son – but I am glad of it – then the Prince of Orange died and left everything in confusion . . . Now the Queen of Denmark is gone! I know I did not love my children when they were young, I hated to have them running into my room, but now I love them as well as most fathers.'[79]

These family deaths created both problems and opportunities for George. On the negative side, Louisa's death removed a possible channel of influence in Denmark. Louisa had never been especially influential at the Danish court but having an insider there, given the strategic importance of Denmark for both British and Hanoverian interests, was potentially advantageous. To compound the problem, it rapidly became clear that Louisa's former husband, Frederick V, was hoping to remarry, partly because of doubts about the mental capacities of their only son, the Crown Prince Christian. One of Frederick the Great's sisters was mentioned as a potential match and George was anxious that his nephew's influence in Copenhagen should not increase. He urged Walter Titley, his long-serving extraordinary envoy at the Danish court, to indicate the unsuitability of a Prussian princess as stepmother to his grandchildren. Titley's representations met with some success as Frederick's new bride turned out to be a member of the senior Guelph house of Brunswick-Wolfenbüttel instead.[80]

[78] Veronica Baker-Smith, *Royal discord: the family of George II* (London, 2008), p. 160.
[79] Horace Walpole, *Memoirs of King George II*, ed. John Brooke (3 vols, New Haven, 1985), i, p. 152.
[80] Baker-Smith, *Royal discord*, p. 173.

The situation in the United Provinces was potentially more promising, although, again, not without difficulties. George's relations with Anne since her marriage to William had been difficult. Shortly after her husband's death, George had written to Anne in a tone which suggested that, in her new situation, a closer degree of co-operation might not only be possible but even desirable. Anne, however, saw through her father's expressions of concern for her health and sympathy at her loss. George hoped that her husband's demise might mean he would be able to exert a greater degree of influence over Dutch affairs. Given the almost constant refrain about Dutch weakness and inactivity during the War of the Austrian Succession, such an outcome would be welcomed in many quarters in Britain. Yet it was precisely because of this that Anne was exceedingly cautious about responding positively to her father's overtures. Her position was difficult enough without opening herself up further to accusations that she was sacrificing Dutch interests to please her father.[81] Perhaps George realized something of the conflicting pressures under which Anne was operating. He did not stop to see, and potentially embarrass, his daughter on either of his journeys through the United Provinces in 1752, although he gained some insight into the tensions between Anne and her advisers from an interview with the commander of Dutch forces, Duke Louis of Brunswick-Wolfenbüttel.[82]

MONARCHICAL ABSENCE AND GOVERNMENTAL CHANGE

George's absences in Hanover could have serious consequences for factional politics within Britain. Newcastle's efforts to outmanoeuvre Bedford in 1750 during George's summer trip were the latest example of what had become almost a traditional rivalry between the secretaries of state for influence via proximity. However, in addition to the specific alterations in the composition of the ministry that followed from these journeys, it might be argued that there were more important structural shifts in the nature of government taking place as well.[83]

Trips to Hanover necessitated putting in place arrangements to govern Britain during the royal absence. The Hanoverian monarchs were familiar with this idea because they had had to make such arrangements for the government of Hanover after 1714 anyway. There was less in the way of recent British precedent, although William III had been a regular visitor to the United Provinces after 1688. There was also, of course, a

---

[81] Ibid., pp. 168–9.

[82] Ibid., p. 153.

[83] For an extended account of these developments, see Andrew C. Thompson, 'The development of the executive and foreign policy, 1714–1760', in Brendan Simms and William Mulligan, eds, *The primacy of foreign policy in British history, 1660–2000* (Basingstoke, 2010), pp. 65–78.

long tradition of providing counsel to the monarch, through the Privy Council and parliament. What was less common, however, was having formalized structures for ministerial meetings that were separate from the monarch, which assumed that he would not attend and which functioned as formal decision-making bodies. George's relatively frequent summer journeys had an important impact on the evolution of such developments.

Another way of talking about this phenomenon is to describe it as part of the history of the evolution of the cabinet. Previous generations of historians have offered rather different accounts of the development of the cabinet as an integral and central organ of government.[84] Much of the emphasis in older accounts was on the link between the development of parliament and the concomitant growth in the independence of the cabinet from the monarch. Chronologically, this separation was often seen as a product of the Glorious Revolution of 1688. The rise of the cabinet was viewed as part and parcel of a series of changes in the governance of Britain which were characterized by the supposed defeat of the absolutist pretensions of James II and the rise of constitutional monarchy that was quickly to follow. Thus described, it is possible to see the broad outlines of a story which would have been recognizable to historians of both the nineteenth and twentieth centuries who wanted to write British history as a story of progress. In historiographical terms, proponents of such a Whig view of history tended to concentrate on internal developments, which they saw as crucial to the development of cabinet government.[85]

By contrast, the account offered here suggests that although domestic pressures played their part, it was largely as a response to external forces and the need to formulate coherent foreign political policies that the cabinet emerged as an independent executive institution. While Whig accounts assumed that monarchical power was declining during the course of the eighteenth century, one of the major points to emerge from George's life is the continuing influence that he exercised on foreign policy. It is also worth re-emphasizing that much of the activity of the state was directed towards foreign policy, rather than the management of domestic affairs. Consequently, it is not surprising that it should be external pressures and the need to meet them that prompted changes in governmental structures.

The key governmental actors when it came to foreign policy were the king and the secretaries of state. Parliamentary management was also important so the attention that was paid to this increasingly crucial task by

---

[84] For classic articulations of a Whiggish account of cabinet development, see T.B. Macaulay, *The history of England from the accession of James II* (5 vols, London, 1848–61), iv, pp. 434–6 and W. Bagehot, *The English constitution*, ed. P. Smith (Cambridge, 2001), p. 9.

[85] Even the most recent account of the development of the cabinet in the period, which is determined to reintegrate the history of government into mainstream history in light of historiographical diversification since the 1960s, maintains a resolutely internal perspective. See Peter Jupp, *The governing of Britain, 1688–1848* (London, 2006), pp. 22–6.

the first lord of the treasury, particularly in the shape of Robert Walpole, Henry Pelham and the older and younger Pitts, is not entirely misguided.[86] Nevertheless, it is also vital to keep means and ends in mind. Parliament's importance, at least for central governmental activity, lay in its role of voting on the funds that were necessary for the military and the Civil List, from which much diplomatic activity was still funded. In crude terms, the task of parliamentary management was essentially an ancillary one. It was needed to ensure that the cogs of government could keep turning but the person charged with that task could not yet automatically claim primacy over his ministerial colleagues as the central figure in any administration.

A look at the background of many secretaries of state in the first half of the eighteenth century indicates something of the qualities and experience that were deemed necessary for high political office. Some, such as Stanhope, had enjoyed successful military careers before being called to political service. Many had some experience as diplomats. Sir Paul Methuen, Craggs, Townshend, Carteret, Harrington, Chesterfield and Holdernesse had all undertaken diplomatic missions. Most of these individuals, in keeping with the profile of diplomats more generally in the period, were either aristocrats or were ennobled prior to taking high office. It was not until the later 1750s, with the rise of Henry Fox and William Pitt the Elder, that there is any evidence that men who were career politicians or closely associated with parliament were plausible candidates for secretaryships. Newcastle, it must be admitted, does not fit easily into either pattern. He did enjoy something of a reputation as a parliamentary figure because, as a wealthy noble and landowner, he, like Bedford, had electoral influence. Yet Newcastle's early political progress had been made through the royal household and he had somehow managed to maintain himself at the centre of political life since the 1720s.

The aristocratic bias in royal councils is striking. This was partly a reflection of the social composition of those holding high offices at court – physical proximity to the monarch was still an important condition for being able to offer advice. But holders of high political office tended to be aristocratic too. When it came to dealing with the king's absence, the same people featured prominently among the lords justices – those who had responsibility for managing day-to-day administration while George was in Hanover. George had been a member of the group himself during his father's 1716 trip. Frederick was appointed to the regency council in 1729, although Caroline was entrusted with the primary responsibility for

[86] It can be taken too far, though: in J.H. Plumb's chapter on George II in *The first four Georges* (London, 1956), pp. 64–86 concentrate on the years 1727 to 1742 and the role of Robert Walpole while the second half of George's reign is covered on pp. 87–91, with Pelham and Pitt playing the starring roles.

leading the regency council on every occasion that George was absent until her death in 1737. This division of responsibilities caused further friction between father and son. The other members of the regency council were drawn from among the chief officers of state and were listed in the surviving minutes in the standard order of precedence. Thus, the archbishop of Canterbury was always among the lords justices, although his attendance at meetings was not as frequent as that of some of the more political appointees. There was, therefore, a close overlap between the composition of the lords justices and of the cabinet council.[87] Given that this was the case, where might it be said that the innovation lay?

Change emerged from the fact that the physical separation of the monarch from his ministers created several sorts of pressure. A recurrent feature of discussions of the political impact of all of George's Hanoverian trips was the fear that decisions were being taken without the knowledge and input of those in London. One possibility was that the travelling secretary was not consulting sufficiently. Another was that the king was acting independently and the new policies reflected his personal views. These might appear to conflict with the ministers' conception of British interests, particularly if it were thought that Hanoverian interests, broadly conceived, had been prioritized. The inability of those left behind to make representations to the king personally meant that they became more concerned about reaching a collective view that could be articulated in an epistolary manner to the travelling secretary in the hope that a united front might have more impact on George.

The crucial period for these developments was the 1740s and the 1750s because it was during these two decades that concerns about the direction of foreign policy were at the forefront of the minds of all involved. George's visit to Hanover in 1741 was overshadowed by concerns about the fate of Maria Theresa and whether a British desire to defend the Pragmatic Sanction would fall victim to a royal wish to defend Hanoverian security. The 1743 trip was dominated by the king's adventures on the battlefield and ministerial concerns that Carteret was making commitments that would prove difficult to uphold in practice. In 1745 it was the concerns of the ministers in London about the situation in Scotland that helped persuade George that it would be necessary to cut short his trip. In 1748 attention was focused on the peace negotiations in Aachen and how easy it would be to reach a settlement and then on Newcastle's nascent interest in how the 'Old System', the traditional British alliance with the Habsburgs to contain French power, might best be preserved. Newcastle's ostensible solution to this problem, the imperial election scheme, was at centre stage in both 1750 and 1752.[88]

[87] Jupp, *Governing of Britain*, p. 24.
[88] See above, pp. 192–7.

The group left in London tended to gather either in the Cockpit, one of the government offices in Whitehall, or at the London residence of Walpole and subsequently Newcastle to agree a line prior to the official meetings of the lords justices. The situation in 1740, '41 and '45 departed from previous visits to Hanover by either Georg Ludwig or George in that it was Harrington who travelled with the king to Hanover. While Harrington had considerable experience and was well liked, at least in the early 1740s, by George, he was not necessarily the senior or more powerful of the secretaries; Newcastle was. This meant that, almost for the first time, the more powerful ministers were all in London. The Old Corps group could therefore feel more confident about voicing their disagreements over the direction of royal policy.

The situation in 1743 was a little different. Carteret had George's ear in a way that Newcastle did not. Nevertheless, the experience of the previous two visits meant that the Old Corps group was reluctant to give up the voice that they felt they now deserved. In 1748 there was a reversion to the norm and Newcastle resumed the right of the senior secretary to accompany the king. Yet those left behind in London were still able to make their views known and the sense of a distinctive 'London lobby' to counter the view from Hanover survived. In this case, the issues tended to focus on Hardwicke and Pelham's fears that Newcastle was signing a series of blank cheques that Britain would not be able to afford, both literally and diplomatically. The issues, though, are less central than the shifts in behaviour caused by George's Hanover trips. Once a certain confidence had developed among the ministers left in London about their right to make their views known, then the genie was out of the bottle and it was impossible to put it back in. The Pelhams were, in one sense, crucial to the development of cabinet government but their contribution lay less in an ability to impress upon a reluctant monarch the necessity of parliamentary management than in the role they evolved in articulating a collective view and in coping with regular monarchical absences. In other words, some of the impetus behind moves towards cabinet government was a by-product of the peripatetic nature of early Hanoverian monarchy.

Political developments of the 1760s provide interesting further support for this view. The 1760s, just like 1742–6 and 1754–7, were marked by persistent ministerial instability. It seemed difficult for administrations to muster sufficient support to gain the confidence of both parliament and the king simultaneously. One way of looking at this problem would be to see in it a reflection of the continuing difficulties that Newcastle and his political heirs had in managing the monarch – nothing especially novel. Yet there was one respect in which the 1760s were different from the previous fifty years. George III, despite various rumours and plans to the contrary, never visited Hanover. His decision was to have important ramifications for how his Electoral subjects felt about the existence of the personal union.[89] In the British context the royal choice was arguably even more important. For the first time in several political generations, the monarch was continuously resident in Britain. George III was, as Jeremy Black has put it, anxious to adopt an executive style of monarchy, 'determined to deploy to the full powers that could be seen as his'.[90] Arguably, George had done this too, although increasing age inevitably diminished his effectiveness. Ministers had grown used in the latter years of George II's reign to making their own views known and often getting their own way. Royal absence had implicitly increased their authority and allowed change. In these circumstances, it is not necessarily surprising that a significant degree of conflict between monarch and ministers ensued. George III's early difficulties indicate the changes that had taken place in the later years of his grandfather's reign. Cabinet government emerged slowly and unevenly but George's summer wanderings were a significant factor in its evolution.

DEALING WITH FREDERICK'S LEGACY

Aside from his long-term contribution to British constitutional development, George had more immediate concerns. Frederick's death meant that problems of political management had abated somewhat. Yet George still had to deal with Frederick's legacy in a variety of other ways. George had been very aware throughout Frederick's life of the difficulties that his son had in relation to money and its management. Frederick was constantly on the lookout for credit and he was happy to exploit sources of finance in both Britain and Hanover. In Hanover, the key figure in organizing funds for Frederick was Ludwig von Schrader and he was already undertaking this task in the early 1740s.[91] Schrader also had a major role in raising bonds to cover the costs of a loan that Augusta had taken out from the prince of Anhalt-Zerbst through the mediation of her brother in 1745. Schrader had persuaded a number of leading Hanoverian worthies to fund these bonds with very little in the form of security being given by Frederick. Having come across to Britain to finalize arrangements with Frederick, Schrader stayed and became effectively part of Frederick's household (although he was not appointed to an official position because he was German).[92] News of Frederick's new source of funding reached his father's ears. In 1747 George wrote to the Hanoverian Privy Council

---

[89] See Torsten Riotte, 'George III and Hanover', in Brendan Simms and Torsten Riotte, eds, *The Hanoverian dimension in British history, 1714–1837* (Cambridge, 2007), pp. 58–85.

[90] Jeremy Black, *George III* (New Haven and London, 2006), p. 51.

[91] Frances Vivian, *A life of Frederick, prince of Wales, 1707–1751: a connoisseur of the arts*, ed. Roger White (Lampeter, 2007), p. 340.

[92] Ibid., pp. 356–62.

asking for a list of the individuals from whom Frederick had borrowed a sum which he understood to be in the region of 50,000 Reichstalers.[93]

George's enquiries met with a limited response in 1747. However, after Frederick's death, the issue became more pressing. Schrader wrote to George shortly after Frederick's demise in an effort to clear his name, as he had discovered that various accusations were being levelled against him.[94] He claimed that his ability to raise credit for Frederick had actually been to the king's service, even though various questions had been asked about the lower interest rates he had been able to procure on these loans. Schrader seems to have found willing lenders in Bremen, Verden and Mecklenburg. His efforts at self-justification failed to convince George. The king ordered that Schrader's Hanoverian pension (he had been an official in the Hanoverian treasury before coming to Britain) be stopped, although Augusta continued to offer financial support to her husband's erstwhile financier. The full extent of Frederick's German borrowings emerged slowly. In 1753 George received a letter from 117 separate creditors in Hanover, none of whom had been repaid. The total sum owed was now 338,400 Reichstalers.[95] Other than disgruntlement at the continued absence of their cash, the creditors also felt that they had been misled. They had been reassured that the loans would not be used to pay off Frederick's other debts but it seems that Schrader had done little more than pay off some of Frederick's larger borrowings by substituting the funds with lower interest rates that he had obtained in Hanover. George does not seem to have been overly sympathetic to requests for help. At least, any help he did provide can only have been partial. By 1761, it was calculated that the interest alone had risen to 145,700 Reichstalers.[96] A relative of the Hanoverian general, Pontpietin, whose original loan to Frederick had amounted to some 7,000 talers, was still trying to recover the sum in 1770. A calculation made for George III at some point in the 1760s valued the capital still owing at £58,000.[97] Whether George III ever paid off this portion of his father's debts is not known.

Frederick's financial problems were one cause of headaches for George. How to deal with disputes about the education of his heir was another. The problem was not so much the way in which Prince George was being educated as the personnel involved. Prince George's tutors had originally been chosen by Frederick, without consulting the king.[98] There was a governor and a sub-governor and the task of educating George and his

---

[93] George to Hanoverian Privy Council, St James's, 29/10/1747 OS and 1/12/1747 OS, NHStA, Hann. 92, 100, fos 1 and 23.

[94] Schrader to George, London, 31/3/1751 OS, ibid., fos 32–4.

[95] Hanoverian creditors to George, 10/4/1753 NS, ibid., fos 46–7.

[96] Ibid., fo. 112.

[97] Ibid., fo. 128.

[98] Vivian, *Frederick*, p. 374, J.C.D. Clark, ed., *The memoirs and speeches of James, 2nd Earl Waldegrave, 1742–1763* (Cambridge, 1988), p. 52.

younger brother Edward fell largely on the preceptor and sub-preceptor. Frederick's death enabled a partial rearrangement of office-holders. Lord North, the governor, was replaced by Lord Harcourt. He, like the new sub-governor Andrew Stone, was thought of as being close to the Old Corps Whigs. The preceptor, Francis Ayscough, was replaced by Thomas Hayter, bishop of Norwich. George made clear his dislike of Ayscough, telling Augusta that even the half-hour that he taught the princes each day was too much.[99] Ayscough had been a close associate of Frederick since the early 1730s and had hoped that his clerical career would take off when Frederick succeeded; instead he had to wait for Prince George to ascend the throne before receiving significant promotion. The only survivor of the previous regime was George Lewis Scott as sub-preceptor.

Relations between Harcourt and Hayter, on the one hand, and Stone and Scott, on the other were not good. Harcourt was determined to exercise the decisive influence over the young princes' education but he was disliked by Augusta, who was not above intriguing against him. Complaints soon reached the king. When George returned from Hanover in November 1752, observers could see that he was angry with Harcourt and the suspicion was that a whispering campaign had been started against him. Harcourt eventually managed to secure an audience with George. Perhaps he felt that attack, in the circumstances, was the best form of defence because he claimed that Stone and Scott, along with Augusta's secretary James Cressett, were men of Tory principles and closet Jacobites and therefore inappropriate educators for the princes. George refused to believe the accusations and Harcourt and Hayter were left with no option but to resign. However, the ruptures at court prompted what remained of the opposition to indulge in a little mischief. Stone and William Murray, the solicitor-general and future earl of Mansfield, were accused of having toasted the health of the Old Pretender while students at Oxford. The matter was formally investigated and while both Stone and Murray were cleared of any wrongdoing it was an unfortunate turn of events.[100] George was so worried by the affair and the tribulations caused by the accusations against Stone that it was rumoured that he was not sleeping properly.[101]

Stone retained his place in Prince George's household, as did Scott. Hayter was replaced by John Thomas, bishop of Peterborough and the role of governor was taken on by one of George's lords of the bedchamber, James, second Earl Waldegrave. Waldegrave, whose memoirs provide an important insight into court life in the mid-1750s, had already acquired one office in the shake-up following Frederick's death – warden of Stannaries

[99] Newman, ed., 'Leicester House politics', p. 208.
[100] Clark, ed., *Waldegrave memoirs*, pp. 54–7.
[101] Rigby to Bedford, 17/2/1753, Russell, intro., *Bedford correspondence*, ii, p. 123.

in the duchy of Cornwall – and had now gained another. Waldegrave's new posts were evidence of the way in which the political tide had started to flow in the king's direction again. While Prince George had succeeded his father as prince of Wales, the duchy of Cornwall was traditionally reserved for the sovereign's eldest son so it now reverted to the crown. Both the valuable income from the duchy and the political patronage, which the warden dispensed, were now back in the hands of George and his ministers, reducing the material and human resources available to the opposition. The prospects for a period of relative political calm seemed good but these hopes were quickly dashed.

Chapter 8

NO MORE PEACE

At the beginning of March 1754, Henry Pelham died. The timing could not have been worse. A general election was due within a matter of weeks. George greeted the news of Pelham's departure with dismay, noting that 'now I shall have no more peace'.[1] Pelham proved to be a hard act to follow and ministerial wrangling was once more to become central to political life over the next few years. From George's perspective two features of the future shape of the administration seem to have been crucial. It should not contain anybody who was personally objectionable to him, and it must support the Whig interest. George also seems to have been more than willing to listen to the advice of his ministers before making a decision about who should succeed to Pelham's offices.[2]

FILLING THE GAP

Pelham had combined several roles. One issue that therefore had to be resolved was whether it would be necessary to find a successor or successors to the posts of first lord of the treasury, chancellor of the exchequer and leader of the Commons. A number of figures were mentioned as potential replacements but, of these, three emerged as central. Henry Fox, the secretary at war and close associate of Cumberland, was seen as having the ability to manage the Commons. William Murray, solicitor-general, was also talked of, despite his recent difficulties with accusations of Jacobitism from his student days. Finally, William Pitt was regarded as an able Commons orator, although he himself recognized that his claims for promotion were far from overwhelming and that it was unlikely that Pelham would be replaced by a single individual.[3] Fox had been first off the mark in canvassing for the job, seeking support from the political great and good almost as soon as he had learned of Pelham's death.

In the confusion following Pelham's death, Newcastle was too overcome with grief at the loss of his brother to think sensibly about how the various vacancies were to be filled. Consequently, Hardwicke assumed a leading

[1] W. Coxe, *Memoirs of the administration of the Right Honourable Henry Pelham* (2 vols, London, 1829), ii, p. 302.
[2] J.C.D. Clark, *The dynamics of change* (Cambridge, 1982), p. 51.
[3] Ibid., pp. 46–7.

role in safeguarding the Old Corps inheritance. George favoured approaching the duke of Devonshire to take on some of Pelham's responsibilities but when he arrived in town, Devonshire politely indicated that he had no inclination to do so and other solutions must be found. The arrangement that emerged was that Newcastle would become first lord of the treasury himself. Henry Legge would be made chancellor of the exchequer and Fox would be promoted to a secretaryship of state. Holdernesse would switch to the northern secretaryship vacated by Newcastle, allowing Fox to have Holdernesse's place as southern secretary. Hardwicke discussed the plan with George and gained his approval before presenting it to the other ministers for ratification.[4]

Almost as soon as the plans had been agreed, they began to unravel. The problem was the extent of the powers that had been offered to Fox. One of the reasons that Hardwicke had been reluctant to fill Pelham's various offices with a single individual was his fear that, unless he was of unimpeachable loyalty to the Old Corps, such an individual might pose a considerable threat to Old Corps political dominance. Newcastle's position at the treasury meant that the patronage power that went with that office had been properly secured. The resources available to Fox to act independently were therefore curtailed from the start. Newcastle and Fox traded blows about what had been promised to whom by whom and when, particularly in relation to their roles in the management of the secret service fund. This issue was crucial because it was this fund that bankrolled government efforts to gain favourable election results and a general election was imminent.[5] The net result was that Fox refused to accept the secretaryship. George, no doubt appropriately briefed by Newcastle and Hardwicke, made it very clear to Fox in their only audience during the immediate post-Pelham upheavals that he was not prepared to let Fox have sole management of the secret service fund and that he had only agreed to advance a commoner to the lofty position of a secretaryship on the understanding that Fox would follow Newcastle's lead. Fox's plans for personal advancement failed, although he was able to retain his previous office of secretary at war.[6]

The vacant secretaryship was now given to Sir Thomas Robinson, who had had considerable diplomatic experience as the British minister plenipotentiary in Vienna for many years and latterly had been one of the plenipotentiaries negotiating the peace of Aachen. Robinson had entered the Commons in 1748, as MP for Christchurch, with strong backing from Pelham and he gained a place at the board of trade shortly afterwards. In parallel to his political advancement, he had also acquired the reasonable

---

[4] Ibid., pp. 50–8.

[5] On the uses of the secret service fund, see L.B. Namier, *The structure of politics at the accession of George III* (2nd edn, London, 1957), ch. 4.

[6] Clark, *Dynamics of change*, pp. 66–8.

court sinecure of the mastership of the great wardrobe. Although some thought that his long service in Vienna had led to him going native, Robinson was part of an inner circle of diplomatic experts in whom George placed his trust so it was not altogether surprising that he was promoted when the opportunity arose.

From the foreign political perspective, the various changes that Pelham's demise had precipitated did little to alter the direction of policy. Despite his transfer to the treasury, Newcastle remained concerned to maintain the system that he and George had worked on over the last few years with an emphasis on a strong attachment to Austria and the defence of the Barrier fortresses against potential French encroachments. Robinson was, in many ways, the ideal choice to support these schemes. The domestic position, however, was less straightforward. Although George, Newcastle and Hardwicke had been anxious not to give Fox too much power, he would have been able to fulfil one of the important tasks of any administration: managing the Commons. It was much less certain that Robinson had either the ability or the gravitas to succeed in this regard. His parliamentary experience was limited and, as Waldegrave put it in his memoirs, when he 'play'd the Orator, which he too frequently attempted it was so exceeding ridiculous, that those who loved and esteem'd him, could not always preserve a friendly composure of Countenance'.[7]

The general election meant that worries about Robinson's managerial competence could be temporarily shelved. The results were generally pleasing for Newcastle. His own calculations suggested that there had been a slight increase in the number of ministerial Whigs with a steep decline in the number of opposition Whigs, mainly supporters of Bedford, and a much smaller decrease in the number of Tories.[8] He triumphantly told Bentinck that 'there is certainly a greater number of real good Whigs in it [the Commons], than in any Parliament, which has been since the Revolution'.[9] Newcastle and Hardwicke both observed the pleasure with which George greeted the results.[10] Hardwicke was keen to stress to the king both the important role that Newcastle had played in securing this outcome and that it suggested a degree of national confidence in the direction of the administration that had previously been lacking.

Fox was still, however smarting from his perceived betrayal by Newcastle in March 1754. During the summer of that year he courted

[7] J.C.D. Clark, ed., *The memoirs and speeches of James, 2nd Earl Waldegrave, 1742–1763* (Cambridge, 1988), pp. 160–1.

[8] L.B. Namier and John Brooke, *The House of Commons, 1754–1790* (3 vols, London, 1964), i, p. 62.

[9] Newcastle to William Bentinck, Newcastle House, 17/5/1754, very private, BL, Add. MSS 32849, fo. 155r.

[10] Hardwicke to Newcastle, Powis House, 24/4/1754 and 5/5/1754, BL, Add. MSS 32735, fos 178 and 234.

Lady Yarmouth as a potentially useful ally to try to press his case for further advancement.[11] As the start of the new parliamentary session approached, the management of the Commons became a more urgent issue. George was aware that Robinson's position suggested that he ought to take on the task but he also knew that Murray, Legge, Fox and Pitt all had either the ability or the desire to act in that capacity.[12]

PROBLEMS ABROAD

It was into this context of concern about parliamentary management that the news broke of the failure of Colonel George Washington to capture Fort Duquesne in the Ohio valley and his subsequent surrender at Fort Necessity in early July 1754.[13] The news from the colonies was significant on several levels. In the broader strategic sense, it was a reminder of the precariousness of the position of the British colonies on the eastern seaboard. With the French controlling Quebec to the north and wanting to move up the Mississippi and then the Ohio from Louisiana in the south there was a serious risk that the thirteen colonies would be encircled. One of the subsidiary motivations of Washington's mission, in addition to interdicting French forces, was to assert the British claim to the lands to the west of the Appalachian mountains: the sense of the threat under which they lived was not lost on the colonists themselves. The news from America was also an opportunity for the ongoing debate between continentalists and 'blue water' advocates about the relative priorities of British foreign policy to be intensified. In the domestic context, Fox used the news to express his disquiet that, as secretary at war, he had not been fully consulted on the orders sent to the troops in America.[14] Holdernesse was forced to defend his actions but how best to respond to the growing French threat in America was to become something of a domestic political football.

While his ministers jostled for position, George seemed less interested in the problems in America than in ensuring that the administration ran as smoothly as possible. This is not to say that he had lost interest in government. In many ways, he was just as active as he had always been in making sure that his views were known, on those things about which he cared. Newcastle had to remind Halifax in early August that although, as first lord, Newcastle enjoyed considerable patronage powers, there were limits to what he could achieve. Newcastle could not 'force the King to do what He may be disinclin'd to; or justify me, in breaking my Word to others,

---

[11] Newcastle to Hardwicke, Claremont, 1/9/1754, BL, Add. MSS 32736, fo. 388.

[12] Clark, *Dynamics of change*, p. 90.

[13] For the background to Washington's actions, see Fred Anderson, *Crucible of war* (London, 2000), chs 4–5.

[14] Clark, *Dynamics of change*, p. 87.

whom I may neither honor, or love, one quarter as much as I do you. Your Lordship is mistaken, if you think, I can do what I please. The King has His own Way of thinking, & acting, in the Disposal of Preferments, and particularly Ecclesiastical ones.'[15] To reinforce his point, Newcastle then listed a number of instances where the requests of the well-connected to have this or that office bestowed upon one of their friends or relations had failed in the face of royal opposition. George remained, even in his advancing years, determined to keep tight control of the reins of patronage.

Another area in which George continued to take a great interest was the affairs of the empire, particularly as they affected his family. George's daughter Mary and her husband Friedrich of Hessen-Kassel had been frequent guests in Hanover during the king's summer visits since their marriage in 1740. Indeed, of those of his daughters not resident in Britain, Mary was probably the child that George saw most after her marriage. The match, whose origins lay in dynastic politics and the value of Friedrich's father's troops, was far from happy. Perhaps this was one of the reasons why Friedrich and Mary's visits to Hanover were rarely simultaneous. Friedrich embodied a number of the vices common to the ruling elite. He was a big spender, a heavy drinker and violent in his personal relationships. He also took mistresses, although this was regarded more as a socially acceptable mark of virility than a vice. What was to prove considerably less acceptable was Friedrich's decision to abjure his Protestant upbringing and convert to Catholicism, ostensibly to increase the likelihood of being united with one of his mistresses in the afterlife. The conversion had taken place in 1749 but it was only made public in late 1754.

George was not best pleased to discover that his son-in-law had turned papist. Hardwicke reported to Newcastle that George was very affected by the news, although even in his distress he could not resist the opportunity of demonstrating his extensive genealogical knowledge to Hardwicke. The chancellor was surprised to be told that George feared that his son-in-law was mad, just as his mother had been before him, and could not quite work out whether this was meant as an insult or in the strict medical sense.[16] News of Mary's predicament had also reached her sister Anne in the United Provinces. This prompted Joseph Yorke, Hardwicke's son and British minister at The Hague, to ask Newcastle what might be done to help. Newcastle responded that George would try to ensure that his grandsons were educated as Protestants and he hoped that the United Provinces (and Anne) might join him in efforts to extract guarantees about the future religious status of Hessen-Kassel.[17] Although the peace of Westphalia had

---

[15] Newcastle to Halifax, Newcastle House, 8/8/1754, BL, Add. MSS 32736, fo. 182v.
[16] Hardwicke to Newcastle, Powis House, 3/11/1754, BL, Add. MSS 32737, fo. 255.
[17] Newcastle to J. Yorke, Newcastle House, 1/11/1754, BL, Add. MSS 32851, fos 123–4.

supposedly fixed the religious map of the empire, there had been sufficient princely conversions from Protestantism to Catholicism and consequent attempts to alter the confession of their territories since 1648 to make the acquisition of further reassurances advisable.

George did more than just make noises about the new situation in which Mary found herself. He dispatched a trusted envoy, Count von der Schulenburg, to Kassel to work out a negotiated settlement,[18] and he expressed his concerns to Landgrave William about the broader impact of his son's conversion on the confessional balance of the empire.[19] Mary's letters to her sister Caroline provided an additional means for George to inform himself of her situation.[20] Schulenburg was able, after a long round of negotiations, to reach agreement about Mary's future fate. The landgrave and Friedrich agreed to an arrangement whereby a formal separation would occur between Mary and Friedrich. Mary would be allowed to keep custody of her sons and to bring them up as Protestants. To ensure that she had the means to look after herself and her family, the revenues of the county of Hanau would be placed at her disposal.

The seriousness with which the king viewed these developments can be illustrated in several ways. Although the issue was, in some sense, a domestic matter that needed to be resolved between the landgrave and his son, George and his Hanoverian privy councillors were anxious that any guarantees that were given should be ratified by the Corpus Evangelicorum, the umbrella organization for Protestants within the empire. He wanted the guarantees to be backed by more than just goodwill. Secondly, George dispatched Ernst von Steinberg, one of his most senior ministers, to Kassel to oversee the final stage of the negotiations. Thirdly, George sought the opinion of Lord Chancellor Hardwicke on the comprehensiveness of the guarantees that Friedrich had offered. While Hardwicke was keen to stress that his knowledge of imperial law made him little more than an informed amateur, he was perfectly happy to raise various legal quibbles about the draft documents. Overall, though, he was certain that George ought to add his royal guarantee to the agreement, noting that it would be 'an Act highly becoming His Majesty's greatness of mind; his care of His Royal Family, & of the Protestant Religion; and I hope the States General will concur with the King in this Guaranty'.[21]

[18] Much of what follows is based on NHStA, Hann. 92, 1991.

[19] George to William of Hessen-Kassel, Kensington, [October 1754], draft, NHStA, Hann. 92, 1991, fo. 27.

[20] Mary had remained close to her sisters. She had visited Caroline at Bath in 1746 and also spent time with Louisa in Denmark when she could. See Fanny Russell to Charles Russell, Bath, 11/10/1746, HMC, *Report on the manuscripts of Mrs Frankland-Russell-Astley of Chequers Court, Bucks* (London, 1900), pp. 355–6 and Veronica Baker-Smith, *Royal discord: the family of George II* (London, 2008), pp. 173–4.

[21] Copy of Hardwicke to Holdernesse, Powis House, 13/12/1754, NHStA, Hann. 92, 1991, fo. 238r.

George himself had admitted after Louisa's death that he might not have been the best of fathers to his children when they were young.[22] However, his prompt action to ensure Mary and his grandchildren's well-being shows something of his paternal care. It was also, however, likely to have been prompted by a broader awareness of the importance of maintaining the position of Protestantism in the empire. George was, in that sense, a dynastic Protestant more than anything else, doubly constrained by his position in both Britain and Hanover to be seen to be doing something to right the wrongs inflicted on his co-religionists. It was for these reasons that George was keen to involve both his British and Hanoverian officials in working out a viable agreement in this particular case; when George eventually signed the guarantee, it was passed from the office of the British secretary of state to Privy Councillor von Behr in Hanover.

MANAGING MINISTERS

In addition to the difficulties that George faced in looking after his family interests, the domestic situation continued to cause concern. Robinson, as had been widely predicted, was not enjoying his managerial role in the Commons. Henry Legge, Henry Fox and William Pitt were all engaged in a series of manoeuvres designed to illustrate their own virtues and their consequent claims for either increased power or improved office, or both. They hoped to achieve this through covert or overt attacks on Robinson's managerial skills. Pitt launched a vitriolic assault on the corruption in the Commons, following the hearing of the petition against the election result in Berwick, and mocked Robinson's handling of the petition against the Reading result. While Fox did come to Robinson's aid in the latter case, his satirical defence of the secretary of state did more harm than good to Robinson's reputation.[23] Newcastle began to wonder if dismissing Pitt from his post as paymaster-general and using the concomitant reshuffle to improve Fox's position might relieve the pressure on Robinson. George also thought that something had to be done. He saw Fox on 2 December and urged him to support his business in the Commons. Fox was evasive. Whether this was because of some sort of formal understanding that he had with Pitt about a joint assault on Newcastle's position is unclear. Fox was also cagey about George's talk of a greater role for him, albeit conditional on acknowledging Newcastle's seniority. He thought that Pitt would not take kindly to Fox being promoted but not him. The net result would be that trouble would continue.[24] Nevertheless, Fox did open up negotiations and these resulted in him accepting a seat on the cabinet council, although without enhancement of his office. The king hoped this would

[22] See above, p. 213.
[23] Clark, *Dynamics of change*, pp. 117–18.
[24] Ibid., pp. 126–7.

make the parliamentary situation easier. He had taken an active interest in the course of the negotiations, not least because he was keen to ensure that Pitt, who was still persona non grata (being paymaster-general did not require attendance on him), derived as little benefit as possible from the disturbances. George would have been happy for Pitt to be dismissed altogether but he was persuaded that Fox's unwillingness to act against Pitt made this impolitic.

Just as it looked as if the situation had calmed down, Newcastle's relationship with George went through one of its periodic downturns. The occasion was vacancies in the royal household. Earl Gower and the second earl of Albemarle both died in December 1754. Between them, they had held a number of important offices. Gower had become lord privy seal in 1742 and held that post, with one brief interruption, until his death. He was also master of the harriers. Albemarle was ambassador to Paris, groom of the stole, governor of Virginia, a knight of the Garter and colonel of the Coldstream Guards. Hardwicke and Newcastle both thought that the deaths created opportunities for them to ease some of their other political worries. Ideally they wanted to use the redistribution of offices to do something for Legge and the earl of Egmont, erstwhile chief political adviser of the late prince of Wales. George, however, had other ideas.

Hardwicke and Newcastle were pressing for a place in the bedchamber for George, third earl of Orford. As Robert Walpole's grandson, Orford had impeccable Old Corps credentials. The king was not impressed, wanting instead to reward the earl of Essex.[25] However, George was even more incensed by the Old Corps' preferred candidate for the new groom of the stole. Hardwicke and Newcastle had thought that bringing the duke of Dorset back from Dublin, where he was lord lieutenant, to become groom of the stole would give them increased flexibility in strengthening the ministry, perhaps by giving Dorset's job to Bedford and thus neutralizing the largest oppositional Whig group in the Commons.

George disagreed. Hardwicke had a very difficult meeting with him when he attended a levee on 3 January 1755. At first the king seemed quite civil, although he had only spoken to Granville and Hardwicke. Hardwicke explained that he had returned to London earlier than he had indicated at a drawing room in the previous week because he wanted to press the claims of his son Joseph for a vacant colonelcy – Joseph was a not implausible candidate for this position; he was already a lieutenant colonel of the Grenadier Guards, having served with distinction under Cumberland during the War of the Austrian Succession. George was noncommittal but Hardwicke's supplication led to a royal explosion about Newcastle's recent conduct. Newcastle 'meddles in things he has nothing

---

[25] Newcastle to Hardwicke, Claremont, 2/1/755, most private, BL, Add. MSS 32852 fos 28–9 and Newcastle to Horace Walpole, Claremont, 2/1/1755, fos 41–2.

to do with. He would dispose of my Bedchamber, which is the personal Service about my Self, & I won't suffer any body to meddle in.'[26] Hardwicke sought to reassure George that neither he nor Newcastle were seeking to impose any particular individuals on the king, although he did mention again the idea of doing something for Dorset. George responded caustically that it was impractical to have a seventy-year-old as groom of the stole.[27] Finally Hardwicke tried to pour oil on troubled waters by reminding the king that the responsibilities of the first lord of the treasury inevitably meant more than simple financial management, not least because it was necessary for the political nation more generally to have a single figure to whom they could address applications for George's favour. Hardwicke pessimistically concluded that, like Newcastle, he felt that relations in the closet were as bad as they had ever been.[28]

However, the storm was relatively short-lived. A few days later, Hardwicke noted that, despite the recent disagreements, George had been civil to him both at the levee and in the drawing room. The conversation had turned to the traditional levee topic of the weather.[29] George was able to get his own way in some respects. Dorset was not imposed upon him as groom of the stole. Instead, William Henry van Nassau van Zuylestein, fourth earl of Rochford,[30] who had previously been George's extraordinary envoy and plenipotentiary in Turin, was rewarded. The resignation of the second earl of Poulett, who had held a bedchamber post since 1733, meant that both Essex and Orford were given posts as lords of the bedchamber, as this created another vacancy in addition to the one created by Rochford's promotion. George had shown himself unwilling to be dictated to in his own domain of the household. Yet his behaviour at the cabinet around this time did not suggest any burning desire for a wholesale alteration in the ministry. According to Robinson, he listened carefully to the letters that were read to him before their dispatch and signed them without much comment.[31]

Newcastle clearly felt that he had been unfairly attacked by George. He worried that the king's recent emphasis on the importance of clarity about the distribution of patronage was the result of hints from Fox about the desirability of curbing Newcastle's power. The promotions in the household also showed worrying signs of royal independence. Rochford was a client of Cumberland while Essex was Bedford's nephew. On the other hand, Joseph Yorke was promoted to the colonelcy of the 9th Regiment of

[26] Hardwicke to Newcastle, Powis House, 3/1/1755, ibid., fo. 63v.
[27] Ibid., 64v. George was being unfair – Dorset was only 66.
[28] Ibid., 65r.
[29] Hardwicke to Newcastle, Powis House, 5/1/1755, ibid., fo. 91.
[30] The fourth earl's grandfather had been a Dutch confidant of William III, naturalized and enobled after 1688. The fourth earl was the first holder of the new familial title to be born in Britain.
[31] Robinson to Newcastle, Whitehall, 3/1/1755, BL, Add. MSS 32852, fo. 61.

Foot. The net effect of all the changes seemed to do little to the balance between the Old Corps, Cumberland and Bedford. Rather, it illustrated George's continuing ability to get what he wanted. Newcastle did still have other cards to play, though. Privately he suggested to Hardwicke that if the king were so determined to retain control of the distribution of places in his household or of Garter knighthoods, then the Old Corps should insist on the quid pro quo of being able to make the parliamentary arrangements that they wanted. Moreover, given the king's known propensity for prioritizing foreign affairs, Newcastle could suggest that if the king were insistent on the first lord not extending his remit beyond the treasury, then Newcastle would withdraw from participation in foreign affairs. The king knew Newcastle's experience and worth in this area and so would have to accept, albeit reluctantly, that he must continue to show a certain degree of favour towards the Old Corps.[32]

Following the excitement of the early part of the parliamentary session, Newcastle and the king were relieved that the first months of 1755 passed without much incident. Neither the international situation nor domestic political wrangling suggested that such relative tranquillity could be anything other than temporary, however. In early April, it became apparent that Lord Poulett, still angry about Rochford's household promotion over him, intended to bring forward a motion attacking Newcastle and condemning the king's projected trip to Hanover. Newcastle was worried that Poulett was part of an organized bid to oust the Old Corps from the position of primacy among the Whigs and replace them with Cumberland's faction, although Poulett's move was probably driven by nothing more sinister than sour grapes.[33] The composition of the regency council also caused some controversy. There was talk that Cumberland might be made sole regent, although Newcastle's contacts with Lady Yarmouth suggested that George was unlikely to go for this option.[34] Instead, Cumberland found himself at the head of sixteen lords justices. Holdernesse, as senior secretary, was given the task of accompanying the king to Hanover. Newcastle stayed in London, partly because his new role as first lord meant that he had no real reason for travelling with the king and partly because he was anxious to keep an eye on political developments at home. Waldegrave identified the key figures, who 'determined all affairs of consequence' as Cumberland, Hardwicke, Granville, Newcastle, Admiral Anson, Robinson and Fox.[35] Cumberland, Fox and Granville were viewed as the more hawkish elements within the regency but the deteriorating nature of the international situation was at the forefront of everyone's minds.

[32] Clark, *Dynamics of change*, pp. 138–9.
[33] Ibid., pp. 153–4.
[34] Ibid., p. 156.
[35] Clark, ed., *Waldegrave memoirs*, p. 168.

DEEPENING INTERNATIONAL WORRIES

In addition to the worsening situation in America, with French incursions up the Ohio, British prospects in Europe were not looking rosy either. Newcastle's efforts since 1748 had been focused on breathing new life into the idea of the 'Old System'. He had hoped that he could restore relations with the Habsburgs and, at the same time, induce Maria Theresa to take seriously her responsibilities to maintain the Barrier fortresses in the Low Countries. The problem was that, while Austrian ministers and even Maria Theresa herself were perfectly happy to make all the right noises about the importance of the Barrier, they did nothing. Habsburg strategic thinking was changing focus. Implacable hostility towards France was softening in the face of the new imperative of recovering Silesia from Prussia. Consequently, by late 1754 it was becoming apparent that Newcastle's efforts in ostentatiously courting the Austrians over the previous six years were unlikely to yield much in the way of tangible results. The Dutch, too, seemed reluctant to do much.[36] The result of this was a temporary move away from a primary concern with Europe to an emphasis on the need to combat France at sea and in the colonies.[37]

The decision to move towards a more aggressive stance in America was also bound up with the factional struggles within Britain. The news of Washington's defeat had led to calls for a strong British response in the autumn of 1754. Newcastle's initial reaction had been that the crisis could be handled by sending a few officers and some half-pay troops. The idea was that a small force might be put at the disposal of the activist governor of Virginia, Robert Dinwiddie. Part of the problem of dealing with the emergent colonial crisis was that there was no centralized structure for making policy or raising troops. This was partly why Cumberland and Fox along with the vigorous president of the board of trade, the earl of Halifax, favoured a more active response. Instead of relying on the colonists to defend themselves with some aid from Britain they proposed that a larger force of regular troops be sent to reinforce the existing British presence of three regular regiments in Nova Scotia. The new force was to comprise two Irish regiments under the command of Major General Edward Braddock. Newcastle was concerned, even after he had agreed to the dispatch of the troops, that such an action might be deemed overly aggressive by the French. He tried to back away but Fox was able to gain George's direct sanction for the dispatch of the troops so there was little that Newcastle could do to resist. Even then, he cavilled at the extent of Braddock's orders, arguing that anything beyond resistance to recent French claims in the Ohio valley might trigger a more general war. He hoped to contain the conflict in America. Cumberland and Fox tended

---

[36] Yorke to Holdernesse, The Hague, 1/4/1755, secret, BL, Add. MSS 32854, fo. 1.
[37] Brendan Simms, *Three victories and a defeat* (London, 2007), pp. 396–8.

towards a more bellicose attitude than the moderation of Newcastle and Hardwicke.[38]

Part of the problem that George faced in early 1755 was that if the British were going to concentrate on the colonial struggle with France, then it was imperative that conflict did not escalate on the continent. Newcastle was much more conscious of this than Halifax, whose trade brief meant his perspective was narrower. The desire for peace on the continent meant in turn that it was important to try to assure Hanover's security. So, as on previous occasions, the royal visit to Hanover was as much about larger questions of diplomacy and politics as an opportunity to take a break from British factional struggles. Newcastle was anxious about how George might be able to navigate the complicated paths of continental politics without his guiding hand, as well as worried about how his dispatches from London would be received by the king. He agreed with Holdernesse that he would always include a separate postscript in his letters to George, designed for Holdernesse's eyes only. He also urged Holdernesse to let him know what George's reactions to his letters were, especially if there were complaints about their length. Newcastle was aware of his tendency to be verbose but claimed that it was only by this means that he could ensure that he had thought of everything relevant to the matter in hand.[39]

Prussia was still seen as the primary threat to Hanoverian security, particularly if Frederick were able to maintain cordial relations with the French court. Some efforts were made in the summer of 1755 to secure Hanover via diplomacy.[40] The irony was that any efforts to concentrate on the colonial struggle presupposed that the continent had been neutralized which in turn meant that an active diplomatic strategy had to be pursued to protect Hanover. One of the traditional ways in which this had been achieved was through subsidy arrangements with other German princes to provide some sort of military cover for the Electorate should the French, or any other power, decide to attack. Understandings were reached with both Hessen-Kassel and Ansbach while George was in Hanover. Holdernesse assured Newcastle that George had only permitted the agreement with Hessen-Kassel to be reached on the lowest possible terms for Britain, such was his desire to minimize the costs to the British taxpayer.[41] Worries about the future availability of Hessian regiments was one of the reasons why George had been so concerned to ensure that the marital problems

[38] Reed Browning, *The duke of Newcastle* (New Haven and London, 1975), pp. 210–12, Anderson, *Crucible of war*, ch. 6, T.R. Clayton, 'The duke of Newcastle, the earl of Halifax, and the American origins of the Seven Years' War', *HJ*, 24 (1981), pp. 571–603.

[39] Newcastle to Holdernesse, Claremont, 9/5/1755, Postscript apart, BL, Add. MSS 32854, fo. 464.

[40] Walther Mediger, *Moskaus Weg nach Europa* (Braunschweig, 1952), pp. 500–9.

[41] Holdernesse to Newcastle, Hanover, 25/5/1755, BL, Add. MSS 32855, fo. 210v.

of his daughter and the landgrave's heir did not lead to Hessen-Kassel disappearing from the north German mercenary market. Mary visited her father in Hanover for six weeks over the summer before returning to Hanau.[42] George did as much as he could to enjoy the summer as well, adopting his usual pattern of dining with Lady Yarmouth and various other ladies from the court. However, the court diarist also recorded several occasions on which his health was deemed sufficiently bad to drive him to physic.[43]

It was difficult to forget the diplomatic situation entirely, though. Newcastle's worries about the French reaction to the dispatch of regular troops to the American colonies had turned out to be partially justified. In response to the British deployment of regular forces, irrespective of the fact that both the regiments had been under strength when they left Ireland, the French decided to provide reinforcements of their own. Moreover, attempts to reach an accommodation by negotiation were proving difficult. The French ambassador in London, the duc de Mirepoix, had taken the lead in efforts to reach a settlement; Albemarle had not yet been replaced as George's representative in Versailles. The problem was the conditions under which full negotiations could take place. The French wanted an armistice to be in place, fearing that British and colonial expeditions might hand the initiative at the negotiating table to George and his ministers if left unchecked. The British, on the other hand, feared that an armistice would simply ensure that the French would be able to move sufficient reinforcements into America to allow them to regroup.[44]

By the time George departed for Hanover, these negotiations had collapsed. Instead of an amicable settlement, orders had been sent to the Royal Navy to prevent the French from landing reinforcements at Louisburg. Vice-Admiral Edward Boscawen was charged with the task. His dispatch was used by Braddock to animate the colonists into vigorous action, both in support of his own expedition to drive the French from the Ohio and to provide the necessary men and materiels for a separate attempt to take Fort Niagara on Lake Ontario using two colonial regiments, mothballed since 1748 but revived for the occasion. Braddock was determined to reverse Washington's defeat of the previous year and take Fort Duquesne. His force was a mixture of the regular troops and colonials who had been recruited to bring the regiments up to strength. He advanced to within ten miles of Fort Duquesne where he was confronted by a force composed mainly of Native Americans but with some French regulars and Canadian militia, numbering around 800 in total. Braddock and his troops had forded the Monongahela river when they spotted the

---

[42] NHStA, Dep. 103, IV, 324, fo. 169r.

[43] E.g. ibid., fo. 166v (8/5/1755).

[44] Browning, *Newcastle*, pp. 216–17, Clayton, 'Duke of Newcastle', pp. 600–1.

opposing French forces, who immediately gave battle. The regular troops proceeded to fight in the only way they knew how – attempting to fire volleys at an invisible enemy. The opposing forces were, meanwhile, able to run amok, moving up and down the British column using the cover of the woods and picking off redcoats with impunity. Braddock's force suffered heavy casualties while his opponents escaped virtually unscathed. Braddock himself suffered a shot to the chest and died as the remainder of his force retreated towards what they regarded as civilization.[45]

News of a second debacle on the Ohio took its time to filter back to London. In the interim other arrangements had been made to sort out the European situation. Promises of troops from German princes were useful but they were unlikely, in themselves, to be a sufficient deterrent. With Maria Theresa refusing to help for anything less than a reciprocal British promise of aid in the recovery of Silesia, British attention turned further eastwards. Sir Charles Hanbury Williams was sent to St Petersburg in April 1755 with the single aim of securing Russian support for the containment of Prussia. Britain had turned to Russia during the War of the Austrian Succession but on this occasion the Russians were well aware of the diplomatic advantages they held.[46] They drove a hard bargain. They did agree to provide a large force to be kept in readiness on Prussia's eastern border should Britain or Hanover be attacked. Yet they were careful to limit their liabilities. An attack on the disintegrating Barrier fortresses was not sufficient to trigger a Russian march into Prussia; neither would an Italian dispute nor the outbreak of a conflict restricted to North America. At least some protection had been found for Hanover, which was, Newcastle and Hardwicke thought, the best that could be hoped for in the present circumstances.[47]

The king's absence in Hanover was making Newcastle distinctly jumpy. The ebb and flow of negotiations in June and July 1755 were a cause for concern both because of worries about whether a suitable alliance could be secured but also because of the knowledge that any agreement, almost regardless of with whom, would have financial implications for Britain. Holdernesse informed Newcastle while talks with the Austrians were still continuing that the king had spoken of the necessity of 'some assistance' from Britain to help finalize an alliance that he wanted to make in his Electoral capacity. What this meant was something that Holdernesse was struggling to discover.[48] Newcastle even thought the situation was

[45] Anderson, *Crucible of war*, ch. 9.

[46] For the importance of Russia to British attempts to achieve continental security, see Walther Mediger, 'Great Britain, Hanover and the rise of Prussia', in Ragnhild Hatton and M.S. Anderson, eds, *Studies in diplomatic history* (London, 1970), pp. 199–213.

[47] Newcastle to Holdernesse, Claremont, 11/7/1755, BL, Add. MSS 32857, fo. 4.

[48] Holdernesse to Newcastle, Hanover, 6/7/1755 (in his own hand), BL, Add. MSS 32856, fo. 551.

becoming so serious that he and Hardwicke should advise George to return to Britain. Newcastle felt it might be possible to persuade George that proper support from him for the Old Corps in the face of the current domestic factional difficulties would go some way to mitigating the foreign problems which remained the king's primary concern.[49]

Newcastle foresaw that the need for subsidies to bolster alliance commitments would have significant domestic political consequences. Subsidies would have to be voted through parliament and would probably entail tax increases. It would be an opportunity for troublemakers to revive patriotic rhetoric about the dangers and costs of the king's continental entanglements, even as Newcastle tried to prioritize the colonial struggle. It would be impossible, as had been done to fund Braddock's expedition, to put the costs through the Irish establishment. Newcastle and Hardwicke's thoughts turned, therefore, back to Pitt and the possibility that he might be won over to the role of parliamentary manager. As well as sounding out Pitt himself, Newcastle wrote to Holdernesse as the first step in laying the groundwork with the king for an alteration in domestic arrangements.[50] It was hoped that simply allowing Pitt to attend cabinet meetings, without further enhancement of office, would satisfy him. The king's reaction to Newcastle's proposals was one of guarded acceptance, although he was quick to remind Newcastle of his personal dislike of Pitt.[51] In a separate letter to Newcastle, Holdernesse revealed that he had achieved such a positive response by utilizing his usual means of talking to Lady Yarmouth first before tackling the king. Earlier George had been irritated with Holdernesse's suggestion that Pitt might be satisfied with a kind word rather than a place on the cabinet council. It was only when Holdernesse had pointed out that it would be advantageous for George's reputation if it were known that he had allowed Pitt in, rather than Pitt forcing his way into the closet, that the king's demeanour altered.[52] Holdernesse's attempts to induce an early royal return from Hanover were less successful.[53]

Unusually the optimist, Newcastle continued to hope that the American conflict might be contained and not escalate into a more general war. Consequently, he oscillated over the orders to be given to Admiral Hawke's squadron in the Channel. Newcastle's hopes rested on a decisive British victory in America deterring the French from further action and making them seek peace instead.[54] Initially, others within the regency had favoured

---

[49] Newcastle to Hardwicke, Claremont, 6/7/1755, ibid., fos 559–60.
[50] Newcastle to Holdernesse, 11/7/1755, private, BL, Add. MSS 32857, fos 37–8 and idem to idem, 11/7/1755, private and particular, ibid., fos 40–2.
[51] Holdernesse to Newcastle, 20/7/1755, private, ibid., fo. 256v.
[52] Idem to idem, 20/7/1755, first ps entre nous, ibid., fo. 262.
[53] Idem to idem, 23/7/1755, entre nous, ibid., fo. 313.
[54] Clayton, 'Duke of Newcastle', p. 601.

an aggressive stance in home waters with Hawke given permission to take any French ships that he came across. There were potentially lucrative commercial prizes to be had but such acts would lead very quickly to war. Newcastle, therefore, put his foot down and insisted that Hawke should be limited to attacks on French warships. Given that Boscawen had already been authorized to prevent French reinforcements from landing in America, it is easy in hindsight to argue that the ship of peace had already sailed. Boscawen failed to stop the French landing at Louisburg but had taken two prizes in the process. He had, therefore, failed in his primary objective and provided the French with ample grounds for portraying Britain as the aggressor.[55] With the French now unlikely to settle the American disputes and subject to attack in European waters, the chances of a general conflict increased.

MORE FAMILIAL TENSIONS

The domestic political situation was being complicated by George's actions in Hanover. Newcastle received word from the elder Münchhausen that the duchess of Brunswick-Wolfenbüttel and her two daughters, Sophia and Amelia, had arrived in Hanover.[56] The Brunswick princesses had been born in 1737 and 1739 respectively and George evidently thought that one of them might be an appropriate bride for his grandson, George, who was fast approaching his eighteenth birthday. The duchess of Wolfenbüttel had the additional advantage of being one of Frederick II of Prussia's sisters so a match might provide a useful means of improving relations with Hanover's dangerous neighbour. Sophia, in particular, caught George's eye. Waldegrave reported George's comment that had he been but a little younger, he would have had no hesitation in marrying her himself. Whether the remark was anything other than flippant is unclear, although it does serve as a useful reminder of the king's continued admiration for the feminine form.

What was of greater concern to George, as Waldegrave was quick to point out, was that his grandson's marriage be sorted out by him and not left to the wiles of Princess Augusta of Wales, who would almost certainly use the opportunity to promote the claims of one of her other relations. The Brunswick-Wolfenbüttel family were not of Electoral status but they were deemed worthy to provide brides for both Charles VI and Frederick II. They were certainly of greater political importance than the dukes of Saxony-Gotha. Nevertheless, the fact that selecting a bride for a future British monarch might come down to a choice between two German

---

[55] Browning, *Newcastle*, pp. 221–2.

[56] G.A. von Münchhausen to Newcastle, Hanover, 11/7/1755, BL, Add. MSS 32857, fo. 60. Their arrival was also recorded in the Hanoverian court diary. See NHStA, Dep. 103, IV, 324, fo. 177r.

princely families, one relatively more powerful than the other, was a reminder that the necessity of marrying Protestants did place certain obstacles in the way of a grand dynastic strategy. News of the king's intentions quickly found its way back to Augusta. She was keen to stymie her father-in-law's plans, fearing that her son's marriage would lead to a reduction in her influence. Consequently, Augusta was quick to play up Sophia's potential faults. She also suggested to her son that his marriage was 'merely to gratify the King's private Interest in the Electorate of Hanover' through an attempted rapprochement with Prussia via Sophia's mother. Waldegrave dated the prince of Wales's loss of 'duty and obedience' to George from this point.[57] Following a period of relative calm, it appeared that relations between the king and his successor's court were worsening again.

George returned to London in the middle of September 1755. He was quickly apprised of the complicated domestic situation and the intrigues that were being hatched at Leicester House.[58] Newcastle's attempts to sort out the Commons by one means or another had continued throughout the summer. The king was growing tired of the furore. He told Holdernesse, with considerable feeling, that 'there are kings enough in England. I am nothing there, I am old & want rest and should only go [back to Britain] to be plagued and teased there about that D——d House of Commons.'[59] Newcastle had seen Pitt at the start of September and made every effort to win him over. Accommodating Pitt would entail some substantial changes to the administration. Pitt was trenchant about the need to put an adequate parliamentary manager in place and that such a person must have an office of advice as well as execution. Pitt objected strongly to the projected treaty with Russia and also thought that the Hessian troops were being bought at too high a price, although Newcastle countered that the Hessian treaty should be seen as part of a broader defence of Protestantism and of George's grandchildren.[60] This cut little ice with Pitt. He claimed subsequently that Newcastle had virtually offered him the seals as the price of an accommodation, although Newcastle recollected Pitt's demand for them, rather than his own promise.

MORE MINISTERIAL MANOEUVRES

In the light of the conversations with Pitt, Newcastle identified three possible courses of action. He could resign and make way for Fox, Pitt could somehow be given the seals with Newcastle continuing where he was

---

[57] Clark, ed., *Waldegrave memoirs*, pp. 164–5.

[58] Ibid., p. 169.

[59] Holdernesse to Newcastle, Hanover, 3/8/1755, entre nous, BL, Add. MSS 32857, fos 553v–554r.

[60] Newcastle to Hardwicke, Newcastle House, 3/9/1755, BL, Add. MSS 32858, fos 422–7. Clark's summary (*Dynamics of change*, pp. 183–5) is more succinct than the original.

or, finally, Fox could be raised to the leadership of the Commons with Newcastle again remaining where he was. Hardwicke feared that adopting the first course of action risked the objection that Newcastle was trying to use the same tactics that had worked so well for securing the position of the Old Corps in 1746. The second plan would be difficult, not least because George would have to agree to part with a secretary of state whom he liked and trusted and replace him with somebody he found personally objectionable.[61] Pitt's continued objections to subsidy diplomacy were gradually forcing Newcastle to favour the third option. Unaware of all that was going on in London, Holdernesse was doing his best to persuade George of the wisdom of taking Pitt in. His arguments were couched very much in terms of the necessity of such an action. His chosen channel was again through the countess of Yarmouth.[62] Lady Yarmouth was a critical point of contact for various politicians and her influence, albeit behind the scenes, a reminder of the extent to which court connection was still crucially important in ministerial politicking and appointments.[63]

By the end of September 1755 Newcastle had persuaded George that an accommodation with Fox was the only viable option. Fox was to be given leadership of the Commons. Sir Thomas Robinson gratefully returned to his position as master of the wardrobe with a large pension to compensate him for the loss of the secretaryship. He was thankful for a return to the quiet life once it became clear that Fox was keeping his promise to do the king's business in the Commons. Newcastle, to his friends, was also quietly congratulating himself on the shrewdness of his political manoeuvres. He felt that promoting Fox might actually reduce the influence that Cumberland had over him because his new job drew him away from Cumberland's military power base. Newcastle also felt confident that the rearrangement of various other offices which had enabled him to promote some of his own following without George consulting Cumberland was a mark of the confidence that the king was once more placing in him.[64] Unfortunately for Newcastle, his decision to favour Fox over Pitt was to have longer-term consequences. Princess Augusta had been informed by Philipp von Münchhausen of the need to reach an accommodation with

---

[61] For George's fondness for Robinson and his limited political pretensions, see Clark, ed., *Waldegrave memoirs*, p. 171.

[62] Holdernesse to Newcastle, Helvoetsluys, 13/9/1755 entre nous, BL, Add. MSS 32859, fo. 74.

[63] It should be noted that George did suggest that Lady Yarmouth 'never meddled in Matters of so high a Nature, & he would not have her brought upon the carpet' (Lincolnshire Archives, Lincoln, Brownlow archives, Berkeley diary, BQ 2/1, fo. 16). The force of the comment was probably more about George's irritation that politicians sought to influence him through her than anything else.

[64] Newcastle to Lady Katherine Pelham, Newcastle House, 26/9/1755, ibid., fos 219–20.

Fox but she was obviously unhappy about it.[65] Pitt was slowly being driven into the arms of Leicester House and the prospects of formed opposition increased. Newcastle, on the other hand, felt confident enough to speed up this process by finally dismissing Pitt, Legge and some of their associates from their posts in November 1755.[66]

George, by contrast, was evidently more concerned about the prospects of his grandson setting up an open opposition stall again. He interviewed the prince of Wales in the closet and proceeded to quiz him on his political knowledge, tested him on the critical (from George's point of view) subject of the importance of Hanover and generally warned him about the dangers of surrounding himself with ill-intentioned advisers. The young prince did not take particularly kindly to the harangue. The interview was typically concise and conducted, according to Waldegrave, in an affectionate but not quite gracious manner. Waldegrave thought that the king had erred in one crucial respect: his lecture would have been better delivered to Augusta. George should have offered to forgive what was past but warned her that he held her responsible for her son's future conduct and that any further political intrigues would be dealt with severely.[67]

Against this background of political manoeuvring and jockeying for place, the early part of the parliamentary session proved relatively incident free. Newcastle ensured that Hardwicke's draft speech from the throne was tweaked to emphasize more forcefully both the extent of British activity in the colonial sphere and the ways in which the recent subsidy arrangements had been designed specifically to avoid the prospect of continental war.[68] Although difficulties with the acceptance of the recent subsidy agreements with Hessen-Kassel and Russia had been widely predicted, they did not emerge in practice. Pitt did his best to denounce them but his speeches were not enough to defeat the measures.

THE PRUSSIAN ALLIANCE

Pitt's disquiet about money for Russia was to be overtaken by events. As early as July, when Münchhausen had informed Newcastle of the duchess of Wolfenbüttel's arrival in Hanover, there had been hints that her brother, Frederick, might be willing to enter into some sort of agreement for 'inactivity' in Germany.[69] The reasons that lay behind Frederick's offer were clear. Frederick retained a healthy respect for Russian power, having been warned by his father to fear it,[70] and the prospect of an agreement

[65] Newcastle to Hardwicke, Claremont, 4/10/1755, ibid., fo. 357.

[66] Browning, *Newcastle*, pp. 227–8.

[67] Clark, ed., *Waldegrave memoirs*, p. 170.

[68] Newcastle to Hardwicke, Claremont, 11/10/1755, BL, Add. MSS 32860, fo. 1.

[69] G.A. von Münchhausen to Newcastle, 11/7/1755, BL, Add. MSS 32857, fo. 60.

[70] 'Letzte Ansprache Friedrich Wilhelm I', in Richard Dietrich, ed., *Die politische Testamente der Hohenzollern* (Cologne, 1986), p. 246.

between Britain and Russia, which he knew was a real possibility, was worrying for him. At first Newcastle kept thoughts of a Prussian accommodation a closely guarded secret, although Hardwicke was made aware of the duke's new policy initiative. Hardwicke was sceptical, as always, about costs. However, Newcastle had begun to see the merit of persuading Prussia not just to be inactive but to enter into a formal neutrality agreement. Münchhausen promptly responded that the good offices of Hessen-Kassel and Wolfenbüttel might be used to persuade Prussia and Frederick to adopt a position of neutrality.[71] Holdernesse was also made aware of Newcastle's intentions and began negotiations with Prussia. Münchhausen made use of the duke of Brunswick as an intermediary as well.

These talks continued while the Russian treaty was being finalized. Newcastle hoped that agreements with Russia and Prussia might be complementary or at least mutually reinforcing, in the sense that conclusion of the first would lead to an arrangement with the second. The Russian price for achieving Hanoverian security was high so if Frederick agreed to a neutrality arrangement then the likelihood of having to pay out to Russia would be reduced. Newcastle proved to be right about Prussia's reaction but he did not fully apprehend what Russia's intentions were. The Russian chancellor Bestuzhev was decidedly anti-Prussian in his outlook. He saw an agreement with Britain as an easy way to get the funds to maintain a substantial Russian force on Prussia's eastern border without having to raise the revenue himself. Empress Elizabeth had been angered by some of Frederick's less than complimentary comments about her penchant for alcohol and handsome men. The vice-chancellor Vorontsov favoured closer co-operation with France but was happy to pursue an anti-Prussian line.[72] Hardwicke expressed some doubts about whether an agreement with Prussia might serve to harm British interests by driving the other major powers together but these fears were swept aside in the summer of 1755.[73]

An agreement between Britain and Prussia was eventually signed in January 1756. The Convention of Westminster fell short, in many respects, of a full alliance. In place of detailed commitments it had a series of vague formulations. Britain and Prussia agreed not to attack each other, which was important from the perspective of securing Hanover, and to stop any incursion of foreign troops into the empire. The British had worries about a French invasion of Hanover in mind, while Frederick continued to fear the aggressive designs of Russia, aided and abetted by Austria and Saxony, on his territories. Despite George's earlier anger at Frederick's perceived

[71] The exchanges can be followed most easily in NHStA, Hann. 91 von Münchhausen I, 22, which conveniently gathers together Newcastle and Münchhausen's letters on the subject.
[72] H.M. Scott, *The birth of a great power system, 1740–1815* (Harlow, 2006), p. 88.
[73] Uriel Dann, *Hanover and Great Britain, 1740–1760* (Leicester, 1991), p. 94.

impertinence in wanting to pursue an independent line in foreign policy, the differences between the powers were relatively small. Each, to a certain extent, was worried by the other's associates: Austria and Russia on the one hand and France on the other. Nevertheless, the convention had been deliberately formulated by Frederick to give him a certain amount of fexibility. The Austrian Netherlands, although technically part of the empire, had been specifically excluded. Frederick hoped that this would be seen by the French as leaving the door open to an attack on Britain from there and would contribute to a sense that the convention was of limited importance and not incompatible with an ongoing friendship with Versailles.[74]

Although the convention was to have several unintended and unanticipated consequences in the longer term, it did provide a solution to some of the disagreements between George and Frederick. By confirming a guarantee of Prussian possessions given in 1745, George had, in effect, renounced any claim to East Friesland. Various disputes between the Admiralty and Prussian merchants were sorted out. Frederick also agreed to settle the outstanding sums on Silesian loans. He had assumed responsibility for the money that various Dutch and British financiers had lent to Charles VI on the strength of his Silesian revenues under the treaty of Breslau in 1742 but payments had been withheld because of Frederick's irritation with George over various other issues.[75]

The convention had been agreed with the aim of Hanoverian security in mind and Hanoverian ministers had been active in promoting its benefits. Yet it was an agreement that George undertook in his royal, rather than Electoral, capacity. Münchhausen subsequently congratulated Newcastle on the achievement of an agreement that he had been instrumental in suggesting originally, noting also the value of a Prussian alliance in defending Protestantism in the empire and the crucial role that the Royal Navy played in defending Britain.[76] Whether out of desperation or because he really believed it, Münchhausen sought to minimize the extent to which the convention had been agreed solely to defend Hanoverian interests by placing it within the broader European system that was so appealing to Newcastle.

DIPLOMATIC REVOLUTION

The reaction of the other European powers to the newly found amity between Britain and Prussia was a mixture of incredulity and delight. It gave further impetus to the plans that Count Anton Wenzel von Kaunitz, a Moravian noble who had risen via a diplomatic posting to Versailles to

---

[74] Dennis E. Showalter, *The wars of Frederick the Great* (Harlow, 1996), pp. 127–8.

[75] Dann, *Hanover*, p. 95.

[76] G.A. Münchhausen to Newcastle, Hanover, 24/21756, NHStA, Hann. 91, von Münchhausen I, 22, fos 41–2.

the position of Austrian chancellor, had been pushing for some time.[77] As early as 1749, Kaunitz had suggested that to achieve Maria Theresa's fundamental objective of the recovery of Silesia, it might be necessary to rethink the Austrian alliance system. What was needed was friendship with Russia and an accommodation with France. Initially, his proposals had been met with extreme scepticism by the more senior members of the Austrian *Konferenz* (the central body for the discussion and formulation of policy). They regarded the threat from France as still too great and so wanted to retain some form of alliance with Britain and the United Provinces. Kaunitz was prepared to tolerate continued good relations with Britain but he was doubtful that Britain would ever provide the necessary support for the recovery of Silesia. Instead he felt that the interests of Austria and Russia, with their mutual distrust of both Prussia and the Ottoman empire, were more naturally aligned.

Kaunitz was aware from his service in France that Louis XV was prone to conducting diplomacy in person and outside official channels through a 'secret de roi'. As the colonial situation deteriorated and war between Britain and France became ever more likely, Kaunitz authorized a cautious approach by Georg Adam von Starhemberg, Austrian ambassador to Versailles, to see what the offer of Austrian neutrality in any Anglo-French conflict might achieve. Neutrality was just the beginning. Starhemberg was made aware of various other issues that could be put on the table to turn neutrality into active alliance. The primary Austrian objective of the recovery of Silesia was not to be mentioned at first. Starhemberg's approach was also a little unusual. Kaunitz had cultivated Madame de Pompadour, Louis XV's mistress, during his own sojourn at Versailles so it was decided to use this route to contact the king in the hope that it would appeal to Louis's penchant for personal diplomacy. Starhemberg therefore began talks with the abbé de Bernis, a close confidant of Madame de Pompadour. The talks during the autumn of 1755 achieved little, though. Louis was nervous about giving too much away, especially as most of his ministers retained a profound suspicion of Austria and had been kept in the dark about the negotiations. News of the Convention of Westminster transformed the scene. French ministers were reminded of how slippery an ally Frederick could be; he had, after all, withdrawn from the War of the Austrian Succession, having made peace separately, on no fewer than three occasions.

France refused to renew the alliance with Prussia when the matter was discussed in February 1756. Instead the talks with Austria were given a new lease of life and their ultimate outcome was the first treaty of Versailles in May 1756. This included a neutrality convention for the empire, similar to

---

[77] Max Braubach, *Versailles und Wien von Ludwig XIV bis Kaunitz* (Bonn, 1952) is still a valuable study of the background to the diplomatic revolution, although this should now be supplemented with Lothar Schilling, *Kaunitz und das Renversement des Alliances* (Berlin, 1994).

that detailed in the Convention of Westminster but, more importantly, it moved beyond general aspirations into specific commitments of support. It was a defensive alliance by which Louis and Maria Theresa promised each other 24,000 troops in the event of an attack on either party. Austria agreed to remain neutral in the Anglo-French conflict but would not have to provide troops for it. France undertook not to attack the Austrian Netherlands. The secret provisions allowed for negotiation of a broader offensive alliance to begin and made clear that the provision of troops would be required if either power were attacked by an ally of Britain. The strong implication was that these provisions would probably only come into effect in the event of a Prussian attack on either France or Austria.[78]

As diplomatic activity went into overdrive in the aftermath of the Convention of Westminster, George and his ministers still hoped and believed that there was a chance that a conflict on the continent had been prevented. Intelligence from Versailles continued to suggest that France intended some sort of assault on England, even following the treaty with Prussia.[79] The widely held assumption among the British ministers, backed to some extent by the reports that were arriving from inside France, was that the French too had succumbed to colonial visions and had realized the folly of getting drawn into continental distractions. Newcastle also thought that Frederick had been, in some sense, integrated into the 'Old System' – a favourite phrase – and that all Britain's allies were singing the same tune about the necessary containment of France.[80] Some hopes were even entertained that Austria might now return to a British alliance – Starhemberg's mission to Versailles remained unknown. What nearly everybody failed to anticipate was that a fundamental principle of European international relations over the previous two centuries – enmity between Habsburg and Bourbon – was about to be broken. As Brendan Simms points out, there was a failure of imagination, despite, or perhaps because of, the British thinking that they were well informed about what was going on inside France.[81]

Nevertheless, rumours of a possible French invasion did trigger some defensive preparations. The British looked first, as they had become accustomed to do, to the United Provinces to help defend Britain's borders and invoked a treaty dating from 1678 which provided for 6,000 Dutch troops in the hour of need. The Dutch response was noncommittal. Privately, Anne promised her father that she would be able to provide the troops if really necessary. She had ascertained from the French representative in The Hague that an invasion was unlikely so thought that her bluff would not be

---

[78] Scott, *Birth of a great power system*, pp. 92–5, Franz A.J. Szabo, *The Seven Years War in Europe, 1756–1763* (Harlow, 2008), pp. 14–16.
[79] Intelligence from Versailles, 9/2/1756, BL, Add. MSS 32862, fo. 402.
[80] Newcastle to Bentinck, Newcastle House, 10/2/1756, fo. 434r.
[81] Simms, *Three victories*, p. 409.

called. Unfortunately for her, the recalcitrant States-General refused to be drawn into her diplomatic game and, when the matter became public, Anne faced a backlash for her overly Anglophile tendencies.[82]

Instead, Newcastle and George took advantage of their recent subsidy agreements to fill the gap left by the Dutch. Parliament voted at the end of March to bring over some 8,000 Hessian troops. Further reinforcements were added by taking 9,000 Hanoverians into British pay and shipping them across the North Sea as well. The decision was made against a backdrop of royal illness. Newcastle was sufficiently concerned to make frequent enquiries of Lady Yarmouth as to George's condition and received updates from one of the royal physicians.[83] The willingness of George and the Hanoverian ministry to agree to this deployment is evidence of how successful they felt their efforts to neutralize the empire had been. Such a move could not have been contemplated if the threat to Hanoverian territory was deemed to be immediate. George was also insistent that he, or rather the Hanoverian treasury, received levy money, to ensure parity of treatment with the Hessians. The troops, of course, did not have to be raised but George did make one concession: he did not demand levy money for the officers, thus reducing the bill by £4,000 to a total of £58,000.[84] There was some debate about the relative merits of Dutch, Hessian and Hanoverian troops and even an attempt to suggest that the employment of foreign troops in Britain was a temporary expedient that would be rendered superfluous by the construction of a proper British militia, although Newcastle ensured that the Militia Bill was killed in the Lords in May 1756, taking the time to write to George immediately after the debate to let him know the outcome.[85]

MINORCA AND THE DESCENT TO WAR

By this point the prospect of open war with France had moved a step closer. At the start of April, Admiral John Byng had been dispatched from Spithead with ten ships of the line to prevent the French Mediterranean fleet under the marquis de La Galissonnière from taking Port Mahon on Minorca. Minorca had been captured by the British in 1708 and served as an important military base in the Mediterranean, extending the reach of British naval power. The French thought that Minorca would be a useful bargaining tool that could be traded in negotiations to end the colonial conflict. Instead, the invasion contributed to the conflict expanding into the European theatre.

[82] Baker-Smith, *Royal discord*, p. 179.

[83] See Wilmot to Newcastle, 26/3/1756 and 27/3/1756, BL, Add. MSS 32864, fos 1 and 8.

[84] Barrington to Newcastle, Cavendish Square, 25/4/1756, ibid., fo. 397.

[85] Newcastle to George, 24/5/1756, BL, Add. MSS 32865, fo. 102.

By the time Byng reached Gibraltar at the start of May, French forces had already landed on Minorca. Byng felt that even with the ships that Commodore Edgcumbe had sailed over from Minorca, he lacked the resources to counter La Galissonnière effectively. He was also misled about the ability of St Philip's Castle to hold out in the face of the French landing. The problem was that Byng had direct orders to transport troops from the Gibraltar garrison over to Minorca to prevent the capture of Port Mahon. Despite this, a council of war decided that sending more troops would simply prolong what was already a lost cause so Byng wrote back to London justifying his decision with the claim that he did not want to put Gibraltar at risk through precipitate action. The king was highly displeased, remarking angrily that 'this man will not fight'.[86] He and the ministry believed that, if properly garrisoned, St Philip's could hold out for some considerable time and so they were infuriated by Byng's decision not to follow the King's orders. Hopes that Byng might redeem himself through a naval victory floundered. Byng engaged La Galissonnière off Minorca on 20 May but the action was indecisive and he returned to Gibraltar. Without reinforcements, the garrison of St Philip's held out for another month but surrendered on 28 June.

Britain had formally declared war on France on 17 May. A reciprocal French declaration followed on 9 June. Although this did little more than formalize a conflict that had effectively been going on since at least 1754, the reaction to the news of Byng's misadventures was to have a more destabilizing impact on British domestic politics. As Waldegrave put it, 'this loss was the principal cause of that popular discontent and clamour which overturn'd the Administration; or rather occasion'd the Panick which obliged our Ministers to Abdicate'.[87] The Minorcan disaster was a useful populist stick with which to beat the ministry, encapsulating fears about British naval decline, yet it also coincided with a growing realization by the ministry that their strategy of European neutralization was also beginning to unravel.

There was a sense of disbelief in the air as news of the treaty of Versailles began to leak out. An intelligence report received at the end of May noted that 'it's whispered that something hath been concluded between this Court [i.e. the French], and that of Vienna' but went on to doubt the veracity of the rumours.[88] Confessional issues were given a certain degree of prominence in the rhetoric concerning the developing European situation. The same intelligence report noted that if any agreement had been reached, then it would probably centre on defending Catholicism in the empire and include some provisions to ensure that

---

[86] Horace Walpole, *Memoirs of King George II*, ed. John Brooke (3 vols, New Haven, 1985), ii, p. 158.

[87] Clark, ed., *Waldegrave memoirs*, p. 173.

[88] Intelligence from Versailles, 25/5/1756, BL, Add. MSS 32865, fo. 110.

when Landgrave William of Hessen-Kassel died, his son (George's former son-in-law) would be able to enjoy all his rights without the various impediments that had been put in his way during the separation agreement. Robert Keith, the British minister plenipotentiary in Vienna, had tried to explain to Kaunitz and Maria Theresa that the Convention of Westminster was designed to preserve the peace of the empire but, as he told Holdernesse, Maria Theresa had insisted that British actions marked a betrayal of her and the Old System and that she might have to join another party. Keith interpreted this as partial confirmation of rumours that attempts were being made to join the Catholic powers in the empire together to oppose what was seen as the 'Protestant League' (itself an emotive phrase, which conjured up memories of the outbreak of the Thirty Years War) formed by Britain and Prussia.[89] Maria Theresa could, of course, complain about British perfidy secure in the knowledge that she had already made alternative arrangements. Newcastle was not above invoking Protestant concerns himself. Writing to Andrew Mitchell, the newly appointed British minister to Prussia, Newcastle hoped that the new friendship between Britain and Prussia would be useful in encouraging the Dutch. A united Protestant front might help the Dutch to stand firm when faced with a tricky international situation.[90]

Newcastle was whistling in the wind. A powerful commercial lobby in the United Provinces was anxious to avoid war and profit from Britain's colonial distractions. By the middle of June the Dutch had formally agreed to remain neutral in the forthcoming European war. In exchange Louis XV promised not to invade, thus rendering the defence of the Barrier unnecessary. France subsequently sought to take advantage of neutral Dutch shipping to increase its own trade. George wrote personally to Anne to see if she could do something to prevent this, but with little immediate effect.[91] The start of June also brought final confirmation from inside the French court that a treaty had been signed between Versailles and Vienna. Newcastle's intelligence sources, backtracking wildly, claimed that they had long hinted that such an agreement was on the cards but that discovering whether it had actually been signed had turned out to be uncommonly difficult.[92]

The foreign political situation provided ample opportunity for critics of the administration to vent their spleen. Pitt made much of the inability to deal properly with the invasion of Minorca. George was also faced, however, with distractions from within his own family. The prince of Wales would come of age in June 1756, thus rendering otiose the Regency Bill that had previously been the source of such tension. Prince George's

---

[89] Keith to Holdernesse, Vienna, 16/5/1756, most secret, ibid., fo. 17v.
[90] Newcastle to Mitchell, Newcastle House, 28/5/1756, private, ibid., fo. 131r.
[91] Baker-Smith, *Royal discord*, p. 181.
[92] Intelligence from Versailles, 1/6/1756, BL, Add. MSS 32865, fo. 167.

attaining his majority created a new set of problems. He now needed an establishment separate from that of his mother, as well as a proper financial settlement. The king had agreed in the middle of April to Newcastle's proposal that the prince be moved to apartments in St James's and Kensington, closer to the king and away from his mother's influence, and that an allowance of £40,000 be granted to him. Bearing in mind the trouble that the issue of allowances for the prince of Wales had previously caused the king, it is unsurprising that George was keen both to settle matters quickly and to avoid the prospect of a parliamentary ambush on the issue by prolonging the session beyond the prince's birthday.[93] George had always found it difficult to exercise control over Augusta. Waldegrave's appointment as Prince George's governor in 1752 had been one way he had sought to do so but Waldegrave admitted that, although he held some sway with Augusta and her son, his efforts to ensure that the prince was properly educated had not always met with resounding success.[94]

Waldegrave was now asked to break the news to Prince George that the king wanted him to cut loose from his mother's apron-strings. Chesterfield was not convinced that where the prince slept would make much difference if he still had the same advisers around him.[95] Newcastle was aware of this and had begun to formulate plans for the composition of the prince of Wales's household. Waldegrave was viewed as a safe pair of hands for the important post of groom of the stole, the senior lord of the bedchamber and effective head of the household. Once the news that the king intended to increase the size of Prince George's establishment leaked out, though, requests for preferment exploded. Any attempt to finalize the composition of the prince's household ran into the difficulty that the prince politely but firmly refused to leave his mother and insisted that a position be found for his close friend and adviser, John Stuart, third earl of Bute. Ideally, the prince wanted Bute as his groom of the stole. Neither George nor Newcastle were taken with the suggestion. One reason was George's insistence on his prerogative rights when it came to household appointments. Another was a dislike of Bute. He was viewed as a friend of Pitt and a fomenter of opposition and consequently not a good person to have around the prince. Negotiations continued throughout much of the summer in parallel with yet more efforts to secure the ministry's position within the Commons. George made his feelings on the shape of his grandson's household clear, doing so not just in the closet but in larger ministerial gatherings as well.[96]

---

[93] Clark, *Dynamics of change*, p. 241. Newcastle subsequently reported to Hardwicke that George was unhappy with the size of the prince's allowance. It is unlikely he thought it too small (Newcastle to Hardwicke, Claremont, 12/6/1756, BL, Add. MSS 32865, fo. 283v).

[94] Clark, ed., *Waldegrave memoirs*, pp. 176–7.

[95] Chesterfield to Newcastle, Blackheath, 17/5/1756, BL, Add. MSS 32865, fo. 37.

[96] Clark, ed., *Waldegrave memoirs*, p. 178.

News of the loss of Minorca did not reach London until after the close of the parliamentary session but it had been clear for some time that the campaign had not been going well. Fox realized that he would have to defend the administration's conduct of the war before an angry Commons in the autumn. He had already done as much as he could to distance himself from the Minorca debacle and he was rapidly losing confidence in Newcastle's leadership. Prince George's majority also reduced the prospect of serious political influence for him under a Cumberland-led regency. Newcastle's difficulties in managing the Commons were further compounded by the death of the lord chief justice, Dudley Ryder. William Murray, attorney-general, quickly made his desire to succeed Ryder known but his price was a peerage (Ryder had been lord chief justice since 1754 and the process to ennoble him was in train at the time of his death). While Murray was certainly legally qualified for the post, his ennoblement would remove an important ministerial spokesman and debater from the Commons. Newcastle was anxious to avoid this, particularly given his own growing doubts about whether Fox was willing to perform the task of Commons management that had led to Fox's promotion in 1755. George was reluctant to have his hand forced when it came to the peerage – he had already created four peers in that year, more than in any year since 1749.[97] Murray's promotion was delayed. Newcastle thought that he could cement the administration's position in the Commons in the interim. Murray hoped the king would change his mind about his title. Fox felt that it was all part of a Newcastle plot to marginalize him.

George was losing faith in Fox as reports of his disloyalty to the administration began to multiply. The two had a fierce argument in the closet in the middle of July, news of which was soon widely known.[98] The king's new antipathy towards Fox and his continued dislike of Pitt were deeply unhelpful to Newcastle from a political point of view. One of them would be necessary as a support in the Commons to ensure that the king's business was done and that Newcastle's administration survived. George was persuaded that he should extend an olive branch to Leicester House by indicating that he was willing to show some mark of favour towards Bute but not grant him a household office. Murray, again proving his general utility, and Argyll were to act as go-betweens.[99] Newcastle was also keen to test whether there might be any possibility of a change in the king's attitude to Pitt by sounding out Lady Yarmouth.

Newcastle was haunted by the prospect that Fox and Pitt might somehow combine to supplant him. A letter suggesting the desirability of

---

[97] He told Hardwicke he was anxious not to set the precedent that the office of lord chief justice would automatically and immediately entail a peerage. See Hardwicke to Newcastle, Powis House, 28/6/1756, BL, Add. MSS 32865, fo. 450r.

[98] Clark, *Dynamics of change*, p. 248.

[99] Newcastle to Murray, Kensington, 9/71756, BL, Add. MSS 32866, fo. 103.

an administration constructed in this manner appeared in the *Public Advertiser* in the middle of August. Hardwicke used its publication to test the waters with George and was pleased to discover that the king seemed suitably averse to the idea.[100] What the king really wanted, though, was unclear. Hardwicke thought that he and Newcastle should make further overtures to Pitt. Lady Yarmouth hinted that George might be willing, albeit grudgingly, to accept Pitt but would continue to resist Bute's appointment, although this may have been because there was a suggestion that Pitt was falling out with Leicester House.[101] George seemed to be in slightly better spirits by the beginning of September anyway, having been reassured by Grafton that popular discontent could melt away as quickly as it appeared.[102]

The domestic political wrangles of the summer were brought to an unexpected conclusion, triggered by a change of royal heart. The king claimed that Barrington, secretary at war, and Fox had made him see the wisdom of acceding to his grandson's request for Bute as his groom of the stole.[103] Whether this was a face-saving measure or evidence of a Newcastle strategy to blame pressure for Bute's promotion on Fox in a ruse with complete deniability is uncertain. A reconciliation between George and his grandson was tentatively pursued. Not only would Bute be brought into Prince George's household but the prince would also be allowed to remain with his mother. Augusta penned a suitably grateful note to her father-in-law.[104]

Newcastle and Hardwicke were still not happy, though. They worried that Prince George thought that it had been his grandfather who had resolved the political impasse and that his pledges of loyalty were to the king, rather than to the administration as a whole, so they were still vulnerable to oppositional pressure.[105] As it turned out, they had more to worry about from Fox. Fed up with shouldering the blame for everything, Fox had decided to resign. Newcastle was irritated to discover that Fox was telling all and sundry that he thought Newcastle treated George as a mere cipher. The king, meanwhile, was angry both at Fox's perceived betrayal and the mess that Newcastle now found himself in. At the same time, the king was probably also aware that Fox might be induced to stay, at least for one parliamentary session. Unfortunately for Newcastle, George was extremely reluctant to turn now to Pitt, complaining repeatedly that he did not think

---

[100] Hardwicke to Newcastle, Powis House, 20/8/1756, ibid., fo. 492.

[101] Newcastle to Hardwicke, Newcastle House, 2/9/1756, BL, Add. MSS 32867, fos 178–9.

[102] Ibid., fo. 176v.

[103] Idem to idem, Newcastle House, 18/9/1756, ibid., fo. 325v.

[104] Augusta to George, 4/10/1756, RA GEO/52957.

[105] Hardwicke to Newcastle, Wimpole, 7/10/1756 and Newcastle to Hardwicke, Claremont, 10/10/1756, BL, Add. MSS 32868, fos 120 and 163.

that Pitt would do his German business.[106] Nevertheless, both Hardwicke and Newcastle felt that an approach to Pitt was the only way to salvage the administration.

Hardwicke's consultations with Pitt did not yield the outcome for which either he or Newcastle had hoped. Pitt refused pointedly to serve in an administration with Newcastle. He demanded an inquiry into the loss of Minorca and the conduct of the North American campaign. He wanted a Militia Bill to be introduced and the Hanoverian and Hessian troops sent home. Disquiet about the presence of the Hanoverians had been aroused by an incident in Maidstone when a Hanoverian soldier had been arrested over the theft of some handkerchiefs, and then released through the intervention of Holdernesse.[107] George had been incensed at the prospect of the Hanoverian soldier being subject to English law, rather than military discipline, and so had supported Holdenesse's action.[108] Newcastle toyed with the idea of resignation but tried to present his decision to George as something that he was prepared to do solely to allow others, like Pitt, to be brought into the administration. He hoped, therefore, that George's well-known aversion to being forced to do anything would be his ultimate salvation.[109] The problem was that Newcastle was unable to find a solution to the problem of Commons management that did not involve Pitt or Fox so on 26 October he finally had to resign. George called for William Cavendish, fourth duke of Devonshire. His initial hope was that Fox might reach an accommodation with Pitt to allow both to serve under Devonshire. Pitt refused and so Devonshire replaced Newcastle as first lord and Pitt succeeded Fox as southern secretary.

The period of ministerial instability that had begun with Henry Pelham's death in 1754 was not quite at an end – there was still a final shuffling of the pack to come. Nevertheless, an event at the end of August 1756 was to alter dramatically British politics and put ministerial squabbles into a larger perspective. Its transformative impact was felt well beyond Britain's shores and it was to dominate the last years of George's reign. On 29 August 1756, Frederick II marched into Saxony, the dagger pointing at the heart of Brandenburg, precipitating the outbreak of the Seven Years War in Europe.[110]

---

[106] Newcastle to Hardwicke, Newcastle House, 14/10/1756, ibid., fos 281–7; Clark, *Dynamics of change*, pp. 267–8.

[107] For further details and a discussion of the extent to which the incident was taken up within patriot discourse, see Matthew McCormack, 'Citizenship, nationhood and masculinity in the affair of the Hanoverian soldier, 1756', *HJ*, 49 (2006), pp. 971–93.

[108] Newcastle to Hardwicke, Newcastle House, 18/9/1756, BL, Add. MSS 32867, fo. 328v.

[109] Clark, *Dynamics of change*, p. 272.

[110] Frederick had discussed the value of overrunning Saxony in his 'Political Testament' of 1752. See Dietrich, ed., *Politische Testamente*, pp. 368–77.

Chapter 9

ULTIMATE VICTORY?

Frederick's invasion of Saxony was designed as a preventive measure. Since news of the first treaty of Versailles had become public, Frederick had become increasingly worried that an offensive alliance was being formed against him. Russian troop movements and rumours of approaches to Maria Theresa gave him particular cause for concern. The Austrians had been approached by the Russians with a plan for offensive action. However, the Austrian desire to ensure that their new allies, the French, were kept sweet, not least because of hopes that the French could provide subsidies, meant that the Russians were persuaded to postpone offensive moves against Prussia until 1757. Frederick was not aware of all his opponents' plans but nevertheless thought that he was sufficiently threatened to justify a pre-emptive strike. He delayed marching into Saxony until the late summer of 1756 to ensure that neither France nor Russia would be able to come to the aid of the Saxons and Austrians.[1]

WAR IN EUROPE AND HANOVERIAN SECURITY

Frederick was in a relatively strong position to wage war. The Prussian recruitment system meant that Prussia was able to support a large army from a not particularly large civilian population. The war treasury was also well stocked. Although Frederick's first two Silesian wars had depleted the 8 million taler that he had inherited from his father, Frederick had made it a priority to replenish it since signing the Peace of Dresden. Nevertheless, he did not want to get dragged into a long war – his attack on Saxony was designed to prevent this.

The problem he faced was that the invasion of Saxony was to have serious repercussions. From a military perspective, Frederick's assault met with immediate success. Saxon forces had been compelled to surrender by October 1756. The Elector, Augustus III, had no option but to go into exile in Poland, where he was also king, taking his officers and court with him. The rest of the Saxon army was forcibly incorporated into the Prussian,

---

[1] For two recent accounts of the origins of the war, on which the following draws, see Franz A.J. Szabo, *The Seven Years War in Europe, 1756–1763* (Harlow, 2008), introduction and Matt Schumann and Karl Schweizer, *The Seven Years War: a transatlantic history* (London, 2008), ch. 1.

increasing its size if not its reliability. Frederick's difficulties were twofold. At a political level his actions were widely condemned. He was portrayed as an aggressor who had transgressed the norms of European society by invading a neutral state in pursuit of his struggles with Austria and Russia. Frederick had also upset the delicate legal balance that held the empire together. The Habsburgs quickly sought to take advantage of the public outcry by putting Frederick under imperial ban.

At a diplomatic level, Saxony's humiliation was also counterproductive. Although nominally neutral, Augustus III had strong ties to Frederick's other opponents. It had been Russian and Austrian pressure that had secured and maintained his election to the Polish throne in the first place. He was married to a Habsburg archduchess and his daughter was married to the Dauphin. The invasion of Saxony was important in pushing the French to undertake a more active role and gave new impetus to the negotiations to conclude an offensive alliance between France and Austria. The precise details took a little time but by the start of the 1757 campaigning season, Russia had both acceded to the first treaty of Versailles and signed a new offensive alliance against Prussia. France, through the second treaty of Versailles (May 1757), had also concluded an offensive alliance with Austria.

The cloud of a European war hung over Newcastle's attempts to survive in September and October 1756. Its onset may have encouraged the king to ensure that the row over his grandson's household did not develop into a more serious split within the royal family, as he knew that his attention would have to be elsewhere in the coming months. The changed European situation gave cause for concern among George's Hanoverian ministers. They had convinced themselves that the arrangement with Prussia offered the best option for ensuring the security of the Electorate but Prussia's new status as imperial pariah created doubts about the wisdom of George's strategy. As early as the middle of September 1756, they began to press George on what the likely threat to Hanover now was, given its association with Prussia.[2]

In the short term, Frederick's invasion of Saxony prompted George to think again about the security of his German lands. By the beginning of November he had decided that the Hanoverian troops stationed in Britain would be better deployed closer to home so they were ordered back to defend the Electorate. The decision was taken just as the Pitt–Devonshire ministry was establishing itself. George was almost certainly driven by worries about the defence of Hanover but the unnecessary presence of the Hanoverian troops had also been a consistent theme of Pittite rhetoric since their arrival.

---

[2] The ministers' concerns are mentioned in Newcastle to Hardwicke, Newcastle House, 18/9/1756, Add. MSS 32867, fo. 330v.

The Hanoverian Privy Council remained concerned, however. August Wilhelm von Schwicheldt, the most strident critic of friendship with Prussia, thought that any arrangement with Frederick was now null and void because it had been based on a defensive agreement, rendered inoperative by Prussian aggression. Others were more pragmatic. The Prussian agreement, for all its problems, was all that Hanover had. Consequently, efforts should be made to keep Frederick on side but at the same time ensure that France was not unnecessarily provoked. Prussian military assistance would be necessary in the case of a French invasion but otherwise military co-ordination and co-operation with the Prussian monarch should be kept to an absolute minimum.[3]

The political situation that the Hanoverian ministers faced was deeply troubling. Frederick was an unreliable ally at the best of times. They felt themselves exposed both because of their association with him and through the connection to Britain. The Holy Roman Empire was knitted together by a sense of legal authority and precedent, and friendship with a power that had purposefully and deliberately stepped outside that system was uncomfortable. Uncertain of British resolve to defend the Electorate, it is unsurprising that the Hanoverian ministers adopted several strategies to guarantee their survival. One of these involved negotiations with the Austrians.

The Hanoverian envoy in Vienna, Georg Friedrich von Steinberg (son of the minister Ernst von Steinberg) had an extensive exchange of letters with Münchhausen between December 1756 and July 1757 discussing the progress of attempts to reach some sort of neutrality arrangement with Maria Theresa.[4] Steinberg's initial claim was that it had been the errors of the British ministry that had got Hanover into the mess in which it now was. Instead of wasting money on the Hessian and Hanoverian troops, offers of subsidies to the Saxon and Bavarian courts would have yielded more tangible results.[5] In reply, Münchhausen set the scene for Steinberg's contacts with Vienna by providing a summary of recent Anglo-Austrian and Austro-Hanoverian relations.[6] His theme was a mixture of admonition and regret. Austria had departed from the well-established and vital path of containing France through the maintenance of the balance within Europe. Hanover's approach to Prussia had been necessary to ensure its security and avoid the fate that had now befallen Saxony. Any hope that the Austrians had of quickly overcoming Prussia must be set aside because of the difficulties of neutralizing the maritime powers and it was bizarre that Austria had deserted her old allies to join with powers whose interests were completely incompatible with her own. Further letters warned of the

[3] Uriel Dann, *Hanover and Great Britain, 1740–1760* (Leicester, 1991), pp. 104–5.
[4] NHStA, Cal. Br. 24, 4510.
[5] Steinberg to G.A. von Münchhausen, Vienna, 20/11/1756, ibid., fo. 17v.
[6] G.A von Münchhausen to Steinberg, Hanover, 18/12/1756, ibid., fos 1–4.

dangers facing the empire if the crisis was allowed to escalate into a more general conflict. Münchhausen also indicated his desire to stay aloof from the whole thing because of his fear that the empire was about to be torn apart by confessional conflict.[7]

Steinberg, meanwhile, was assiduously reporting the Austrian view of Britain's recent conduct. The British must have been aware of Frederick's plans to invade Saxony and had they not realized that it was likely to lead to a French invasion of Westphalia and Hanover being put in danger? The thought, or more accurately hope, was expressed that financial problems and the deteriorating situation in America would lead to a rapid settlement of Anglo-French disputes.[8] Early in 1757, Steinberg's efforts bore fruit of a sort with an Austrian offer of neutrality for Hanover under certain conditions. Steinberg was keen that the neutrality offer be considered seriously.[9] The ministry in Hanover gradually warmed to the idea, although the king was less taken with it.[10] The problem was the terms involved. The Austrians demanded promises that no aid of any sort be given to Frederick and also wanted assurances that there would be no objections to marching troops through Hanoverian territory en route to invade Prussia.

Further meetings between Steinberg and Kaunitz revealed Austrian disquiet about the activities of Andrew Mitchell, British minister in Berlin, and suggested that the Austrians saw their Hanoverian counterparts as rather put upon; the real source of Austrian anger was Britain.[11] It did not take a diplomatic genius to work out what the Austrians were trying to do. Once more they were attempting to play upon the ambiguity of George's position as king and Elector, either to create dissent between the two ministries or to achieve their own aims with minimal fuss. Even as discussion moved on to whether the agreement George had signed in 1741 might serve as a useful model for a neutrality agreement, George and Münchhausen were aware of the dangerous path they were treading. George did think that a neutrality arrangement would provide a means for preserving both Austrian authority and the integrity of the imperial system.[12] Yet keeping their approaches to Vienna entirely secret from Frederick was likely to provoke his ire. George may also have realized the risk of history repeating itself in another respect. The British ministers had been extremely irritated in 1741 at being kept in the dark about the

[7] Idem to idem, Hanover, 26/12/1756 and 23/1/1757, ibid., fos 4–5 and 8–9.

[8] Steinberg to G.A. von Münchhausen, Vienna, 4/12/1756, 15/12/1756, 29/12/1756, ibid., fos 18r, 19r and 19v.

[9] Idem to idem, Vienna, 5/1/1757, ibid., fo. 20r.

[10] Walther Mediger, 'Hastenbeck und Zeven. Der Eintritt Hannovers in den Siebenjährigen Krieg', *Niedersächsiches Jahrbuch für Landesgeschichte*, 56 (1984), pp. 143–5.

[11] Steinberg to G.A. von Münchhausen, Vienna, 12/2/1757 and 23/2/1757, NHStA, Cal. Br., 24, 4510, fo. 21 and 22.

[12] G.A. von Münchhausen to Steinberg, Hanover, 6/3/1757, ibid., fo. 11r.

prospects of a Hanoverian neutrality arrangement. Given the ministerial instability of the last few years, did George really want to provoke another period of domestic crisis, especially given Pitt's patriot proclivities?[13] Ultimately, the Austrians were able to force George's hand. They demanded that neutrality be conditional on allowing Hanoverian territory to be used as a base for Austro-French activity against Prussia. George found these conditions unacceptable. It would have been humiliating and dangerous to allow Hanover to be occupied for such a purpose. The growing popularity of Frederick in Britain meant that it would have been politically inexpedient as well.[14]

DOMESTIC DISQUIET

The domestic situation in Britain remained difficult. Pitt, now secretary of state for the southern department, had his own set of political minefields to negotiate. George had not wanted to bring him in because of his perceived reluctance to undertake the king's German business, despite Newcastle's reassurances that the king's servants had no choice but to do the king's bidding. Pitt therefore faced the perennial ministerial problem of worries about the disfavour of the closet. The easiest way to win that favour quickly was to embark on an extensive programme of support for continental measures, thus playing to royal prejudices. The problem with such a strategy was that it risked alienating those elements of patriot support that Pitt had been able to muster in his critiques of Newcastle's misconduct of the war. Pitt was also shackled with health worries as he and Devonshire tried to build their new administration. Yet it did not take long for Pitt to come to a firm appreciation of political realities. Out-of-doors support was useful but it was not vital in the way that royal favour was. Like others, such as Newcastle, before him, Pitt was to discover the intellectual and practical benefits of continental strategy as a means to facilitate political survival. Newcastle, properly out of office for the first time in over thirty years, remarked to Hardwicke when the new administration was little more than a month old how willing Pitt now appeared to be to divert funds to the continental struggle.[15] In February 1757 Pitt addressed the Commons on the necessity of allocating £200,000 for the defence of Hanover. His advocacy of the importance of the Prussian connection suggested that the scourge of subsidies had undergone a political conversion.

---

[13] The difficulties of squaring neutrality with British demands is apparent in idem to idem, 24/3/1757 and 27/3/1757, ibid., fos 13r and 15.

[14] Dann, *Hanover*, p. 109, Manfred Schlenke, 'England blickt nach Europa: Das konfessionelle Argument in der englischen Politik um die Mitte des 18. Jahrhunderts', in P. Kluke and Peter Alter, eds, *Aspekte der deutsch-britischen Beziehungen im Laufe der Jahrhunderts* (Stuttgart, 1978), pp. 27–38.

[15] Newcastle to Hardwicke, Claremont, 11/12/1756, BL, Add. MSS 32869, fo. 328r.

Yet, even in these circumstances, George's support could not be taken for granted. Various sources close to the king make this plain. One is the diary of John, fifth Baron Berkeley of Stratton (1697–1773), which has recently become available to researchers through its deposit in Lincolnshire County Record Office.[16] Berkeley, a supporter of Granville and then of Fox, became treasurer of the household in January 1756 before being moved sideways to the captaincy of the gentleman pensioners in the political crisis provoked by the onset of the European war.[17] He was a frequent attendee at court and his diaries provide a vital insider perspective on George's last years. His account of the autumn of 1756 is peppered with references to the king's irritation at his political predicament, particularly the need to pacify Pitt and Leicester House.[18] Shortly after Christmas 1756 Sir Thomas Robinson, out of the political firing line and back in his household position, reported to Newcastle a conversation he had had with Philipp von Münchhausen in which the latter, on the king's instructions, had expressed George's wish for Newcastle to come back into the ministry by one means or another.[19] Several other approaches were made in the early part of 1757. Aside from the usual difficulties in working out a disposition of places acceptable to the king and enough of the others concerned to enable changes to be carried through, the problem of how best to deal with the political fallout from the Minorca fiasco remained.

Much of the anger and disquiet about the conduct of the Minorca campaign had become focused on the fate of Admiral Byng. His court martial was convened aboard the *St George* at Portsmouth at the very end of December 1756. The charges centred on whether Byng had done his utmost in the naval battle in May 1756 and in assisting the garrison. Prior to the court martial, there had been a heated pamphlet debate on whether Byng had been dispatched in time and whether he had been given adequate resources to undertake his orders. Anger at the Newcastle administration's conduct of the war had the corollary of eliciting some sympathy for Byng. Nevertheless, after hearing evidence for a month, Byng was found guilty of the charges levelled against him. The articles of war specified a mandatory death sentence in such cases. The court, however, seemed reluctant to see it enacted. All of its members joined together in a plea for clemency to the Admiralty.

[16] Lincolnshire Archives, Lincoln, Brownlow archives, Berkeley diary, BQ 2/1–64. There is an excellent introductory discussion in Nigel Aston, 'The court of George II: Lord Berkeley of Stratton's perspective', *Court Historian*, 13 (2008), pp. 171–93. I am grateful to Dr Aston for discussion on a number of points relating to the diary.

[17] Aston, 'Court of George II', pp. 176–8.

[18] Berkeley diary, BQ 2/1, fos 8–10.

[19] Robinson to Newcastle, Whitehall, 28/12/1756, Robinson from Newcastle, Whitehall, 28/12/1756, BL, Add. MSS 32869, fo. 410.

Politically, it looked as if showing mercy might be a viable option. After all, Pitt had been constantly critical of Newcastle's conduct of the war and might plausibly claim that Byng had been a scapegoat when responsibility really lay higher up the chain of command. Yet this was problematic for two reasons. The lengthy court martial had been extensively covered in the press and the descriptions of Byng's conduct that had been revealed were, to say the least, uninspiring. Popular opinion, ever fickle, seemed to be moving against Byng. George's own attitude was also a barrier. He seemed reluctant to pardon somebody whom he still viewed as a coward.

Nevertheless, efforts to save Byng persisted. Newcastle suggested the king should consult members of the cabinet council over Byng's fate, although George declined to pursue this course.[20] The first lord of the admiralty, Richard Grenville, second Earl Temple, sought the opinion of the courts as to whether the sentence was legal. They found that it was but Byng's status as an MP led to further attempts to help him through parliament. Members of the court martial were summoned to the Lords and on 2 March, having been absolved from their traditional vow of silence, were asked about the sentence. They replied that they had not seen anything wrong with process but the sentence was still harsh. Temple's single-minded pursuit of a pardon for Byng was clearly irritating George. One of the duke of Bedford's correspondents reported that Temple had been pestering the king about Byng, only to be told that as the admiral was guilty of cowardice, pardoning him would mean that George would be breaking the promise that had been forced out of him not to pardon delinquents. Temple had then had the temerity to ask what George would do if Byng died bravely. The king had been hard pressed to contain his anger.[21] Byng, therefore, had to pay the ultimate price, execution by firing squad on the quarterdeck of the *Monarque* on 14 March 1757. Voltaire was memorably to claim that his death was a futile gesture 'pour encourager les autres'. The king's stern attitude towards the importance of military discipline had prevailed. Yet the only person who believed that he had done nothing wrong seemed to be Byng himself. Both the ministry and his fellow officers were appalled by his dilatory conduct but they wondered whether a death sentence was suitable punishment for his failings.

The treatment that George had received from Temple, Pitt's brother-in-law and close political associate, did little to endear the new ministers to the king. The king had warned Pitt in late January that Sir Robert Walpole had been made to work hard to win his confidence and it was only once Walpole had proved his worth and shown zeal in the king's

---

[20] Reed Browning, *The duke of Newcastle* (New Haven and London, 1975), p. 257.

[21] Rigby to Bedford, Bedford House, 3/3/1757, Lord John Russell, introduction, *Correspondence of John, fourth duke of Bedford with an introduction by Lord John Russell* (3 vols, London, 1842–6), ii, p. 238.

service that George had started to trust him.[22] George stepped up his efforts to entice Newcastle back into office, using Waldegrave as his chosen intermediary, during February and March 1757. Newcastle remained somewhat coy, although he also, in the words of his biographer, 'basked in his role as the sine qua non of government', courted by the king and by his fellow politicians alike.[23] Newcastle was unwilling to resume major office until what he viewed as the witch-hunt against him, in the shape of a parliamentary inquiry into the conduct of the war, was stopped. As he told the king directly after one of his approaches, he was happy to support George's measures in parliament and would continue to serve him in that capacity but the political climate made it impossible to come back in at present and he was unwilling to take the blame for all that had gone wrong.[24] George remained insistent, though. Waldegrave sought Newcastle's advice on how the duke would restructure the administration if either Pitt or Temple resigned or were obliged to leave.[25] The agreed Old Corps position was that George should wait until the end of the session to see if any vacancies arose before determining how they should be filled. The rather vague answers that Newcastle had given were unsatisfactory to George. Newcastle learned the king was disappointed that he had not provided anything more specific and he had even been accused of selfishness by George. The king felt that he had been through enough ministerial travails to merit more consideration.[26]

Newcastle and his colleagues may have been biding their time, either waiting for the political storm to blow over or their general indispensability for good government to be recognized, but George was less patient. He was anxious about the conduct of the war on the continent and fed up with what he viewed as the insolence of Pitt and Temple in the closet. The two issues became intertwined. Pitt had spoken about the necessity of forming an Anglo-Hanoverian 'army of observation' to monitor the situation in Westphalia when he spoke in the Commons on 18 February. He had also spoken in favour of a sizeable subsidy for Prussia. The Hanoverian troops returning to the Electorate after their sojourn in Britain would form part of the force but the decision to dispatch British troops as well was indicative of a determination to fight in Europe, as well as America. The question of the command of this force was a vexed one. George had, according to Berkeley, initially thought of commanding himself but he then wanted Prince Louis of Brunswick-Wolfenbüttel, commander-in-chief of Dutch forces to take on the role.[27] George enjoyed

[22] Berkeley diary, BQ 2/2, fos 14–15 (23/1/1757).

[23] Browning, *Newcastle*, p. 256.

[24] Newcastle to George, 16/3/1757, BL, Add. MSS 32870, fos 287–90.

[25] Newcastle's notes of a conversation with Waldegrave at Newcastle House, 25/3/1757, ibid., fo. 335.

[26] Stone to Newcastle, Whitehall, 26/3/1757, ibid., fo. 343.

[27] Berkeley diary, BQ 2/3 fo. 5 (1/4/1757), Dann, *Hanover*, p. 109.

good relations with Prince Louis and had consulted him often during his continental visits. Prince Louis refused. The decision of the Dutch to remain neutral may have played its part. George's thoughts then turned to Louis's younger brother. Ferdinand of Brunswick-Wolfenbüttel was learning the art of soldiering under Frederick the Great's expert tutelage but the Prussian monarch was anxious not to lose him so suggested instead that George place his trust in Cumberland. Cumberland had already been mentioned in London and George agreed to give the command to his son.

Cumberland was an active political figure as well as a soldier and saw an opportunity to neutralize his opponents. He refused to depart for the continent while Pitt continued to hold office, claiming that he would find it impossible to conduct a successful campaign if hampered by an administration containing Pitt.[28] Cumberland calculated that Fox and other members of his faction would be likely beneficiaries of a ministerial shake-up. George saw a golden opportunity to rid himself of Pitt and the despised Temple. Temple was dismissed from the Admiralty on 5 April 1757. George may have hoped that history would repeat itself and that dismissing Temple would lead Pitt to resign, just as Sandwich's removal had triggered Bedford's departure in 1751. In this he was to be disappointed. Pitt appeared at court, much to the king's irritation. Faced with Pitt's refusal to go quietly, George sent Holldernesse round to demand the return of his seals of office on the evening of 7 April. The political merry-go-round was set in motion again.

MINISTERIAL INSTABILITY – AGAIN

George hoped that his intervention would force either Newcastle or Fox to declare their hand more fully. His preference was for an administration led by either one of them, or a combination of the two, provided that Pitt and Temple were kept out.[29] In such a difficult foreign situation, the king might have hoped that a reasonably rapid resolution would be found and that the politicians would focus on the critical business of fighting the war. Instead, there was to be a further period of protracted negotiation and intrigue just as the military situation on the continent was deteriorating. Horace Walpole described this time as the 'interministerium'.[30] Newcastle's role as administration-maker in these months was generally acknowledged. Concerned, as ever, to pick up every trace of what the king thought about him, he was anxious about any perceived slight and sought constant

[28] J.C.D. Clark, *The Dynamics of change* (Cambridge, 1982), p. 354.

[29] J.C.D. Clark, ed., *The memoirs and speeches of James, 2nd Earl Waldegrave, 1742–1763* (Cambridge, 1988), pp. 191–2.

[30] Horace Walpole, *Memoirs of King George II*, ed. John Brooke (3 vols, New Haven, 1985), ii, p. 259. Walpole's first use of the term was in a letter written to Horace Mann in July 1743.

reassurances that he remained in good odour in the closet.[31] Nevertheless, Newcastle's strategy had two distinct elements: to ensure that the king was brought to accept the necessity of including Pitt in the new administration and to seek to forge an alliance with Pitt on the lowest terms possible. Tactics to achieve these ends involved negotiations with Pitt but also included talking to others, just to make clear to Pitt that there were plenty of options that Newcastle could pursue if Pitt proved too demanding or intransigent.

There had been very little evolution over the previous few years in the political groupings.[32] Cumberland remained close to Fox and enjoyed some support from both Bedford and Waldegrave. They might almost be described as a court faction, were it not for the fact that George's relationship with Cumberland remained somewhat ambiguous. Pitt and Temple were close to Princess Augusta, Bute and the prince of Wales – a classic reversionary interest. They retained their suspicion of Cumberland and concomitant desire to keep Fox from office. They were also less enthusiastic about continental war than Cumberland. Finally, there were Newcastle and Hardwicke, representatives of the Old Corps and eager to return to office once the Minorca inquiry had been concluded.

The inquiry finally got under way on 19 April. It managed to expedite its business inside a fortnight. Given the need to sort out a new administration which would probably include Newcastle, it is perhaps not surprising that the inquiry found that the ministry had been justified in looking first to the strength of the fleet in home waters, especially given the widespread rumours of French invasion plans in the early months of 1756. Consequently, little evidence was found to support the contention that Byng had been the victim of shortages of ships and supplies, rather than the author of his own demise.

George now accepted that some sort of accommodation would have to be reached with Leicester House. In the ensuing negotiations the main sticking points proved to relate to the disposition of places rather than substantive policy issues. Pitt's initial demands were heavy. He wanted to return to his position as secretary of state, as well as having Henry Legge as head of the admiralty and George Grenville, Temple's younger brother, as chancellor of the exchequer. Given the king's known antipathy to Temple, all that was asked for him was a place on the cabinet council. The demand to replace Viscount Barrington as secretary at war with Lord George Sackville was refused by the king. George was not especially enamoured with any of those associated with Leicester House but Barrington had also been an effective member of the royal household. As Sir Thomas

---

[31] See the typical exchange: Newcastle to Hardwicke, Claremont, 8/4/1757, BL, Add. MSS 32870, fo. 378v and Hardwicke to Newcastle, Wimpole, 9/4/1757, ibid., fo. 396v.

[32] For a pithy narrative of the manoeuvrings of this period, see Richard Middleton, *The bells of victory: the Pitt–Newcastle ministry and the conduct of the Seven Years' War, 1757–1762* (Cambridge, 1985), pp. 15–18.

Robinson's successor as master of the great wardrobe, he had shown a suitable sense of economy.

Negotiations dragged on. The king, tired by the strains of finding a workable administration, ordered Newcastle to come back in on 27 May.[33] Newcastle continued to insist that Pitt should get back the seals and that something should be done for Temple. He was reluctant to accede to the king's demand that Fox be granted the paymastership. Beginning to see that the king might be serious about constructing a ministry without him, Pitt started to moderate his demands. The king realized that none of his own desires had been met in the new Pitt/Newcastle scheme and ordered that the talks be terminated at the start of June. George briefly entertained hopes that Waldegrave might form an administration with Fox, and talks with him began on 8 June. They were brought to a crashing halt by the decision of Holdernesse to resign, apparently independently of any direct prompting from Newcastle. The king was dismayed to see Holdernesse go, particularly as his rise had been largely down to royal favour and he had been kept in post during the upheavals of the previous few years by George's intervention.[34]

With Waldegrave's attempts to form an administration going nowhere, George reluctantly agreed to recommence negotiations with Newcastle and Pitt. Lord Chief Justice Mansfield was chosen as the initial mediator, although he was soon replaced by Hardwicke. To the very last, George stuck to his demands that Fox be given the paymastership and that Temple should not have any office that brought him into frequent contact with the king in the closet. He also wanted to ensure that the secretary at war was to his liking, a not unreasonable demand given the state of the nation. Hardwicke was able to ensure that his son-in-law, Anson, was returned to the position of first lord of the admiralty. Henry Legge, who had been intended for the position under the scheme agreed between Newcastle and Pitt, instead became chancellor of the exchequer (again). Holdernesse got the seals of the northern secretaryship back, although George's displeasure with him was apparent for some time afterwards. One example of it was the king's decision to grant the vacant Garter stall to Waldegrave rather than Holdernesse. Newcastle returned to the treasury, Pitt to the southern secretaryship. Henry Fox became paymaster, Barrington was retained as secretary at war and Temple became lord privy seal which entitled him to attend the king's councils but did not necessarily entail close contact with the monarch.

The Pitt–Newcastle administration which finally came into being in late June 1757 was to survive even beyond George's death in 1760. What had been at the root of the ministerial instability since 1754 and what

[33] Berkeley noted frequently during these months his fear that the political crisis was having a deleterious effect on the king's health. See, for example, Berkeley diary, BQ 2/3, fo. 8 (10/4/1757), fo. 25 (18/6/1757).
[34] Clark, ed., *Waldegrave memoirs*, pp. 196–202.

contribution, if any, did the king make to that instability? Part of the answer lay in the difficulty of managing the Commons after Pelham's death. Yet there was much more going on than just debates about parliamentary management. Newcastle did face a tricky task in determining which of several potential candidates might take on leadership of the Commons but the problem of heading an administration from the Lords was a practical, not a constitutional, one. The other difficulty that Newcastle, and all his assorted political partners and rivals, faced was finding a compromise between political necessities and royal preferences. Pitt was only grudgingly accepted by George and Newcastle had to utilize his considerable skills of political persuasion to achieve this. In a very crude sense, it might be said that Newcastle had been able to prevail and that George's attempt in April 1757 to reassert his authority by dismissing Pitt had failed. The king had not had a workable alternative to put in place and, as previously, attempts to construct a ministry without the Old Corps proved to be mere phantoms. Yet George had not surrendered everything. In areas that mattered to him – those with whom he was obliged to have close contact in the closet and who was to manage the land war – he had prevailed. War and how to deal with its impact hung over the ministerial crises of 1754–7, just as it had in 1742–6. While the outcome of the struggle for places might not have been entirely to George's liking, he could console himself with the fact that the foreign political direction that all his ministers pursued, regardless of their professed positions when out of office, was largely to his taste.

This did not stop George from feeling sorry for himself. As he pointed out to Waldegrave, who had just advised him that he would be unable to form a ministry and that George 'should give way to the necessity of the times' and take Pitt in, his situation was far from agreeable.[35] While his ministers, and the public at large, seemed angry about his supposed partiality for Hanover, he was doing nothing more than Britain should do for any country that had been endangered by British policies. The British were rightly proud of their constitution and laws, continually talking of the liberties they enjoyed, but George challenged anybody to produce a single instance in which he had overstepped the marks of constitutional propriety. Indeed, the only person who appeared to lack liberty was himself as he did not even seem to have the right to veto those who were to be his supposed servants. He found it unusual that the aristocracy seemed keener to stay on good terms with Newcastle than with him.

CUMBERLAND AND KLOSTER ZEVEN

What was really important to George, however, was the progress of the continental war. News of Frederick II's advance into Bohemia at the begin-

---

[35] Ibid., pp. 206–7.

ning of the 1757 campaigning season had been welcomed. However, by the time that the ministerial wranglings had been completed less positive news was emerging from the Bohemian theatre as reports reached London of Frederick's defeat at Kolín on 18 June. Meanwhile, the situation in Westphalia was also giving cause for concern. Cumberland had departed for the continent in April, preceded by instructions from his father to his Hanoverian servants to ensure that Cumberland was served proper meals while on campaign.[36] Although he was generally of a hawkish disposition, his actions during the 1757 campaign were largely defensive. Given the circumstances, this was hardly surprising. The French army under Marshal d'Estrées was at least 75,000 strong. By contrast, Cumberland's 'Army of Observation' numbered no more than 47,000 – 27,000 from Hanover itself, including the troops recently returned from Britain, with the rest made up of troops from Hessen-Kassel, Wolfenbüttel, Saxony-Gotha and Schaumburg-Lippe.[37]

George continued to encourage his son from London, telling him of reports that d'Estrées's army had been severely depleted through desertions and urging him to take as full advantage as possible of the provisions available in the ecclesiastical states of Westphalia, while checking the French advance.[38] There was little that Cumberland could do to stop French forces, though. By late June, the French were at Bielefeld. They then proceeded to close the net around Hanover. The Prussian port of Emden was captured, making communication with London more difficult. Hessen-Kassel was quickly occupied and Landgrave William fled towards Hanover. Cumberland himself retreated further towards the Electorate. By the middle of July, d'Estrées's army had crossed the Weser, occupied the area around Göttingen and was closing in on Cumberland's position near Hameln. Cumberland had drawn up his forces on raised ground near the village of Hastenbeck. Although the French army was nearly twice the size of his own, his forces occupied a strong defensive position. On 26 July the French began an assault on Cumberland's position, suffering heavy casualties in the process. The encounter was hardly decisive militarily but Cumberland quickly decided that the strategic situation was impossible. Faced with such a large opposing force, he began a retreat towards Verden in the north of the Electorate. Hanover was now open to French occupation.

The news of Cumberland's defeat and withdrawal northwards was greeted with relative equanimity by the king. Berkeley was somewhat surprised because he had worried about how George would cope, given

---

[36] George to von Reden, St James's, 29/3/1757, NHStA, Dep. 103, XXIV, 2653.

[37] For a useful summary of the Hanoverian side of the story, see Mediger, 'Hastenbeck und Zeven', pp. 147–53.

[38] George to Cumberland, St James's, 5/5/1757, RA, GEO/52967 and idem to idem, Kensington, 20/5/1757, RA, GEO/52968–9.

his capacity for extreme happiness or anger over small matters.[39] In a letter to Cumberland at the start of August, George professed to be convinced of Cumberland's 'sense and capacity, and zele for my Service'. The king was insistent that neither Cumberland nor his troops should shoulder the blame for the reverse and that they had behaved honourably. Fate had simply dealt them a bitter blow. Consequently George was entrusting Cumberland with full powers to negotiate a separate peace for the Electorate. He was to use all his skills to save both George's army and his Hanoverian subjects from the 'misery and slavery they grown under'. The letter concluded with a warning to negotiate cautiously and expressions of paternal concern about the state of Cumberland's health.[40]

There was little else that George could do. The disposition of responsibility within the new British administration was such that Pitt had taken charge of the war effort, with Newcastle overseeing finances and patronage. There was little enthusiasm for sending British forces to Hanover's aid and Frederick's military position meant that there was little prospect of Prussian help.[41] Meanwhile the military pressure on the Electorate was building. Marshal d'Estrées had been given only a few days to celebrate his victory at Hastenbeck. He found himself the victim of court intrigue, blamed for the tardiness of his advance towards Hanover, and was replaced by the duc de Richelieu who had led the successful French invasion of Minorca in the previous year.

Richelieu was quick to take advantage of Cumberland's retreat. The duchy of Wolfenbüttel was rapidly overrun and much of the Hanoverian Electorate followed. Hanover itself was occupied and many of the Hanoverian ministers retreated to Stade, although Münchhausen remained in the city. Stade had been selected long before as the best location from which to govern the Electorate in case of invasion. Its fortress was large and its proximity to the Elbe made it easy to reinforce. George had drawn up a plan for moving his jewels and valuables from Hanover to Stade in 1741 and the plans used in 1757 had been revised following fears of a Prussian attack on the Electorate in 1753.[42] The French advanced as far north as a line defined by Bremen in the west and Harburg in the east. It was only when his military supremacy had been established that Richelieu deigned to negotiate.

From the Hanoverian ministers' point of view, fair terms would include the dispersal of the army of observation, with the constituent forces being allowed to return to barracks, a promise on George's part not to involve himself further in the continental war either by supporting or opposing

---

[39] Berkeley diary, BQ 2/41, fo. 3 (7/8/1757).

[40] George to Cumberland, Kensington, 9/8/1757, RA, GEO/52970.

[41] On Pitt's refusal to send British troops, see Pitt to George Grenville, St James's Square, 11/8/1757, William James Smith, ed., *The Grenville papers* (4 vols, London, 1852–3), i, p. 206.

[42] See the plans in NHStA, Hann. 92, 98 and 99 for the earlier and later periods.

Prussia, French withdrawal from George's German territories and those of his allies, all of which would be sealed by a separate peace.[43] Negotiations between Cumberland and Richelieu were facilitated by a Danish intermediary. Although Richelieu was anxious to conclude an agreement so his forces could be diverted to the campaign against Frederick, he was aware that he was negotiating from a position of strength. Talks began at the start of September. On 8 September 1757 Cumberland signed the Convention of Kloster Zeven at Bremervörde. Richlieu added his signature in Kloster Zeven itself two days later. The terms proved worse than either George or his ministers had wanted or expected. The army of observation was disbanded but the bulk of Hanoverian forces had to be confined to a small area in the north of the Electorate with only a few regiments left in Stade. There was nothing about a French withdrawal so the occupation would continue. While the convention was technically a neutrality arrangement of the sort that George had desired, it was effectively also a surrender.

News of the agreement was greeted with dismay in London. George's British ministers had been well aware for much of August that some sort of deal was on the cards. Holdernesse had explained the king's unusual serenity in the closet following news of Cumberland's defeat at Hastenbeck by his suspicion that instructions had been issued to reach a separate deal.[44] The British ministers had already been sounded out about the question of neutrality.[45] They were reluctant to say too much to George directly, feeling that they were not equipped with all the facts and were not really able to comment on purely Hanoverian issues. Nevertheless, their anxiety was apparent. The spectre of 1741 loomed large. How easy would it be to fulfil commitments made to Prussia, particularly about the provision of subsidies, if George reached a separate peace as Elector? While the fiction of George's two persons, Elector and king, was an occasionally useful political device, it was unlikely that either Austria or France would accept that George could carry on a continental war as king from which he had withdrawn as Elector.

As in other instances, George's initial panic when faced with a setback slowly gave way to a greater degree of resolution. Newcastle saw a copy of a letter to Cumberland in which George made clear the importance of doing all that he could to save the army of observation.[46] As the weeks went by, he became more adamant that Cumberland must refrain from signing anything that ruined the army or was generally disadvantageous. The rediscovered determination was almost certainly genuine but it had the added bonus of enhancing the king's credibility with a sceptical

[43] Dann, *Hanover*, p. 113.
[44] Holdernesse to Newcastle, London, 12/8/1757, BL, Add. MSS 32873, fo. 42.
[45] Newcastle to Hardwicke, Newcastle House, 3/8/1757, BL, Add. MSS 32872, fos 426–7.
[46] Copy of George to Cumberland, Kensington, 16/8/1757, BL, Add. MSS 32873, fo. 111.

ministry. Despite the public posturing, disquiet remained. Frederick conveyed his extreme displeasure at the way in which events had unfolded to Andrew Mitchell, claiming that the Hanoverians had managed to dupe the British. He began to ask difficult questions about where the support guaranteed by the Convention of Westminster was.[47] George's new-found resilience even led him to urge Cumberland to defend Stade, in which he would be helped by the dispatch of a naval squadron, or try to link up with Prussian forces to the east, but it was already too late.[48]

Once the precise terms that Cumberland had agreed became known, George reacted angrily. Newcastle was surprised by how unhappy George seemed, as he complained that Providence had abandoned him.[49] He condemned his Hanoverian ministers for their lack of resolution. Cumberland was recalled, knowing full well what the king thought of the convention. The king did not mince his words. He described the convention as 'shameful' and 'ruinous'.[50] George tried to claim that Cumberland had exceeded his authority: he had been instructed to negotiate an agreement that had to include French evacuation of Hanoverian territory as one of its conditions.[51] Few believed that Cumberland had acted alone.[52] While George's tone may have altered during August, there is little doubt that Cumberland had not gone beyond that which he was empowered to do. Philipp von Münchhausen tried to explain what had led to the agreement, in a written account presented to Newcastle. Its content was such that Newcastle and Hardwicke agreed that it could not possibly be published because of the harm it would do to Anglo-Prussian relations.[53]

Cumberland returned home in disgrace. He arrived at Kensington to discover his father playing cards with his sister Amelia. Their meeting lasted a matter of minutes. The king accused Cumberland of ruining his country, the army and his reputation. Cumberland presented a paper justifying his conduct, at which point George angrily departed. Cumberland's response was to tell his sister to inform the king that he intended to resign all his military appointments and he then returned to Windsor, where he was warden of the Great Park.[54] George was still trying, unsuccessfully, to convince the British ministry that Cumberland had overstepped the mark. Fox, who was hardly a disinterested party, told Bedford that Münchhausen had been permitted by the king to show the letters supposedly illustrating how Cumberland had acted without orders

---

[47] Mitchell to Newcastle, 28/8/1757, private and most secret, ibid., fo. 323.

[48] Middleton, *Bells of victory*, p. 36.

[49] Newcastle to Hardwicke, Newcastle House, 19/9/1757, BL, Add. MSS 32874, fo. 148v.

[50] George to Cumberland, 20/9/1757 quoted in Middleton, *Bells of victory*, p. 37.

[51] Dann, *Hanover*, p. 115.

[52] Berkeley diary, BQ 2/4, fo. 1 (20/9/1757).

[53] Hardwicke to Newcastle, Wimpole, 5/9/1757, BL, Add. MSS 32873, fo. 468.

[54] Veronica Baker-Smith, *Royal discord: the family of George II* (London, 2008), p. 188, Newcastle to Hardwicke, Newcastle House, 12/10/1757, BL, Add. MSS 32875, fo. 56.

to a selection of British ministers. The conclusion that the ministers had drawn was the precise opposite of that which George had intended.[55] Berkeley initially thought that George's anger with his son was largely for effect – Cumberland was present at a levee and a drawing room on 13 October – although Cumberland's determination to resign gave him pause for thought.[56]

FIGHTING ON

In the interim Pitt and his ministerial colleagues had begun the process of disowning the convention. News of the terms reached London on 17 September. On the 18th, Holdernesse constructed a diplomatic circular that made plain that the convention had been negotiated without the knowledge of the British ministry, with the distinct implication that they did not feel bound by it. Given George's anger at the terms, it was easy to persuade him that this was the right course of action, although a public repudiation of the convention was not immediate. The ministers trod carefully. The news from the front was not especially positive – the Russians had defeated a Prussian army at Gross-Jägersdorf and in consequence Frederick, commanding another Prussian force, had halted his attempts to pursue the Franco-Imperial forces ranged against him. He had also, while admonishing the British for keeping him in the dark about the terms of Kloster Zeven, begun to explore whether he could reach a separate peace deal with France. Naturally, he failed to inform his uncle of these talks.[57]

There was one glimmer of hope. The Russian commander, Apraxin, had determined not to press home the advantage he had gained at Gross-Jägersdorf and had, instead, decided to retreat to the security of Tilsit. Apraxin's caution, which led soon afterwards to his dismissal, relieved the immediate pressure on Frederick. It was sufficient to suggest that Prussia was still worth backing. In a meeting between Philipp von Münchhausen and the leading British ministers (Newcastle, Pitt, Holdernesse and Granville, with military advice supplied by Anson and Sir John Ligonier) on 7 October, the latter let it be known that while they did not presume to offer the king advice on how to conduct his Hanoverian business, they felt that were the king to disown the convention, they could see their way to taking the army of observation into British pay as soon as it recommenced operations.[58] This gave further support to George's determination to act. He had already issued

[55] Fox to Bedford, Holland House, 12/10/1757, Russell, ed., *Bedford Correspondence*, ii, pp. 276–8.
[56] Berkeley diary, BQ 2/4, fo. 10 (13/10/1757) and fo. 13 (16/10/1757).
[57] Szabo, *Seven Years War*, p. 86.
[58] Middleton, *Bells of victory*, pp. 37–8. For the note of the meeting, dated 7/10/1757, see BL, Add. MSS 32874, fo. 475.

orders to his Hanoverian ministers to find reasons for breaking the agreement. His eventual grounds for repudiating the convention were typical. The French had insisted that the Hessians disarm before returning home – an apparent contravention of the agreement. George was irritated that Cumberland had not resisted this more strongly, describing him as 'his rascally son' and exclaiming that his 'blood was tainted'. When Newcastle expressed some disquiet at the king's language, George retorted that 'a scoundrel in England one day may be thought a good man, another. In Germany, it is otherwise; I think like a German.'[59]

The initial reaction of the Hanoverian ministers to the new plan was less than enthusiastic. They remained concerned that, with a French army on their doorstep, they would bear the brunt of any French anger at the repudiation of the convention. Nevertheless, they were slowly won round. Philipp von Münchhausen was dispatched to Stade to insert some steel into the exiled ministry there. The broader military situation had begun to swing back in Hanover's favour as well. Richelieu had been anxious to neutralize Hanover as quickly as possible because of his desire to divert his forces to the attack on Prussia. Aware of the threat on his flank, Frederick had diverted a small force under Ferdinand of Brunswick-Wolfenbüttel to delay Richelieu's progress. Ferdinand was so successful that at the beginning of October Richelieu agreed to halt campaigning for the year. Frederick, meanwhile, suspecting that he might now force the Franco-Imperial army that had been pursuing him to give battle, concentrated his forces and was victorious at Rossbach, to the west of Leipzig, on 5 November 1757. In the aftermath of the battle Frederick suggested Ferdinand as a candidate to fill the request of George and his ministers for a Prussian general to command the army of observation. This offer was accepted with alacrity and the Hanoverian ministers were reassured that the new commander of their forces was a Guelph.[60]

THE CONSEQUENCES OF KLOSTER ZEVEN

The aftermath of Kloster Zeven was felt in several ways. It prompted George to revise his 1751 will. A codicil in the Royal Archives, dated 6 October 1757, introduced significant changes. Some were a matter of necessity, others of deliberate choice. As Prince George had come of age the previous provisions that dealt with how Cumberland would govern Hanover in the event of a regency (§12) were now superfluous. However, the clauses that had created a fund of some 3 million taler and stipulated how Cumberland could use it (§3–7) were revoked. Instead the interest on the capital was to be used 'towards the supporting of our military

---

[59] Newcastle to Hardwicke, Newcastle House, 8/10/1757, BL, Add. MSS 32874, fos 471–2.
[60] Szabo, *Seven Years War*, pp. 94–100; Dann, *Hanover*, p. 116.

Establishment in Germany, or, according to circumstances, to other purposes, tending to the Good & Welfare of our German dominions & subjects'.[61] Whilst the king may have been concerned about the future well-being of his German subjects, it is difficult to avoid the conclusion that he was also expressing pique at Cumberland's recent conduct.

George raised the question of the future of the dynastic union between Britain and Hanover again in the aftermath of Kloster Zeven.[62] In late September, Philipp von Münchhausen advised his brother that the issue of the continuing union of the territories might be discussed in the next parliamentary session and there was some concern (from unspecified parties) about how the Electorate would fare under a monarch who knew little of it.[63] The clear subtext was worries about George's age and the attitudes of the prince of Wales but these had been heightened by the inability of the king and his ministers to prevent the occupation of the Electorate that had occurred, in large measure, because of British disputes with France.

Unlike in 1744 there was no collective ministerial reply and the privy councillors responded individually. They had been asked by George to consider what the political consequences of a separation of the two territories would be, as well as whether and/or how this could be achieved. Gerlach Adolf von Münchhausen, the senior minister, wrote from Hanover, as did Johann Clamor August von dem Bussche, Levin Adolf von Hake and Burchard Christian von Behr. The three ministers who came between Münchhausen and Bussche in order of seniority – Ernst von Steinberg, Karl Philipp Diede zum Fürstenstein and August Wilhelm von Schwicheldt – had relocated to Stade and it was from there that their replies came.

The responses were all measured, with a careful discussion of the pros and cons of the current arrangements, and varied in length from a few pages to extensive essays. Münchhausen was sure that there were no insuperable difficulties involved in bringing a separation about but felt that, given the complicated way in which Hanover's territories had been brought together, it was best not to give the emperor any opportunity to raise questions of inheritance and succession. Münchhausen's general view was that the dynastic link was useful, provided that Britain continued to accept it. He argued that the connection added prestige to the British crowns, as well as giving an easy entrée into the affairs of the empire. Britain had increased access to troops while Hanover enjoyed additional

---

[61] Codicil to George's will, Kensington, 6/10/1757, RA, GEO/52971–3.

[62] The following account draws on the individual ministerial responses contained in NHStA, Hann. 92, 70 along with the analyses in Mitchell D. Allen, 'The Anglo-Hanoverian connection, 1727–1760', unpublished Ph.D. dissertation, University of Boston, 2000, pp. 260–71 and Nick Harding, *Hanover and the British empire 1700–1837* (Woodbridge, 2007), pp. 169–74.

[63] Dann, *Hanover*, p. 134.

protection against powerful neighbours such as Prussia. British financial support was also welcome. However, Münchhausen, while accepting that a continuation of the union was probably best for the moment, could foresee a time when separation might become desirable. It would allow the Hanoverian Elector to concentrate his resources and attention entirely on the protection of the Electorate and it might even encourage the British to be more forthcoming with aid if they were no longer able to assume Hanoverian co-operation.

Steinberg's analysis made extensive reference to the advantages of keeping Britain involved in continental politics and the ways in which the union had facilitated access for British forces and alliances and helped to preserve Protestantism within the empire. Both sides had benefited. What was important now was that Britain recognize its responsibilities in extricating Hanover from the mess in which it had been placed by British policies.

The lengthiest analysis was provided by Schwicheldt. His central concern was to stress the vital importance of a return of amity with Austria. It was only through this that Hanoverian interests could be preserved: Schwicheldt had been a sceptic about the alliance with Frederick since its inception. If the Old System were not revived, then it was probably best for the union to be dissolved and for Hanover to achieve a separate reconciliation with the emperor. Schwicheldt thought that territories with resident princes generally seemed well ruled but noted that, even in George's absence, Hanover remained a generally contented place.

Behr's contribution was considerably more concise than Schwicheldt's. He favoured the preservation of the union, not least because of the advantages it had for preserving Protestantism and, more pragmatically, because of the need for aid in removing the occupying French forces. Hake's opinion was similarly positive about the connection, although he entertained doubts about how well Hanover could be ruled by somebody unaccustomed to its ways. He was also anxious about how to deal with the Austrians now that they had allied with France. Bussche, taking advantage of his extensive diplomatic experience, drew comparisons with other multiple monarchies, noting that the resources of the weaker state tended to be absorbed by the stronger. He worried that France would always take advantage of Hanover as a bargaining chip in future wars with Britain, although he hoped, perhaps forlornly, that the costs to France of an invasion might discourage her from pursuing this course.

Diede offered a considered analysis, looking beyond the immediate context of French occupation to argue that tying Britain into the empire was useful because it increased the likelihood of British co-operation with the emperor. This, in turn, helped to protect states like Hanover by keeping the empire strong. He was also convinced that local knowledge, both of the territory itself and in selection of ministers, was vital for Hanover's future success. If the link were to end, Diede could see no other course for Hanover but that of building up a stronger army than it had at present. He was a cautious advocate of continuing union.

The overall impression from the differing opinions is of the necessity of maintaining the link in the present circumstances but pessimism about the future, either because of fears about what George III might think of the Electorate or because of the difficulty of coping with the incredible diplomatic situation of Habsburg/Bourbon friendship. George was not moved to take any particular action and, as recent work has shown, the ministers' expectations about his successor were, to a certain extent, confounded.[64] There is little doubt, though, that the Seven Years War in general and the experience of French occupation in particular led to an increased desire among Hanoverians to consider the utility of the connection with Britain and to re-evaluate it.[65] Although Ferdinand's assumption of command of what was now styled 'His Britannic Majesty's army' in December 1757 did lead to some immediate relief for parts of the Electorate, his advance southwards was halted at the Aller. It was not until spring 1758 that Ferdinand was able to evict the French from Westphalia.[66] French forces continued to occupy the city of Hanover throughout the winter. One group that suffered because of this were George's troop of French comedians. Instructions had been issued that all performances should cease in the aftermath of Princess Caroline's death in December 1757 because the Hanoverian court, even when occupied and in only tenuous contact with the king via the uncertain postal route through Stade, had to go into mourning.[67] The comedians faced a larger problem, however. When it became known that they had performed for the occupying French forces on 20 December, the king was so incensed that he sacked them all and dissolved the troupe completely.[68]

The French advance through Westphalia had also led to the displacement of someone a little closer to the king. As the French occupied Hessen-Kassel, Mary and her father-in-law, Landgrave William, had fled. By the middle of September Mary had joined her brother at Stade. Amidst the worries about how to disengage himself from the commitments made by Cumberland, George found time to consider Mary's future financial security, which had been rendered uncertain by the

---

[64] See the path-breaking T.C.W. Blanning, ' "That horrid Electorate" or "ma patrie germanique"? George III, Hanover and the Fürstenbund of 1785', *HJ*, 20 (1977), pp. 311–44 and the more recent summary in Torsten Riotte, 'George III and Hanover', in Brendan Simms and Torsten Riotte, eds, *The Hanoverian dimension in British history, 1714–1837* (Cambridge, 2007), pp. 58–85.

[65] For a powerful argument in favour of seeing the period as a watershed moment, see Hermann Wellenreuther, 'Die Bedeutung des Siebenjährigen Kriegs für die englisch-hannoveranischen Beziehungen', in A.H. Birke and Kurt Kluxen, Kurt, eds, *England und Hannover/England and Hanover* (Munich, 1986), pp. 145–75.

[66] Szabo, *Seven years war*, pp. 131–6.

[67] Philipp von Münchhausen to von Reden, London, 31/1/1758, NHStA, Dep. 103, XXIV, 3272.

[68] Rosenmarie Elisabeth Wallbrecht, *Das Theater des Barockzeitalters an den welfischen Höfen Hannover und Celle* (Hildesheim, 1974), p. 156.

invasion of the lands on which she relied for revenue to support her and her sons. Newcastle approached Bedford, who had become lord lieutenant of Ireland as a result of the recent ministerial moves, to see if a pension could be found for Mary on the Irish establishment. The figure the king had in mind was £6,000 per annum, although he was aware that the Irish establishment already had to shoulder considerable burdens.[69] Bedford's response was carefully crafted. He did not want to stand in the way of the king's liberal impulses but the costs of pensions to the Irish establishment had increased by some £17,400 since 1727 when they had stood at nearly £38,000. Bedford was worried that he already had to make up shortfalls to fund existing pensions out of general funds and he feared that revenues would decrease even further during the war. His suggestion was that it would be more appropriate for the Westminster parliament to pick up the bill, not least because it was British actions that had given rise to Mary's exile in the first place.[70]

Figures for pensions on the Irish establishment in the Royal Archives confirm Bedford's analysis of increasing costs but also show that an Irish pension had been a traditional way to get round the prohibition on rewarding non-Britons from royal funds; German ministers, Georg Ludwig's mistress and her daughter and non-British diplomats were all rewarded by this route prior to 1727.[71] George was unwilling to be held back by Bedford's obfuscations. He decided to establish a pension immediately and pay it out of his Civil List, despite his previous protests that it was already overstretched, and then defer the decision on whether it would be permanently charged to Irish or British funds.[72] It seems not entirely coincidental that it was shortly after these exchanges that the Irish parliament began to worry about the number of pensions to non-residents that had been granted on the Irish establishment.[73] The king's pleas of poverty were, it has to be said, a little overdone. Following a parliamentary grant to pay off Civil List debts of some £457,000 in 1747, George had entered a new era of frugality and this, plus increasing Civil List revenues, meant that he had accumulated a surplus on the Civil List by the late 1750s.[74]

Concerns about his family and inner circle were increasingly bearing down on the king. His close friend Charles Fitzroy, second duke of

---

[69] Newcastle to Bedford, Newcastle House, 3/10/1757, BL, Add. MSS 32874, fos 416–17. The letter is also printed in Russell, ed., *Bedford correspondence*, ii, pp. 270–1.

[70] Bedford to Newcastle, Dublin Castle, 13/10/1757, BL, Add. MSS 32875, fos 67–8.

[71] Pensions on the Civil List of Ireland as at Midsummer 1727, RA, GEO/52758.

[72] Newcastle to Hardwicke, Newcastle House, 23/10/1757, BL, Add. MSS 32875, fo. 231r. Berkeley was eventually appointed one of the trustees of the pension with Hertford and Hardwicke. See Berkeley diary, BQ 2/47, fo. 5 (27/7/1758).

[73] Berkeley diary, BQ 2/43, fos 5–7 (17 and 20/11/1757).

[74] Sir John Sainty and R.O. Bucholz, *Officials of the royal household, 1660–1837* (2 vols, London, 1997–8), i, pp. lxxiv–lxxxv.

Grafton, had died on 6 May 1757. Fitzroy had been lord chamberlain since 1724, having succeeded Newcastle in that role. Waldegrave viewed him as the consummate courtier whose long acquaintance with George enabled him to address the king in ways and on subjects where others feared to tread. He had a particular skill in managing Newcastle. Waldegrave thought that the crisis of 1757 might have been less protracted had Grafton lived.[75] Grafton's loss was not just felt by George. His daughter Amelia had always been very close to Grafton, even though he was the same age as her father. Grafton was replaced as lord chamberlain by William Cavendish, fourth duke of Devonshire. Devonshire had not particularly enjoyed his stint as first lord of the treasury in coalition with Pitt and was happy to take a lesser office, having overseen the caretaker administration that kept things going before the final establishment of the Newcastle–Pitt administration. Like Grafton, though, he continued to attend meetings of the inner cabinet.

The king's own health had deteriorated somewhat. There had been considerable interest in its state for some time, with correspondents noting the ups and downs of royal coughs and colds.[76] However, George was now largely deaf, and blind in one eye. His assorted medical complaints did little for his temper. He remained a great survivor, though, both politically and personally. George's family life continued to be complicated. Two of his children were already dead and a third, Caroline, followed them to the grave after months of illness in December 1757. Caroline had not been active in court life for some time. It was claimed she had weak limbs, although Berkeley thought that she preferred solitude and disliked the English. Her death was a further blow to the king but Berkeley was surprised that George saw company at a levee before she had been buried.[77] Mary settled in Hamburg with her two sons as the Seven Years War swept over Westphalia. George had already made some efforts to secure her future financially and he was able to offer her permanent support via an annuity. The king's relations with both Anne and Cumberland were difficult but for different reasons. Both had disappointed their father in some way, Cumberland militarily and Anne through her inability, or unwillingness, to bring the United Provinces into the war.

[75] Clark, ed., *Waldegrave memoirs*, p. 199.

[76] Berkeley made frequent comment on the king's health, whether good or bad. In June 1757, he was pleased to see George looked well on the thirtieth anniversary of his succession. By the middle of October, he noted how the king looked better than for some weeks past and he was described as being in 'perfect health' on his birthday in November. Berkeley diary, BQ 2/3, fo. 29 (22/6/1757), BQ 2/4 fo. 15 (23/10/1757) and BQ 2/43, fo. 2 (10/11/1757).

[77] Berkeley diary, BQ 2/4, fo. 25 (26 and 28/12/1757) and BQ 2/43, fo. 18 (1/1/1758).

RAIDING AND RENEWAL?

The news from the various theatres of war was not especially positive as
1757 drew to a close. Although Frederick's victories at Rossbach and
Leuthen offered a glimmer of hope on the continent, elsewhere British
efforts had met with little success. An expedition to attack Louisburg,
combining troops from the colonies with support from the Royal Navy,
failed. Moreover, the marquis de Montcalm who commanded French
forces in Quebec had used the opportunity of the earl of Loudoun
concentrating most of his forces for the attack on Louisburg to capture
and destroy Fort William Henry at the head of Lake George. Although the
feared French advance down the Hudson valley did not eventuate,
Loudoun was recalled to London. His appointment as commander-in-
chief in America had come about through his close association with
Cumberland and Fox and they were no longer in a position to defend him
so he was replaced by Major-General James Abercromby.

Moreover, Pitt's initial foray into raids on the French coast had also met
with distinctly limited success. Pitt was keen on a raiding policy for several
reasons. It was a way of fighting in Europe that did not look like just
another means of defending the Electorate and the naval component
offered a sop to 'blue water' advocates. At the same time, it allowed Pitt to
claim that Britain was doing something practical to divert French forces
from attacks on Frederick.[78] The attempt to land at Rochefort in
September 1757 miscarried. It proved impossible to find an appropriate
landing site that would allow cannon for a land attack on Rochefort to be
offloaded so the commanders of the expeditionary force felt unable to risk
disembarkation and returned to Britain without having engaged the
enemy. Unsurprisingly, this outcome was met with incredulity in London
which rapidly turned into a desire for answers. George was urged to investigate what had gone wrong. Instead of simply convening a court martial,
George appointed a board of inquiry to investigate the raid. Three senior
officers concluded that there had been little to prevent a landing so
blamed the decision taken by the council of war that led to the return
home. General Sir John Mordaunt, the senior army commander on the
raid, was subsequently court-martialled for disobeying orders but was
acquitted. George, who had named Mordaunt and his fellow officers for
the expedition specifically when asked to approve the raid, indicated his
displeasure by dismissing Mordaunt from his personal staff.[79]

George had also been pressed to deal with military matters in another
respect. Cumberland had kept his word and resigned all his military
appointments. Many of the ministers were relieved. Neither Pitt nor
the remainder of the Old Corps were sorry to see the back of Fox's

[78] Brendan Simms, *Three victories and a defeat* (London, 2007), pp. 434–5.
[79] Middleton, *Bells of victory*, pp. 40–3.

patron and his enforced departure from ministerial deliberations. Yet Cumberland's resignation left a vacancy for the post of commander-in-chief. Filling the vacancy quickly would ensure that there was no easy route back for Cumberland, should the king change his mind.[80] A memorandum pressing the ministerial case for a rapid replacement was presented to George on 19 October.[81] The king's initial response was unpromising. Still the armchair general, he claimed that he would be his own commander-in-chief, as well as leaving the command of the Grenadier Guards, which Cumberland had held since 1742, vacant. The ministers objected that this solution was impracticable. Instead, Pitt pressed the claims of Sir John Ligonier, who was even older than the king, having been born in 1680, to fill the gap. Ligonier, a Huguenot exile, had the advantage of being trusted by both George and the ministers so the king eventually agreed to his appointment. He succeeded to nearly all of Cumberland's posts, taking over command of the Grenadiers, being created field marshal and raised to the Irish peerage. He was, however, merely commander-in-chief, rather than captain-general. Whereas Cumberland had enjoyed authority over all forces both at home and abroad, Ligonier was limited in that he could only send orders to commanders in America in consultation with civilian ministers.[82] Throughout these comings and goings, Newcastle continued to place great faith in his cultivation of the countess of Yarmouth as a means both of getting his views across to the king and of making suggestions about the stream of patronage requests that Cumberland's departure had generated.

Despite his age, Ligonier had a significant impact on the conduct of the war. The renewed sense of vigour has often been attributed to Pitt himself, although Richard Middleton has emphasized the extent to which Pitt was the figurehead of a more collective effort.[83] Ligonier played his part by the promotion of officers like Amherst, Forbes and James Wolfe for a renewed assault on the French in Canada during 1758. Whether stemming from Pitt directly or not, the American offensive was part of a larger effort to prosecute the war more widely and successfully which emerged in that year. There were further offensives against Louisburg and Fort Duquesne, as well as moves against Quebec and Montreal. Elsewhere a raid on the French coast took place, with an attack on St Malo in May and June 1758. Most importantly, though, direct efforts to alter the course of the continental war were stepped up.

A necessary precursor to these efforts was to mend fences with Prussia. Negotiations took place in the early months of 1758. Frederick wanted a

[80] Hardwicke to Newcastle, Wimpole, 16/10/1757, BL, Add. MSS 32875, fo. 143.

[81] Memorandum for the king, 19/10/1757, ibid., fos 191–2.

[82] Newcastle to Hardwicke, Newcastle House, 23/10/1757, fos 223–4; Middleton, *Bells of victory*, pp. 45–6.

[83] Middleton, *Bells of victory*, *passim* but especially pp. 211–32.

British squadron to be dispatched to the Baltic, as well as British troops added to Ferdinand's forces. Pitt was hesitant about both ideas, aware of his patriot credentials and the widespread resistance to British troops on the continent. In the end, though, it was agreed that the British should garrison the coastal town of Emden and that George should, from British funds, maintain an army of at least 50,000 in Germany.[84]

The attack on St Malo was not an overwhelming success, although at least the expeditionary force did manage to land and destroyed shipping along the coast without laying siege to St Malo itself. Nevertheless, it provided a sufficient diversion to enable other plans to come to fruition. Ferdinand wanted to break out of his position and force the French out of Westphalia into the Austrian Netherlands. His plan needed an element of surprise because it would be difficult to accomplish without moving his troops on to the west bank of the Rhine unmolested. He was able to do this, although he violated Dutch neutrality in the process, by the start of June. Ferdinand proceeded southwards and met a French force under the comte de Clermont on 23 June near Krefeld. But for miscommunications among the French commanders, Clermont's troops would have been reinforced by another French corps that was bound for Bohemia. Nevertheless, Clermont's forces still outnumbered those of his opponent. Despite his inferior numbers, Ferdinand was able to make Clermont give up his position and retreat south eastwards.[85] It was further evidence that a corner had been turned in the continental war. The news was timely. Berkeley had been concerned about the king's health for much of 1758. In May he had caught a cold, having spent too long in the garden. He had intended to see the guards march past but had arrived earlier than he had originally planned, so had to wait around. At the beginning of June his pulse had been so low that his physicians had thought it unwise to bleed him. A few weeks later he had declined so much that Berkeley feared he would be dead by the winter. There were worries that he would lose his sight completely.[86]

Even before news of the victory at Krefeld reached London, Pitt had already hinted at a change of direction in his approach to continental affairs. The 6,000 soldiers who had participated in the raid on St Malo could be redeployed to where they were needed most. The implication of Pitt's statement, made during a ministerial meeting on 20 June, was that they could be sent to Germany. The timing of Pitt's change of heart is noteworthy. It occurred on the day on which parliament was prorogued for the summer, thus pushing the opportunity for hostile questioning of Pitt's volte-face into the distant future.[87]

[84] Ibid., pp. 57–63.
[85] Szabo, *Seven Years War*, pp. 142–7.
[86] Berkeley diary, BQ 2/46, fo. 8 and 16 (10–11/5/1758 and 1/6/1758) and BQ 2/5, fos 22–3 (19 and 22/6/1758).
[87] Middleton, *Bells of victory*, p. 73.

The decision to commit British forces to the continent came at an important moment. It precipitated a rush among the higher ranks of the officer corps to be assigned to the German war, rather than amphibious raiding or, worst of all, the backwater of the colonial campaigns. Charles Spencer, third duke of Marlborough, was at the head of the queue to get to the continent to emulate the exploits of his famous grandfather. Although Marlborough had been lord steward since 1749, there had been much in his earlier career to irritate George. He had been a close associate of the prince of Wales in the 1730s and had spoken out against the conduct of the Hanoverians during the Dettingen campaign, even resigning his bedchamber post in protest. There had been a rapprochement in 1745 but Marlborough and Lord George Sackville were not George's first choice of officers for the German campaign.[88] The king's instincts seem to have been sound. On arriving in Emden, Marlborough threatened to resign unless his superiority over the Hanoverian general, Baron August von Spörcken, was acknowledged, which involved Pitt in some hasty negotiations to smooth matters over.[89]

If Ferdinand enjoyed some success in the early summer of 1758, elsewhere the military picture on the continent was less rosy. Frederick had confidently advanced into Moravia, hoping to besiege and capture Olmütz. Unfortunately, the capture of his supply train and an Austrian advance forced him to break the siege and retreat northwards in late June. Frederick continued back towards Silesia and then decided to take personal control of the campaign against the Russian forces that had advanced into East Prussia. Frederick engaged the advancing Russians at Zorndorf on 20 August. Casualties were heavy on both sides but the ability of the Russians to march away unharassed and in good order suggested that Frederick had been unable to fulfil his hopes for a total destruction of the forces opposing him. Ferdinand himself spent much of the summer engaged in a war of manoeuvre around Westphalia. Following his victory at Krefeld, he endeavoured to give battle to the French army of the Rhine again but, unable to find advantageous ground, decided that the safest course of action was to withdraw to the east bank of the Rhine. A second French force had overrun Hessen-Kassel and was advancing towards Hanover, adding to the pressure on Ferdinand to retreat. Ferdinand did not fall back immediately. Instead, he countered by deploying his own forces over a wide area, highlighting the over-extended French lines and forcing them back instead. The cat and mouse game continued until October when Ferdinand established his winter quarters in Münster and the French, having exploited Hessen-Kassel fully, had to withdraw southwards.[90]

---

[88] Ibid., pp. 74–5.

[89] Marlborough to Pitt, Coesveldt, 18/8/1758, *Correspondence of William Pitt, earl of Chatham* (4 vols, London, 1838–40), i, pp. 337–8 included the complaint that Spörcken had been promoted faster than Marlborough so whereas Marlborough had formerly been senior, the roles had now been reversed.

[90] Szabo, *Seven Years War*, pp. 179–87.

There had been several glimmers of good news in August 1758. A second raid, this time on Cherbourg, had resulted in its capture. The raiding party, commanded by Lieutenant-General William Bligh who had been unable to effect a transfer to Ferdinand's army, took several privateers and pieces of ordnance which were subsequently triumphantly paraded in Hyde Park. The problem was that Ferdinand's barrage of requests for further reinforcements to face the ever-increasing French army on the Rhine under the marquis de Contades strongly suggested that the raiding strategy was failing in one of its primary objectives. It was not keeping French forces from Germany because the French realized the raids were only a diversion. At home, the king seemed to be fighting his various ailments and, by the beginning of September, his condition appeared much improved.[91]

Elsewhere the news was mixed. In America, although Amherst had managed to capture Louisburg, destroying several French ships in the process, Abercromby's assault on Fort Ticonderoga was a failure and he had to withdraw to the other end of Lake George.[92] Bligh's earlier success at Cherbourg was tempered by his attempt to take St Malo. His second foray ended in heavy losses as he attempted to withdraw his troops on to the accompanying naval vessels. George was displeased by the loss of precious soldiers and let it be known that Bligh was no longer welcome at court. Although George quickly decided that social ostracism was more than Bligh deserved, it was too late to prevent Bligh from resigning.[93]

Following his reversal against the Russians in August, Frederick was to suffer a second, against the Austrians in October at Hochkirch. Frederick was subsequently able to prevent the Austrians from wintering in Silesia. Yet it seemed that the offensive advantage, which he had enjoyed since the start of the war, was slipping away from him. Despite these setbacks, Frederick remained a popular figure within Britain, celebrated as a Protestant hero both in print and artefact.[94] However, popularity alone did not win wars and Frederick was ever anxious that his allies contributed as much as possible to the war effort.

One area of particular concern was the continued passivity of the Dutch. The Austrians had allowed the French to garrison the Barrier fortresses since 1757, thus freeing up their own troops for service against Frederick in Germany. If the Dutch could be induced to enter the war on the side of the allies then it would be possible to provide material assistance to Ferdinand's army in Westphalia, as well as forcing Austria to reconsider its deployment of troops and potentially reducing the pressure on Frederick. In addition to the strategic value of renewed friendship with

[91] Berkeley diary, BQ 2/48, fo. 12 (10/9/1758).

[92] Lake George had been renamed after the king in 1755.

[93] Middleton, *Bells of victory*, pp. 79–83.

[94] Manfred Schlenke, *England und das friderizianische Preussen 1740–1763* (Munich, 1963), pp. 225–53 and 393–408.

the Dutch, the British were anxious about trade disputes. British observers tended to attribute the hostility of Dutch commercial interests to Britain to the results of French troublemaking. Dutch traders, however, had sufficient complaints about the high-handed attitude of the Royal Navy for the French to need to do little to arouse anti-British feeling. The development that most irked London during the Seven Years War was the French use of neutral Dutch shipping to carry on trade with the French West Indies. The ending of this trade was the precondition for renewed British friendship. These demands were delivered to Anne without any indication of reciprocal British concessions, such as a willingness to expedite the various complaints about harassment of Dutch shipping pending in the admiralty courts. Anne was aware that the proposals would be very difficult to sell to an already angry States-General and expostulated to her father's representative in The Hague, Joseph Yorke, about the impossible situation in which the request had put her.[95]

Efforts to induce the Dutch to participate in the war were fruitless. Anne was caught, as so often before, between a rock and a hard place. For the mercantile interest in Holland and the other provinces, her inability to stop the capture of Dutch shipping by the Royal Navy was a sign of her closet British sympathies. The British meanwhile remained incredulous that she could allow the trade with the French West Indies to continue, thus providing France with a valuable revenue stream at a critical moment. The pressures of the European situation were taking their toll on Anne's health, as were the efforts to ensure the acceptance by the States-General of her plan to marry her daughter Carolina to Prince Charles Christian of Nassau-Weilburg. She died on 12 January 1759 of dropsy. The court in the United Provinces went into mourning but instructions were also issued for official mourning in both London and Hanover. The king did not see company or go to chapel. With an unusual degree of candour, Berkeley observed that much more notice had been taken of Anne's death than of her brother's eight years before.[96] Even in the middle of a war, the Hanoverian court tried to give the impression of business as usual, requesting precise details of what the ladies at the court in London were wearing to ensure that they could do the same.[97]

ANNUS MIRABILIS

Although 1759 had not begun in an auspicious manner, it was to be a remarkable year for George. There had been renewed concerns about his health during autumn 1758. Berkeley noted that his 'intellects are much impair'd. There is no doing business with him but through my Lady

---

[95] Baker-Smith, *Royal discord*, pp. 204–5.
[96] Berkeley diary, BQ 2/6, fos 18–19 (21/1/1759).
[97] NHStA, Dep. 103, XXIV, 3274.

Yarmouth; who is a weak woman, tho' inoffensive.'[98] George managed to visit the ball given in celebration of his birthday but was laid up subsequently with gout. He surprised the court by attending a drawing room in late November. The courtiers fell over themselves to compliment him on how well he looked and the king, although carrying a stick, affected not to use it. Berkeley even thought that curiosity about George's condition was increasing court attendance. By Epiphany 1759, though, the king was well enough to make his usual offering at the altar and then play cards in the evening.[99]

On the political level, the prospects were better. From the king's perspective, the balance of British commitments was slowly shifting in the right direction. There were some 20,000 British regulars in the North American theatre, aided and abetted by 25,000 locally raised troops. Ten thousand British regulars had been committed to Ferdinand and another 7,000 were stationed at Gibraltar. At first glance, this suggests that greater resources were being devoted to the colonial war. It has to be remembered, though, that Anglo-Prussian agreements ensured that a further 50,000 troops were in British pay in Germany and that during the course of 1759 an additional 12,000 British regulars were added to that number.[100]

The war effort remained finely balanced. In February rumours that the French planned to invade Britain began to circulate. Choiseul had decided that this was the best way of preventing Britain's growing colonial dominance.[101] Following the capture of Louisburg in the previous year plans were already afoot for a further assault on French Canada. Major-General James Wolfe had embarked to lead the expedition down the St Lawrence on 14 February 1759. Choiseul hoped to stop the British offensives against Quebec and the French West Indies dead by an attack on the centre. The ministry in London realized that any invasion plan would entail the French seeking to combine their Atlantic and Mediterranean fleets so Boscawen was dispatched with a squadron to prevent the French Mediterranean fleet passing through the Straits of Gibraltar.

In Germany, the French plan was to force Ferdinand back towards Hanover. Their campaign had begun brightly with a victory over Ferdinand's forces at Bergen, just outside Frankfurt, in April. The French advance continued northwards. By the start of July it was clear that the primary French objective was to cross the Weser and advance into Hanover. Ferdinand attempted to halt French progress by sending a force under his nephew to secure Minden but they arrived too late to prevent the French from seizing the bridge and taking the city. Ferdinand was becoming increasingly despondent. One of the conditions of his accepting

---

[98] Berkeley diary, BQ 2/6, fo. 1 (5/10/1758).

[99] Ibid., fo. 2 (10/11/1758) and fo. 18 (6/1/1759), BQ 2/50, fo. 2 (17/11/1758) and fo. 5 (26/11/1758).

[100] Simms, *Three victories*, p. 451.

[101] Szabo, *Seven Years War*, p. 213.

the command of George's army was that he would have direct access to the king and would not have to filter his requests through civilian ministers. He sought guidance from George at this point on the best course of action and urged the king to have plans in place should an evacuation of his forces from Emden become necessary. Remembering what had happened in 1757, he also sought assurances that he had royal permission to stand and fight.[102]

Ferdinand managed to turn his position around, despite this relatively unpromising situation. By the end of July he had advanced his forces to take up positions in an arc to the north-west of Minden. His opposite number, Contades, remained confident that the French positions were impregnable. Nevertheless, Ferdinand conducted a series of manoeuvres, including dispatching a force to harry French supply lines, to suggest that his troops were more widely dispersed than was actually the case. This was sufficient to draw the French out to give battle. On 1 August Contades marched his men on to the plain west of Minden and drew them up opposite Ferdinand's troops. A second French corps under Broglie was to march on the French right, take Ferdinand's left flank, commanded by the Hanoverian general Georg August von Wangenheim, and overrun Ferdinand's army. Broglie did manage to take Wangenheim by surprise but he did not press home his advantage quickly enough. Wangenheim was therefore able to deploy his own artillery and halt the French advance. In the interim, Ferdinand had thrown three Hanoverian and six British battalions under General von Spörcken forward. They advanced on the French centre where they faced, rather unusually, cavalry rather than infantry. Lacking the firepower to check the advance, Charles Fitz-James, the French commander and illegitimate grandson of James II, decided to charge the advancing infantry instead. A first and second charge were both effectively repelled by infantry volleys. At this juncture, Ferdinand was keen to exploit the gap in the French centre and ordered Lord George Sackville, commander of the British cavalry, to attack. Sackville was subsequently to claim that the orders he had received had been unclear and so the opportunity to take full advantage of the French position was missed. A third French cavalry charge failed and Ferdinand consequently pressed further forward. By late morning Contades withdrew to Minden. He had suffered some 7,000 casualties to a mere 2,800 on the Anglo-Hanoverian side. During a council of war at Minden that evening, Contades expressed the view that the French position had become overstretched and decided that a tactical retreat was in order. The threat to Hanover had passed for another season. When news of the victory reached London, the royal drawing room was so packed that it resembled the height of winter, rather than the dead summer season that it was.[103] By the start of September

[102] Ibid., pp. 217–20, Berkeley diary, BQ 2/6, fo. 33 (2/7/1759).
[103] Berkeley diary, BQ 2/56, fo. 9 (9/8/1759).

Contades had been forced back as far as Giessen, partly because Ferdinand had followed up the victory at Minden with further pressure on French lines.[104] The king was still interested enough in military affairs to reject Bedford's suggestion that Major-General Kingsley be given Waldegrave's regiment with the retort that he did not want to waste a good foot officer by giving him a cavalry regiment.[105]

While the victory at Minden was widely welcomed, the way in which the battle had unfolded gave rise to further tensions. Ferdinand was sufficiently irritated by Sackville's conduct to issue a general order afterwards stating that if Granby had been in command of the cavalry, then the victory would have been more complete.[106] It was hardly surprising that relations between Sackville and Ferdinand had deteriorated to the point of boiling over into a public dispute. Sackville had succeeded Marlborough as the senior British commander in Germany following the latter's death in October 1758. Marlborough's own complaints about lines of command and his superiority to Hanoverian generals had already caused problems. Berkeley had thought that the limits placed on his power would probably lead Sackville to refuse the command.[107] Sackville had also been connected politically with Leicester House and shared some of its suspicion of continental wars, although not to the extent of being willing to forgo the opportunity for personal advancement and glory that the German war offered. Following the public slight to his reputation that Ferdinand's comments implied, Sackville felt he had little option but to write a letter of resignation and forward it to the king. He did, however, take the precaution of instructing the aide-de-camp who was dispatched with it to Britain that it should only be delivered after seeking the advice of the earl of Bute, by now chief political adviser to the prince of Wales.

George displayed little sympathy for Sackville. He had no liking for commanders whom he perceived as having failed to do their duty and promptly dismissed him from all his military appointments. This created a difficult situation because as Sackville was now technically a civilian, it was uncertain whether he could still be court-martialled. A period of legal wrangling followed, during which Sackville was the object of continued opprobrium from the press. When the court martial finally commenced in February 1760 it was on a charge of disobedience. George had suggested that he would be happy to pursue Sackville with the same vehemence that he had used against Byng. In the end, the court agreed that George had been justified in dismissing Sackville and found him guilty of disobedience

---

[104] Szabo, *Seven Years War*, pp. 256–62.

[105] Berkeley diary, BQ 2/7, fo. 4 (20/9/1759).

[106] For the broader context of the relationship between Sackville and Ferdinand, see Piers Mackesy, *The coward of Minden* (London, 1979). The aftermath of the battle is covered in ch. 6.

[107] Berkeley diary, BQ 2/50, fo. 1 (5/11/1758).

but stopped short of the death sentence. Instead, Sackville was found to be unfit to serve in a military capacity.[108]

The contrast with earlier public outcries over military failures is interesting. Disputes about the behaviour and treatment of British and Hanoverian forces in the aftermath of Dettingen in 1743 had led the then British commander, Earl Stair, to resign and had been one of the triggers of a bout of anti-Hanoverian rhetoric.[109] On this occasion, with a ministry more united in its commitment to a continental strategy, the outcome was different. Sackville found little support in elite circles and Leicester House was unable to fan the flames of opposition in quite the way that had been possible previously. The reaction to Byng's behaviour in 1756 provides a further point of comparison. Sackville was, admittedly, not in overall command but he was to be the butt of a number of attacks invoking cowardice. Byng had paid the ultimate price, despite the efforts of those who had condemned him. In Sackville's case, the court, perhaps aware of the king's unbending attitude to military indiscipline, did not run the risk of a royal refusal to exercise mercy. Yet the context was different as well. The capture of Minorca took place in a situation where British military power seemed to be in decline on all sides. By the time that Sackville faced his accusers, Minden had proved to be the herald of a sustained upturn in Britain's military fortunes.

Some good news from America had already made its way back to Britain.[110] British control of the Great Lakes had been established with the fall of Fort Ticonderoga and the seizure of Niagara. Initial reports from Wolfe's expedition against Quebec had been less optimistic. Wolfe had navigated down the St Lawrence to Quebec without too much difficulty but had discovered that the French were well entrenched so had not been able to find a suitable site from which to launch an attack. The ministry was consequently a little surprised to learn that Wolfe had managed to identify a narrow path up the Heights of Abraham and had successfully got his force ashore and up the cliff to the plain above on 13 September. The two sides were reasonably equally matched in numbers: about 4,500 each. The major difference was that Wolfe's men were entirely regular troops while Montcalm had a mixture of regulars, militia and Native American forces. Convinced that he had little choice but to fight, Montcalm ordered his troops to advance but discipline quickly broke down. Wolfe had ordered his men to wait until the enemy was sixty yards distant before opening fire. When they did, the effect was devastating. The

[108] Macksey, *Coward*, chs 7–9. Sackville's insistence on trying to clear his name meant that the affair was kept in the public eye for longer than the ministry wanted. For the comparison with Byng, see p. 167.

[109] Simms, *Three victories*, pp. 452–3.

[110] For an extended narrative of the 1759 campaign in America, see Fred Anderson, *Crucible of war* (London, 2000), pp. 297–384.

French advance quickly turned into a retreat. Wolfe was fatally injured but Brigadier George Townshend was able to assume command and the British troops were soon digging in for a siege. Within a matter of days the disheartened garrison had surrendered.[111]

News of the victory in Quebec reached London in late October. There was to be one final occasion for ringing the bells of victory in 1759. Choiseul, despite the military setbacks that France had already faced, was determined to proceed with his plans for the invasion of Britain. Attempts to unify the French Mediterranean and Atlantic squadrons lay at the heart of this strategy. Boscawen had led the successful blockade of Toulon for much of 1759 but when he was forced back to Gibraltar to refit the French were able to slip through the Straits. Boscawen quickly gave chase. One French column sought refuge in Cadiz. The bulk of the other made its way to neutral Portuguese waters off Lagos. Boscawen, feeling the opportunity was too good to miss, promptly captured two French ships and sank two more. The French Mediterranean fleet's break-out had been held back. The Atlantic fleet had been trapped in Brest by Hawke, who had managed to keep up a continuous blockade by having sufficient ships to enable sequenced refitting and resupply. However, bad weather at the start of November forced him back into Torbay. This allowed several French ships from the Caribbean to sneak back into Brest, where the crews were quickly redeployed. Admiral Conflans left Brest on 14 November with a fleet of twenty-one ships. His destination was Quiberon Bay where the transports and troops for the invasion of Britain were assembled. Hawke with twenty-three ships intercepted Conflans's fleet as it reached Quiberon Bay on 20/21 November. Instead of following the standard line of battle, Hawke ordered his ships to engage the enemy in a general melee. The results were devastating for the French. Six ships were captured, taken or run aground. Of the remainder, half escaped to other ports and the others sought refuge in the mouth of Vilaine, although they had to unload their guns in the process. Two British ships ran aground. The result was a decisive British victory that destroyed Choiseul's invasion plans.[112]

The public reaction to this series of victories was suitably adulatory. The first verse of a song performed at the Theatre Royal in Covent Garden shortly after news of the victory at Minden boldly proclaimed that

> In Story we're told,
> How our Monarchs of Old
> O'er France spread their Royal Domain:
> But no Annals shall shew
> Her pride laid so low,

---

[111] Ibid., ch. 36.
[112] Szabo, *Seven Years War*, pp. 265–7.

As when brave George the Second did reign, Brave Boys
As when brave George the Second did reign.

Subsequent verses compared British triumphs to the military prowess of
the ancient world and cited success in America, at Minden and on the seas
as evidence of it. The penultimate verse paid tribute to the ability of the
militia to repel any potential French invasion.[113] Although the amount of
direct credit that could be attributed to George for this year of victories
was necessarily small, he provided an excellent focus for public outpour-
ings of joy at the *annus mirabilis*.

The king seems to have had a change of heart over his will, and added
a further codicil in the middle of September. In it he sought to explain the
reasons that had moved him to add the 1757 codicil. He stated that his only
grounds for making the earlier alterations had been 'that our Funds &
Stocks were exhausted, and that our German Dominions & Our Subjects
themselves, were by unhappy times, for the greatest part & for a long time
to come, disabled from making the usual contributions'. Lest anyone still
doubt his motivation, he added that Cumberland 'has always behaved to
us as a good & dutyfull Son'. The death of several of his children had
rendered the earlier division of funds obsolete. Instead he now wanted to
divide the sum of 200,000 talers equally between his three surviving children. He added in his own hand an additional 10,000 talers each for
Gerlach Adolf von Münchhausen and Ernst von Steinberg.[114] The military situation had certainly improved since George's last amendments in
1757 and the death of Anne probably necessitated further revision but it is
also likely that time had begun to heal the wounded relationship with
Cumberland. Thoughts of his mortality were clearly on the king's mind.
In February he had written a note stating that he wanted the bank bills
that Lady Yarmouth held to become hers on his death.[115]

Amid the celebrations an ugly dispute about patronage erupted.
The king's dislike of Temple was common knowledge, and insisting that
Temple did not gain a place that required frequent personal contact with
the monarch had been one of George's triumphs in the protracted negotiations that led to the Pitt–Newcastle administration. Nevertheless,
Temple still hankered after a mark of favour. The highest honour attain-
able was a Garter knighthood. Ultimate appointment lay in the king's
hands but it was common practice for potential candidates to solicit the
support of the first lord of the treasury to make representations on their
behalf. Waldegrave had been the last beneficiary of royal largesse and
there were now two further vacancies, created by the deaths of the earl of

[113] Song performed by Mr Beard at the Theatre Royal, Covent Garden, 9/8/1759, RA,
GEO/52982.
[114] Further codicil, Kensington, 15/9/1759, RA, GEO/52984–6.
[115] George's note, 10/2/1759, RA, GEO/42878–9.

Carlisle and the duke of Marlborough. Temple had expressed his interest
in one of these as early as September 1758. Holdernesse, who had been
disappointed at Waldegrave's advancement, was also interested, as were
the marquis of Rockingham, the earl of Halifax and Lord Bristol.
Newcastle had responded to some initial enquiries by mentioning the need
to satisfy Ferdinand. His case became immeasurably stronger in the aftermath of Minden but the question of how to fill the second vacant garter
stall remained.

Pitt began to hint that the only means to satisfy Temple would be by
giving him the Garter. George had other ideas. He was aware that Temple
wanted a mark of favour, ideally the Garter. However, he also knew that if
it became known that such a mark had been forced from him then its
cachet would be significantly diminished. He therefore decided to dig in
his heels. George held the line throughout October 1759. Newcastle was
worried that the crisis might threaten the ministry's survival. Although
good news had started to trickle in, there was still uncertainty about the
position both on the continent and outside Europe. Some thought that
George was seeking to provoke a crisis that would remove Pitt because
he feared that his British ministers would not be willing in a future peace
settlement to return British gains outside Europe as a means to secure
Hanoverian territorial expansion. The king was almost certainly right
that neither Pitt nor the rest of the administration would stomach such a
strategy, though whether it was part of George's calculations is unclear. In
the event, Temple called the king's bluff. He resigned on 14 November and
George grumpily agreed to his reinstatement on 16 November with the
promise of the Garter.[116] Still smarting from the reverse, George was char-
acteristically short with Newcastle, telling him that if the British ministers
would not support his plans for territorial acquisition, then he would press
for a separation of his territories.[117]

LAST YEAR

Although by the end of 1759 George could sit back feeling a certain degree
of contentment about the performance of his armed forces, other belligerents were already thinking about ways of bringing the conflict to a conclusion. Both the French and the Prussians were beginning to baulk at the
costs. Frederick, in particular, after his defeat by an Austro-Russian force
at Kunersdorf in August 1759 was increasingly anxious to begin negotiations. Even Newcastle was experiencing sufficient difficulties in raising
funds in the City to give him pause for thought.[118] Part of Britain's

---

[116] The toings and froings can be followed in the relevant sections of *Pitt correspondence*, i
and there is a succinct summary in Middleton, *Bells of victory*, pp. 140–2.

[117] Newcastle to Hardwicke, Newcastle House, 21/11/1759, BL, Add. MSS 32899,
fos 6–7.

[118] Szabo, *Seven Years War*, pp. 267–8; Middleton, *Bells of victory*, pp. 113–19.

maritime success had depended on the inability of France to enhance its navy by bringing Bourbon Spain into the war as well. Ferdinand VI had relatively good relations with Britain. The prospects after his death in August 1759 and the succession of Charles III were much less clear. Moreover, with the raft of successes, it seemed that Britain's war aims had largely been achieved. There was, therefore, a willingness to negotiate and talks between Britain and France began at The Hague in the early months of 1760, although it was apparent by May that they were getting nowhere and so were broken off.

Expectations about the campaign season in Germany were high. The size of Ferdinand's army had been increased by reinforcements from both Hanover and Britain and a concomitant rise in costs to the British taxpayer. It was hoped that the run of victories would continue and even be surpassed. Given the circumstances, it was always going to be difficult for Ferdinand to match concrete achievements to the heightened sense of what might be possible. His activities followed a pattern that had been established in previous years. The French tried to move from their bases near Frankfurt to seize as much territory as possible and Ferdinand sought to halt their advance. The French managed to overrun Hessen-Kassel, again, by the middle of the summer and took Göttingen but were unable to advance further into Hanover. Ferdinand retaliated with attempts to force the French back but neither side had sufficient momentum for a decisive breakthrough.[119]

Dissatisfaction with Ferdinand's conduct was growing. The king was frustrated by the lack of progress and did little to disguise it, leading Berkeley to comment adversely on his lack of mastery of himself.[120] Pitt had begun to think about revisiting the question of maritime raiding as an addition or even an alternative to a continental strategy. Frederick's campaigning in 1760 had reached a virtual stalemate. Pitt was also concerned that the French seemed to be pouring troops into the German theatre and was anxious to revive his diversionary options. Thoughts had turned to the possibility of an attack on Belleisle. Hawke, the hero of Quiberon Bay, was asked for his views. His reply reached London on 24 October. Anson took it to St James's to show George. Hawke had been unusually forthright in expressing his doubts about the wisdom of the plan. Pitt arrived, irritated both by Hawke's response and Anson's actions in showing it to the king. George made clear to Pitt his unwillingness to divert troops to the operation. In the aftermath of the audience, Pitt continued to tell anyone who would listen how Hawke had let him down.[121]

George rose at his usual hour of six the next day and drank his hot chocolate. He continued with his morning routine and retreated to the

[119] Szabo, *Seven Years War*, pp. 300–8.
[120] Berkeley diary, BQ 2/10, fo. 15 (20/7/1760).
[121] Middleton, *Bells of victory*, pp. 166–9.

privacy of the royal toilet. His faithful valet, Schröder, waiting outside, heard a noise followed by a decisive thud and rushed in to find the king lying on the floor. The king had tried to ring for assistance and had sustained a deep cut to his face from his fall. He was dragged to bed where the standard medical procedure of blooding was accompanied by tradi- tional levels of success. The post-mortem revealed that he had suffered a ruptured ventricle.[122]

George was buried on 11 November in Westminster Abbey. The funeral, like that of Caroline before him, was private. Cumberland took on the role of chief mourner, despite the stroke that he had suffered in August 1760. In accordance with George's request, the side of his coffin was removed so that his decomposed body could mingle with that of his late wife. The court and the country went into mourning. In Hanover both the time and the date of when the official instructions about mourning had been received were noted. Philipp von Münchhausen sent precise details to ensure that the plans that had been worked out with Holdernesse about what would happen in Britain were imitated exactly in Hanover. When it came to dress, 'the ladies to wear black Bombasines plain muslin or long lawn linen, crape hoods, Shamoy shoes and gloves and crape fans. Undress, dark Norwich crape. The men to wear black cloth without buttons on the sleeves and pockets, plain muslin or long lawn cravats and weepers, shamoy shoes and gloves, crape hatbands and black swords and buckles. Undress, dark grey frocks.' It was eventually decided that in Hanover only the coaches of ministers and those above the rank of major- general needed to be decked out.[123] A new era for both Hanover and Britain had begun.

---

[122] Walpole, *Memoirs*, iii, p. 118.
[123] Pro Memoria from Philipp von Münchhausen, London, 26/10/1760, NHStA, Dep. 103, XXIV, 3275.

CONCLUSION

The reaction to George's death was swift – many of the shops in London were bedecked with mourning almost as soon as the news became public.[1] The king's will was opened in the presence of George III, the duke of Cumberland, Princess Amelia and Philipp von Münchhausen on 31 October. Princess Amelia had the 1751 will, while the other two had been kept by Münchhausen. Cumberland renounced his legacy and Berkeley was shocked to hear that provision did not seem to have been made for the pages and valets. By the time that George was buried on 11 November, his successor had decided that he would hold drawing rooms on Sundays and Thursdays, levees on Monday, Wednesday and Friday and keep Tuesdays and Saturdays for himself. Sackville had already taken advantage of the king's demise to resume his attendance at court. George's body was removed from Kensington to the Prince's Chamber in Westminster on 10 November – his seventy-seventh birthday.[2]

Assessments of his life varied. Berkeley, who had observed his declining years at close quarters, noted his passion for money and his inclination to justice. He wondered at the providential nature of how George's narrow designs to protect Hanover seemed to have yielded so many benefits for Britain in the recent war. More generally, though, he thought that George had never intended to infringe his people's liberties and that posterity would think of him as a good prince, if not an amiable man. He 'had extreme good parts, improved by reading and reflexion, but wanted resolution' when faced with insolent ministers (although this last remark may have reflected Berkeley's dislike of the Old Corps). At the end of his life, he had left his domains in a strong position within both Europe and the wider world and he was one of the best, if not one of the greatest, monarchs ever to sit upon the throne.[3]

Chesterfield was less sympathetic, commenting adversely on George's love of money and seeing it as the prime motivator of much of his conduct. Unlike Berkeley, Chesterfield thought the king socially and intellectually unaccomplished. He preferred the easy company of women to

---

[1] Philip Mansel, *Dressed to rule* (New Haven and London, 2005), p. 137.

[2] Lincolnshire Archives, Lincoln, Brownlow archives, Berkeley diary, BQ 2/13, fos 4–7 (1 and 3/11/1760) and BQ 2/14, fo. 4 (5/11/1760).

[3] Berkeley diary, BQ 2/12, fos 18–20 (27/10/1760).

the refined social life of a gentleman. Although he had a good memory for factual information and spoke German, French, English and Italian well, he lacked a real facility for belles-lettres. Yet even Chesterfield was prepared to acknowledge that he had been a weak, rather than a bad, king.[4]

Horace Walpole thought that George had often found himself in humiliating circumstances with his ministers but had tended not to exact revenge when the tables were turned and the opportunity arose. Like Berkeley and Chesterfield, he noted the interest in money and Hanoverian affairs. He also commented on the king's seeming lack of interest in literature and the arts. Walpole was not impressed by the accusations of 'bookish men', noting that 'the advantages to their country resulting from authors must be better ascertained, before the imputation becomes a grave one. Had he [George] pensioned half a dozen poets, and reaped their incense, the world had heard of nothing but his liberality.' Walpole was clearly unconvinced that there was much general benefit from supporting 'Atterburys and Drydens'.[5]

In their different ways, all these assessments of George's reign acknowledge that he did little harm to Britain. Is it possible to say something more positive and speak of his achievements? One thing that deserves mention is the length of his reign and the impact this had both on the European system and the domestic situation within Britain. It is easy to forget because of the sixty-year reign that came afterwards that George was the longest reigning British monarch since Elizabeth I. More interestingly, even though George became king at the relatively late age of forty-four (only six of the forty-one post-Conquest monarchs were older), at the time of his death no British monarch had lived longer than George and only three (George III, Victoria and Elizabeth II) have done so subsequently. This is important for more than record-keeping and breaking. In an age in which the monarch was still, as this work has amply demonstrated, crucial for the daily conduct of government, longevity was an important asset. Only Newcastle could claim anything close to George's experience of the practicalities of government. Even in his old age, with failing sight and an increasing variety of ailments, the king continued to work hard, reading his letters daily and talking to his ministers about them. The business of government took priority over all other activities.[6]

[4] BL, Stowe 308, fos 3v–5v (printed in Chesterfield's *Characters of eminent personages* (London, 1777)).

[5] Horace Walpole, *Memoirs of King George II*, ed. John Brooke (3 vols, New Haven, 1985), iii, pp. 118–19.

[6] In April 1759 Berkeley noted that George had spent so long reading the letters from the Dutch mail that his attendance at chapel had been delayed until 12.30 p.m. His servants had thought that something extraordinary must have taken place but, although Ferdinand had broken camp, the news was largely routine. See Berkeley diary, BQ 2/53, fo. 20 (8/4/1759).

George had also ruled for longer than nearly all his European contemporaries – only Louis XV had acceded earlier and his period of effective rule, following his minority, had only really begun after George had become king. When it came to diplomacy, George's obsession with who was related to whom and how was a considerable asset. He had a firm grasp of the dynastic politics and connections which remained vital for building alliances and in settling territorial disputes; it was not for nothing that so many eighteenth-century wars were 'succession' conflicts of various types. George's central importance for the conduct of foreign policy has been a key theme of this work. The decision to take his domains to war was one that had a direct impact on his subjects in terms of the taxes and armies and navies that needed to be raised. Yet there were indirect impacts as well. By engaging in conflict for significant periods, particularly in the second half of his reign, George transformed the lands he ruled. Governmental and fiscal structures changed and adapted to cope with these pressures. The need to consider both Britain and Hanover was also crucial in this respect.

The king's continued interest in his German domains had a number of effects. His determination to preserve Hanoverian security in 1741 and 1757 left him with severe domestic difficulties and did little to enhance his reputation with his British subjects. Ministers faced a difficult choice. While patriot rhetoric was very much in vogue in the 1740s and '50s, it was an uncertain friend for those wishing to enter high office. The king wanted ministers willing to do his business, including supporting his European strategy. Newcastle and Pitt, both of whom toyed with the patriots at various points for strategic reasons, came to realize that power was more valuable than popularity. In this respect, 1760 was to prove to be a watershed. George III, although he retained an active interest in his Hanoverian domains, was less wedded to their strategic centrality, which created more options for politicians. George III's decision not to visit Hanover also had other implications. As the discussion of the evolution of the cabinet in Chapter 7 suggested, royal absence from London had been a significant factor in the notion of a formed ministerial opinion in contradistinction, and sometimes even opposed, to that of the monarch emerging as significant political factor. The king's omnipresence after 1760 meant that clashes between a young, vibrant executive monarch and ministers grown used to presenting their collective opinions were more likely.

From the point of view of George's Electoral ministers the shock of 1757 was to have significant consequences. It led to a rethink of how valuable the personal union with Britain was. The invasion of Hanover had come about because of British, rather than Hanoverian, policies and if Britain was unwilling or unable to offer support in times of crisis then it is unsurprising that this precipitated a re-evaluation of the utility of the link. Part of the problem related to the increasing importance of colonial affairs within British politics. Another was the difficulty of thinking about relations with Prussia. From the perspective of most British ministers

Prussia was a potentially useful (junior) alliance partner. From George's perspective, Frederick's accession in 1740 had seemed to offer an opportunity for renewed Anglo-Prussian amity, with Frederick accepting avuncular advice and co-operating with George's plans. These hopes had been rapidly dashed by Frederick's inconvenient habit of pursuing an independent, and often devious, line of his own. Yet the residual possibility remained that he might be assimilated into British schemes. The Convention of Westminster and the subsequent lauding of Frederick as a Protestant hero in Britain seemed to suggest that these goals were achievable. Yet the Hanoverian ministers found it difficult to concur. While their attitudes towards Prussia displayed some variation, they tended to see their Hohenzollern neighbour as part of the problem rather than the solution. They felt that the threat from Prussia to their position within the empire needed to be countered. In this, George's wider European perspective led him to take a different view. He had to balance British and Hanoverian concerns. The fact that both British and Hanoverian ministers complained at various times about his seeming preference for the other side suggests that he was getting the balance about right.

George's ability to adopt different roles, suited to his circumstances, is one of the most striking features of his reign. His use of court culture and ceremonial was far more complicated than a simple account of declining ritual and relevance would suggest. In his daily life, he wanted to preserve the traditional habits of formal dressing in a way that his father had not. His interest in procedure and process meant he was keen to ensure that etiquette and the formal rules that surrounded court life were preserved. Consequently, on his 1743 Dettingen campaign he kept his British and Hanoverian stables separate and did not allow officials from the one to interfere with the running of the other. This caused the duke of Richmond considerable irritation but even he, harsh critic of George as he could be, admitted that the king was innocent of the charge of leading only his Hanoverian troops and ignoring the British. George had been all over the battlefield, leading by example.[7] The king's personal bravery both at Dettingen and at Oudenarde, when he earned the epithet 'young Hanover brave', was not in doubt.

Yet his sometimes bluff exterior and his desire to play the general belied a more skilful political operator. George had shown during his time as prince of Wales, when he had used his father's absence in Hanover to mount his own public relations campaign, that he could make use of the resources available to him effectively. He regularly attended the theatre and seemed to enjoy appearing in public. This continued once he became king, although the loss of his wife seems to have made him retreat into the confines of his court circles. Although the London cultural market had

[7] Richmond to Newcastle, Hanau, 5/7/1743 and 10/7/1743, Timothy J. McCann, ed., *The correspondence of the dukes of Richmond and Newcastle, 1724–1750* (Lewes, 1984), pp. 102–3.

become too diverse for the monarchy to retain a monopoly over it, George might be regarded as patron-in-chief, the one whose patronage was eagerly sought, not least because it was economically valuable.

In Hanover, by contrast, George's court was much more the centre of social and cultural life; the continued Sunday gatherings of the Hanoverian nobility even when George was absent in London provide ample evidence of this. When in the Electorate, George was perfectly at home playing the role of benefactor and *Landesvater*, be it as observer of Harz silver mines or as the interested visitor to the university named after him in Göttingen. There may have been tensions between the more commercial and the more courtly aspects of George's life but he was prepared to live with them and negotiate his own path through them. In this respect George's rule was characterized by the interaction of several worlds. He was too aware of the constitutional and, more importantly, financial limitations under which he had to operate in Britain to seek to govern in the representational mode of some of his continental counterparts. His royal building was distinctly limited – not even Versailles-lite – but that which he did undertake reflected his more general interests. Between 1731 and 1733 the Royal Mews in Charing Cross on the site of what is now Trafalgar Square were rebuilt. The Treasury was also rebuilt in the 1730s, as was Horse Guards in the late 1740s and early 1750s.[8]

Generations of historians, influenced by Whig historiographical myth, have created the impression that George was a weak excuse for a king, easily manipulated by clever statesmen and scheming women. His genuine achievements have been overshadowed by a concentration on Sir Robert Walpole and George's grandson, George III. As such, he has been too readily consigned to the historical margins. This is both unfortunate and unfair. George had a better command of all aspects of administration than Walpole and he was able to meet the demands of ruling a diverse group of territories more successfully than his successor. The sorts of skills that George needed were not unusual for monarchs in this period. The patchwork nature of many European states, held together by the personal dynastic inheritance of the ruler, meant that an appreciation of the different rights, privileges and customs of the constituent territories was a necessary prerequisite for successful rule. George was alive to the intrinsic difficulties of his position and showed considerable skill and judgement in finding an appropriate path. Politicians are sometimes praised for their ideological consistency. Adapting to circumstance, by contrast, is not always viewed in such a positive light. It would be difficult to argue that George was always consistent but he did have a canny ability to identify the politically possible in most circumstances.

---

[8] H.M. Colvin, J. Mordaunt Crook, Kerry Downes and John Newman, *The history of the king's works: volume V, 1660–1782* (London, 1976), pp. 127, 212–13, 431–40.

Britain and Hanover were both very different places in 1760 from what they had been in 1714. Hanover had come to terms with absentee rule and the situation of non-residence was accepted, albeit grudgingly. Britain was undergoing a series of economic, social and political transformations. Much of this was taking place independently of the action of individuals, even powerful ones like George. However, as Britain maintained an active position in European politics, George made a significant contribution to ensuring that Britain's global position was consolidated and even enhanced.

George was not a figurehead monarch who stood aside from the political process, providing an uncontroversial focal point around whom the country could unite. He was still very much involved in the rough and tumble of quotidian political debate and decision-making. Eighteenth-century commentators, when considering the various types of people who filled the benches of the House of Commons, often noted the necessity of the 'man of business', someone who could stand aside from partisan struggles and get things done. It was a job description not exclusive to members of parliament. It could apply with equal force to monarchs. George was the ultimate 'man of business' in both Britain and Hanover.

BIBLIOGRAPHY

MANUSCRIPT SOURCES

Farmington, Connecticut, Lewis Walpole Library
Charles Hanbury Williams papers, vols 1–6

Hanover, Niedersächsisches Hauptstaatsarchiv
Calenberg Brief 15: 2684
Calenberg Brief 24: 4510
Dep. 84 (Königlichen Hausarchivs): A, 42, 51; B, 188, 365
Dep. 103 (Königlichen Hausarchivs): I, 160; IV, 227–8, 249, 300, 311, 323–4; XXIV, 250, 541, 1329, 1557, 1717, 1914, 2118, 2225, 2281, 2488, 2587, 2616–17, 2643, 2647–9, 2652–3,2957, 3266, 3269–70, 3272, 3274–5, 3547–52, 3632
Hannover 47 (Army): I, 45
Hannover 91 (Nachläβe): von Hattorf 54; von Münchhausen I, 22
Hannover 92 (Deutsche Kanzlei, London): 70, 98–100, 1991

Lincoln, Lincolnshire Archives
Brownlow archives, Berkeley diary, BQ 2

London, British Library
Stowe MSS 231
Stowe MSS 308
Additional MSS 7072
Additional MSS 22627
Additional MSS 32694–723, 32735–7, 32795–816, 32849–75, 32899 (Newcastle papers)
Additional MSS 35407–10, 35870 (Hardwicke papers)
Additional MSS 61234
Additional MSS 61492

London, National Archives, Kew
Lord Chamberlain's department: LC 2/24
Lord Steward's department: LS 13/269
State Paper office: SP 90/26 (Prussia)
SP 43/25–7 (Regencies)
Office of Works: Work 21/1

Windsor, Royal Archives
EB/P 4–8
GEO/52758, 52777, 52795–803, 52808–24, 52850–4, 52880–5, 52921–31, 52933, 52936–50, 52957, 52967–73, 52980, 52982, 52984–6

PRINTED PRIMARY SOURCES

A true dialogue between Thomas Jones, a trooper, late return'd from Germany and John Smith, a serjeant in the First Regiment of Foot Guards (London, 1743).

Bielfeld, Jakob Friedrich, *Letters of Baron Bielfeld translated from the German by Mr Hooper* (4 vols, London, 1768–70).

Bodemann, Eduard, ed., *Aus den Briefen der Herzogin Elisabeth Charlotte von Orléans an die Kurfürstin Sophie von Hannover* (2 vols, Hanover, 1891).

Chesterfield, Philip, fourth earl of, *Characters of eminent persons* (London, 1778).

Clark, J.C.D., ed., *The memoirs and speeches of James, 2nd Earl Waldegrave, 1742–1763* (Cambridge, 1988).

Cobbett, William, *Parliamentary History of England* (36 vols, London, 1806–20).

Cowper, Spencer, ed., *Diary of Mary Countess Cowper, lady of the bedchamber to the Princess of Wales, 1714–1720* (London, 1865).

Coxe, William, *Memoirs of the life and administration of Sir Robert Walpole* (3 vols, London, 1798).

——, *Memoirs of the administration of the Right Honourable Henry Pelham* (2 vols, London, 1829).

[Croker, J.W., ed.], *Letters to and from Henrietta, countess of Suffolk, and her second husband, the Hon. George Berkeley; from 1712–1767* (2 vols, London, 1824).

Deutsch, Otto, *Handel: a documentary biography* (London, 1955).

Dietrich, Richard, ed., *Die politische Testamente der Hohenzollern* (Cologne, 1986).

Drögereit, Richard, ed., *Quellen zur Geschichte Kurhannovers im Zeitalter der Personalunion mit England 1714–1803* (Hildesheim, 1949).

Forster, Elborg trans. and ed., *A woman's life in the court of the Sun King: letters of Liselotte von der Pfalz, 1652–1722* (Baltimore and London, 1984).

Gay, John, *The poetical works of John Gay* (3 vols, London, 1797).

Grieser, Rudolf, ed., *Die Memoiren des Kammerherrn Friedrich Ernst von Fabrice (1683–1750)* (Hildesheim, 1956).

[Hardwicke, Philip, second earl of], *Walpoliana* (London, 1781).

Hervey, John, Lord, *Some materials towards memoirs of the reign of King George II*, ed. Romney Sedgwick (3 vols, London, 1931).

Historical Manuscripts Commission. *Eleventh report, Appendix, part IV. The manuscripts of the Marquess Townshend* (London, 1887).

Historical Manuscripts Commission. *Fourteenth report, Appendix, part IX. The manuscripts of the earl of Buckinghamshire, the earl of Lindsey, the earl of Onslow, Lord Emly, Theodore J. Hare esq., and James Round, esq.* (London, 1895).

Historical Manuscripts Commission. *Fifteenth report, Appendix, part VI. The manuscripts of the earl of Carlisle* (London, 1897).

Historical Manuscripts Commission. *Report on the manuscripts of his grace the duke of Portland* (10 vols, London, 1891–1931).

Historical Manuscripts Commission. *Report on the manuscripts of Mrs Frankland-Russell-Astley of Chequers Court, Bucks* (London, 1900).

Historical Manuscripts Commission. *Report on the manuscripts of the earl of Denbigh, preserved at Newnham Paddox, Warwickshire* (London, 1911).

Journals of the House of Commons.

King, Peter, 'Notes on domestic and foreign affairs' in idem, *The life of John Locke: new edition* (2 vols, London, 1830).

Köcher, Adolf, ed., *Memoiren der Herzogin Sophie nachmals Kurfürstin von Hannover* (Leipzig, 1879).

Linnell, C.L.S., ed., *The diaries of Thomas Wilson, D.D.* (London, 1964).

McCann, Timothy J., ed., *The correspondence of the dukes of Richmond and Newcastle, 1724–1750* (Lewes, 1984).

The memorial of the E—— of S—— (London, 1743).

Mosheim, Johann Lorenz, *Beschreibung der grossen und denckwürdigen Feyer die bey der allerhöchsten Anwesenheit des allerdurchlauchtigsten, grossmächtigsten Fürsten und Herren, Herren Georg des Andern, Königes von Grossbritannien, Frankreich und Irrland, Beschützers des Glaubens, Herzoges zu*

Braunschweig-Lüneburg, des Heil. Röm. Reiches Ertzschatzmeisters und Churfürsten, auf deroselben Georg Augustus hohen Schule in der Stadt Göttingen im Jahr 1748. am ersten Tages des Augustmonates begangen ward (Göttingen, 1749).

[Perceval, John], *Faction Detected, by the evidence of Facts* (London, 1743).

Phillimore, Robert, ed., *Memoirs and correspondence of George, Lord Lyttelton* (2 vols, London, 1845).

Pitt, William, *Correspondence of William Pitt, earl of Chatham* (4 vols, London, 1838–40).

Rose, G.H., ed., *A selection from the papers of the earls of Marchmont* (3 vols, London, 1831).

Roberts, R.A., ed., *Diary of Viscount Percival afterwards first earl of Egmont* (Historical Manuscripts Commission, 3 vols, London, 1920–3).

Rosenthal, Norman, ed., *The misfortunate margravine: the early memoirs of Wilhelmina margravine of Bayreuth* (London, 1970).

Russell, Lord John, intro. to *Correspondence of John, fourth duke of Bedford with an introduction by Lord John Russell* (3 vols, London, 1842–6).

Ryder, Dudley, *The diary of Dudley Ryder, 1715–1716*, ed. William Matthews (London, 1939).

Saussure, César de, *A foreign view of England in the reigns of George I and George II*, trans. and ed. Madame van Muyden (London, 1902).

Schaer, Friedrich-Wilhelm, ed., *Briefe der Gräfin Johanna Sophie zu Schaumburg-Lippe an die Familie von Münchhausen zu Remeringhausen, 1699–1734* (Rinteln, 1968).

Smith, William James, ed., *The Grenville papers* (4 vols, London, 1852–3).

Toland, John, *An account of the courts of Prussia and Hannover* (London, 1714).

[Waller, Edmund and Philip Dormer Stanhope], *The case of the Hanover forces in the pay of Great Britain, impartially and freely examined: with some seasonable reflections on the present conjuncture of affairs* (London, 1743).

[Walpole, Horace], *The interest of Great Britain steadily pursued* (London, 1743).

Walpole, Horace, *Reminiscences written by Mr Horace Walpole in 1788 for the amusement of Miss Mary and Miss Agnes Berry* (Oxford, 1924).

—— *Memoirs of King George II*, ed. John Brooke (3 vols, New Haven, 1985).

Wortley Montagu, Mary, *The complete letters of Lady Mary Wortley Montagu*, ed. Robert Halsband (3 vols, Oxford, 1965–7).

SECONDARY WORKS

Alcorn, Ellenor M., ' "A chandelier for the King", William Kent, George II, and Hanover', *Burlington Magazine*, cxxix, no. 1126 (January 1997), pp. 40–3.

Alvensleben, Udo von and Hans Reuther, *Herrenhausen: Die Sommerresidenz der Welfen* (Hanover, 1966).

Anderson, Fred, *Crucible of war* (London, 2000).

Anderson, M.S., *The war of the Austrian succession, 1740–1748* (Harlow, 1995).

Arkell, R.L., *Caroline of Ansbach* (London, 1939).

Aston, Nigel, 'The Court of George II: Lord Berkeley of Stratton's perspective', *Court Historian*, 13 (2008), pp. 171—93.

Bagehot, W., *The English constitution*, ed. P. Smith (Cambridge, 2001).

Baker-Smith, Veronica, *Royal discord: the family of George II* (London, 2008).

Baldwin, David, *The Chapel Royal ancient and modern* (London, 1990).

Barmeyer, Heide, 'Hof und Hofgesellschaft in Hannover im 18. und 19. Jahrhundert', in Karl Möckl, ed., *Hof und Hofgesellschaft in den deutschen Staaten im 19. und beginnenden 20. Jahrhundert* (Boppard am Rhein, 1990), pp. 239–73.

Beattie, John M., *The English court in the reign of George I* (Cambridge, 1967).

Bertram, Mijndert, *Georg II* (Göttingen, 2003).

Birke, A.M. and Kurt Kluxen, eds, *England und Hannover/England and Hanover* (Munich, 1986).

Biskup, Thomas, 'The university of Göttingen', in Simms and Riotte, eds, *Hanoverian dimension in British history*, pp. 128–60.

Black, Jeremy, 'George II reconsidered. A consideration of George's influence on the control of foreign policy, in the first years of his reign', *Mitteilungen des österreichischen Staatsarchivs*, 35 (1982), pp. 35–56.
—— ed., *Britain in the age of Walpole* (Basingstoke, 1984).
—— 'Parliament and the political and diplomatic crisis of 1717–18', *Parliamentary History*, 3 (1984), pp. 77–101.
—— *British foreign policy in the age of Walpole* (Edinburgh, 1985).
—— 'Fresh light on the fall of Townshend', *Historical Journal*, 29 (1986), pp. 41–64.
—— ed., *Knights errant and true Englishmen* (Edinburgh, 1989).
—— 'Parliament and foreign policy in the age of Walpole: the case of the Hessians', in idem, ed., *Knights errant*, pp. 41–54.
—— *Parliament and foreign policy in the eighteenth century* (Cambridge, 2004).
—— *George III* (New Haven and London, 2006).
—— *George II* (Exeter, 2007).
—— 'Debating Britain and Europe, 1688–1815', *British Scholar*, 1 (2008), pp. 37–52.
Blanning, T.C.W., ' "That horrid Electorate" or "ma patrie germanique"? George III, Hanover and the Fürstenbund of 1785', *Historical Journal*, 20 (1977), pp. 311–44.
—— *The culture of power and the power of culture* (Oxford, 2002).
—— *The triumph of music* (London, 2008).
Borkowsky, Ernst, *Die Englische Friedensvermittlung im Jahre 1745* (Berlin, 1884).
Borman, Tracy, *Henrietta Howard* (London, 2007).
Braubach, Max, *Versailles und Wien von Ludwig XIV bis Kaunitz* (Bonn, 1952).
Brauer, Gert, *Die hannoversch-englischen Subsidienverträge, 1702–1748* (Aalen, 1962).
Brewer, John, *The sinews of power* (London, 1989).
—— *The pleasures of the imagination* (London, 1997).
Browning, Reed, 'The Duke of Newcastle and the Imperial Election plan, 1749–1754', *Journal of British Studies*, 7 (1967–8), pp. 28–47.
—— *The duke of Newcastle* (New Haven and London, 1975).
—— *The war of the Austrian succession* (Stroud, 1993).
Bruce, Anthony, *The purchase system in the British army, 1660–1871* (London, 1980).
Burke, Peter, *The fabrication of Louis XIV* (New Haven, 1992).
Burrows, Donald, *Handel* (Oxford, 1994).
—— *Handel and the English Chapel Royal* (Oxford, 2005).
Campbell Orr, Clarissa, 'New perspectives of Hanoverian Britain', *Historical Journal*, 52 (2009), pp. 513–29.
—— ed., *Queenship in Britain, 1660–1837* (Manchester, 2002).
Carswell, John, *The South Sea bubble* (Stroud, 2001).
Clark, Christopher, *Iron kingdom* (London, 2006).
Clark, J.C.D., *The dynamics of change* (Cambridge, 1982).
Clayton, T.R., 'The duke of Newcastle, the earl of Halifax, and the American origins of the Seven Years' War', *Historical Journal*, 24 (1981), pp. 571–603.
Colley, Linda, *In defiance of oligarchy* (Cambridge, 1982).
Colvin, H.M., J. Mordaunt Crook, Kerry Downes and John Newman, *The history of the king's works: volume V, 1660–1782* (London, 1976).
Cust, Lionel, 'On a portrait of Sophia Dorothea of Zell', *Burlington Magazine for Connoisseurs*, vol. xix, no. 101 (August 1911), pp. 301–2.
Dann, Uriel, *Hanover and Great Britain, 1740–1760* (Leicester, 1991).
Davies, J.D. Griffith, *A king in toils* (London, 1938).
Dean, Winton, *Handel's Operas, 1726–1741* (Woodbridge, 2006).
Dickson, Patricia, *Red John of the battles* (London, 1973).
Dickson, P.G.M., *The financial revolution in England* (London, 1967).
Drögereit, Richard, 'Das Testament König Georgs I. und die Frage der Personalunion zwischen England und Hannover', *Niedersächsisches Jahrbuch für Landesgeschichte*, 14 (1937), pp. 94–199.
Droysen, Johann Gustav, *Geschichte der Preußischen Politik* (14 vols, Leipzig, 1868–86).

Duffy, Christopher, *The '45* (London, 2003).

Eagles, Robin, ' "No more to be said"? Reactions to the death of Frederick Lewis, prince of Wales', *Historical Research*, 80 (2007), pp. 346–67.

Edwards, Peter, *Horse and man in early modern England* (London, 2007).

Elias, Norbert, *The court society* (Oxford, 1983).

Ellis, Kenneth, *The post office in the eighteenth century* (Oxford, 1958).

Fähler, Eberhard, *Feuerwerke des Barock* (Stuttgart, 1974).

Feuerstein-Praßer, Karin, *Sophie von Hannover* (Regensburg, 2004).

Frensdorff, F., 'G.A. von Münchhausens Berichte über seine Mission nach Berlin im Juni 1740', *Abhandlungen der Königlichen Gesellschaft der Wissenschaften zu Göttingen. Philologisch-Historische Klasse*, neue Folge 8,2 (1904).

Fritz, Paul S., 'The trade in death: the royal funerals in England, 1685–1830', *Eighteenth-century Studies*, 15 (1982), pp. 291–316.

Gerrard, Christine, 'Queens-in-waiting: Caroline of Anspach and Augusta of Saxe-Gotha as princesses of Wales', in Campbell Orr, ed., *Queenship in Britain*, pp. 143–61.

Gibbs, G.C., 'English attitudes towards Hanover and the Hanoverian succession in the first half of the eighteenth century', in Birke and Kluxen, eds, *England und Hannover*, pp. 33–51.

Gregg, Edward, 'France, Rome and the exiled Stuarts, 1689–1713', in Edward Corp (with contributions from Edward Gregg, Howard Erskine-Hill and Geoffrey Scott), *A court in exile* (Cambridge, 2004), pp. 11–75.

Grieser, Rudolf, 'Die Deutsche Kanzlei in London, ihre Entstehung und Anfänge', *Blätter für deutsche Landesgeschichte*, 89 (1952), pp. 153–68.

Griffin, Emma, *Blood sport: hunting in Britain since 1066* (New Haven and London, 2007).

Habermas, Jürgen, *The structural transformation of the public sphere* (Cambridge, 1989).

Handrick, Wolfgang, *Die pragmatische Armee 1741 bis 1743* (Munich, 1991).

Harding, Nick, *Hanover and the British empire, 1700–1837* (Woodbridge, 2007).

Harris, Bob, *Politics and the nation* (Oxford, 2002).

—— 'Hanover and the public sphere', in Simms and Riotte, eds, *Hanoverian dimension*, pp. 183–212.

Harris, Tim, *Politics under the later Stuarts* (London, 1993).

Hatton, Ragnhild, *George I: Elector and king* (London, 1978).

Hatton, Ragnhild and M.S. Anderson, eds, *Studies in diplomatic history* (London, 1970).

Havemann, Wilhelm, *Geschichte der Lande Braunschweig und Lüneburg* (3 vols, Göttingen, 1853–7).

Hayes, James, 'The royal house of Hanover and the British army, 1714–60', *Bulletin of the John Rylands Library*, 40 (1957–8), pp. 328–57.

Hegeler, Britta, 'Sophia von Hannover – ein Fürstinnenleben im Barock', *Niedersächsisches Jahrbuch für Landesgeschichte*, 74 (2002), pp. 147–88.

Herman, Eleanor, *Sex with the queen* (London, 2006).

Hogwood, Christopher, *Handel: Water Music and Music for the Royal Fireworks* (Cambridge, 2005).

Holmes, Geoffrey, *British politics in the age of Anne* (revised edn, London, 1987).

Hoppit, Julian, *A land of liberty? England, 1689–1727* (Oxford, 2000).

Horn, D.B., 'The origins of the proposed election of the King of the Romans, 1748–50', *EHR*, 42 (1927), pp. 361–70.

Hughes, Michael, *Law and politics in eighteenth-century Germany* (Woodbridge, 1988).

Hunter, David, 'Rode the 12,000? Counting coaches, people, and errors en route to the rehearsal of Handel's *Music for the Royal Fireworks* at Spring Gardens, Vauxhall in 1749', *London Journal* (forthcoming).

Ilchester, earl of (G.S.H. Fox-Strangways), *Henry Fox, first Lord Holland* (2 vols, London, 1920).

—— *Lord Hervey and his friends, 1726–38* (London, 1950).

Jones, Clyve, ' "Venice preserv'd; or a plot discovered": the political and social context of the Peerage bill of 1719', in idem, ed., *A pillar of the constitution*, pp. 79–112.

—— 'The "reforming" Sunderland/Stanhope ministry and the opening of the 1718–19 session of parliament in the House of Lords', *Historical Research*, 78 (2005), pp. 58–73.

—— ed., *A pillar of the constitution* (London, 1989).

Jubb, Michael, 'Economic policy and economic development', in Black, ed., *Britain in the age of Walpole*, pp. 121–44.

Jupp, Peter, *The governing of Britain, 1688–1848* (London, 2006).

Kalthoff, Edgar 'Die englischen Könige des Hauses Hannovers im Urteil der britischen Geschichtsschreibung', *Niedersächsisches Jahrbuch für Landesgeschichte*, 30 (1958), pp. 54–197.

Kluke, P. and Peter Alter, eds, *Aspekte der deutsch-britischen Beziehungen im Laufe der Jahrhunderts* (Stuttgart, 1978).

Kroll, Maria, *Sophie: electress of Hanover* (London, 1973).

Küster, Sebastian, *Vier Monarchien – Vier Öffentlichkeiten: Kommunikation um die Schlacht bei Dettingen* (Münster, 2004).

Lampe, Joachim, *Aristokratie, Hofadel und Staatspatriziat in Kurhannover* (2 vols, Göttingen, 1963).

Langford, Paul, *The excise crisis* (Oxford, 1975).

Lodge, Richard, 'The treaty of Abo and the Swedish succession', *EHR*, 43 (1928), pp. 540–71.

—— 'The mission of Henry Legge to Berlin, 1748', *Transactions of the Royal Historical Society*, 4th series, 14 (1931), pp. 1–38.

Macaulay, T.B., *The history of England from the accession of James II* (5 vols, London, 1848–61).

McCormack, Matthew, 'Citizenship, nationhood and masculinity in the affair of the Hanoverian soldier, 1756', *Historical Journal*, 49 (2006), pp. 971–93.

McKay, Derek and H.M. Scott, *The rise of the great powers, 1648–1815* (Harlow, 1983).

Mackesy, Piers, *The coward of Minden* (London, 1979).

Malortie, C. E. von, *Beiträge zur Geschichte des Braunschweig-Lüneburgischen Hauses und Hofes* (6 vols, Hanover, 1860–72).

Mansel, Philip, *Dressed to rule* (New Haven and London, 2005).

Marschner, Joanna, 'Queen Caroline of Anspach and the European princely museum tradition', in Campbell Orr, ed., *Queenship in Britain, 1660–1837*, pp. 130–42

Mediger, Walther, *Moskaus Weg nach Europa* (Braunschweig, 1952).

—— 'Great Britain, Hanover and the rise of Prussia', in Hatton and Anderson, eds, *Studies in diplomatic history*, pp. 199–213.

—— 'Hastenbeck und Zeven. Der Eintritt Hannovers in den Siebenjährigen Krieg', *Niedersächsisches Jahrbuch für Landesgeschichte*, 56 (1984), pp. 137–66.

Michael, Wolfgang, *England under George I*, trans. Annemarie and George MacGregor (2 vols, London, 1936–9).

Middleton, Richard, *The bells of victory: the Pitt–Newcastle ministry and the conduct of the Seven Years War, 1757–1762* (Cambridge, 1985).

Millar, Oliver, *The Tudor, Stuart and early Georgian pictures in the collection of Her Majesty the Queen* (2 vols, London, 1963).

Müller, Angelika, 'Das Bild der Hannover-Könige des 18. Jahrhunderts in der neueren und neuesten englischsprachigen Geschichtsschreibung', in Rohloff, ed., *Grossbritannien und Hannover*, pp. 194–226.

Namier, L.B., *The structure of politics at the accession of George III* (2nd edn, London, 1957).

Namier, L.B. and John Brooke, *The House of Commons, 1754–1790* (3 vols, London, 1964).

Newman, A.N., 'Leicester House politics, 1748–1751', *EHR*, 76 (1961), pp. 577–89.

—— ed., 'Leicester House politics, 1750–60, from the papers of John, second earl of Egmont', *Camden Miscellany XXIII*, Camden 4th series, 7 (1969), pp. 85–228.

—— *The world turned inside out: new views on George II* (Leicester, 1987).

Owen, J.B., *The rise of the Pelhams* (London, 1957).

—— 'George II reconsidered', in Whiteman, Bromley and Dickson, eds, *Statesmen, scholars and merchants*, pp. 113–34.

Patze, Hans, 'Zwischen London und Hannover. Bemerkungen zum Hofleben in Hannover während des 18. Jahrhunderts', in Peter Berglar, ed., *Staat und Gesellschaft im Zeitalter Goethes* (Cologne and Vienna, 1977), pp. 95–129.

Pedicord, Harry William, *'By their majesties command': the house of Hanover at the London theatres, 1714–1800* (London, 1991).

Plumb, J.H., *Sir Robert Walpole* (2 vols, London, 1956–60).

—— *The first four Georges* (London, 1956).

Pocock, J.G.A., *Virtue, commerce, and history* (Cambridge, 1985).

Reitan, E.A., 'The Civil List in eighteenth-century British politics: parliamentary supremacy versus the independence of the crown', *Historical Journal*, 9 (1966), pp. 318–37.

Richter-Uhlig, Uta, *Hof und Politik unter den Bedingungen der Personalunion zwischen Hannover und England* (Hanover, 1992).

Riotte, Torsten, 'Das Haus Hannover in der angelsächsischen Forschung', *Niedersächsisches Jahrbuch für Landesgeschichte*, 79 (2007), pp. 325–34.

—— 'The kingdom of Hanover and the Marienburg sale', *Court Historian*, 12 (2007), pp. 49–61.

—— 'George III and Hanover', in Simms and Riotte, eds, *Hanoverian dimension*, pp. 58–85.

Rohloff, Heide N., ed., *Grossbritannien und Hannover: die Zeit der Personalunion, 1714–1837* (Frankfurt/Main, 1989).

Roolfs, Cornelia, *Der hannoversche Hof von 1814 bis 1866* (Hanover, 2005).

Rose, Craig, *England in the 1690s* (Oxford, 1999).

Roseveare, Henry, *The financial revolution, 1660–1760* (London, 1991).

Sainty, Sir John and R.O. Bucholz, *Officials of the royal household, 1660–1837* (2 vols, London, 1997–8).

Schaich, Michael, 'The funerals of the British monarchy', in idem ed., *Monarchy and religion*, pp. 421–50.

—— ed., *Monarchy and religion: the transformation of royal culture in eighteenth-century Europe* (Oxford, 2007).

Schaumann, A.F.H., *Sophie Dorothea, Prinzessin von Ahlden und Kurfürstin von Hannover* (Hanover, 1879).

Schieder, Theodor, *Frederick the great*, ed. and trans. Sabina Berkeley and H.M. Scott (Harlow, 2000).

Schilling, Heinrich, *Der Zwist Preußens und Hannovers 1729/1730* (Halle, 1912).

Schilling, Lothar, *Kaunitz und das Renversement des Alliances* (Berlin, 1994).

Schlenke, Manfred, *England und das friderizianische Preussen 1740–1763* (Munich, 1963).

—— 'England blickt nach Europa: Das konfessionelle Argument in der englischen Politik um die Mitte des 18. Jahrhunderts', in Kluke and Alter, eds, *Aspekte der deutsch-britischen Beziehungen*, pp. 24–45.

Schnath, Georg, *Geschichte Hannovers im Zeitalter der neunten Kur und der englischen Sukzession, 1674–1714* (4 vols, Hildesheim, 1938–82).

—— *Der Königsmarck-Briefwechsel* (Hildesheim, 1952).

—— (with contributions from Rudolf Hillebrecht and Helmut Plath), *Das Leineschloss: Kloster, Fürstensitz, Landtagsgebäude* (Hanover, 1962).

—— *Ausgewählte Beiträge zur Landesgeschichte Niedersachsens* (Hildesheim, 1968).

—— 'Der Fall Königsmarck', in idem, *Ausgewählte Beiträge*, pp. 52–123.

—— 'Eleonore v. d. Knesebeck, die Gefangene von Scharzfels', in idem, *Ausgewählte Beiträge*, pp. 124–65.

—— 'Die Prinzessin in Ahlden', in idem, *Ausgewählte Beiträge*, pp. 166–257.

Schumann, Matt and Karl Schweizer, *The Seven Years War: a transatlantic history* (London, 2008).

Schwencke, Alexander, *Geschichte der Hannoverschen Truppen im Spanischen Erbfolgekriege, 1701–1714* (Hanover, 1862).

Scott, H.M., *The birth of a great power system, 1740–1815* (Harlow, 2006).

—— 'Hanover in mid-eighteenth-century Franco-British geopolitics', in Simms and Riotte, eds, *Hanoverian dimension*, pp. 275–300.

Sedgwick, Romney, *The House of Commons, 1715–1754* (2 vols, London, 1970).

Sheppard, Edgar, *Memorials of St James's palace* (2 vols, London, 1894).

Showalter, Dennis E., *The wars of Frederick the Great* (Harlow, 1996).

Sichart, L. von, *Geschichte der königlich-hannoverschen Armee* (5 vols, Hanover, 1866–98).

Simms, Brendan, 'Pitt and Hanover', in Simms and Riotte, eds, *Hanoverian dimension*, pp. 28–57.

—— *Three victories and a defeat* (London, 2007).

Simms, Brendan and William Mulligan, eds, *The primacy of foreign policy in British history, 1660–2000* (Basingstoke, 2010).

Simms, Brendan and Torsten Riotte, eds, *The Hanoverian dimension in British history, 1714–1837* (Cambridge, 2007).

Smith, Hannah, 'The court in England, 1714–1760: a declining political institution?', *History*, 90 (2005), pp. 23–41.

—— *Georgian monarchy* (Cambridge, 2006).

Smith, Hannah and Stephen Taylor, 'Hephaestion and Alexander: Lord Hervey, Frederick, prince of Wales, and the royal favourite in England in the 1730s', *EHR*, 124 (2009), pp. 283–312.

Speck, W.A., *The butcher: the duke of Cumberland and the suppression of the '45* (Oxford, 1981).

Starkie, Andrew, *The Church of England and the Bangorian controversy, 1716–1721* (Woodbridge, 2007).

Strong, Roy, *Coronation: a history of kingship and the British monarchy* (London, 2005).

Sykes, Norman, *William Wake* (2 vols, Cambridge 1957).

Szabo, Franz A.J., *The Seven Years War in Europe, 1756–1763* (Harlow, 2008).

Szechi, Daniel, *1715: the great Jacobite rebellion* (New Haven and London, 2006).

Taylor, Stephen, ' "The Fac Totum in Ecclesiastic Affairs"? The duke of Newcastle and the crown's ecclesiastical patronage', *Albion*, 24 (1992), pp. 409–33.

—— 'Queen Caroline and the church', in Taylor, Connors and Jones, eds, *Hanoverian Britain and empire*, pp. 82–101.

—— 'The clergy at the courts of George I and George II', in Schaich, ed., *Monarchy and religion*, pp. 129–51.

Taylor, Stephen, Richard Connors and Clyve Jones, eds, *Hanoverian Britain and empire: essays in memory of Philip Lawson* (Woodbridge, 1998).

Thompson, Andrew C., *Britain, Hanover and the Protestant interest, 1688–1756* (Woodbridge, 2006).

—— 'The development of the executive and foreign policy, 1714–1760', in Simms and Mulligan, eds, *Primacy of foreign policy*, pp. 65–78.

Townend, G.M., 'Religious radicalism and conservatism in the Whig party under George I: the repeal of the Occasional Conformity and Schism Acts', *Parliamentary History*, 7 (1988), pp. 24–44.

Trench, Charles Chenevix, *George II* (London, 1973).

Übersicht über die Bestände des Niedersächsischen Staatsarchivs in Hannover (4 vols, Göttingen, 1965–92).

Vaucher, Paul, *Robert Walpole et la politique de Fleury (1731–1742)* (Paris, 1924).

Vivian, Frances, *A life of Frederick, prince of Wales, 1707–1751: a connoisseur of the arts*, ed. Roger White (Lampeter, 2007).

Wallbrecht, Rosenmarie Elisabeth, *Das Theater des Barockzeitalters an den welfischen Höfen Hannover und Celle* (Hildesheim, 1974).

Wellenreuther, Herman, 'Die Bedeutung des Siebenjährigen Kriegs für die englisch-hannoveranischen Beziehungen', in Birke and Kluxen, eds, *England und Hannover*, pp. 145–75.

Werrett, Simon, *Philosophical fireworks* (Chicago, 2010).

Whiteman, A., J.S. Bromley and P.G.M. Dickson, eds, *Statesmen, scholars and merchants* (Oxford, 1973).

Wilkins, W.H., *The love of an uncrowned queen* (2 vols, London, 1900).

—— *Caroline the illustrious* (2 vols, London, 1901).

Wilson, Kathleen, 'Empire, trade and popular politics in mid-Hanoverian England: the case of Admiral Vernon', *Past and Present*, 121 (1988), pp. 74–109.
—— *A sense of the people* (Cambridge, 1995).
Wilson, Peter H., *German armies* (London, 1998).
Woodfine, Philip, *Britannia's glories* (Woodbridge, 1998).
Worsley, Lucy, *The courtiers* (London, 2010).

UNPUBLISHED DISSERTATIONS

Allen, Mitchell D., 'The Anglo-Hanoverian connection, 1727–1760', Ph.D. dissertation, University of Boston, 2000.

INDEX

Printed and bound by CPI Group (UK) Ltd, Croydon, CR0 4YY

24/01/2025

14631926-0001